THE WORLD WE WANT

Also by Catherine Bishop

Female Entrepreneurs in the Long Nineteenth Century, edited with Jennifer Aston (Palgrave, 2020)

Minding Her Own Business: Colonial Businesswomen in Sydney (New South Books, 2015)

Too Much Cabbage and Jesus Christ: Australia's 'Mission Girl' Annie Lock (Wakefield Press, 2021)

Women Mean Business: Colonial Businesswomen in New Zealand (Otago University Press, 2019)

About the Author

Dr Catherine Bishop is an award-winning historian and writer who lives in the Blue Mountains in Australia. She currently holds a postdoctoral fellowship at Macquarie University.

THE WORLD WE WANT

The New York Herald Tribune Youth Forum
and the Cold War Teenager

Catherine Bishop

Australian Scholarly Publishing
Melbourne & Galway

© Catherine Bishop 2024

First published 2024 by
Australian Scholarly Publishing
7 Lt Lothian St North
North Melbourne, Vic 3051
tel: 61 3 93296963
contact@scholarly.info / www.scholarly.com

ISBN 978-1-923267-00-8

ALL RIGHTS RESERVED

Cover Design: Amelia Walker

Cover images:

1. JFK meets 1962 delegates: L–R Sverrir (top of head), Aino, Ashish (kneeling), Jehangir, Sanaa, Kirsten (presenting model ship), Ayzer, Maarten (looking like a young JFK), Chiseko, Karin (neck only), Andreas, Suheil. Abbie Rowe, US NPS, JFK Presidential Library and Museum

2. Opening credits of 'The World We Want' showing 1955 delegates NET, IULMIA

3. Nebiat (56) makes a VOA broadcast USIS

In memory of my beloved aunt Susan, whose diary began it all.
For the Forum Alumni, without whom there would be no book.

Contents

List of Illustrations	*viii*
Acknowledgements	*x*
Author's Note	*xii*
Abbreviations	*xiii*
Preface	*xv*

1.	An Invitation	1
2.	Genesis	10
3.	Leading the Way	25
4.	Follow the Money	44
5.	The Chosen Ones	61
6.	Coming to America	90
7.	'Walking Textbooks' at Host Schools	102
8.	Part of the Family	119
9.	Adolescent Ambassadors	140
10.	Media Darlings	152
11.	'Reds Under the Bed'… and Other Obsessions	169
12.	Beyond New York	196
13.	Hamburgers, Milkshakes, Sex, Drugs, & Rock 'n' Roll	213
14.	What a Delegate Did Next	228
15.	Americans Abroad	252
16.	'An Exercise in Futility?'	268
17.	A Forum Phoenix	282
18.	Changing the World One Teen at a Time	301

Appendix 1: Tables	*313*
Appendix 2: List of Delegates	*318*
Notes	*339*
Bibliography and References	*374*
General Index	*390*
Index of People	*394*

List of Illustrations

Cover

1 JFK meets 1962 delegates
2 Opening credits of 'The World We Want' 1955
3 Nebiat makes a VOA broadcast 1956

Section 1 between pages 118–119

1 Jona poses for Pan Am 1960
2 Per appreciated his free Pan Am flights in 1961
3 Ibrahim and Naila with a milkshake 1958
4 First snow for Dorothy & Thac 1962
5 Judith at Montclair High 1956
6 Learning to type was a novelty for Monika 1965
7 Hee Joon, Inga & a dishwasher 1956
8 Tissa as 'walking textbook' 1959
9 Gus & Ida at water bubblers in 1959
10 Johan & Judith at Charles Gorton High 1956
11 Ibrahim and Vivian in a car 1958
12 Eddie shoveling snow 1965
13 National costumes as visual symbols 1960
14 Ylang and boy delegates in 1961
15 Waldorf Astoria Finale 1956
16 Michael doing a haka at the finale 1967
17 Santi addresses a school assembly 1952
18 Saroj performing at Orientation 1958

Section 2 between pages 168–169

19 TV debate in 1955
20 Filming educational TV in Hagerstown 1960
21 Israeli and Arab delegates on TV debates 1956
22 Sherille's evidence of TV appearances 1971
23 The 'Arab League' 1958

24 African delegates all friends 1962
25 Arriving in Berlin on a field trip 1956
26 1949 Forum program cover
27 Less glamorous bus travel 1962
28 Traveling light? On the road again 1962
29 Arriving at Orientation 1958
30 Helen Waller on the bus 1959
31 Bob Huffman at the Capitol 1965
32 Yvette and Vinod exchanging views 1969
33 The inevitable group photo at the UN 1949
34 Eddie at a 'Mini UN' at Princeton 1965
35 Probal and General Naguib 1953

Section 3 between pages 212-213

36 Meeting President Truman 1952
37 Meeting President Eisenhower 1957
38 Delegates with Juan Trippe & his helicopter 1957
39 Pete Seeger with delegates 1959
40 Santi & Salika meet Yul Brynner for VOA 1952
41 Amos dancing at informal party 1969
42 Raimondo & protestors at the White House 1969
43 High jinks on field trips, Mike & Eddie 1965
44 Girl delegates in the cold 1972
45 Summer 1964 delegates in Berlin
46 Maria sketched at Auschwitz trials 1964
47 Summer Forum on trains in Europe 1964
48 Alumni volunteers as Orientation kitchen staff 1960
49 Cora wearing her '59ers scarf
50 Alumni Reunion Delhi 1999
51 The author interviewing Annemarie on Capri 2018
52 Nga in 2024 watching herself on TV in 1958

Acknowledgements

I have been researching and writing this book for a decade—as an unpaid side-project to my day job as an academic historian. It is not a commissioned history, but The Herald Tribune World Youth Forum Alumni Association have been very supportive, allowing me access to their records and enabling me to trace delegates. The Association also committed to buying copies for their members, facilitating publication.

I am enormously grateful to the Forum alumni, host families, staff, and others, who responded to many emails and participated in online and in-person interviews, generously sharing their time, stories, and Forum memorabilia. This project has been a great excuse to travel. I was privileged to be invited to several Forum reunions, which included a VIP visit to Singapore's Gardens by the Bay, a party in a home overlooking Rome's Pantheon, and an interview on Capri, with the sea sparkling in the sunshine.

Many interviewees went above and beyond: traveling to meet me, providing accommodation and meals, acting as tour guides, or gathering groups of alumni for joint interviews. A few visited me in Australia. All provided fascinating conversation and good company. We found unexpected connections. Maarten Engwirda's friend and political party leader, Els Borst, was at the 1949 UK forum with my aunt. Diana Bedini's business, Rome's famous Babington's Tea Rooms, was founded by her New Zealand grandmother, who features in my book on NZ colonial businesswomen. When Christoph Bertram said his successor at the International Institute for Strategic Studies in London was an Australian, it was one of my neighbors (of course).

I have been honored by the trust placed in me. I have respected requests for anonymity and have also anonymized some stories to avoid harm or embarrassment. Journalist Ginger da Silva and academic Haider Khan (both Forum alumni) read the whole of an early draft, while others read parts. Ibrahim Houri provided generous support for a NY book launch.

Above all, I am especially grateful to Catherine Marin, the Alumni

Association chair, for championing the project from the outset, for bringing the Alumni Association on board, for her ongoing friendship and passion for the project, and for giving her *blanquette de veau* recipe to my partner.

Thank you to Rachael Stoeltje at Indiana University Moving Image Archive for (enthusiastically) digitizing the surviving Forum television programs, and to filmmaker Richard Hall of Nerds Make Media, for tracking down other films, and for making a new Forum film with me: 'The World We Wanted'.

Thank you to Kate Robinson, Lucia Oesterlund, Jared Olar, to archivists and librarians, and to all those who found delegates, sent documents, and shared information. Photographs were provided by delegates and archives. I am grateful for copyright permission from delegates (for their snapshots), Victoria Parmentier (for her father's photo), Guy Smiley, the Pan Am Foundation, Queen's Library, NY (for the *NYHT* morgue), and the JFK Library. State Department photographs are in the public domain. I have tried to trace copyright holders of all photos, but some were impossible. They were probably taken by *NYHT*, Pan Am, or State Department staff photographers, who followed delegates around, or by local press photographers.

I am grateful to Mabel Gardner, Anna Fett, and other scholars who generously shared their expertise, including the anonymous reviewers of the manuscript (especially Reviewer 2, whose positive, productive engagement helped me clarify the book I wanted to write.) Thanks to my university colleagues for their support and friendship, and to the Australian Academy of Humanities for a 2015 Travelling Fellowship.

It was a delight to meet people who were *actually there*—a new experience for me, more used to writing nineteenth-century history. Some have not lived to see the book published: I wish I had written faster.

Last, but never least, I thank my partner Richard, who has willingly shared this process with me, reading every word and providing (as always) expert suggestions, and whose *blanquette de veau* is now nearly as good as Catherine's.

Author's Note

The World Youth Forum's name changed over time. It began as the *New York Herald Tribune* Forum for High Schools, by 1962 was the *New York Herald Tribune* World Youth Forum, and from 1967 was just the World Youth Forum. In this book, the Forum (capitalized) refers to the program. Students who attended were called delegates. At the end of the three months was a grand finale, also advertised as the 'Forum', but here it is called the finale. The *New York Herald Tribune* is also referred to as the *Herald Tribune* and the *Tribune.*

Delegates are identified in the text by first name (country represented, year of Forum). A full list of delegates, with interview details, is in Appendix 2.

I have referred to countries by their names as they were at the time of the Forum. Ceylon is used in preference to Sri Lanka, Rhodesia for Zimbabwe, Turkey for Türkiye, and the Czech Republic is called Czechoslovakia. Yugoslavian delegates came from what are now separate countries but represented Yugoslavia at the Forum. For consistency, Egypt is used instead of UAR, although several delegates were labelled as UAR (but all were Egyptian), and Ghana instead of Gold Coast, although the first delegates were from the Gold Coast. The Forum celebrated the renaming with Amelia (Ghana 57). I have used Germany, Korea, and Pakistan in the text: Delegates were from West Germany but were said to represent Germany. Korean delegates were said to represent Korea rather than South or North Korea. Delegates identified as representing Pakistan came from both West Pakistan and East Pakistan (later Bangladesh). The United States of America is variously called the United States, the US, or America, reflecting common usage. Russia, the Soviet Union and the USSR are all used. Malaya became Malaysia in 1963.

In the endnotes short references are used. Archival references identify Box (B), Folder (F), the collection, and archive. Full details are in the bibliography.

Abbreviations

ADST	The Association for Diplomatic Studies and Training
AFS	American Field Service
AFSC	American Friends Service Committee
ASIO	Australian Security Intelligence Organisation
Bio(s)	Delegates' autobiographies written when selected: now in various archives: Reid, LOC, NET, Wisconsin, Alumni Association website, personal papers.
CAP	Civil Air Patrol
CBS	Columbia Broadcasting System
CEWC	Council For Education in World Citizenship
CIA	Central Intelligence Agency
CORE	Congress of Racial Equality
D	*The Delegate*, Alumni Association magazine
DP	Displaced Person
FAO	Food and Agriculture Organization of the UN
FT	*Forum Tribune*, newsletter produced annually by delegates and Forum staff
HHW	Helen Hiett Waller
HRR	Helen Rogers Reid
HTWYFAA	*Herald Tribune* World Youth Forum Alumni Association
ILO	International Labour Organization
Int(s)	Interview: by author, see Appendix Two
IOS	Investors Overseas Service
IULMIA	Indiana University Library Moving Image Archive
JHW	John 'Jock' Hay Whitney
KFC	Kentucky Fried Chicken
LOC	Library of Congress
MIT	Massachusetts Institute of Technology
MOMA	Metropolitan Museum of Art, New York
N	Forum Newsletter; quarterly newsletter from Forum staff to alumni

NARA	National Archives and Records Administration
NATO	North Atlantic Treaty Organization
NET	National Educational Television
NHS	National Health Service (UK)
NJ	New Jersey
NYC	New York City
NYHT	*New York Herald Tribune*
NYT	*New York Times*
NYU	New York University
NZ	New Zealand
OR	Ogden 'Brown' Reid
Oram Report	Sidney W Green 'Interim Report' in HTWYFAA archives
PTA	Parent Teacher Association
RH	Robert Huffman
SA	South Africa
SLC	Sarah Lawrence College
SNCC	Student Nonviolent Coordinating Committee
The Met	Metropolitan Opera House, New York
TVA	Tennessee Valley Authority
UN	United Nations
UNA	United Nations Association
UNESCO	United Nations Educational, Scientific and Cultural Organization
UNHRC	United National Human Rights Council
US	United States
USIA	United States Information Agency
USIS	United States Information Service (known as USIA overseas)
USSR	United Soviet Socialist Republic
WR	Whitelaw 'Whitie' Reid
WYF	World Youth Forum

Preface

'Oh London—so exactly how I had always imagined it.'

This book was supposed to be about my aunt, Susan Maclean. After she died in our home town of Whanganui, New Zealand, in December 2011, I found her diary, written as a 16-year-old, along with scrapbooks, photograph albums, and letters. I vaguely knew she had won a trip to London as a teenager, but I had never asked her about it. She had traveled frequently since, and I too, a child of the 1970s, took overseas travel for granted. I did not realize that she had won a nationwide competition, and in 1949 had flown to London for three months (when inter-continental flying was still a novelty and New Zealand to London meant half-a-dozen stops along the way) to be part of the *Daily Mail* World Youth Forum run by the Council for Education in World Citizenship.

With a New Zealand boy delegate, Susan joined twenty-four other teenagers from seven European countries and six 'Dominions' (the US was included as a 'dominion'!). The delegates met in the UK to discuss 'The World We Want' in a series of live forums in front of large audiences of British school children. They lived with British families and attended British schools. They trooped around tourist sites, 'were photographed, of course, all over the place', and met political and media heavyweights, including Sir Frank Whittle, who Susan described (starry-eyed or slightly bored?) as 'the greatest expert alive on jet propulsion'. Susan's diary was full of youthful exuberance and refreshing frankness. 'I love it already!', she wrote breathlessly, within twenty-four hours of her arrival in London, 'so exactly how I had always imagined it'.

I thought the diary worth publishing so began researching the 1949 *Daily Mail* Forum and tracing former delegates. While my aunt became a well-respected high school teacher and wrote a biography of a New Zealand church architect, her fellow delegates seemed to outshine her: they included an archbishop, a deputy prime minister, a high-ranking civil servant, a renowned lawyer, and several academics, including world-famous philosopher, Charles Taylor.

Then the project took an unexpected turn. My aunt's forum had been inspired when, in 1948, the *Daily Mail* covered the experiences of six British delegates to the *New York Herald Tribune* Forum for High Schools in the US. The *Daily Mail* Forum was but a pale imitation lasting just three years: the *Herald Tribune* Forum was a whole different kettle of fish.

The nice, manageable tale of my aunt's trip to London in 1949 would have to wait, as I realized there was a different, much bigger story to tell across the Atlantic in New York.

Chapter 1

An Invitation

In early 1994, Parisienne Catherine Marin received an intriguing invitation forwarded from a long-ago address. It was from someone she had never met, inviting her to a place she had never been. When she arrived at the sprawling manor house on the island of Corfu, the garden was unkempt, the house itself was barely furnished, there was no sign of her host, and the other guests, most unknown to her, were as mystified as she.

It was a scenario that could have graced an Agatha Christie novel. That summer, nineteen people, some with a friend or family member, arrived at I Kourti in the tiny, idyllic rural village of Vouniatades, thirty minutes' drive from Corfu's main center. They ranged in age from about 45 to 65 and they came from seventeen countries across the world. Like Catherine, most had never met each other. Neither had many met Jordan Arzoglou, whose personal invitation had summoned them to his home. Fortunately, unlike Agatha Christie's *And Then There Were None*, this was a scene not of death, but of rebirth—the beginning of a new phase in a then near 60-year-old phenomenon.

The perplexed guests had one thing in common, enough to make the week in Corfu a success. They had all been teenage delegates to a world youth forum that ran annually for twenty-five years from 1947, mostly under the auspices of the *New York Herald Tribune*. They had attended in different years, however, and most were strangers to each other. Seven were from continental Europe; others were from India, Singapore, Nigeria, Israel, and North America. They included an ambassador, journalists, translators, senior public servants, teachers and academics, an architect, homemakers, and business executives. An amiable chaos prevailed. The newly appointed British ambassador to Turkey spent at least one night on a thin palliasse on the landing, while Catherine, who had been the 1959 French delegate, proved her culinary and organizational skills producing elaborate meals for all with few provisions and minimal kitchen facilities—three small pots and one stove-top element (the prewar oven was defunct). The women wore their lovely frocks, brought in anticipation of a grand house party; they unearthed a large round table in the long grass with a mismatched assortment of old chairs, and had 'great dinners and lovely receptions'. Amid the disarray, the group, joined a few days later by their host, also a former delegate, bonded over their Forum experiences. This was the unlikely beginning of the Forum Alumni Association, whose members had been involved in the long-lived *New York Herald Tribune* World Youth Forum.[1]

The Forum

The *New York Herald Tribune* Forum for High Schools began in 1946 as a forum for American students, developing into an international exchange program the following year. Its aims were educational and internationalist, within the context of Cold War anxieties pitting American democracy against Soviet communism.

Each year, from 1947 to 1972, about thirty 16-to-18-year-olds from around the world were selected as their country's representative and flown free of charge to New York. Between January and March, these students stayed with three or four different American families while attending schools, mainly in the New York and New Jersey areas. From 1953, they gathered in smaller groups each week to film panel discussions on current issues, broadcast on television. They met an A-list of senators and celebrities, including Eleanor Roosevelt, Henry Kissinger, Ingrid Bergman, Harry Belafonte, and occasionally the US president. They traveled to Washington DC and sometimes went further afield—to Boston, St Louis, and Tennessee, where this multicultural group were confronted by segregation. In some years, they enjoyed an additional excursion 'on the way home'—variously to Berlin, London, Geneva, Cairo, and Accra. The climax of the three-month exchange was a grand finale forum. Delegates debated and performed for an audience of over two thousand high school students, gathered from their host schools. These forums were held most often in the Grand Ballroom of the Waldorf Astoria Hotel, *the* place for international conferences in New York, and later at the Lincoln Center. The *Herald Tribune* printed stories about the delegates throughout their three-month stay, as well as a multi-page feature in its educational supplement, including photographs and speeches. The Forum was a pet project of the newspaper, which provided staff and a small amount of funding. Other foundations and corporations also contributed sponsorship sporadically. There was no direct government funding until the late 1960s, but the United States State Department provided in-kind logistical assistance, as did airlines, local schools, universities, and others. After the *Herald Tribune* folded in 1966, funding became a more critical issue as we will see. The last proper Forum was in 1972, after which a much-diminished program limped on until the mid-1970s.

The 807 delegates who attended the Forum in its 25-year existence varied in their perspectives and attitudes. They came from eighty-four different countries and a range of social backgrounds. They also—crucially—spanned a quarter of a century. The delegates to the first Forum in 1947 were born around 1930, with Depression childhoods and teenage experience of World War II. Britain still had an empire, Europe had disintegrated, and the US and USSR were beginning to flex their muscles in a struggle for world dominance, each framing policies against the dire threat of the opposing political system. Those who appeared at the last Forum in 1972 were born around 1954. They experienced other wars, depending on where they lived: the Cold War, the Vietnam War, civil wars around decolonization, upheavals in the Middle East. Taking television for granted, they had witnessed a moon-walk, the events of 1968 in Europe, the beginnings of second-wave feminism, and the American civil rights movement. Youth culture had been transformed with the arrival of the 'teenager', especially pronounced in the US. An American term first coined in 1941, the 'teenager' was a 'social invention' in which compulsory secondary education played a central role, teaching American youth 'what they shared in common and in what ways they differed from others'. The delegates came to define themselves within that framework: they, like their fellow American students, 'became teenagers'.[2]

The Forum had three overlapping aims—internationalism, Cold War politics, and American education—which competed with and complemented each other over its three decades. Forum publicity loudly proclaimed its ambitions to promote peace and understanding by bringing together carefully chosen teenagers from around the world. As a 'baby UN', potential future leaders would get to know each other and thus contribute to a more peaceful world. This idealistic internationalism was genuine (if a little naïve), but was intertwined with the second somewhat disparate element, a desire to engage with young people in a Cold War battle for hearts and minds. The Forum was a soft power weapon in the United States' cultural cold war against the Soviet Union. These 'future leaders' would be exposed to American democracy and modernity and would hopefully develop life-long feelings of friendship and gratitude towards the US.[3] The third element, education, looked inward. The foreign teenagers were 'walking textbooks', introducing American students to the wider world, ideally helping to create more internationally aware American citizens.

In the 1940s, a war-weary world often associated youth with hope. Historian Mischa Honeck has described the US during the fifties as 'a world rotating around the needs of the young'. Children and young people became central to post-war idealism around a better, more prosperous, and more peaceful world. They were a moral lode stone for the future. Young people might, suggested *Seventeen* magazine, teach their parents and friends to 'build a better world'. 'Youth', of course, is a fluid concept, and has been applied to anyone from children to those in their thirties. There were also race and gender-based judgements and expectations about 'youth'. Youth were never a cohesive mass, as the Forum showed.[4]

At the same time youth spawned moral panics around juvenile delinquency and teenage rebellion. The Forum and similar initiatives were a form of containment. This was explicitly recognized in 1968 by consultant Sidney Green, reporting on the Forum's viability. Young people 'seek participation in the decisions that affect their lives', he wrote. 'A communications medium that they can trust must be established so that their ideas can be heard and presented'. Without it, 'they will move violently to change the existing societal structures which deny them this role'. Young people 'were in the vanguard of change', he declared, 'much of it erratic and at times destructive'. He was writing on June 8, 1968, two months after Martin Luther King's assassination, and just two days after Robert Kennedy was shot by a 25-year-old Palestinian America.

There were growing student protests in Europe, as well as civil rights and anti-Vietnam War activism in the US. Although Green was specifically commenting on the 'sense of alienation' felt by young people in the late 1960s, when youth were 'determined to be heard', commentators in the late 1940s were already concerned about juvenile delinquency and the Forum was a way to give teenagers a means of expression that put the brakes on any rebellious tendencies.[5]

Above all, young people were a central focus of Cold War policy-planning initiatives on both sides of the Iron Curtain, as has been shown in a growing literature on the history of youth engagement in internationalism, especially during the Cold War.[6] Mass festivals, university exchange programs, and even scouts and guides were all soft power weapons.[7] Encouraged to be 'global ambassadors of world friendship', young people supposedly also embodied their idealized Western or communist cultures.[8] The rhetoric of peace and friendship co-opted young people into the Cold War, as 'little cold warriors'.[9] They were not mere pawns, however. Those 'global ambassadors' could also sometimes behave inappropriately, as historian Marcia Chatelain discovered in the case of American Girl Scouts. Youth festival participants or pen pals communicating across borders did not always keep to the script.[10] Young backpackers crisscrossing Europe in the post-war decades created an international youth culture that ignored the Iron Curtain, in essence undermining their nation states' Cold War priorities.[11] The young also participated in the civil rights movement—high school desegregation was at the forefront—and wrote letters protesting the Vietnam War, asserting their rights to citizenship and political activism.[12] Forum delegates could, upon occasion, be similarly uncooperative, particularly in the 1960s, embracing controversy, challenging conventions, and disobeying rules.

The Forum, too, was more than simply a player in the Cold War struggle for hearts and minds. Like many Cold War initiatives, it found itself somewhere betwixt and between: its organizers' internationalist idealism was genuine but so was their confidence in the superiority of American democracy. The Forum was never completely and uncritically pro-American, however. Despite the restrictions of McCarthyism in

5

the early years, when any expression of sympathy for socialism or even internationalism was regarded as suspicious, open-ended discussion about communism was part and parcel of the Forum. The presence of delegates from political systems many Americans imagined as 'socialist' opened up rather than closed down debate.

Uncovering the Story

To unearth the Forum story, I have become (to resort to another Agatha Christie analogy) a historical Poirot as well as an embarrassingly adept google-stalker. There is no one set of Forum archives: bits and pieces were scattered across the globe, held in private hands and buried in various individuals' papers in multiple public institutions across the US. The Forum's Alumni Association's website have digitized records and Alumni throughout the world have treasured scrapbooks of memorabilia, albums of official photographs interspersed with snapshots, folders of 'autobiographies', instructions, and itineraries, diaries, and letters. Together, these provide the behind-the-scenes conversations, the debates about money, the frank memoranda about delegates and staff, the planning specifics and personal revelations that enrich the story of the Forum.

A serendipitous internet search led me to stumble upon the icing on the cake. The Indiana University Moving Image Archive holds a wonderful treasure trove of films—sixty-nine of the half-hour Forum television programs broadcast in the 1950s. Archivist Rachael Stoltze was as excited to find someone who knew about the films as I was to locate them. Now they have been digitized and many excerpts have gone viral on YouTube, adding another layer to the Forum story by prompting a new generation of young people to voice their reactions (and be surprised by their elders). The National Archives in Washington holds some USIS propaganda films of the Forum and a few audio recordings of later television programs. I also co-produced a short film with documentary filmmaker Richard Hall, interviewing groups of panel participants together in 2022 as they watched themselves on television decades earlier. Some had not seen each other since.

Television programs were just one part of the public record of the Forum. Until 1965 the *New York Herald Tribune* published multi-page features about the Forum each year.[13] The publications of Forum sponsors, Pan Am, TWA Airlines, and *Scholastic* Magazine, now available online, all carried Forum stories. The Forum's newsletter, diligently produced by Forum staff quarterly until 1962, was fortuitously preserved by Forum alumni and *The Delegate* was distributed by the Alumni Association biannually from 1993 to 2020. Scholarly interest in the Forum has been limited to a 1961 Columbia University MA thesis by Emily (Lee) Workum, who had privileged access to Forum records through her neighbor, Forum director, Helen Waller.[14]

Easily the most valuable and exciting source for this project were the delegates themselves and others associated with the Forum. Not only did they hold many archives, but the Alumni Association had contact details for nearly half the delegates. Tracking down the others—those who avoided the Alumni Association as well as those who were delighted to be 'found' and put in touch—was both a challenge and tremendous fun. I have discovered just how powerful an internet search engine can be. But not just the search engine. Emails sent to complete strangers led me to delegates through random acts of human kindness. A Danish man who had absolutely nothing to do with the Forum received my email because he shared a (quite common, I now realize) name with the co-author of an article written with one early delegate. He not only replied, but tracked down my delegate, who did not have email; he telephoned her to get her address so that I could be in touch.

A key tool in my search was the collection of 'autobiographies' I managed to gather. To be selected for the Forum, delegates wrote an essay, usually on 'The World We Want', and an 'autobiography'. Sadly, only a handful of essays survived, but many of the 'autobiographies' did, and are a fascinating window into the ways young people presented themselves to the world. But they also enabled me to identify and trace delegates. Many included birth dates, full names, parents' names and occupations, schools, hometowns, and ambitions for future careers, all helpful in narrowing down the search for delegates, fifty, sixty, or seventy years later. Even the littlest detail helped. For instance, young Tomas Estrada (Argentina 57) hoped in his autobiographical essay to 'make new friends, learn a lot, and on my way *see those beautiful American girls*, if I have the chance'. My internet search led to a magazine article written in 2014 by a South African visitor to an Argentinian polo club. 'Raconteur Thomas de [sic] Estrada held court, an elderly former banker turned horse dealer with a wicked sense of humour and *whose attention never left the women at the table*'. (my emphasis.) Of course it was the same man, his desire to 'see those beautiful ... girls' undimmed.[15] Other times, more tangible information proved critical, such as the name of a high school, or intended university. Peter Lewis (UK 65) was indistinguishable in internet search engines from a plethora of Peter Lewises. But his biography revealed he was off to Oxford's St Peter's College, which fortunately had an active (and obliging) alumni association, allowing me to track him down.

Finding delegates was just the beginning. Over the last decade I have interviewed delegates, staff, and hosts, as well as family members of those who have died. I have met 135 in person (pre-COVID) and spoken with another fifty-four by Zoom, Skype, or telephone. I have had substantial email correspondence with these as well as another thirty-two delegates and family members of twenty-five delegates. I have also been in touch with several host families, Forum staff, and teachers. I have interviewed people from each year of the Forum and from sixty of the eighty-four countries.[16] I was privileged to attend a few reunions, including the 50-year reunion of delegates from 1969. Several had not met since; it was fascinating witnessing their reconnection.

Best of all, the process of uncovering the history of the Forum has been a series of moments of connection, as I reintroduced long-lost delegates to each other, linked family members of long-dead delegates with television programs showing their parents and grandparents as starry-eyed teenagers, and discovered a range of intelligent, interesting individuals from across the world.

Telling the Story to Win Hearts and Minds

The next three chapters of this book place the genesis of the Forum idea in its post-war context, and introduce those who led it and those who paid for it. We then follow the delegates as they experience the Forum, focusing on different aspects—their selection, Orientation program, host schools and families, the public appearances, televised debates, discussion topics, field trips, and homecoming. The final chapters look at the later initiatives—the Summer Forum, what happened after the *Tribune* folded in 1966, and the development of the Alumni Association, before I assess the Forum's impact and legacy.

The Forum involved 807 young people from eighty-four countries, along with the directors, newspaper owners, moneymen, and staff who created the Forum, and the American teenagers they encountered. The impressionable delegates—imagined as potential world leaders, diplomats, politicians, civil servants, academics, and business tycoons—shared the powerful drug of hope and idealistic internationalism against a background of modern American democratic prosperity and unparalleled world influence. Did the *Herald Tribune* World Youth Forum capture their hearts and minds? To answer this question, we start the story at the very beginning—a very good place to start—with the genesis of the Forum idea.

Chapter 2

Genesis

In April 1946, 12-year-old Laura Marvin of Mansfield, Pennsylvania read 'The World We Want', a new regular column in the *New York Herald Tribune*, printing letters from high school students about current issues. This month, there was a ten-page special feature describing the recent Forum held in New York's famous Waldorf Astoria Hotel, attended by 3600 American students from 400 high schools.[1] Eminent speakers included New York Mayor William O'Dwyer, Eleanor Roosevelt, the Chancellor of Syracuse University William P Tolley, US Supreme Court Justice Owen J Roberts, atomic energy consultant David Lilienthal, Dr Eelco van Kleffens of the UN, as well as a general, a major-general, and a vice-admiral from the armed forces.

Alongside these authoritative and overwhelmingly male speakers were scattered voices of youth, including 19-year-old Cushing Niles of the Student Federalists, 16-year-old Ivan 'Gus' Gavrilovic, son of a Yugoslavian member of the UN Headquarters Commission, and Richard Glasgow, president of the Oak Ridge Tennessee Youth Council on the Atomic Crisis, and whose father worked on the Manhattan Project. Alice Horton, 21-year-old ex-president of the US Student Assembly, told how 'with a seven-woman crew of bricklayers, she pushed wheelbarrows of bricks and cement to construct a worker's home' as a guest of the Soviet Anti-Fascist Committee in the Soviet Union. Student Federalists' founder, 20-year-old Harris L Wofford Jr, and UN Youth president, 17-year-old Stephen M Schwebel, fiercely debated the wisdom of World Government. The two victors of the Forum's high school speaking competition, Leonard Polisar, who had political ambitions, and Nancy Philips, a 17-year-old aspiring opera singer, reprised their winning speeches on 'The World We Want'. These youngsters were all smart and politically engaged and several went on to have significant careers.[2]

Laura devoured the newspaper's Forum coverage, which included

'Who's Who at the Forum', and the texts of all the speeches. She wrote to the organizers, endorsing the 'worthwhile and wonderful' Forum that gave 'the youth of your city a chance to express their opinions on subjects of great importance'. She proposed an improvement: 'If we could have a Forum consisting of high school students from <u>all over the world</u> to discuss problems of world importance, I believe that we would be better prepared to accept and understand the responsibilities which must some day be placed upon our shoulders' (her emphasis).[3] Forum staff at the *Herald Tribune* were impressed, replying, 'if such a gathering could be assembled it would be a very fine thing', suggesting that 'some day you can help work on such an idea'. That day came sooner than expected, although there is no evidence that young Laura Marvin was involved.

Just a year later, in 1947, the fledgling *Herald Tribune* Forum for High Schools became international, inviting selected students from Central and South America, as well as from Canada. In 1948 and 1949 the focus was Europe; in 1950 and 1952 they invited students from Asia and the Middle East and by 1953, buoyed by success, the Forum expanded to include students described as coming from 'all over the world'.

Laura's suggestion was not, of course, solely responsible for the refashioning: the Forum's genesis lay in the convergence of several factors already at play. It involved collaboration between media, schools, and the US government, representing their mutual interest in creating an engaged and informed American citizenry. It was born in an era of Cold War fears and renewed internationalist fervor, with an increasing focus on youth as the hope of the future. It was not alone either as a youth forum, providing an appropriate outlet for youthful expression, or as an educational exchange program, introducing American students to the world and vice versa, although it was unusual in being both.

The Herald Tribune, Helen Rogers Reid, & the Forum on Current Problems

It all began with a newspaper and a well-connected, internationally-minded feminist. Newspapers had a vested interest in literate populations. Serious newspapers like the *Herald Tribune* sought a reputation for public service and reliability, and the respect of their readers. The *Herald*

Tribune was owned by the Reids, a prominent Republican family whose formidable and well-connected matriarch, Helen Rogers Reid, was at the helm by the late 1940s.

Having inherited the *New York Tribune* from his father, Whitelaw Reid, in 1912, Ogden Reid had appointed his wife Helen Rogers Reid director of advertising in 1918; advertising revenue soared by 90 per cent in two years. By 1922 Helen was vice president and a primary force behind Ogden's purchase in 1924 of the rival *New York Herald*. The merger of the two papers spawned a new publication: the *New York Herald Tribune*. Helen was ambitious, while Ogden, as Richard Kluger put it bluntly in his history of the paper, 'was a drunk'. Helen called herself Ogden's 'first mate' but was represented in the media as 'Queen Helen'. Nevertheless, the partnership worked. Helen's feminism and activism took the paper to a younger and more liberal audience, while Ogden's conservativism comforted traditional readers. Ogden died in 1947, leaving the paper in Helen's hands. She appointed her older son, Whitelaw 'Whitie' Reid, as editor and vice president, but remained a powerful guiding hand, though Richard Kluger was scathing of her management of the business. 'I'll have to check with Mother' became Whitie's constant refrain. Ogden 'Brownie' Reid followed his brother as editor in 1955. By the middle of the century, Helen's was a well-connected, wealthy, and powerful voice, representing progressive, liberal Republicanism, promoting women, encouraging inclusion of African Americans, and (carefully) challenging McCarthyism. This was a different breed of Republicanism from that associated with Donald Trump in the twenty-first century and had a strong, idealistic strand of internationalism running through it. The *Herald Tribune* continued as an independent liberal Republican paper after the Reid's family friend John Hay 'Jock' Whitney bailed them out and bought it in 1958. A hugely wealthy, idiosyncratic, and energetic businessman, philanthropist, and Republican, 'Jock' Whitney was Eisenhower's friend and his Ambassador to Britain in 1960.[4]

Looking back in 2006, journalist Alan Feuer remembered the *Tribune* fondly as 'a printed playground for Joseph Mitchell, Herbert Asbury, St Clair McKelway, Alva Johnston, and Tom Wolfe'. It was also, notably, 'a place that employed a female sportswriter, who, in off hours, raced

Ferraris'. This was Denise McCluggage, an award-winning journalist, race car driver, and one of the many female journalists and editors appointed and promoted by Helen Rogers Reid.[5]

Reid's connections were impeccable. She had an overflowing folder of membership cards of most women's clubs in New York.[6] And she did not just collect memberships but was actively involved, seeing the club movement as a vehicle for women's self-improvement and a means for elite and educated women to exert influence. To that end, in 1930 she launched the annual *Herald Tribune* Women's Conference on Current Problems, run by Marie 'Missy' Meloney, editor of the *Herald Tribune's* Sunday magazine.

Clubwomen from all over the Eastern states gathered at the Waldorf Astoria Hotel. In September 1932, 2000 women heard speeches on national and international issues from the likes of International Federation of University Women founder and Dean of Barnard College, Virginia Gildersleeve, novelist Fannie Hurst, and writer and political commentator Walter Lippman. Reid's connections meant President Herbert Hoover delivered a message to the conference by radio, which was rebroadcast widely. Reflecting the growing preoccupation with engaging young people in political and social issues in the interwar period, philosopher Irwin Edman spoke on 'the youth movement in the world today'.[7]

By 1935, the conference had expanded, targeting audiences beyond women's clubs, although not much beyond a white, middle-class elite. The *New York Herald Tribune* Forum for Current Problems became an annual event, attracting notable speakers from around the world and from a range of political and career backgrounds. Katherine Hepburn and Shirley Temple added star power in 1938, the latter reappearing in 1945 alongside Walt Disney and Orson Welles. The President of the United States usually made an appearance, as did Eleanor Roosevelt. The 1949 speakers' list was a 'Who's Who of American politics', along with Indian Prime Minister Jawaharlal Nehru and his sister, Vijaya Lakshmi Pandit, India's Ambassador to the US, who offered international political interest, while Edith Piaf provided a musical interlude. In 1952 UN Secretary General Trygve Lie gave the opening address.[8] The last Forum for Current Problems was in 1955. It was canceled at short notice the following year, probably for financial reasons, since the newspaper was beginning to struggle.

The High School Forum was an offshoot of this Forum and outlasted its progenitor. Young people provided attractive copy for the newspaper, with their optimism, fresh views, and fresh faces. They were potential new readers—and writers. In 1948 the *Tribune* hosted a workshop for budding reporters writing for an 'all-high-school' page of the newspaper, and sponsored an annual 'High School Journalism' award. Never one to miss a cross-promotional opportunity, the *Tribune* offered the six winners in 1949 an assignment to cover the High School Forum at the Waldorf Astoria that March.[9] The *Tribune* was positioning itself as high school students' newspaper of choice, by engaging with them through the Forum and by providing free copies focusing on Forum discussions for classroom activities, thereby keeping 'the *Trib.*' front of mind as they browsed newsstands.

Not the Only Youth Forum

The *Tribune* was not the only newspaper in the game, however, and two other major media players were already in the 'forum' market, alongside a raft of other forums sponsored by educational institutions. Their shared aim was to engage young people in positive and productive ways, giving them a sense of being heard, at a time when civil unrest protesting racial discrimination, as well as muggings and street fighting involving young people, seemed rife. Mayor La Guardia was explicit when addressing the first *New York Daily Mirror* forum in November 1943: 'Youth to me is not a social problem ... Childhood is not a headache—it is a joy complete and the glorious promise for the future'.[10] The tabloid *Daily Mirror* was hosting 200 American teenage delegates representing twenty-two organizations interested in 'the problems of youth' at the Hotel Astor, for an all-day meeting.

Mirror Forum participants heard from adult speakers and held panel discussions, passing resolutions about improving life locally for youth and the need for a 'permanent group to fight juvenile delinquency and racial discrimination'—a harbinger of the increasing engagement by high school students in the civil rights movement.[11] In 1943 African American teenagers were prominent participants, with 16-year-old Walter L Wallace of the Youth Builders organization reportedly making 'an impressive appearance' presiding over the forum after being elected as MC. (Young Walter would continue to be impressive, becoming a renowned sociologist at Princeton, hitting headlines in 2008 when identified as Michelle Obama's thesis supervisor.) [12]

The *Mirror* forum became an annual event: by 1946 there were 540 American delegates representing fifty-four youth organizations. As well as perennial topics of racial discrimination and juvenile delinquency, delegates widened their perspective, calling for 'unity to eliminate the causes of war' after hearing the UN's Benjamin Cohen speaking about UNESCO. In 1948, the *Mirror* forum followed the *Tribune*'s example and went international, including seven foreign students. In 1952, twelve young international delegates joined 2500 students from ninety US youth organizations, packed into the Hotel Astor to hear from worthies, including Ambassador Carlos Romulo of the Philippines, past president of the UN General Assembly. The *Mirror* thenceforth involved a few international participants annually. In 1951, foreign students were from Australia, Austria, Portugal, Venezuela, the Gold Coast, Scotland, Canada, Haiti, and Jamaica, as well as from the territories of Alaska, not yet a state, and Newfoundland, only recently part of Canada.[13] Unlike the *Herald Tribune* Forum, the *Mirror* forum's international participants were all boys. This gendered focus was not unique but becoming increasingly unusual. While boys dominated exchange programs more generally, there were few that were exclusively male.[14] The *Mirror*'s panel discussants did include both male and female American students and there were some notable adult female speakers. Ruth Clinton, author of a plan for combating juvenile delinquency in Moline, Illinois, spoke in 1946, and the first female president of the UN General Assembly, Vijaya Lakshmi Pandit, appeared in 1954.

The *Mirror* forum preceded the *Herald Tribune* Forum but was never on the same scale. Australian Robin Room, a delegate in 1956, was aware of playing second fiddle: 'The *New York Mirror* was a tabloid paper, and its youth forum was quite self-consciously competing with and trying to catch up with the *New York Herald Tribune* equivalent.' The *Mirror* forum lasted until at least 1961, when Anders Mellbourn, later a journalist and director of the Swedish Institute of International Affairs, attended. Although unaware of the rival *Tribune* Forum, he was disappointed with the lack of engagement with American teenagers in the *Mirror* forum: the foreign boys stayed in hotels and were basically tourists. He also remembered the New Zealand boy Graeme Gainsford stole the headlines by delivering a 'fiery anti-communist' tirade during the forum. Decades later Graeme himself had forgotten this, but it was feasible in the context of a forum that occurred just months after the Bay of Pigs crisis in Cuba. Untroubled by the lack of Latin American participants, the group passed resolutions on 'How Can We Meet the Communist Challenge?' and 'How Can We Improve Our Relations with Latin America?'.[15] The newspaper folded in 1963 and the *Mirror* forum did not survive its demise.

Also harnessing young people for the greater good—and reader-friendly copy—was the *New York Times*' High School Forum. This teenage panel discussion program was broadcast on radio and from 1952 on television. Run by Dorothy Lerner Gordon, a one-time folk singer with a career in children's broadcasting, from 1943 until her death in 1970, it was re-named Dorothy Gordon's Youth Forum after the *Times* ceased sponsorship in 1960. Only American students participated, but topics included international relations. In 1947, a panel of three boys and three girls discussed 'Are World Affairs our Business?', concluding pessimistically that the partition of Palestine and resulting civil war would be 'a tinder-box for another world war'. Other topics included the Marshall Plan, the English ban on tobacco imports, and food for Europe.[16] American teenagers were being encouraged not only to understand world affairs, but to have opinions and express them.

Alongside forums run by New York newspapers were others, ranging in size, purpose, and sponsorship. Many were localized, but all were, like the *Tribune* Forum, designed to give youth a voice. A few were larger. The Columbia Scholastic Press Association had conventions for young representatives of high school newspapers from 1925: 3700 attended its twenty-fourth in 1948. High school newspapers had a long history in the US as a seedbed for educating teenagers in citizenship and American democracy.[17] Like forums they offered young people a means of expressing their views, along with the all-important sense of being listened to, if not always heard. In an age when the teenager was becoming a recognizable identity, providing such outlets was important.

Also an Exchange Program

The *Herald Tribune* Forum differed from other forums in its ambition, its international focus and its second core mission: an exchange program. (The *Mirror*'s foreign boys did not have extended home stays or attend American schools in the same way as *Tribune* delegates.) As such, it is part of a much longer history of educational exchange programs, stretching back to the nineteenth century, but blossoming particularly in the interwar period, alongside a growth in idealistic internationalism. Interwar exchange programs were aimed mainly, but not exclusively, at university students and were often for American students going overseas. The Experiment in International Living, for instance, was founded in 1932 by Syracuse University's Donald Watt. It initially focused on Europe, was quickly co-educational, and was the first American organization to have local home stays for Americans in Europe. As Watt said, people 'learn to live together by living together', an idea also at the core of Forum philosophy.[18]

This was also the period when international youth organizations such as Boy Scouts began to flourish. The enormous scout jamborees that began in 1920 and the girl guides' world camps (from 1924) were promoted as exercises in world friendship, with scouting describing itself as a 'Junior League of Nations'. But it was internationalism with an agenda: as Mischa Honeck put it, 'For most Anglophone organizers, embracing internationalism was about transforming empires, not dissolving them.' After 1945 a growing number of initiatives aimed at bringing international young people together, ranging from pen pal networks to actual exchanges, and with the development of the Cold War, the underlying cultural imperialism intensified.[19]

This was epitomized by the AFS (American Field Service) high school exchange program, which was contemporary with the Forum. From 1947, it brought foreign high school students to American schools and sent Americans overseas. From 1971 it also sponsored non-American students traveling between other countries. Unlike the Forum, students spent a whole year immersed in the host country's life; it was a social and cultural experience, albeit one with US cultural diplomacy objectives at its heart, alongside internationalist ideals. AFS organizers hoped that the 'personal experience' of the exchange would give foreign 'young men and women ... a true understanding of American democracy in their minds and a warm, lasting friendship for America in their hearts'.[20] AFS students did not specifically engage in political discussions or 'forums' until a brief period in the 1970s, when, as we shall see, the Forum joined forces with AFS, the Experiment in International Living, and International Christian Youth Exchange (ICYE).

Hand in Hand with the US Government

It was no accident that educational exchange programs were popular in the US, which sought to embed itself as the modern leader of the future in a rapidly escalating Cold War. The Forum developed in the context of a series of crises: the nuclear arms race, the Korean War, the Chinese Communist Revolution, the division of Germany, and later, Soviet intervention in Hungary and Czechoslovakia, the Cuban missile crisis, and the Vietnam War.[21]

In the US, it was 'reds' or communists, rather than monsters, who proverbially lurked 'under the beds' of American children in the 1950s and 1960s. Communism, with Soviet power behind it, was a very real 'clear and present danger'. The Cold War was, as historian Brian C Etheridge noted, 'the decisive prism through which Americans understood the world around them'.[22] In the first half of the 1950s, Senator McCarthy's notorious campaign to winkle out supposed home-grown communists added fuel to the fire. Targeting government, media, and arts figures, it used fear, intimidation, and hearsay to create a pervasive atmosphere of suspicion that 'reds' were indeed under every bed in the country.

The soft power Cold War was a serious business, and the US State Department effectively co-opted the Forum. Most delegates recalled some contact with the United States Information Agency (USIA), also known (particularly overseas) as the United States Information Service (USIS).[23] The communications arm of the US State Department between 1953 and

1978, the USIA's officers were attached to US embassies around the world.

USIA's 'public diplomacy' program aimed to 'help achieve US foreign policy objectives' through soft power, by improving 'perceptions and understanding between the people of the United States and the people of other countries'. It also sought to understand 'foreign public opinion' for US government 'policy making purposes' and then, to 'influence public attitudes in other nations' by giving 'foreign peoples the best possible understanding' of those policy decisions. This was a sort of internationalism, but primarily to serve the cause of American foreign policy. As Mark Blitz, ex-USIA Associate Director, wrote bluntly in 1985, 'public diplomacy' was 'the decent term for what would otherwise be called propaganda'. The USIS established libraries, showed films, and engaged with locals. Phillip Pillsbury, USIA Junior Officer in Florence, loved his job because it was 'a very personally based operation'. It was 'an opportunity to meet people and yes, distribute literature and yes, it could be called propaganda, indeed it was'. But, he 'never felt anything wrong with that'.[24] One of his responsibilities was interviewing potential Italian delegates for the 1961 *Herald Tribune* Forum.

Academic exchange programs were thus weapons in the cultural Cold War, critical to offset the threat of 'leftist or neutralist thought especially among many influential persons in academic, cultural, and press circles who are too inclined to accept leftist propaganda at face value', as Secretary of State John Foster Dulles put it. Supporting the Forum was a logical extension of this strategy, targeting teenagers regarded as future 'influential persons'. And it was a long game. The results of such youth exchanges 'may not be seen for several years, but such youths with their enthusiasm and drive will some day [sic] be the core around which regimes are built', predicted US foreign service officer E Wilder Spaulding in 1953.[25]

The Forum had logistical support from the US State Department, but no actual funding until the late 1960s. The State Department favored year-long high school exchange programs, in which foreign students were embedded in American families, high schools, and communities, exposing them to American democracy in action. From 1949, the US government 'worked very closely with competent private organizations' to 'stimulate programs' introducing 'young people of many countries to each other at an age especially productive of close understanding and friendship'. Despite this global-sounding statement, 'Teen-age Program' funding was limited to foreign students coming *to* the US, rather than Americans traveling abroad, underscoring its soft power role. The US State Department financially supported high school exchange programs such as the American Field Service, the American Friends Service Committee, International Christian Youth Exchange, the Michigan Council of Churches, the US Catholic Conference, and Youth for Understanding. The true extent of State Department involvement and funding was not widely advertised. In 1956, 700 students visited under the auspices of these programs. By 1959, 1930 teenagers from forty-eight countries were involved; by 1962, 3220 from fifty-nine countries. $200,000 (still only 1 per cent of the private programs' total costs) was provided in 1967, allowing 4000 foreign students from sixty-six countries to come to the US. Nevertheless, emphasized the State Department that year, trying to keep at arm's length, nearly 90 per cent of the 100,000 foreign students then in the US remained 'non-sponsored' (they were mainly university and college students).[26]

The State Department gave administrative assistance to other exchange programs, a subtle way to keep tabs on their activities. USIS officials often helped select delegates for the Forum, also enabling them to identify and connect with the best and brightest (or best connected) of a nation's high school students. The extent of USIS involvement varied from country to country, but it was sufficient for NYU Education Professor and proponent of international education, F L Redefer, to dub the Forum 'an arm of our State Department in spreading understanding among our young people'. The Forum's involvement with the US government through the USIA was a mixed blessing. On the one hand, it lent legitimacy to the program, ensuring that foreign governments took it seriously. It allowed the Forum privileged access to Ministries of Education, ensuring the greater visibility of the program, which was competing for delegates with the likes of AFS. On the other hand, reliance on US officials for connections in foreign countries dictated which countries were invited, with Department of State officials screening the invitation list. Too close an identification with the US government also laid the Forum open to accusations of promoting US interests rather than true internationalism. The dilemma deepened as the Cold War intensified. Historian Sara Fieldston identified a shift in US youth programs from post-war idealistic internationalism to a 'more sharply nationalist tone', promoting the American democratic way of life in opposition to communism in the 1950s.[27] The *Tribune* Forum was not immune from this shift, but while communism was a perennial topic of interest, several international Forum delegates commented on the frankness of discussions. 'Free speech', after all, was promoted as central to American democracy, part of the 'openness' promoted by US soft power diplomacy.

The USIA realized that US interests were best served by 'openness'. As director Edward R Murrow put it, 'Truth is the best propaganda ... to be persuasive we must be believable, to be believable we must be credible, to be credible we must be truthful'. Diplomats were of course adept at 'spinning' the 'truth' and when exposing the US, 'warts and all', the USIA picked which warts to show.[28] Nevertheless, the key to US 'public diplomacy', like the key to the Forum, was demonstrating that free debate, openness, and 'honesty' were American, while restrictions, secretiveness, and lies were emblematic of more tyrannical and undemocratic regimes.

The co-opting of American intellectuals, writers, artists, and musicians as willing soft power ambassadors of democracy, extended even to those who openly criticized the government and highlighted America's problems, notably racial segregation and the gap between rich and poor. For example, Nobel prize-winning American writer William Faulkner, a vocal critic of segregation, spent much of the 1950s being rolled out around the world as a cultural ambassador (sometimes literally, his developing alcoholism requiring careful management by long-suffering USIS functionaries). The very fact that Faulkner did not shy away from criticizing the US while abroad increased the attraction of his pro-Western message. There was 'comfort in the knowledge that criticism of the American way of life and of the American attitude is not subversive', opined the *Manila Chronicle* during Faulkner's visit in 1955.[29]

On the Other Hand

The US was not alone in wanting to win the hearts and minds of the world's youth. The World Federation of Democratic Youth and the International

Union of Students, both supported by the Soviets, organized enormous World Festivals of Youth and Students from the late 1940s. These were at the opposite end of the scale from the *Herald Tribune* Forum, both in size and approach. The largest festival, in 1957 in Moscow, catered for 34,000 young men and women (generally in their twenties) from 131 countries. They attracted participants from both sides of the Iron Curtain. While the Forum often invited communist countries, only Yugoslavia and (once) Czechoslovakia ever sent delegates. Two Forum delegates who also attended a World Festival recognized them as entirely different animals. The World Festivals were far less subtle than the Forum in their partisanship. Ollie (Finland 62) remembered feeling intimidated at the 1962 Helsinki Festival, with its rigid conformism and consistent messaging, in contrast to the Forum, where he appreciated the range of views. Kaarina (Finland 59), who decided against attending the Helsinki Festival, reminded Alumni firmly in a newsletter that the Festival was held 'against the protests of the government, public opinion and the headquarters of youth and student associations in Finland'.[30]

Mack (US 61) was invited by Gloria Steinem to join an informal student group going to the 1962 Helsinki Festival. It was a free trip with 'a couple of meetings beforehand and regular meetings there'. Mack was 'suspicious' and worried about the consequences of attending. He visited the State Department, where a 'very grey person' told him that while officially not supporting participation, 'unofficially we are glad to have respect-worthy Americans present to represent a better model'. Mack was relieved to hear 'you won't get into trouble if you go'. Steinem claimed the trip was 'privately funded' with 'State department approval'. Her fellow organizer, 'a much more spooky-seeming person with a military quality', recalled Mack, was more 'aggressive', telling the group, 'when you get there we are going to want to know what you say and what they say to you'. His rationale was unclear. Neither he nor Steinem suggested the information was for the State Department, and Steinem has always maintained that she was 'never asked to report on other Americans or assess foreign nationals I had met'. In any event, Mack was assigned the West Africans, and sent on a three-week intensive French language course at Columbia University, before a pleasant two weeks in Paris, practicing

French 'and trying to pick up girls'. Then he was off to Helsinki, where, he remembered, 'it didn't work ... I was conscientious enough to try to talk to West Africans when I saw them but it was a non-event'. With the other 8000 participants he had an 'exciting' time, including witnessing 'riots and teargas and mounted police'.

Mack was surprised when asked to compare the Festival and the Forum. They were so very different, he said. The Festival was 'a large scale propaganda' exercise, with self-selecting, significantly left-leaning, activist participants, who were less open minded and more interested in speaking than listening. In contrast, the Forum was 'carefully crafted' with 'high quality participants ... chosen for their emotional intelligence and articulateness, interested in having an impact in a gracious, articulate way' rather than arguing. With 'a media outlet' and 'participation by a large number of non-self-selecting students' in high schools, it was 'effective at conveying the value that we should know more about the world'.[31] While possibly a rose-tinted view of the Forum, which had its share of dogmatic arguments, his description highlighted the essential differences in scale and selectivity which meant the Forum was a far more subtle Cold War exercise.

Creating Informed Citizens

Aside from global politicking, the US government was also interested in the Forum's domestic aims, sharing the desire of educationalists and the media to give American teenagers a better understanding of the wider world. One version of the Forum's origins emphasizes this: 'One day in '46, in Helen Reid's apt. over luncheon', members of the New York Board of Education grumbled that 'though war had changed the map of the world, the textbooks had not caught up with the changes'. If the *Tribune* could bring in international students as 'walking textbooks', then the Board 'would make arrangements for hospitality' for them.[32] There are obvious problems with this story, not least that the *first* High School Forum was for local students—not a 'walking textbook' in sight. It nevertheless demonstrated that education, for the benefit of *American* rather than international students, was central to the Forum from the outset. It would become increasingly important over time. Although highly selective in its international cohort, the Forum sought a much broader American student audience, as Mack (US 61) pointed out. The Forum was a familiar format for American students: the US had a long tradition of encouraging informed discussion and debate through high school newspapers, clubs, and societies.[33] The program also connected specifically with 'World Affairs' clubs and 'International' societies at schools. Domestic students were exposed to the best and brightest of foreign counterparts, who in turn were introduced to the marvels of American democracy.

The Forum meshed neatly with the *Tribune*'s interest in serious issues, public service, and reaching new readers, and with US government interest in soft Cold War diplomacy. This collaboration between media, government, and educational establishments made the Forum unique as both a high school international exchange program and as a contained public platform for the voice of youth. It epitomized the hopes placed in young people by an insecure and apprehensive post-war world.

Chapter 3

Leading the Way

Forum Directors

Who do you get to turn a collection of thirty smart, articulate, culturally and linguistically diverse teenagers, far from home, some for the first time, into a cohesive group, inculcating them in the ongoing Forum mystique? The Forum experience was shaped for a large part by those who led it. These Forum directors needed not only to mold this motley crew into 'the Forum', but also to quickly identify the leaders and the followers, the talkers and the listeners, the rebels, the jokers, the shy and retiring, those with something intelligent to say, and those who were the social glue. The Forum director needed to be intelligent, with a deep knowledge of international affairs and an ability to communicate with teenagers, to facilitate discussion, and to create good headlines for the *Tribune*. In choosing Helen Hiett in 1946, *Tribune* owner Helen Rogers Reid found someone to get the ball rolling and put her stamp on the Forum, shaping its culture for years to come.

The 'Most Bombed US Woman'

NBC war correspondent Helen Hiett gained fame in 1940 as the 'most bombed US woman' after her experiences in war-torn Europe. She was also the first woman to win a National Headliner Award that year, for 'the best exclusive radio reporting of a news event' after her broadcast on the bombing of Gibraltar. According to one newspaper, she obtained her scoop by 'making friends with chorus girls en route to entertain the troops' and joining their number. This tale, which was a fabrication, was typical of the sorts of stories that circulated around Helen. She was, nevertheless, present on the Rock when it was bombed. By the time she joined Helen Rogers Reid at the *Herald Tribune*, she had already had a remarkable career.[1]

Helen Hiett was born in 1913 in Chenoa, Illinois. Her father, 46-year-old Asa Hiett, was a schoolteacher and later school superintendent. Her mother, Stella, ten years his junior, was also a trained teacher. By the mid-1920s, the family were in Pekin, Illinois, where Asa swopped education for real estate, and Helen attended school. Pekin was, as historian Mabel Gardner has pointed out, 'an unlikely developmental location for an international and political scholar'. A Ku Klux Klan stronghold, Pekin was a sundown town, where African Americans made sure they were out of town by nightfall, and it had a strong working-class culture. Helen, however, was a high achiever—an active and enthusiastic participant, volunteer, and leader in numerous school activities. In her final year she was one of fifteen National Honor Society students, who 'have excelled in scholarship and proved themselves most capable as leaders'. She was good at languages and her mother's parents were German immigrants, giving Helen an outlook that reached beyond the boundaries of the small administrative capital of Tazewell County. She was well-placed to engage the smart young people who would later attend the Forum. She also established her journalistic credentials early, as a member of the Quill and Scroll Society and working part-time for the *Pekin Daily Times* during her last three years of high school.[2]

Helen Hiett was ambitious, with a clear understanding of where she was heading from early on. 'Ever since I first heard about the League of Nations in high school, I knew I wanted to work for the League, for internationalism—that's why I took political science at the University of Chicago.' Although university was no longer a strange choice for women (in 1930, 43 per cent of undergraduates at American universities were women), political science was still a male domain. Hiett won a scholarship to Chicago, where she completed her Political Science degree in three (rather than the usual four) years, graduating in 1934. She studied with political scientist Harold Lasswell, whose innovative research and ideas on power, propaganda, and public opinion doubtless had an impact. She was Treasurer of the Freshman Women's Club and lived in the University of Chicago's International House in her second year, immediately embedding her in an expanding international community. Here she developed the skill at massaging networks and connections that would be so apparent during the Forum years, and she focused on her next step—getting to Europe. She applied for 'every kind of scholarship there was', finally obtaining funding for further study from the Students' International Union.³

Helen Hiett spent 1935 and 1936 in Geneva developing the passion for hiking and mountaineering that she would later share with her husband and children, and which would ultimately take a tragic turn. She also made her mark at the League of Nations as part of a small cohort of interns from ten different countries. That most of the group were males did not faze her. Helen was never one to let her sex stand in her way. She networked relentlessly. When her scholarship ran out, she became secretary to Geneva Research Centre Director, Raymond L Buell, an American foreign policy expert known for his opposition to American isolationism. She was also writing, sending articles to the *Pekin Daily Times* back in Illinois and working on more academic pieces. By 1936, having 'reached the saturation point in League ideologies and wishful thinking', she returned to the US, where she developed a reputation on the public speaking circuit before winning a doctoral scholarship to the London School of Economics from the Federation of American Women's Clubs Overseas. But she also continued reporting from the European continent, with a summer visit to a girls' labor camp in Germany and travels in Spain touring recently active civil war battlefields. With war looming, her PhD fell by the wayside.⁴

In 1938 she was back in the US giving talks about the developing European situation, particularly to student audiences. One US newspaper aptly dubbed her 'American girl and world citizen'. Hiett was in France when war broke out in Europe in 1939. She remained for two years, joining NBC as a war correspondent in 1940. It became a badge of honor for her that she managed to charm her way to great stories through difficulties that other journalists failed to navigate, particularly if those journalists were men. She returned to the US in 1941 and broadcast her own daily quarter-hour news commentary on the NBC network for the next eighteen months—a rare feat. While female voices were often heard on the wireless, they were generally found discussing 'women's issues'.⁵

Helen Hiett also wrote a book. *No Matter Where* appeared in 1944 and was a manifesto of internationalism that prefigured much of the Forum philosophy. It was similarly optimistic and idealistic. As one reviewer noted, her solutions were 'over simple', with no idea 'how—beyond wishing—youth will attain' the undefined international organization for peace that she advocated. As 'a wartime book', adhering to government regulations for paper conservation, it displayed the rather alarming logo of the Council for Wartime Books: a determined-looking, swooping eagle, with a book in its claws and carrying a banner declaring that 'books are weapons in the war of ideas'. This publication indicated how Helen's philosophies, while stridently internationalist, were not out of step with some government's thinking. Describing her experiences in Europe during the first two years of the war, the book told of friendships between young people from different backgrounds. 'The hope of a better world tomorrow is in the hearts and minds of the world's young people', began the blurb on the inside of the dust jacket. This book was also (in some senses quite literally) a call to arms for young Americans in particular. 'Our time is now', Helen declared in the final paragraphs, inviting them to 'contribute to the common enterprise' of rebuilding to 'win an ordered world'.[6] It went without saying that the 'ordered world' would subscribe to democratic principles with the US leading the way.

Helen and the Forums

Helen's own opportunity to contribute was about to appear. In 1945, Helen Rogers Reid commandeered Helen Hiett to help run the Forum for Current Problems. Missy Meloney had died in 1943 and Reid needed a replacement. Hiett passed the test, becoming Forum director in 1946, adding to her established skills as journalist and political commentator. In November 1945, the *Tribune* reported that a high school class in the Bronx was using the texts of the Forum's speeches printed in the newspaper to have their own forum to discuss world issues. In March 1946 the *Herald Tribune* launched its Forum for High Schools, about which young Laura Marvin read so avidly. It had the backing of the well-connected Helen Reid and was built on the recognition factor and capacity of Helen Hiett.[7]

The High School Forum was arguably less prestigious than the Forum for Current Problems, where Helen Hiett was chairing discussions between international political heavyweights in front of an audience of adults. But for Helen it meant more employment, it fitted neatly with her own philosophies, and it maintained her connections with the great and the good. The expansion of the High School Forum into an international exchange program provided Helen with direct influence over the delegates as well as with teenagers more broadly. Youth were seen as the key to the future, and Helen was at the coalface. As a woman, Helen might have struggled to get ongoing employment as a serious journalist, despite her wartime experience. The Forum offered an attractive alternative, with youth, education, and international peace more easily justified as women's concerns. Helen was not unusual in using the combination of internationalism and youth as a vehicle for her own emancipation and advancement. Despite ongoing systemic and structural gender discrimination, upper-middle-class, educated women across the Western world found that the international arena was one in which they could exert influence, and if that arena involved young people, even better. The Forum was an exemplar of this phenomenon, in which the two Helens personified modern American career women, ironically while promoting the ideal American family to delegates.[8]

Helen Hiett became synonymous with the High School Forum held annually January to March, running it in tandem with the Forum for Current Problems each October. She directed the Forum's development from a local New York High School program to one with international reach, putting into practice the principles outlined in *No Matter Where*. As with the book, Helen's shaping of the Forum was in line with the US government's celebration and promotion of American democracy. She never let delegates forget that the encouragement of their free speech was a fundamental tenet of the US way of life and not necessarily available elsewhere. Helen was ambitious for the Forum (and for herself), keeping it front and center at the *Herald Tribune*, but, ever the journalist, also made the Forum work for the newspaper too. Some others at the *Tribune* considered the Forum merely an exercise in corporate social responsibility, but Helen saw it as a core part of the newspaper, and herself a key figure. She advised Ogden 'Brownie' Reid (editor 1955–58) on his editorials, fought for control over her budget, challenged boundaries, and often rubbed people up the wrong way, although she could also be persuasive and charming when required.

Helen was the face of the Forum, a strong and memorable presence. She polarized delegates. She was 'a typical American lady—forthright, forthcoming, confident, and loud', said one. She exemplified the career woman, a type unfamiliar to some male delegates used to women remaining in the background. Hameeda (Pakistan 52) thought Helen 'had a very good sense of humour and a lot of understanding', and admired Helen's management skills, 'the way she could take this troop of over twenty people and make them all [a group], without letting them wander off too much, but giving us a good time'. She regretted that they had not 'had more time to talk to her, because she was always so much on the run, she didn't really have time … she used to sit with us occasionally.' Some found her motherly, others thought she was a calculating woman, who played favorites and was principally concerned with her own ambitions. Some recognized that she was a journalist first-and-foremost—with an eye for the stories that would sell newspapers. Far from avoiding controversy, she courted it. She 'really didn't care about individual delegates in any way but cared a lot about "her" Forum', said one delegate. Another summed it up, 'She was very pleasant to everyone, but you sort of had the feeling that because she had done this so many times and one girl from Iceland is just like the other girl from Iceland, and one kid from Indonesia is just like another kid from Indonesia … of course that's what you'd expect. I mean she did this every year.' She was 'not especially warm, although she tried to give the impression' that she was, noted one delegate perceptively.[9]

Helen certainly had her favorites, but equally, she tailored her behavior to what delegates needed. She could be motherly for those who required it but did not waste time nurturing those who did not. She could certainly be intimidating and had high expectations. She challenged delegates to think and express well-thought-out opinions and had more time for those who were smart and articulate. Arnlaug (Norway 58) enjoyed Helen's unpredictability. One day she grabbed Gerd (Germany) and Arnlaug: 'Come on you two, you're coming with me', and took them to meet soon-to-be German Chancellor, Willie Brandt, who was in New York. For Arnlaug this was a highlight of the Forum. Helen expected delegates to step up and be prepared for anything, she was impatient with dilly dalliers. Susan (SA 57) described her as 'very, very smart—very ambitious', certainly with 'an agenda' but with charisma—she 'coaxed' rather than bullied. Other delegates were less generous in their assessments. But Susan stood up to her, calling her out when she was being manipulative. Helen seems to have enjoyed this—she appreciated smart, intelligent people who had something to say, were willing to argue, and expressed themselves in interesting ways, particularly when they did so on television.[10] She was dismissive of those who did not meet her high expectations.

Helen and 'Whitie'

Initially, Helen was not the only face of the Forum. She liaised with *Tribune* staff and had the support of Helen Rogers Reid and her son Whitelaw. Whitie Reid, a bachelor, also in his thirties in the late 1940s, was heavily involved in the Forum and there are conflicting stories about their relationship. One rumour had it that they were 'as good as engaged' at one point—Helen 'having ambitions'. According to Richard Kluger's history, Helen Rogers Reid decided that 'what Whitie Reid badly needed was a managing woman behind him' and placed 'at least two comely candidates' in front of him, including Helen Hiett. Helen apparently later told a colleague that she would have married Whitie 'if he'd only proposed'. Yet another version suggests Helen Rogers Reid told Helen she would support her career on the condition that she did *not* become involved with her son Whitelaw.[11] Any of these versions are possible, and all fit with Helen Hiett being an ambitious career woman.

Mrs Waller: Wife and Mother

In March 1948, coincidentally in the same week as Whitie Reid announced his own engagement, Helen married Theodore (Ted) Waller, three years her junior, just eight months after Ted had arrived in New York. This may have been a whirlwind romance, or they may have been old friends. They met through Harold Lasswell, who became 'Uncle Harry' to their children. He had taught them both at the University of Chicago, where their paths may even have crossed. Ted graduated in 1937 and was probably a freshman when Helen graduated in 1934. Although barely 32 when he married Helen in 1948, Ted had already been married twice. His second wife, Ruth, had died tragically of meningitis aged just 25 after saving a drowning child in Minsk in August 1946. Ted and Ruth both worked for the United Nations Relief and Rehabilitation Association. After Ted returned to the United States, he became Field Director for the Committee for the Marshall Plan, and then head of the Washington Office of the United World Federalists. These connections tied in neatly with Helen's Forum activities.[12]

Along with an internationalist agenda, Ted and Helen shared a love of mountaineering. Family friend and Sarah Lawrence College student helper at the Forum, Lee Workum, wrote of a holiday in Switzerland in 1957: 'You will not be surprised to hear that no Alp was too dangerous nor too high to keep Mrs Waller from taking off from the top with enthusiasm and abandon. She left 19-year-old Peter Workum trailing behind and Ma Workum gazing up from below in trembling admiration.' The Wallers had regular holidays in the mountains with their three children, Jonathan (Jay) (born February 1949), Mark (born May 1950), and Margaret (Margi) (born January 1954). (Observant readers will realize that this meant that Helen was quite literally giving birth during two Forums and heavily pregnant during a third. Fascinatingly, one (male) delegate from 1949 did not even notice!) The Waller family lived in a rambling old farmhouse in Katonah in Westchester County, New York. Helen and Ted both had careers while their children were growing up, Ted rising in the ranks of educational publisher Grolier Inc., and they had domestic staff, including nannies. Helen mothered her children like she ran the Forum: multitasking. Margi remembered her mother driving her to school, steering 'with her knees, with a cup of coffee in one hand and a cigarette in the other ... she smoked three packs of L&M's [Ligget and Myers]—unfiltered—a day'. She was a no-nonsense mother, telling her daughter to be 'a good sport—a mountain girl'. Crying was not encouraged. Margi understood that 'there was something wrong with acting like a girl'—she had to be 'as tough as the boys'. But Helen was also a personality—she could 'charm her way into anything'. The Wallers hosted some wonderful parties, particularly when Forum delegates were in town, and Helen knew everybody who was anybody. Margi noted, however, that her mother had 'great disdain for those who flaunted their money'. In the 1950s, Katonah did not have quite the air of exclusivity that it does today, and it was 'a point of pride' for Helen to live in a ramshackle, 200-year-old farmhouse with cat-scratched furniture,some distance from New York. It 'amused' her, remembered Margi, to invite dignitaries from the city to cocktails in the sticks.

Margi also recalled wonderful lively family discussions at the dinner table. Ted would bring home a new 'big word' with which to bamboozle them. Sixty years later her brother Mark could still recollect three of the more startling: 'formication', 'borborygmus', and 'blivet'. They would often spend hours at the dinner table poring over the 'quite massive Oxford English dictionary searching for words to stump the rest of the family', recalled Mark. He also remembered them all sitting on their parents' bed while Helen taught them to play bridge. She was 'an incredibly smart person', a 'strong presence', with a 'wicked sense of humor and endless curiosity', he said. She was impressive: a woman who made an impression. As a small child watching his mother on the little black-and-white television set in his parents' bedroom, he worried out loud to the latest nanny, 'why is Mum locked in that box?'

Both Mark and Margi also recalled their father's drinking—this was the era of long liquid lunches, martinis in the club car on the train out to Katonah, and a pick-me-up when he got home. By the late 1950s, Helen and Ted were living relatively independent lives. Mark did not think it a particularly 'good marriage' for his father. Helen was 'not necessarily a good mate', he said. As a 1950s career woman, Helen might have attracted criticism, but one wonders whether any woman would have been a 'good mate' for Ted—as well as being an alcoholic, he had a wandering eye.[13]

'Alps Mishap' Leads to Tragedy[14]

In the summer of 1961, the family was climbing in Chamonix in France when Helen was 'hit by a falling rock ... fell and rolled for a considerable distance over snow and rocks', suffering no broken bones but 'serious internal injuries'. The *Herald Tribune's* Europe correspondent reported on August 1 that she was 'out of danger' and recuperating in a European hospital after a successful emergency operation to stop internal bleeding. *Tribune* bosses sent flowers and good wishes and breathed a sigh of relief. In her thank you note to Jock Whitney on August 11, Helen was upbeat. 'I'm coming back alive and it's fun especially since no one here at the hospital expected me to!' Ever the journalist, she enthused that 'The Trib. really is an international newspaper', with the 'latest proof' being 'letters & telegrams from Forum Alumni <u>all</u> over the world' after the article about her accident. She joked, 'Sorry it frightened them all so much though!' She asked for another mention in the newspaper, to reassure everyone that she was 'getting well very rapidly' and would return to New York 'before the end of August'. She was full of ideas for the Forum and could 'hardly wait, given all the interesting new developments … especially in school edition plans'. Ted and the children returned to the US on August 12, leaving Helen 'in reasonably good shape', and expecting her to 'be along soon'. Instead, ten days later, at 11am on August 22, aged just 48, Helen suffered an embolism and died. She was buried in Chamonix, with only husband Ted, the general manager of the *Tribune*'s European edition, a few local friends (including the local deputy mayor), and hospital staff in attendance. It was almost exactly fifteen years after Ruth's death in Minsk. Ted did not cope well, locking away his memories of Helen and shutting himself away from their mutual friends. His daughter remembered no memorial services or opportunities to grieve as a family. Within four months of Helen's death Ted married 'his mistress' Irene Kitzing, and Helen was effectively written out of her children's lives.[15]

The Show Must Go On: After Helen

By the time of her death in 1961 Helen had turned the Forum into an institution. Although never financially secure, as we shall see, it had developed from a meeting day for local high schools into a three-month exchange program attracting delegates from around the world, with schools across the New York/New Jersey area clamoring to host students. Helen had fashioned a successful format of homestays, field trips, and televised panel discussions, along with an impressive array of important and famous figures for delegates to meet. Her Forum even inspired the 1949 *Daily Mail* imitation in the UK, but it did not have Helen at the helm and lasted only three years. Helen did not rest on her laurels and was always looking for new initiatives, even in her final days. She had created an ongoing Forum spirit among many alumni, and they were on the brink of becoming a more formal association when she died in 1961. To this day, there is a distinction between alumni from the 'Mrs Waller's time' and those who came after. 'Waller' Forum alumni are certain their version of the Forum was the original and the best, and that without Helen Waller, the Forum was but a pale shadow of itself.

Certainly, it was difficult to imagine a Forum without Helen when she died so suddenly in 1961. Her death had ongoing (and at the time some unrecognized) repercussions for the Forum. It is testimony to its success in raising the profile of the *Tribune*, perhaps, that the newspaper did not just abandon it. Planning was underway for the 1962 gathering, but delegates had not been chosen. It would have been simple to pull the plug. But the Forum was also important for John Hay Whitney, who had owned the *Tribune* since 1958 and was a proponent of internationalism, albeit within a framework of promoting US influence. Historian Frances Stonor Saunders described him as one of the CIA's 'quiet channels', particularly through his ownership of the London-based media service and CIA propaganda operation, Kern House Enterprises, in the 1960s, and family connections. The Forum's aims also meshed nicely with those of the Whitney Foundation, which sponsored educational opportunities for students from diverse backgrounds.[16]

So instead of wrapping it up, at the end of October 1961 the *Tribune* appointed as Forum director the recently widowed Virginia Graves Wieschhoff, a former teacher and educational administrator. Her husband, Herbert, had died in a plane crash in the Congo in April with UN Secretary General Dag Hammerskjold. Stately, elegant, and grieving, 56-year-old Mrs Wieschhoff was not the best choice to engage a group of smart, effervescent teenagers, despite her educational and international experience. She was nearly ten years older than Helen and looked significantly older. By all accounts she did her best with the Forum group of 1962, but it was not a brilliant fit. 'She treats us like 2-year-olds and 40-year-olds simultaneously' and 'doesn't realize we are kids who want to enjoy ourselves', complained one delegate in a letter home. Nevertheless, she did not leave immediately after the 1962 Forum. The '1963 World Youth Forum' booklet included Virginia's picture as director, and in mid-October 1962, Sarah Lawrence College staff were still corresponding with her about the 1963 Orientation program, starting on December 22, 1962. Six weeks later, in early December, they were informed abruptly that Virginia Wieschhoff had left. Ed Solomon, Forum liaison at the college, thought she had been hard done by and gave her replacement 'hell about what was done to' her.[17]

Virginia Wieschhoff had resigned in mid-November. Did she jump or was she pushed? She had certainly had a difficult time with some of her Forum group. Her resignation letter does not survive, but John Hay Whitney's reply does: he regretted that he could not see her in person due to his busy schedule and was sanguine about her departure. He was 'more than sorry' that 'the program is not what you had hoped it would be', given that, as he put it, the 'Forum operates more along business lines than is typical of the kind of philanthropic work you visualized when you took it on'. Was this a dig? He thanked her politely for filling the void left by Helen's 'untimely death' and making it 'possible for the Forum to live'.[18]

Virginia's replacement was 36-year-old Robert Smyser Huffman. Fortunately, given there were just three weeks before delegates arrived, he was familiar with the Forum. He had been running the Greater Metropolitan Program of the World Youth Forum, organizing the selection of the American delegate, and coordinating the relationship between local schools, media, and the Forum since the beginning of 1962. He had previous experience with the United Nations Association in Maryland, the Experiment in International Living, and as a State Department Foreign Affairs Officer. Originally from Ohio, the son of a schoolteacher, he had studied Business Administration at Ohio Wesleyan University. His university yearbook photo shows a clean-cut, bespectacled, pleasant-looking young man. He was six foot tall, ran cross-country, and was in the Men's Glee Club, the orchestra, the Tower Players, and the Varsity Debate team. Married since 1953, and with two young children, in 1963 he lived in Connecticut. His daughter remembered him as 'very intelligent and passionate about fostering better understanding between peoples and international relations'. He had 'an impressive memory and grasp of history and was a good writer'. Haider (Pakistan 71) described him as a 'non-city person', with 'no false sophistication … he didn't know the best restaurants in New York, for example'.[19] Helen Waller had reinvented herself from small-town Illinois reporter to a well-connected, award-winning journalist with international reach. Huffman did not have the same razzle-dazzle, although he was equally as invested in the Forum.

Despite his complaint about the *Tribune*'s treatment of Virginia Wieschhoff, Sarah Lawrence College's Ed Solomon thought Huffman 'a very "nice guy"', who would 'be able to take hold of the program and … have it in good shape'. Pan Am's director of public relations also approved of the new broom, noticing in 1963, 'renewed vigor in the program beginning last year and, while it was late getting started, nevertheless, it offers every hope for a rejuvenated program which, I am sure, will rebound to the benefit of our nation'.[20] (It sounds like he was saying the Forum was ready for a change even without Helen's death.) Huffman remained Forum director until the bitter end, fighting hard in the latter years to attract sufficient funding. His role became more critical after the *Tribune* folded in 1966, when the Forum was rebranded as simply the World Youth Forum and administered by a Board of Trustees.

Bob Huffman was not Helen Waller and had less impact on most delegates. Some described him as remote—professional and good at his job—but neither a father figure nor a confidante. Mikko (Finland 69) remembered 'a nice man who seemed very busy', his chain smoking earning him the nickname 'Huff Puff'. Emmanuel (Ghana 68) was more positive, being 'very impressed with his leadership'. With a 'nice deep voice', Huffman was 'attentive'; he 'knew things' and 'spoke very well'. Aysel (Turkey 64) recalled 'a tall and a serious looking gentleman, who seemed even more serious with his thick black frame eye glasses and his long black overcoat!', but who was 'very kind' and 'a good organizer'. When Monika (Austria 65) learned the term 'WASP' (White Anglo Saxon Protestant) she thought that summed up Bob Huffman. He presented 'the best picture of "America, the beautiful" (which we often sang), at a time of racial riots in the South'. He was 'clearly anti-communist/-socialist' and did not have 'a very positive opinion of the Catholic Church (I learned at the Forum that Catholics were expected to have many children—I didn't know that in Catholic Austria and Bavaria)'. She thought that 'he knew Western Europe, but hasn't been very much on other continents'.[21]

Often delegates remembered other staff more clearly, particularly the Forum alumni enlisted to assist on a casual basis. Certainly by 1970, Bob Huffman seemed a bit superfluous to some, 'out of touch with the world, and young people'. This might also reflect the increasing sophistication and independence of teenagers through the 1960s. Young people were discovering more strident and confident voices of their own, expressed in a youth culture and in political activism that no longer needed an adult moderator. The 'hope of the future' in 1949 had come of age by the late 1960s.[22]

The Workers Behind the Scenes

Helen Waller, Virginia Wieschhoff, and Bob Huffman did not run the Forums singlehandedly. Much of the daily grind was undertaken by a revolving door of paid and unpaid assistants. One assistant was particularly scathing about this, saying Helen was happy to be the face of the Forum, but behind the scenes her staff were the dogsbodies who did the real work. Helen ran two Forums until 1956, the Forum for High Schools from January to March and then the Forum for Current Problems in October. In 1948 the Forum payroll included full-time salaries for Helen Hiett and her main assistant Stella Stern, for Leonore Sanders, and for Mae Wolff Stabler, who was the *Tribune's* director of information well into the 1950s. Margaret Toomey worked half-time. When threatened with budget cuts in 1956, Helen insisted that two assistants were 'ESSENTIAL' for the Forum for High Schools' organization between October and March. She provided a page-long list of Forum tasks, including matching delegates with host students, which was a 'particular puzzle [that] takes two people 2–3 weeks to complete'. Corresponding with delegates, host schools, host families, national selection committees, USIS officials, and dignitaries, as well as organizing Orientation, briefing sessions, the TV series, field trips, and the final Forum also took time. And these were jobs for the assistants. 'My own calendar', she concluded firmly, itemizing an extended inventory of tasks, is 'too long to list'. The assistants had clerical help, with secretaries pulled from the *Tribune* when required, while the newspaper's publicity department did PR. Helen resented her lack of control over this, keen to oversee all Forum budgets and staff. In the 1960s Robert Huffman usually had one assistant and a secretary until the *Tribune* folded, after which staffing levels fluctuated depending on his resources. In 1967 he had a staff of three, for example, but in 1969 he depended upon the volunteer help of Lew (US 64)'s mother Katherine Andrews.[23]

The paid assistants, especially in the 1950s, were generally young women who stayed two or three years. It was a badly paid job with irregular hours, designed for a smart young woman as a stopgap. Significantly, however, marriage and motherhood were not always a barrier to employment. The American family might have been central to US Cold War propaganda, with an idealized stay-at-home mom surrounded by two-and-a-half children and sparkling labor-saving devices in her new suburban home, but employment rates for women also rose in the 1950s. Doris 'Freddie' Friedman started as Helen's assistant in 1952, married in 1953, and continued working (still as 'Freddie') until the end of 1956. Similarly, although Joan Levy arrived straight out of college and departed two years later in 1967 when she married Robert Layton, her colleague, Sylvia Abraham, John Hay Whitney's secretary, remained after she wed in the same year. Sometimes married women returned to the workforce for specific purposes. In 1961 Norma Brent, already in her 40s, joined the team to pay the secondary school and college tuition for her son. Notably, when he graduated, she did not return to domesticity but started a new career as a teacher in her early 50s. Former delegate Christine Dodson (Greece 53) got a job with Helen when she turned up in 1959 to show off her new baby, having moved to the US and married in the interim. Christine's appointment was unexpected on all sides. As she went in with her baby to see Helen, Forum assistant Jeanne Brockman was coming out. 'She was really angry', Christine remembered. Then 'Waller just got up and right there and then said to me, would you like Jeanne's job … I need someone tomorrow'. Had Jeanne been sacked or had she quit? No record remains of why, although Christine herself got an inkling in her own two years working for Helen Waller, whom she found a demanding boss.[24]

At least two assistants were African Americans, surprising some delegates who noticed formal and informal segregation even in New York. Perhaps this was deliberate. Rita Taylor (1956–57) took a temporary pay cut to transfer to the Forum office, with Helen promising to increase her pay in time, being 'extremely anxious to have Rita in my office'. She felt 'her addition to the Forum staff has unique advantages in connection with High School Forum work'. She did not specify those 'unique advantages', but performing diversity may have been one. Another African American, Joan Lee Smith (1959–62), had a great influence on her colleague Christine, who recalled that she was 'the first one who got me involved in racial issues ... her father was a very active black man in the beginning of the equality'.[25]

Helen Waller only ever employed one young man. Johan Holst had been a delegate himself (Norway 56) and was possibly employed at the behest of another employee and former delegate, Judith Perry (Canada 53). They distinguished themselves by quietly getting married in Arlington, Virginia, during the Forum trip to Washington in 1960. Robert Huffman employed more young men, also associated with the Forum. Dave Bromberg, runner up in the 1963 American delegate competition, was an airport greeter and general dogsbody in 1964. Appropriately for someone who would establish himself as a folk musician, he never went anywhere without his guitar. Gus Nasmith (US 62) also started as an 'airport greeter' in 1963. He was earning $100 for his help by 1966. He and another alumnus, Lew Andrews (US 64), met delegates at the airport and delivered them safely to Sarah Lawrence College. By the end of the decade Gus had risen to assistant director and was running much of the Summer Forum program. Correspondence between Bob Huffman and Gus shows that they were a close-knit team, both working hard to keep the Forum alive. Delegates remembered Gus with fondness. For many he was the face of the Forum more than his boss. Emmanuel (Ghana 68) was impressed that 'he knew how to relate to us', probably because 'he had gone through the program'. While Huffman was 'almost like strict', Gus was more easy-going. 'We didn't do anything mischievous, but we felt good.' With Gus, 'it felt he was one of us. I liked him. We all did.'[26] One girl delegate's diary is full of breathless anticipation for the next time she will see Gus, who clearly had made an impression. He was just a year or two older and very personable.

Like Gus, other assistants acted as links between delegates and Forum director. They were less intimidating. Hameeda (Pakistan 52) remembered 'Freddie' (Doris Friedman) 'was very friendly and nearer our age, so she was a lot of fun'. Christine 'was really the person who took care' of the delegates, recalled Snait (Israel 61), although another (male) delegate thought she had too strong a personality. Avri (Israel 68) enjoyed talking with Bob Joyce (1967–68) who was 'more approachable' than Huffman.[27]

No assistant remained for long, but they were critical to the Forum, undertaking the bulk of the administrative work as well as being available to delegates as sympathetic shoulders to cry on and sources of advice. The predominance of young women in these positions, especially in the 1950s, was to be expected given the low pay and 'girl Friday' nature of what was a short-term job. Nevertheless, some used it as a stepping stone to a career, particularly in the international education sector, while one reinvented herself and became a historian and another became a diplomat.[28]

Harnessing the Alumni

Forum directors, paid assistants (and the occasional mom) were supplemented by a raft of alumni volunteers. From the start, Helen Waller created a sense of community, maintaining contact with delegates after they returned home through newsletters and personal visits, and encouraging US-based alumni to drop by the Forum office. She also co-opted them to assist. Late in 1956, Helen asked alumni to contact their country's 1957 delegate, and called for volunteers to 'lend a helping hand' for new delegates traveling through the 'necessary stop-over points like Manila'. Selection committees had written to her, 'worrying about how delegates with limited funds and no travel experience' would cope.[29]

US-based alumni often visited the new batch of delegates during Orientation week and in 1959 Helen saw another way to encourage (or exploit) their engagement (and to save money). The 1958 Christmas newsletter announced enthusiastically that 'the entire staff for the 1959 Orientation (including cooks and dishwashers) will be Forum alumni'. They were unpaid. Chit (India 56), studying at Harvard, saw this as a way of 'giving back', but also appreciated his continued involvement in the 'energy of the Forum'. The initial six volunteers were a diverse group. 'Every continent represented except Europe!', exclaimed Helen in the newsletter, adding that 'if we survive the experiment', Orientation week would 'be run this way in the future'. Helen regretted this arrangement meant that there would be 'no extra beds, or space at meals, for visiting alumni'. She slyly suggested they might apply to be 'Kober House Staff' in later years. The scheme lasted for two years. There were benefits for the alumni, especially when they were studying far from home. Jorge (Uruguay 53) loved his time as an unpaid 'kitchen hand ... in charge of cooking' in 1959 and 1960. It was better than staying in the empty dorm at MIT in Boston over Christmas and there were lots of new people to meet, including Pete Seeger and civil rights lawyer Thurgood Marshall. Jorge told me proudly, 'there was Thurgood Marshall and he was eating *my* food!' Jorge's cohort back in 1953 had not enjoyed an 'orientation' period so doubtless that added to the attraction.[30]

For 1960, the Forum introduced an 'alumni fellowship' scheme, under which 'alumni fellows' were flown back from their countries (or from whichever American college had given them a scholarship) for the whole three-month Forum period. This was one better than the volunteers, who were usually based around New York, and only came to Orientation. Although also unpaid, the alumni fellowships were competitive. The December 1959 newsletter announced that fifty applicants had competed for the first three positions for 1960. It was an inspired innovation. These 20-somethings also bridged the gap between middle-aged Forum directors and teenage delegates. Importantly they were ex-delegates. As the alumni fellows emphasized in the first issue of the annual *Forum Tribune* circular to new delegates in December 1959, 'The one thing we would like you to do is to come to us with your problems, large and small ... remember that one of us might have had the same problem as a delegate!' Accompanying the delegates on their field trips, they were also relatively responsible pairs of eyes, ensuring the teenagers were safe, without having to be too heavy-handed about rules and regulations. Helen also used them to lead discussions, and, in 1960, the three Alumni Fellows appeared with five 1960 delegates on a Forum panel in the Association for Supervision and Curriculum Development Annual Conference. Having their perspective as 25-year-olds undoubtedly enriched the conversation, but was their involvement at the expense of actual 1960 delegates? Alumni fellows reappeared in 1961 and 1962, with the additional requirement that they have a degree of maturity. One of them, Ulrik (Denmark 48), at 31, must have seemed quite old to the delegates, but the Forum now wanted responsible chaperones. In 1962, the third and final year of alumni fellows, Josephine (Australia 53) was probably the most useful as a qualified doctor.[31] Alumni continued to appear in the 1960s as helpers, but the fellowships were discontinued under Bob Huffman's leadership, contributing to the disconnect between 'Mrs Waller's' delegates and those who came later.

Leading the Way

If the Forum relied heavily on the hard work of volunteer alumni and office staff, it was shaped by the personalities and connections of its directors. Helen Waller created and molded the Forum according to the ideals laid out in her prospectus for youth-led world peace, *No Matter Where*. Always a journalist, with an eye for a headline, she cajoled and manipulated the delegates into providing good copy. She also massaged her connections, and those of the *Tribune* owners, the Reids and Whitneys, to great effect. She wanted impact and international prestige for the *Tribune*, the Forum, and herself. Bob Huffman was a different breed, more focused on the educational aspects of the Forum, less well-connected, and less charismatic. He arguably had a more difficult job, corralling more rebellious teenagers in a rapidly changing world, in which the Forum as either an international propaganda machine or Cold War player struggled to hold its own. Helen Waller remained legendary among many delegates, and if Bob Huffman was less memorable, his determination to keep the Forum alive in later years was second to none. That commitment was essential after the death of the *Herald Tribune* in 1966.

Much of the director's job was massaging connections with the great and good, with the influential (to impress foreign delegates) and with the cashed-up or those with relevant services to offer. For, like any such program, the Forum required financial and in-kind support, and it is to this we turn now—to follow the money.

Chapter 4

Follow the Money
Financing the Forum

Running the Forum did not come cheap. Delegates required flights, accommodation, and entertainment. Administrative costs included staff, plus copying, printing, and postage, which all added up, as well as internal transportation. The three-month visit concluded with a grand finale, usually held at the Waldorf Astoria and later the Lincoln Center—both of which charged substantial hire fees. Forum organizers became adept at finding partners to provide financial and in-kind support. Those partners came with their own agendas and included the US State Department. The Forum was a perfect example of the private-public collaboration that characterized the business of Cold War cultural diplomacy, in which idealism, internationalism, and independence sometimes sat uneasily alongside US propaganda interests. The partners in the Forum enterprise found themselves willing bedfellows with convergent aims.[1]

The principal sponsor, until its demise in 1966, was the *Herald Tribune*, for whom the Forum was a public relations, corporate social responsibility, and newspaper-sales-boosting enterprise. Behind-the-scenes correspondence suggested not all *Tribune* bean-counters were fans.

The Budget

The Forum was always on a tight budget. Records from the 1950s illustrate the myriad ways costs were calculated, manipulated, and, as the *Tribune* hit money troubles, trimmed. Helen Waller fought hard for her share of the pie, culminating in what *Tribune* business manager Barney G Cameron described in 1958 as a 'not a very pleasant discussion' about expenditure.[2]

Forum costs varied, depending often on how elaborate and extensive the activities, and the level of external sponsorship. The 1946 Forum for just American students came in at a lean $5462.53. That cost nearly quadrupled the following year, with the expansion of the program to include international students staying for three months. Delegates' travel was free, but that for Forum staff and reporters formed the biggest single item in 1947 at $9368.81. The total cost of the Forum for 1948 more than doubled again to nearly $23,500 because the salaries of Helen and the staff were included. (This was about $285,000 in 2024 dollars.)[3] The costs nearly doubled again in 1949 to an eye-watering $44,418.17. This was not as bad as it seemed, as it included $10,098 for 'space in Monday issue 101 columns 511654 copies'—for a blow-by-blow description of the forum at the Waldorf in a ten-page special feature in the *Tribune*. The inclusion of the newspaper space cost was an in-kind expense, but it indicated that the Forum was assessed independently from the newspaper in its accounting. And the regular costs continued. Printing, postage, and telephone costs were around $4000, travel and entertainment, $5500. The Waldorf Astoria ballroom rent was steep at $2993.82 in 1947, rising to $3591.07 in 1949. Small costs added up. One of the more obscure budget items in 1947 was a payment of $250 to the New York Decorating Company. Was that to decorate the Waldorf for the finale? Or Helen's office? The organist at the Waldorf Astoria, Dr Casimir Parmentier, charged $120 in 1949. Insurance costs were $846.35 in the same year. Some costs were unexpected. In 1947, medical expenses for Erica (Canada 47) cost $513.81, and two boys also visited the doctor at $25 each. In 1949, $835 was spent on medical costs and flying the parent of a sick student from Europe to the US.[4]

Costs plummeted in 1950 to just under $22,500, including the newspaper space. Had the Forum been told to watch spending? The salaries bill dropped from $12,000 to just under $8000. Printing costs halved, and travel costs for staff, speakers, and students were just under $1600, a fraction of the previous costs. The services of the famous Casimir Parmentier had been dispensed with in favor of a cheaper organist (or he performed for a shorter time), paid a mere $25. The newspaper feature was almost halved into fifty-three columns, 'costing' just $6519.85. Creative accounting, which shifted half of Helen Waller's salary to the Forum for Current Problems budget, reduced expenditure still further, to $18,335.52, in 1952. Aside from salaries, the biggest single annual expense was renting the grand ballroom of the Waldorf Astoria. In 1952 the finale moved to the Hotel Astor, where the rival *Mirror* Forum was held, but this was even more expensive than the Astoria at $1542.59 for one day. The Forum moved back to the Waldorf in 1953. The UN General Assembly Hall was the venue in 1954 and 1955. It was a mere snip at $785 and then $1029. But the Waldorf remained the preferred venue from 1956 until 1962. It had prestige. First, it was the setting of the *Tribune*'s Forum for Current Problems, with its global cast of eminent speakers. Holding the High School Forum in the same place raised its status by association, and reinforced the idea that youth were important. It also maintained the image of the *Tribune* and its owners, the Reids and Whitneys, as players in New York society. Ex-president Herbert Hoover, General Douglas Macarthur, and Marilyn Monroe all lived at the Waldorf in the 1950s: it was *the* place to be. Over the years, Forum staff negotiated hard for discounts with some success. Bob Huffman moved the Forum finale to the newly opened Philharmonic Hall at the Lincoln Center in 1963. Orientation week and other gatherings were held for many years at Kober House at Sarah Lawrence College, which did not charge a fee, although there were costs for staff, food, and administration, as well as wear and tear. The *Tribune* (and later CBS) also provided office space.[5]

In 1954 and 1955 Forum costs came in at $16,224 and just under $15,000. By 1966, when the *Tribune* folded, Forum costs had again more than doubled to $40,000, but included the Greater Metropolitan and Summer Forum programs. In subsequent years Huffman cut costs to the bone, as we will see in a later chapter.[6]

Selling Newspapers

The *Herald Tribune*'s core business was not the Forum but newspaper publication. Both the Forum for Current Problems and the Forum for High Schools were pet projects of *Tribune* owner Helen Rogers Reid, but they had to justify their existence, primarily through raising the profile of the paper, demonstrated most tangibly through increased circulation. As well as being 'a public service to bring the best thinking to bear on the issues of the day', the Forum for High Schools, like its Current Problems predecessor, was 'a public relations tool to extend the readership' of the newspaper. During the televised debates, Helen Waller made sure not only to thank sponsors but also to advertise the annual special Forum feature in the *Herald Tribune*. The newspaper's 'Educational Department' wrote to teachers advertising a 'special school rate', which in 1957 was three cents per copy, allowing classes 'to share in this meeting of the world's young minds ... acquiring a grassroots understanding of the people and problems of other nations'.[7]

Marketing the newspaper was at the forefront of Forum decisions. When it was proposed that the students spend some time with host families in rural areas in Maryland, Helen Waller was unsure. On the plus side, it would allay criticism that delegates had a 'rather one-sided picture of American life', staying only in the New York area, as Flemington High School teacher Helen Scharrer suggested in 1949. In addition, the visit would involve no extra work for Forum staff. But was it worth it for the newspaper? The 'people' in Maryland had been 'difficult to deal with in the past' and had 'small compunction about omitting mention of the *Herald Tribune* in publicity relative to the project'. Even 'more important', Waller argued, was the 'real question' as to 'whether we should send Forum students to localities outside our primary circulation area'. She feared that the paper would not 'consider money spent on administration justifyable [sic] for those areas'.[8]

Forum staff worked hard to collect evidence of local and international impact, especially among an up-and-coming generation of newspaper readers. Helen Waller provided numerous endorsements from delegates, host families, and schools in a 1952 memo to Whitie and Helen Reid titled 'more proof of the penetration of the High School Forum'. Forum delegates' visit was the theme of the WC Mepham High School's yearbook. An American embassy official in Iran praised the program for successfully imparting positive understandings of 'American culture, philosophy, and ideals', in contrast to other exchanges, whose participants returned from the US merely 'impressed by the size of our country, its technological development, its material wealth, etc'. Reed Harris, USIA, saw 'many evidences that the impact of your carefully organized trips and discussions is felt all over the world'. A 1954 television program opened with Helen quoting from Malverne High School students' enthusiastic letters: 'Even the teachers learned something ... we learned more in two weeks from the students than in two years of reading books'.⁹

In 1956 *Tribune*'s director of information Mae Stabler wrote to the parents of Gladys (Lebanon 56), ostensibly to advise that Gladys was doing 'an exceptionally fine job' and 'making a unique contribution to better understanding', but also asking them to send 'all the publicity concerning your daughter … published in papers, magazines or school publications in your country'. This was for the annual 'comprehensive scrapbook' with 'clippings from all over the world'.¹⁰ As belts at the *Tribune* tightened, excerpts from this scrapbook along with selected highlights from complimentary correspondence were forwarded to Ogden Reid as ammunition against Barney G Cameron and others, who viewed the Forum as a luxury.

The threat to the High School Forum became serious in 1956, when the twenty-fifth annual *Herald Tribune* Forum for Current Problems was canceled barely a month before it was scheduled to take place in October. It died, apparently without fuss, after nearly a quarter of a century.¹¹ Could the High School Forum be next?

There was a veiled threat in Barney Cameron's May 1956 memo to Helen after one conversation: 'I do hope you understand our concern in wanting to make the *Herald Tribune* itself as strong as possible, so that we may continue to engage in the Forum and other worthwhile activities'.¹² In 1958 they disagreed over staff wages, Helen's expenses, and the inevitable incidental costs from Forum excursions. But underscoring it all was the issue of control. Cameron had to approve every expenditure item. In January 1958 Helen told Barney that she was 'tired of quibbling over Forum expenses' and that she 'would live within' a budget if she was given one, but 'didn't want anyone to tell her how she could spend the money'. She stormed out of his office, announcing she would get Ogden Reid to 'establish new rules' so that she could operate the Forum without consulting Barney Cameron. This did not eventuate, and the pair were still 'quibbling' in May 1958, with Barney refusing to pay 'the avalanche of Forum bills' from the group's trip to Berlin, including some expenses incurred by Helen after delegates had left. Helen had remained in Europe, ostensibly on Forum business. Barney was (understandably) dubious and things came to a head. 'Mrs Waller was not only trying to taunt me into losing my temper, but inviting me to throw her out of the office—neither of which happened', concluded Barney in his report to Ogden Reid. He told Helen 'quite frankly' that he thought the Forum's value 'was negligible from the circulation and advertising standpoint' and it should be undertaken 'only if the *Herald Tribune* was making real money and could afford this sort of thing'.

Helen then upped the ante, threatening to 'take the Forum over to Mr Sulzberger', owner of the rival *New York Times*, who was, she said, 'very anxious to take over the Forum at any time [the *Tribune*] didn't want it'. Was she bluffing? One imagines so, since the *Times* already had Dorothy Gordon running their own American youth forum. Barney was unconcerned, suggesting to Ogden Reid that before approving the budget for the coming year, they should 'sit down and discuss the advisability of continuing the High School Forum'. Despite his reservations, the Forum continued, surviving the sale of the *Tribune* to John Hay 'Jock' Whitney late in 1958. According to Robert Huffman, Jock Whitney 'was urged by many top staffers to scrub the Forum' when he took over the paper; 'he could have saved at least a third of a million dollars by 1966 had he done so'. This was not an unsubstantial sum, 'even to a Jock Whitney'. But he did not. The Forum continued, its position nevertheless remaining tenuous, with Helen writing in January 1961 to new *Tribune* vice president and moneyman, Richard Steele, asking firmly for 'a decision by February 10, 1961, if the Forum is to continue in 1962 under the *Herald Tribune* auspices'.[13]

Helen's death in August 1961 arguably gave the *Tribune* the ideal opportunity to ditch the Forum. Instead, Whitney told the 'many people' who 'urged us to continue', that there was 'great enthusiasm' at the newspaper, where people saw an opportunity for 'broadening and strengthening' Forum activities. Money remained tight, though, and newspaper sales continued to be important. When briefing John Hay Whitney in 1963, Forum assistant director Anne Counes articulated the importance of Louis E Dieruff High School not only by praising the school's long-term cooperation, but adding, 'Incidentally, they buy about 100 copies of the HT issue carrying the proceedings of the Forum'.[14]

The *Herald Tribune* did not outlay vast sums on the Forum, cleverly spreading the burden around government and private enterprise sponsorship and making the most of good-will volunteers. John Hay Whitney put it bluntly when thanking a donor in 1963: 'Although the Forum is a department of the *Herald Tribune*, it is not an income-producing operation ... every dollar saved—or contributed—assumes an importance far out of proportion to the amount of money involved.'[15] Where did that money and in-kind support come from? And what did it really cost?

'An Arm of Our State Department?'

One of the most striking things about Forum is that it received no formal State Department funding until its final years. The US government's 'Teen-age Program' focused on organizations providing year-long exchanges, as we have seen. The government provided the Forum with 'facilitative nonfinancial assistance', which it gave to several organizations working in the field.[16]

The USIA had a heavy hand in selecting delegates, except, that is, for 'invitations to Iron Curtain countries'. American embassies provided logistical assistance and access to local resources. Consul officials, cultural attaches, and USIS staff publicized the program, liaised with foreign governments, assisted in 'screening and selection of candidates', and facilitated visas and travel arrangements. USIS personnel sometimes went above and beyond. During his selection, Emmanuel (Ghana 68) stayed in the home of Cultural Affairs Officer Stella Davis in Accra. His boarding school was 400 miles from the capital. Emmanuel described Stella as a 'very wonderful woman', and certainly she must have been, because playing host to a 16-year-old schoolboy was surely not in her official job description.[17]

At times government support went further. In 1949 the *Chicago Daily Tribune* journalist Arthur Henning, an anti-communist, vented isolationist spleen: 'US Taxpayers Stand Cost of Luxury Tours: Planes at Disposal of "Right" People'. Among the 'right' people attracting his ire were the thirty-four European Forum students. Three Air Force twin-engined C-47s ferried delegates around the US from New York to Dallas to Los Angeles and back on what Henning called 'an internationalist propaganda enterprise'. He claimed the *Herald Tribune*, 'an internationalist organ and Marshall Plan propagandist', had a $100,000 subsidy from Marshall Plan funds through owner Helen Rogers Reid's influence with the Truman administration.[18] (In his diatribe he missed another connection—Forum convenor Helen Hiett's new husband Ted Waller had been a field director for the Committee for the Marshall Plan.) The coast-to-coast jaunt was not repeated.

The Forum knew government support was essential, giving the Forum legitimacy and credibility internationally. Both the Forum and the US State Department nevertheless understood the benefits of an illusion of distance, just as with the 'Teen-age Program' more broadly. When seeking to expand the Forum to Asia and the Middle East for 1950, Helen Waller consulted with the State Department. Its memo to 'Certain American Diplomatic and Consular Officers' in the countries was explicit about the benefits of the Forum, which 'may be extremely useful in promoting friendly relations between the US and countries concerned'. At the same time, officials were asked 'not to discuss the project at the time with the reps of countries'. Both the Department and the *Herald Tribune* 'prefer keeping this a private enterprise'. The newspaper would make first contact with foreign officials. The role of the State Department and its functionaries would be 'to act as technical assistants' to the *Herald Tribune*.[19]

Nevertheless, as far as the rest of the world were concerned, the Forum was inextricably linked with the US government, whether for better or for worse. Alice (Singapore 52) later told a researcher she had won 'an essay competition funded by the United States Information Service'. The *Indonesian Observer* reported the arrest of Permesta rebel Nonna (Indonesia 57) in 1959 and made much of her having been 'sent to the United States with a scholarship under the sponsorship of the United States Information Service'. The implication was clear, particularly as the CIA were providing support to Permesta. And it was not lost on Forum newsletter editors reprinting the story. They were annoyed that 'no mention is made of the fact that it was sponsored by the Indonesian Ministry of Education'.[20] That was true, but the American government were also very much involved.

The World Assembly of Youth was exposed in the late 1960s as a CIA front, but the Forum does not appear to have had any covert interference. Rather the reverse. It seems the only CIA interest in the Forum was investigative. Buried in the archives is a small, typed memo 'just by way of keeping you filled in', from Helen Waller to Ogden Reid in December 1956. She reported that 'John H. Mitchell, C.I.A. was "investigating" the High School Forum'. Mitchell, she said, was 'a good type', who 'honestly doesn't seem to know what angle they are interested in'. She had 'cooperated fully, of course', explaining 'the degree to which the State and USIA have been involved in our operation from the beginning, and the extent to which they make use of our materials around the world'.[21]

There was, of course, no need for CIA intervention. This was a cooperative relationship between partners with converging aims, promoting a pro-American version of 'democratic' internationalism. The Forum worked hand-in-hand with the US government, inspiring NYU professor Redefer's description of it as 'an arm of our State Department in spreading understanding'. Professional, political, and personal connections linked *Tribune* owners, Forum directors, government officials, and politicians. This was indicative of a wider phenomenon, noted by historian Karen Paget: not only did actors on both sides of the public/private divide operate in the same intersecting circles, but individuals also moved in and out of government and non-government positions, some even holding them concurrently. The careers of Ogden Reid and John Hay Whitney epitomize this. Bob Huffman was himself an ex-State Department man and Helen Waller just knew everybody. As she boasted to a potential sponsor, 'Secretary Dulles' sister personally made arrangements for the 1956 Forum group to spend a week in Berlin and is now making plans for a return visit to Berlin in 1957'.[22] *That* was how well connected the Forum was, she was saying. Those personal connections allowed the Forum access to prominent government figures and ensured the government had the ear of those running the program.

Delegates came from countries that were either allies of the US or candidates for a closer political relationship—within the American sphere of influence. Forum officials consulted annually with the State Department over country selection, so it would 'coincide with the national interest'. Like the Forum, the US government saw the specially selected delegates—ideally the cream of the crop of their own countries—as potential future leaders. As Senator (later President) Jack Kennedy told 1957 delegates, 'I am confident that seated here today are the Eisenhowers and the Diems and the Hammarskjolds and the Madam Pandits of the future.'[23] Ten years later, a State Department report was equally explicit about the benefits of hosting foreign exchange students, whether in high schools or universities.

> Many ... will enter the educated group of potential leaders on their return home. The quality of their education here, the connections and friendships they develop, and the views of the United States and Americans they take back with them are thus significant to their country's future understanding of and relationship with the United States.[24]

Forum organizers were complicit in USIS 'public diplomacy'. The USIA made films of the Forum in 1950, 1952, and 1959, along with annual recordings of the the Forum's finale sessions. These were circulated through US embassy channels, as were delegates' Voice of America broadcasts, in which they waxed lyrical about the charms of the US. By 1957, a State Department photographer was 'regularly assigned to follow the Forum group for three months to make picture stories of each delegate in one American host family, school and community'. US cultural affairs officers made 'extensive use of Forum material throughout the world', especially in the 1950s. Helen consistently reminded alumni of their responsibilities in her newsletter: 'Have all of you written to the USIS official who helped you with your trip here?'. The 'USIS should also get a copy of your report to the Ministry of Education' and 'please be sure, all of you, to pay a visit to the USIS office, and explore the variety of possibilities that can be created for you to share your Forum experience with others'. Alumni were told to respond to USIS surveys about the impact of the Forum. A USIS officialin Denmark was impressed with Ejvind (59), who (surprisingly for any of us who have met the effervescent Dane) 'could not find the words to tell how much the Forum meant to him'. He 'showed the great value of the Forum experience' because 'he was able to give a more positive picture of American youth than has been given in the Danish press'. The official continued enthusiastically, 'In inviting Ejvind, we have not only won a firm friend of American youth, but have given him an experience which I think has broadened his view of the world and will make him a more active and politically conscious Danish citizen'.[25]

For the US government, supporting the Forum as an unofficial arm of American 'public diplomacy' was an easy choice, particularly as no actual money changed hands for much of the relationship. Equally, the benefits for the Forum were clear, providing access and assistance, and raising its profile internationally. Informal channels of communication and converging aims meant that there seemed little need for the Forum to tailor its programs or selection of delegates beyond any uncomfortable limits.

Fly Away With Me

Government support was also key to arrangements with Pan Am and TWA (and sometimes other airlines) to provide complimentary flights for delegates. The State Department recommended annually to the Civil Aeronautical Board (CAB), which regulated airlines, that it 'authorize free international air travel' for Forum delegates. The State Department kept itself at arm's length from this significant concession, suggesting strongly in a 1959 background paper that 'it might be inadvisable to make a public statement with regard to this support', because 'the CAB considers the Forum as an exception to the rule against making such authorizations'. This 'exception' lasted for twenty-five years, until 'a change in government policy' in 1972 that meant that the Forum could 'no longer have the free air transportation for delegates', causing it to radically alter its format. Neither was it really an exception. *Mirror* Forum delegates also flew free of charge, and Pan Am sponsored other student flights. Their involvement was in many ways unsurprising. Air travel was emblematic of American modernity, a suitable expression of American global power. Like other American businesses wishing to extend their markets around the world, airlines realized the product that was 'America' was a powerful marketing tool, at least until the later 1960s, when the shine was becoming tarnished by civil rights issues at home and imperialist follies abroad. Like the Forum, airlines enabled the dissemination of American ideas around the world. TWA's president Charles Thomas put it more romantically in

Skyliner Magazine in 1960. The collaboration was 'logical', because 'the ideals of the Forum—to bring nations close and increase communication among people—are similar to those of TWA'.[26]

The real trade-off was publicity. Jona (Iceland 60) was bewildered to be offered an ice cream the moment she landed in New York. She soon realized this was the first of many photo opportunities. 'The Icelandic delegate eating an ice cream' was too good an image to pass up. Pan Am's diligent photographer, Lorraine Kure, posed a smiling and exhausted-looking Jona with an ice cream sundae, her Pan Am travel bag prominently displayed. Other delegates were also snapped as they arrived—carefully arranged around their Pan Am or TWA bags. This was the price for free air travel. It was just as well Lorraine was a 'wonderful person', remarked Jona, because they 'saw a lot of her'. Stories about delegates appeared in airline magazines, especially those aimed at schools.[27] And the names of Pan Am and TWA were front and center during broadcasts and live performances of Forum delegates, with annual puff pieces in the *Herald Tribune* highlighting their mutual admiration. Young Forum delegates were a target demographic, especially in the new age of jet travel.

Other airlines became involved when Pan Am and TWA did not fly to delegates' countries. Occasionally free flights were impossible, leaving Forum officials scrambling. Then, it was all about personal connections. Michael (Kenya 64) almost missed out entirely when Kenya's independence meant that BOAC could no longer fly him from Nairobi to London, requiring an extra flight for $500. Neither he nor the Forum had the funds but Forum staff successfully obtained sponsorship from the 'Cannon Family Fund', which, remarked Forum staff member Anne Counes in some surprise, 'seems to be a small philanthropic fund, located in the south *of all places,* dedicated to furthering the interests of African students'. It was administered by an exceedingly well-connected New Yorker (and ex-girlfriend of JFK), Frances Ann Dougherty. Of course, nothing comes for free, and Michael had to sing for his supper. Anne Counes noted drily that the Doughertys 'had Michael to their home for dinner twice and seem to be very pleased with their "investment"'.[28]

Personal connections were also key to local transportation. Forum secretary Martine Price (an 'outrageous woman who loved people and high society', and who demonstrated personality and entrepreneurship in her business and personal life) was usefully friends with Herbert G. 'Duke' Wellington Snr, a major Greyhound stockholder. She approached Herbert, who made a personal donation in 1963, and enabled the Forum to hire Greyhound buses for their jaunts to Washington and Boston at cost.[29]

Bed and Board

Having arrived in the US, delegates required accommodation. Schools, students, and their families were critical partners in the Forum enterprise. The support of the Metropolitan School Study Council and later of a broader range of schools, including both public and private, was 'in-kind' rather than financial. In contrast to the *New York Mirror* forum, where the delegates stayed in hotels, the *Herald Tribune* successfully outsourced responsibility for housing and entertaining the delegates. It was a win-win situation, with aims of high schools and Forum intersecting, as we will see in a later chapter.

Universities and colleges were also key partners, notably Sarah Lawrence College, a women's liberal arts college in Yonkers New York, where Orientation was held from 1954 to 1967. The College charged no fee, understanding there were mutual benefits in the arrangement. As College president Harold Taylor pointed out, delegates had 'vivid and warm' memories of their time there, taking away an image of American college life which was 'progressive, liberal, and intellectually interesting'.[30] Female delegates were also potential future students.

Files in the College archives detailing negotiations with Forum staff reveal the relationship was not always smooth-sailing, and the level of interaction varied. Initially things were positive. College staff were impressed with the caliber of the 1954 delegates and were keen to support closer ties in 1955, including joint seminars and College student mentors. The idea was that college students and foreign delegates would collaborate on projects relevant to the curriculum. Together the College and the Forum obtained $25,000 (the equivalent of $280,000 in 2023) from the Ford Foundation to cover costs of three sessions at Sarah Lawrence including Orientation week, as well as a whistlestop international tour for a select group of delegates plus two College students.

Combining with the College was a clever way for the Forum to access Ford Foundation sponsorship. As early as 1952 Melvin Fox of the Ford Foundation had suggested the *Tribune* might consider 'getting a Foundation to finance the High School forum'. Fox described it as an attractive proposition for potential sponsors because of the 'tremendous' and 'visible' impact of the Forum 'in so many parts of the world'. He regretted that the Ford Foundation itself was limited by its charter to assisting adults in the field of international exchange. Sarah Lawrence College qualified. Just over $5000 of the $25,000 was spent by the College on a series of workshops, which included their students and Forum delegates. Another $4000 was Helen Waller's director's fee, and the remaining $16,000 was for the trip to England, France, Lebanon, Egypt, Pakistan, and India. Delegates performed and debated in forums in front of high school audiences in each country.[31]

There were potential advantages for both parties in the combined program, not least the publicity value in bringing the College to the 'attention of high school students throughout the country, which should aid our recruitment program', but College staff were skeptical from the outset. College dean, Esther Raushenbush, was suspicious that Helen Waller's suggestion that College students accompany the foreign delegates to their host schools was 'principally a way of getting some check by our students on the schools'. Others saw little real educational value in the workshop scheme which had an overemphasis on social interaction, and 'were disconcerted about the projects and methods which were suggested by the *Herald Tribune*', which did not square with 'the educational practices to which they were accustomed'. The delegates were 'too exploited' and 'driven to point of exhaustion' and 'were so fatigued physically and mentally that most of them used the [workshop] week exclusively for resting', learning little about the way the College worked. The 'chief difficulty', concluded the college, was the 'different aims and different expectations' of the College and *Tribune*, the former concerned with education and the latter with 'publicity'. The *Tribune* valued 'the foreign students chiefly in terms of their external performances; the great international issues of the day become dramatic opportunities to highlight a performance rather than serious topics regarding study'.[32] The workshops were not repeated.

Personality clashes were at the center of the discord. Some College staff disliked 'Mrs Waller's personality' and 'her manipulation of people'. Leading the charge against Helen was Ed Solomon, who accompanied the Forum group on the 1955 overseas jaunt, and whose internal memos to College president Harold Taylor were frank. He made the most of complaints by College students in June 1957, after the delegates' visit, of minor damage to rooms, missing equipment, and unauthorized long distance phone calls. In 1958 Solomon suggested withdrawing from all arrangements with Helen: 'the girls at Kober really don't like to have the Trib. kids', and there was no 'real relationship with Helen or the delegates'. Most tellingly, he had 'serious questions' about the 'quality' of Helen's Orientation program, (although he did not specify his concerns) and feared 'the name of Sarah Lawrence might suffer as a result'. Ed was out on a limb. An equally frank note from Harold Taylor to the College dean noted that 'He don't [sic] like Helen after their round the world trip [in 1955] but I'm trying not to allow him to spoil our show with the Forum because of that'. (One wonders what really happened on the trip). As Harold told Ed himself, 'I realize how you feel about Helen Waller, but the relationship between the Forum and Sarah Lawrence is an important one with ramifications going much beyond the simple housing facility which we can offer them'.[33]

The very real complaints from the girls continued. They disliked having to pack everything up and there was always damage and the odd wandering saucepan. In 1960 a heated exchange erupted over extra charges for cleaning and damage and for missing items including, rather embarrassingly, a book borrowed by Forum staff member Judith Perry, and jewelry from the room occupied by Helen and her small son. It is not clear how this dispute was resolved. Helen certainly took personal offence. Nevertheless, the Forum continued to use Sarah Lawrence College for group gatherings. In November 1966 Taylor Hall girls signed a petition against the Forum delegates, citing the lack of security for their belongings and the inconvenience of packing up. Their protests were ignored or resolved, and college staff noted in 1967 that 'there were no complaints from our students after the visit'.[34] In 1968, however, Forum Orientation shifted to Seabury House in Connecticut, ending the fifteen-year association with Sarah Lawrence.

Other Media

The *Tribune* also forged mutually beneficial links with other media that were crucial to the Forum's success. Forum debates were broadcast on educational radio and from 1953 on television, initially on WOR. The 1958 television programs of forum panel discussions were produced 'in association with *Readers Digest*'. An ongoing cooperative relationship with the *Digest* was first mooted in 1956, 'undertaken wholly on their initiative', according to Helen, who was 'convinced that the primary reason for their interest is the fact that they are in trouble in Washington on postal rate legislation and feel the need for a tie-in with an ultra-respectable international public service', i.e. the Forum. Helen had plenty of ideas for spending *Digest* money, from lunches with political heavyweights to overseas group trips to London and beyond. She also wanted delegates to feature in foreign *Digest* editions, especially the Italian, Arabic, and Australian, increasing the Forum's visibility and encouraging 'a wider base of selection' for delegates.[35] *Readers Digest* demurred, confining itself to contributing to the television programs.

Scholastic Publishing were involved from the early 1950s, having 'an aim shared' with the *Tribune*: 'education of the young people of all countries for good citizenship in national and international affairs'. *Scholastic Magazine* for schools included features about the delegates and their edited debates, 'providing a unique resource for social studies teachers'. Delegates made good copy. 'Senior Scholastic' magazine received 'double its normal number of letters to the editor' from students commenting on the published transcripts of Forum discussions. Delegates also co-authored articles in *Junior Scholastic* describing their lives. In 1958, the enterprising Junior Scholastic editor used the Forum connection for a feature on Iceland. He interviewed the younger relations of two previous Icelandic delegates for his article 'How We Live in Reykjavik' in the World Friendship Series. Nowhere in the ensuing article was the Forum mentioned, undoubtedly annoying Forum organizers. But the Forum benefitted more tangibly. Unlike *Readers Digest*, Scholastic Magazines sponsored some field trips.[36]

Alongside media sponsors were companies ticking the corporate responsibility box. Miller & Rhoads department store in Richmond, Virginia, hosted delegates for two weeks in 1953 and again in 1957, as participants in the store's self-named High School Forum. Reflecting the increasing engagement of American colleges and universities with the Forum, Princeton University's International Affairs Council sponsored the 1966 delegates' visit to their campus.[37]

Money, Money, Money

It is clear then, that money underpinned the Forum. It was at the forefront of the directors' minds as they worked to ensure the Forum's survival. Money became even more critical after the *Herald Tribune* closed its doors in 1966, as we will see in chapter 16, when we follow Bob Huffman's creative attempts to keep the Forum alive. Throughout the Forum years, keeping costs down was important, but so too was being proactive in attracting sponsorship, in cash or in kind. The price of that sponsorship was usually not onerous, as Forum and supporters had shared aims. Nevertheless, the delegates had to pose for photos, give interviews, and provide appealing copy, while the Forum staff had to consult and negotiate with government and corporate sponsors to ensure mutual satisfaction.

Having sorted out the finances (more or less), choosing an appealing cast of delegates was the next priority.

Chapter 5

The Chosen Ones

Fifteen-year-old Cyrus (Iran 50)'s introduction to the *Herald Tribune* Forum was a small announcement in a Teheran daily newspaper in 1949 seeking an Iranian student to visit the United States for three months. Going to the US was a dream for the young schoolboy. He fancied his chances.

Seventy years later, Cyrus told his story with relish. He was shattered when a school friend explained it was already decided: the chosen one was the Minister of Education's son. Cyrus decided to 'do something about that'. He talked his way into the office of F Taylor Gurney, US cultural attaché in Teheran, and gave the startled gentleman a letter to the *Herald Tribune*. In schoolboy script on a long sheet of paper was his complaint about the selection process: 'It was a great opportunity for students in Iran to come to the US and all that, but it seems as though the fix is in and some kid [has already been picked] and so on'. Gurney read the letter 'with a very serious face' and sent Cyrus away.

A few months later Cyrus' school principal told him of a nationwide competition for the Forum delegate. Cyrus was his school's representative. 'We had a discussion with the Ministry of Education and agreed that if there was a contest [in this school] you would win it', said the principal. (Open competition clearly only went so far!)

Cyrus competed with other boys from across the country, including, he remembered with satisfaction, the son of the Minster of Education, 'who had already packed his bags'. After several rounds of essay writing, the final few were interviewed by Iranian education officials and an American representative—none other than F T Gurney, who, Cyrus wryly noted, 'acted as though he had never seen me before in his life!' A month later Cyrus's father, 'who never came home for lunch' from work, arrived in great excitement at midday to tell his son he had been selected. Thus, on Saturday, 7 January 1950, Cyrus, along with an Iranian girl delegate, arrived at La Guardia airport for three months in the US.[1]

Cyrus's was one of the more memorable, although not the only quirky selection story, as you might expect from a program that selected 809 delegates from 84 countries. Of those 809, two did not arrive: Alfredo Larranaga (Peru 47) won a college scholarship to Canada and went there instead, and, tragically, Shirley Kris (Panama 58)'s father died the evening before she was to leave. There was also a ghostly presence in the records of another delegate (number 810), 'Nguyen Hoa Hanoi' from Vietnam, mentioned in correspondence organizing flights but nowhere else.[2] Of the remaining 807, Thelma (Liberia 53) went home early, and at least another two were ill for much of the Forum (Erica, Canada 47, Louise, Belgium 49).

The Forum's 'procedures for the selection of delegates' remained similar throughout the Forum's existence, designed to produce an ideal group of delegates: smart, articulate, engaging youngsters, who would be responsible ambassadors, representative of their nations yet also the best of them. They would be from all parts of the world, speaking different languages, with different religions, cultures, and social backgrounds, but with commonalities: they were all (supposed to be) high school students and able to debate world issues in English.

Curating a Global Forum

What each Forum looked like depended first on which countries were invited, and which accepted the invitation to send an impressionable teenager to experience the seductive charm of American modernity and democracy for three months. Some of the eighty-four countries represented at the Forum were only there once and appeared almost every year. Others, notably most communist states, were conspicuous by their absence. Until 1953 the Forums targeted specific regions, and often countries sent two delegates apiece—usually a boy and a girl. After a preliminary gathering in 1946 for American high school students, in 1947 South and Central American countries sent delegates. At the eleventh hour, Lester Pearson, who was a Forum speaker, intervened. He inquired why Canadian students had not been included in this 'Americas' forum. As a former Canadian Ambassador and UN heavyweight, he could not be ignored.[3] Four young Ottawans were swiftly rustled up to make the trip south. In 1948, with confidence building, the Forum's attention switched to Europe, with a 'Marshall Plan' Forum, including six teenagers each from Britain, Sweden, Norway, and Denmark, along with three Finns and, bizarrely, two Australian boys. Europe more broadly was the focus in 1949, while 1950 and 1952 focused on Asia and the Middle East. A Forum planned for 1951 was called off at the last minute, amid concerns about the escalating conflict in Korea.

From 1953 the Forum spread its wings to include countries from around the globe, although not evenly distributed. Europeans were consistently 25 per cent of delegates in each year. During the 1950s Asian countries made up about 30 per cent of delegates, dropping to 15 per cent in the 1960s, their place taken by South American delegates, who were sparse in the 1950s. African delegates' numbers also increased, building slowly to 15 per cent of delegates in 1957, and remaining between 10 and 15 per cent thereafter. Middle Eastern delegates were between 15 and 20 per cent of delegates in the 1950s but fell to below 10 per cent in the 1960s, while New Zealand and/or Australian delegates appeared in the early 1950s and from 1963.

The reasons for this distribution were not publicly acknowledged, but behind the scenes, global politicking, journalistic priorities, and personal interactions can be glimpsed, combining to provide a geographically and culturally diverse bunch of delegates who would assist American soft power and create appealing headlines.

The Forum wanted global coverage but a small enough group to be cohesive, so countries in the same region competed for places. Small countries struggled. There were no Papua New Guineans and no Pacific Islanders, no one from Guyana or French Guinea. Several African nations never appeared, possibly because they had been Portuguese, German, or French colonies, and English was not widespread. But why no Libya, for example? Of great strategic importance to the US during the 1950s and 1960s, Libya would seem an ideal source of teenage ambassadors. English language teaching was on the ascendence, and university students of English could access scholarships to study abroad.[4] Perhaps, however, neighboring Egypt was a more interesting choice as it shared a border with Israel. Cuba, El Salvador, Venezuela, Haiti, and Honduras were only at the 1947 'pan-American' Forum. Luxembourg and Portugal sent two delegates each to the European-focused Forum in 1949, but none reappeared. The short-lived state of Tanganyika sent a delegate in 1962, the Ryukyu Islands participated in 1954. Cambodia sent the daughter of an ex-Prime Minister in 1960. Cyprus was there in 1964, and Hong Kong only appeared in 1971.

Media Fodder

Media considerations also influenced country choices. Thinking commercially in 1950, Helen Waller argued for the inclusion of Western European countries to enable the European edition of the *Herald Tribune* to 'cooperate with the Forum project in any way that might be useful to it'.[5] Newsworthiness was also an important criterion in selecting countries, creating good television and newspaper headlines, and exposing American students to important world issues. Having both Israeli and Arab delegates promised a certain frisson, as did introducing British delegates to newly independent Indians or Pakistanis or pairing white South Africans and Rhodesians with their black African neighbors.

Asian (and later African) delegates were also important visually. Helen Waller was explicit about this in 1950 when considering invitations. The Forum would benefit from the 'greatly enhanced general interest' in these 'little-known' Asian countries, provided by the 'certain color, even glamor' of their 'native costumes'. This sort of appeal could 'scarcely be duplicated in any other areas'. The idea that the Asian delegates' main purpose was cultural exoticism permeated the Forum, with some European interviewees telling me that Asian delegates were chosen to provide color with their costumes, dances and singing, while Europeans were chosen because they could debate well and were politically aware. It was not altogether true. While some Asian delegates were quiet and retiring, and many had fabulous national costumes, others were as articulate as their sometimes-dowdier European counterparts.

Global Politics

Writing to Whitie Reid about the planned 1951 Asia-focused Forum, Helen Waller explained her first ten choices: Burma, Ceylon, India, Indo-China, Indonesia, Malaya, Nepal, Pakistan, Philippines, and Thailand.[6]

All of these countries' delegates to the 1950 forum had proved 'highly successful' but most importantly: 'These areas will still be of vital importance to United States Foreign Policy'. The next three countries on Helen's list were Korea, Japan, and Australia. The first two were in the same 'general area' as the favored ten, but had not been included in 1950. They had sent 'many queries' about the Forum. As for the last: 'It would be interesting', mused Helen, 'to also include Australia because of its geographical position in the area', a perceptive comment at a time when Australian governments, while adhering to a 'White Australia' policy, were increasingly recognizing the need to engage with their near neighbors to the north.[7] The final seven choices were all from Western Europe: the UK, Germany, France, Italy, Austria, Benelux, and Switzerland.[8] Their inclusion made the Forum 'world-wide in scope' and, reasoned Helen, thinking geopolitically, would 'dramatize America's equal interest in both Europe and Asia'. Although the 1951 Forum never eventuated, the strategic thinking behind this list informed future Forums. As the program gathered momentum, Forum directors met annually with State Department officials 'to agree on a country invitation list that will coincide with the national interest' for the following year's Forum. In 1956, for example, 'Iceland was retained and Morocco and the Sudan added … at State's specific request'. For 1957, Helen added Burma, Sudan, and Tunis to the list and substituted Brazil and Argentina for Guatemala and Mexico, also 'at the request' of the State Department.[9] It is unlikely that these were robust conversations, with Helen vehemently defending her own choices. Given their shared outlooks, it was probably a formality.

The dominance of Western European countries was unsurprising. Although one might expect the US to be more interested in attracting students from 'developing' countries, most foreign exchange students in universities and high schools in the 1950s and 1960s were Europeans.[10] Helen Waller herself was a Europhile, spending her summers climbing in the European alps, and speaking French, German, and Italian, rather than Korean or Urdu. Europe had high standards of education, with many northern Europeans speaking excellent English. The US had a strong presence in post-war Europe and was intent on bolstering NATO as a bulwark against the Soviet bloc in the Cold War.

Some countries appeared annually. The UK, Germany, Israel, and Japan sent delegates consistently; Italy was there each year from 1954. France appeared every year except 1967. This may have been fallout from France's withdrawal from NATO in June 1966 and a nuclear research treaty with the Soviet Union, or just an anomaly. Indian delegates were there every year except 1964 and 1965. Nigeria's first delegate appeared in 1955 and they continued to attend annually, while Vietnam and Yugoslavia sent delegates for sixteen of the possible twenty internationalist forums. Sometimes a change in a country's regime dictated a withdrawal from participation, or its later inclusion. Indonesia signed an arms deal with the USSR in 1962, and no Forum delegates appeared until after the CIA-backed coup deposed President Sukarno in 1966. The 1967 delegate, Agung, was the son of key political figure, a member of Bali royalty, and a leading light in the anti-Communist youth movement. Ghana's presence at the Forum also came to a shuddering halt in 1962. In the same year, the Soviets awarded the International Lenin Peace Prize to Ghana's president and independence leader Kwame Nkrumah (Sukarno had received it two years earlier), an indication of the way political winds were blowing. Ghanaian Forum delegates also reappeared in 1967 following a coup removing Nkrumah and costing over 1600 Ghanaian lives (arguably orchestrated by US agents). Difie (Ghana 1967)'s father, a businessman and opposition party activist, had just returned from five years' exile. Difie and two of her brothers became prominent government figures, Difie a politician and then High Commissioner to South Korea. Ceylonese delegates also vanished between 1963 and 1967. Ceylon boasted the world's first female prime minister in this period, but her nationalist government leaned left. Then, just as Ghana, Indonesia, and Ceylon were returning to the fold, Arab nations boycotted the Forum for two years because of American support for Israel in the Six-Day War in 1967. This might all be just coincidental. Forum publicity made much of the wide range of countries included in the program; sometimes nations missed out to make way for others in the region. But a quick glance at the records of the government-sponsored 'Teen-ager Program' shows a similar pattern of attendance (and non-attendance), suggesting that there was more to it.[11] Politics mattered in this game of soft diplomacy.

Pragmatism vs Politics

Sometimes sheer pragmatism determined the choice of countries. As Helen Waller told Whitie Reid in 1950, it would be 'improvident to simply abandon the organizational know-how and goodwill' in certain places. The Forum should 'capitalize on the organization ... already in existence' from previous Forums. Conversely, the bad behavior or lackluster performance of a delegate one year could influence the choice of countries the next. Egypt, Iran, Iraq, Israel, Lebanon, and Syria all sent delegates in 1950. Helen was reluctant to repeat the experience. *Tribune* readers were more interested in Europe than the Middle East, argued Helen, although she did not specify how she knew this, and host schools and families reported that 'in nearly every case ... Arab students did not know how or were unable to cooperate as effectively as our schools have come to expect from the other delegates'. Perhaps these reports reflected cultural differences or political disagreements rather than uncooperativeness. Nevertheless, Helen was concerned: it left 'some doubt in my mind as to whether we would be justified in inviting delegates from these countries again'.[12] Despite her reservations, Middle Eastern delegates remained part of the Forum cohort. The potential political drama and publicity offered by bringing Israeli and Arab delegates together was too good an opportunity to miss.

Just as Helen had her doubts in 1950, Robert Huffman regarded Muhammad (Jordan 63), 'as a disappointment and, apparently something of a trial as well'. There was a bigger story behind this, which we will revisit in a later chapter, but the upshot was that Huffman suggested that Jordan not be invited in 1964. A frantic exchange of memos and letters followed, with the American Embassy arguing that the diplomatic ramifications of not inviting Jordan would be profound. It would be 'assumed that the decision is entirely the result of the '63 delegate's speaking out vigorously on the Arab-Israeli issue', confirming Jordanians' conviction 'that Americans resent efforts to tell them the "truth" about this issue which to the Arab mind transcends all others in importance'. Ambassador Macumber assured his friend Jock Whitney that they would 'make a particular effort to select as objective and broad-gauged a candidate as possible'. This was bigger than Muhammad or the Forum, as Macumber reminded Whitney. Cold War diplomacy was at stake. 'The present regime in Jordan, unlike that in almost all other Arab states, rejects neutralism and has adopted a policy of friendship to the West', rather than the USSR. This policy was 'not an easy one for the GOJ [Government of Jordan] to pursue'. Huffman quickly backed down and looked forward to welcoming Gaby (Jordan 64), whose selection perhaps centered on just one sentence in his selection autobiography: 'I am easy-going, don't like to hurt people's feelings, but stand up for my principles in a reasonable way'. This was also the year when the significant imbalance between a single Israeli delegate and three or four Arabs was addressed. From 1964 no more than two Arab countries were invited in any one year.[13]

Conspicuous by Their Absence?

Invited countries did not always accept.[14] Yugoslavia was the only communist country to send delegates regularly to the Forum. A Czech delegate appeared once in 1967, in a fleeting moment of rapprochement with the West, just before the Prague Spring of 1968 and a further Soviet crackdown. There were no Russians, no Chinese, no Poles, and no Hungarians. Tellingly, most delegates did not question the absence of China or Warsaw Pact countries. They did not expect to see them there.

Nevertheless, as a Forum pamphlet emphasized in 1967, all countries were eligible 'except for countries with which the US does not have diplomatic relations'. China was therefore excluded, but Eastern bloc countries, including the Soviet Union from 1956, received regular invitations. Whether anyone expected them to accept is unclear, but it was certainly a strategic public demonstration of the Forum's inclusiveness. This was while President Eisenhower was promoting cultural exchanges with the Soviet Union, albeit much to the horror of the State Department, which advocated a more cautious approach. By inviting Eastern Bloc countries, the Forum was also responding to public opinion. Many Americans, like their president, were fascinated by the Soviet Union. The *Tribune* reported in November 1955 that 'ironically, given that the Soviet Union is the only country that has not yet accepted an invitation to send a delegate to the Forum', 54 of the 101 host schools in the New York metropolitan area had named a Russian as one the delegates they would most like to host, 38 naming it as their first choice. Host schools would remain disappointed. Russia, the Ukraine, and Belorussia 'did not reply' to the invitation for 1957, and Poland and the USSR ignored it the following year. The *Tribune* reported that the USSR 'refused to send a student delegate' for 1959.[15]

There was great hope in 1958 when Valentina Titova of the USSR Committee of Youth Organizations was reportedly 'considering' the invitation. Forum staff responded to her letter of inquiry with alacrity, emphasizing they 'sincerely regretted the absence of Soviet representation' at the previous three Forums. No Russian students were forthcoming, although Valentina Titova was certainly interested in the idea. Two years later she was instrumental in arranging a separate 'World Youth Forum', in which '142 students, representing some sixty countries, met to discuss disarmament, co-existence, and other political issues'. American students were sent by the American Friends Service Committee. Later that year Mrs Titova visited the US with the Experiment in International Living.[16] Helen Waller may have felt snubbed. A Soviet student delegate would have been a real coup for her and the Forum.

The Forum persisted in asking Soviet Bloc countries and experimented with others. Forty countries were invited for 1960, Cambodia and Rhodesia for the first time. Four countries declined, including Poland and the USSR. A publicity flyer promoting the involvement of Pan Am and TWA listed the forty-six countries invited to the 1963 Forum. Of those forty-six, thirteen did not send delegates but another six countries not on the original list did appear: Belgium, Iran, Korea, Panama, Spain, and Syria. Perhaps these were on the 'B list'.[17]

The exact combination of countries in each year's Forum differed, but some things were constant. Form 1953, a variety of regions was always represented, with delegates exposed to vastly different cultures, religions, politics, ideas, economies, and geographies. And all delegates were handpicked—theoretically the best and the brightest youngsters of their generation.

Choosing Delegates

Early in 1949 the *Herald Tribune* provided nine 'Rules for Selection' describing desirable delegates. They should be citizens by birth of their respective countries, aged 17–18 years old, and 'preferably of state supported or subsidized schools'. They would fit into an American family and high school and have a 'working knowledge' of English. This last was strongly emphasized, 'fluency in English' being essential for their participation in 'forums and classroom discussions'. They should also have 'an active interest in world affairs', and show 'intellectual curiosity and adaptability to new situations'.[18]

In 1963, when Huffman took over, the Forum produced several booklets outlining the Forum program, formalizing processes. The 'Procedure for the Selection of the Delegate' opened with a list of qualities of a 'properly qualified candidate'. As well as earlier criteria, delegates should be 'in the upper fourth of his [sic] class ... of sound character and integrity', 'willing to work co-operatively with others', and 'personable and neat' (or 'capable of making a good impression in public'). There was now an official application form to be submitted with three 'letters of recommendation'—two from teachers and a character reference from 'an adult (not a relative) who has known him [sic] for several years'. Once selected, the candidate should undergo a 'complete physical examination by a registered medical doctor' and sign a waiver of liability. Clearly by the 1960s insurance considerations were important.[19]

For 1967, an additional stipulation heralded a new era with different priorities. The delegate should be 'a deserving student <u>who has never been to the United States before</u>'. The rules specifically excluded 'a person who has had other opportunities to travel widely', and those 'whose family could easily pay his [sic] way to visit the United States'. This signaled a fundamental change in the Forum aims. Gone was the idea of attracting future leaders from the elite of targeted nations to imbue in them a love of the US and influence global politics. Instead, as international tourism grew and elite youngsters traveled independently to the US, the Forum aimed to expose a less privileged group to America. For some delegates, the Forum provided an otherwise unattainable opportunity. Sherille

(Ceylon 71) found his island home 'kind of isolated'. He told me, 'my mother and I had … an agreement that I would in some way find a way to travel and see the world, even if meant joining a ship as a deckhand'. His mother was doubtless relieved when he won a Forum place, rather than running away to sea.

Officially, the selection process had two stages. Students wrote a 1500-word essay, usually on 'The World We Want', in English, without advance knowledge. Forum guidelines suggested that each school should submit one essay. 'No more than six' candidates should be selected for the final contest: a personal interview and an autobiography written in English. The interview panel of three should include a representative of the Minister of Education, a representative of the American Embassy, with the third panel member chosen by these two.[20]

Responsibility for choosing delegates, however, ultimately lay with national governments, who tweaked the rules and procedures as they saw fit. The level of competition varied across countries, for logistical, linguistic, and political reasons. Nevertheless, almost all delegates wrote an essay, had an interview, and introduced themselves with an autobiography.

'The World We Want'

Only a handful of the selection essays on 'The World We Want' survive. Thor (Norway 48) wanted a world of liberty and mutual respect; Meliton (Philippines 50) gave an impassioned plea for cooperation not because 'we rather like the idea' but because 'we just have to banish war'. Twelve years later Dorothy (Malaya 62) hoped for 'unity in diversity'. Louise (Belgium 49) competed against her older sister, surprising her entire family by winning. She reflected later that her essay about music and internationalism might have been more appealing than her sister's, which had 'rehashed some of our father's [pro-Russian] views'. Sometimes topics varied. Josephine (Australia 53) and Hiranthi (Ceylon 67) both wrote on the UN. Hiranthi told me she thought her frankness was the key to her success. She had written 'there's no point calling it a world body when it's not funded by everybody, and it's funded by the rich countries, and at the end of it they try to deliver, they first look after the people who fund them'. She laughed,

'I mean—I was sixteen years old and I just wrote out all the things that they had done wrong'. In 1963 delegates had to write 500 words on 'Why I believe I should be my country's delegate' and 1000 words on 'My Country'. 1967 had a theme—'living in a world of cities'—requiring delegates to be from urban areas. The essay topics had also changed, thankfully eschewing the ghastly 'Why I should be my country's delegate' for 500 words on 'My country's role in today's world' and 100 words on 'The three major urban problems of my city and possibilities for their solution'.[21]

The actual essay-writing process varied across countries, with some delegates writing under exam conditions, while others worked at home over time, aided and abetted by parents and teachers. By 1969, the Israeli delegate was chosen by interview from a pool of just sixteen schools and only the winner wrote the required essay. This was possibly not the best strategy: Amos (Israel 69) was a procrastinator. He dithered so long over the essay that the Foreign Office threatened to withdraw his trip. This proved the necessary motivation.[22]

The Interview

Generally, selection committees included combinations of local government officials, educators, and US consular staff, but countries had diverging approaches. Towards the end of the 1950s, alumni began to be involved. Adolfo (Argentina 59) was concerned about his country's selection process, having concluded that neither 'the Embassy official who deals with foreign matters', nor the Ministry of Education, understood 'the exact meaning of the Forum nor the organization of it'. He wrote a letter outlining the ideal characteristics of a delegate and got other Argentine alumni to sign it. Alumni were on some selection committees in the 1960s Catherine (France 59) was delighted to be included after she had 'two very long talks with Mr Gorman at the USIS' and 'he said that the Forum was very different from what he expected'.[23]

Delegates remembered traveling to a capital city for an interview, but few remember the questions and answers, unless they had been particularly embarrassed or, alternatively, witty. Yasar (Jordan 59) 'winged it', he said, making them laugh—when asked what he would tell the Americans about Jordan, he replied, 'I would tell them Jordan is a big, big museum without walls'. German selectors told Dieter (Germany 62) they chose him because despite his having clearly 'not the faintest idea what the Munich Agreement was', he 'wiggled out of the situation so beautifully that we had to give [it] to you'.[24] This ability to answer difficult questions under pressure was essential for many Forum delegates.

The Autobiography

> 'That's right,' they said. 'Your story, an autobiography. Write that.' And I tried. And I tried so many times, tried so many different approaches. It was the toughest assignment, yet this writing about myself. Oh, I could write reams about other people. I could say nice things of them, pleasant things kind things, but about myself... I don't know where to begin, in the first place. You could be logical and begin ... "I was born a ... " And that would be like beginning a short story with "Once upon a time ... ". Trite. Odiously, barbarously trite.

Despite his declared diffidence, 18-year-old Meliton (Philippines 50) clearly knew what he was about. His delightful and carefully constructed autobiography is one of 665 that survive in various archives.[25] These texts are unlike other life-writing or self-presentation by young people and are a window into how teenagers from around the globe presented themselves to the world.[26] Forum organizers distributed the autobiographies to host schools, families, other delegates, and media. In some ways the autobiographies were remarkably similar. These were all teenagers, whose lives revolved around family, school, friends, and hobbies. They were all privileged voices, empowered to describe themselves in their own words, but conscious of the need to impress dual adult audiences—their governments and American selectors. Despite their similarities, however, no two were the same—except for those of Singaporean siblings, Yuen Kum Chuen (Singapore 55) and Yuen Chooi Yeng (Singapore 59). Although allowed no 'notes or outlines', Yeng reproduced her brother's autobiography almost word for word, testimony to her memory if not her originality.[27] It was a dangerous strategy, for Chuen's biography had flair; his attempts at humor and self-deprecation memorable enough for this researcher to notice his sister's plagiarism. That it was not picked up at the time suggests either a high turnover of Singaporean administrators, or their lack of interest.

Overall, however, the autobiographies varied greatly—in length, style, and in what delegates chose to reveal. Some were brief, often reflecting delegates' lack of facility in English. Others were like a curriculum vitae—bullet point lists of enviable attainments—even from three British delegates, whose English fluency was not in doubt. The third, Suzanne (UK 62), got a swift response. New Forum assistant Norma Brent enclosed the autobiography of Tan Wee Kiat (Singapore 61) as an exemplar and requested a rewrite: 'Your resumé is complete, but it would be so much warmer and friendlier if it were written in story form'. Suzanne obliged, perhaps to extremes, her quirky 'three major dislikes; all forms of cruelty, bad smells and tapioca' echoing Tan Wee Kiat's equally disparate hates: 'cigars and cigarettes, racial discrimination, butter and cheese'.[28]

Story form did not save all autobiographies from stultifying dullness. One step up from a resumé were the predictable catalogues of (over-) achievement—exams passed, prizes gained, sports played, musical instruments mastered, competitions won, and positions reached. Mostly from Anglophone countries, these were full of information but not self-reflective, revealing little about the writers other than that they were obvious candidates for Forum selection, as head prefects, captains of sporting teams, and academically at the top of their classes. A notable exception was Michael (UK 72)'s autobiography, which was intelligently witty, in that deliciously dry, British, clever-clogs sort of a way so often characteristic of those destined for Oxbridge. 'I had the good fortune to be born with a foreign surname' [Portillo], the 18-year-old began. 'This I have found an immense benefit, not only because it differentiates me on long lists from "Browns" and "Smiths" and serves as a topic to end many an unhappy pause in conversation, but also because it has given me an interest in a foreign country, and a point of comparison with my native Britain, which I would have otherwise have lacked.'[29] He adroitly combined humor with a serious point, a talent that would serve him well in his later political and broadcasting careers.

Biographies like this were entertaining. In a good year there were two or three delegates who used expressive word pictures, philosophical reflections, emotion, and sometimes humor, demonstrating a flair for writing and a self-awareness not always found among teenagers. Often the most expressive were from Asia or non-English speaking countries, suggesting different traditions of story-telling and self-presentation across different cultures. In Korea, for instance, where humility was valued, delegates discussed their achievements 'as a collective effort', which owed much to parental support.[30] Philippines' students were clearly encouraged to use poetic language and imagination, in contrast to the generally matter-of-fact Anglo-sphere and European offerings.

Delegates were invited to reveal strengths and weaknesses, likes and dislikes, dreams and ambitions. In 1957 Helen Waller included examples of questions they might consider: 'what books in English have you read lately?', 'can you jitterbug', 'sports (at which do you excel? Or do you hate all physical exertion?)', 'could you show your host mother how to prepare a special dish?', and 'are you contemplative, gregarious, moody, easy-going, sensitive, gay, shy, aggressive, etc, etc.?' This explained some of the more idiosyncratic inclusions in the biographies: Irjaleena (Finland 57) contributed, 'I cannot jitterbug but I am always eager to learn all new things so perhaps this too.'[31]

Some autobiographies were heartbreakingly honest, some were unintentionally funny, others told harrowing stories of war, loss, and hardship. Graham (SA 61) stood out with his startling revelation of 'an imaginary friend called "Koetie" with whom I used to have the most exciting and hair-raising adventures all over the world' as a child, emphasizing (strategically?) that 'New York was our particular port of call and we had our armies based there as well'. Some delegates thanked the *Tribune* in advance, others waxed lyrical about their desire to see America, a few declared political ambitions or hoped to 'be of service' to the world. Several claimed 'typical childhoods' and 'average families', but also wanted to impress. Pedro (Chile 61) admitted, 'Well, I really don't have many special abilities, but I know how to whistle quite well and when I am happy I don't sing so badly. I am quite a good chauffeur and I drive since I was ten years old'.[32]

Surprisingly there were few gendered differences, although more girls admitted to being able to cook. Only a few girls wrote of marriage and motherhood; Yumiko (Japan 57) stood out: 'I am but a homely being, who desires to get married and settle down, be a good housewife and a good mother in the future'. No boys discussed the issue, although Johnny (Philippines 54) noted that 'if a personable lady ever learns to cook "lumpia" like my mother then she has only to beckon and I shall come'. In other ways, boys and girls wrote similar texts, cultural background more significant than gender in distinguishing them from each other. All were self-representations from youngsters hoping 'to leave a worthwhile trace' of themselves on the global stage.[33]

Why Apply?

What prompted teenagers to apply for the Forum? It had prestige, especially in its early years. In 1947 Australian newspapers declared 'No American, not even the President, is big enough to resist an invitation to address the *Herald Tribune* Forum'. And America was *the* destination—a global power, rich and modern. As Minh (Vietnam 65) told me, there was 'a very, very idealized notion of the US ... if you go to the US you are okay'. Delegates' autobiographies were often full of enthusiasm: their 'dearest wish' was to go to the US. Pietro (Italy 65) had exchange experience, having attended Camp Rising Sun as a 14-year-old in 1961, and was keen to return. Stella (Brazil 64) 'once read in a book that "all good Americans go to Paris when they die." If this was applied to Brazilians the destination would not be Paris but the United States.' Lee Hup San (Malaya 58) thought the US was 'a model nation' and hoped to 'return with useful ideas for the betterment of Malaya'. Marwan (Syria 52) slyly suggested that he needed to go because he had heard different opinions; 'Some denied the very existence of the American Family. Others said that the American Family was very united and I didn't know what to believe.' Veroslava (Yugoslavia 61) wanted 'to meet an average American family' because 'we understand people better when we learn more about their way of living'. Others were pragmatic. Silvio (Brazil 63) thought the Forum 'would be a wonderful opportunity for me' to get 'a practical knowledge of the many nations of the world' to help 'in the furtherance of my career' as 'a diplomat in the future'. Serban (Bolivia 64) was typical of many, seeing the Forum as a stepping stone to an American college, but unusual in admitting it in his biography: he wanted to study nuclear physics in the USA, 'because I believe American universities are the best in this field'.[34]

The Forum compared favorably for many delegates with its competitor AFS. It was shorter, but also 'vastly more glamorous', said Gerhard (Germany 54), who turned down an AFS scholarship. The Forum was also more international. Ceridwen (UK 67) said of a friend and former AFS student: 'She hadn't had the richness of experience', that a Forum delegate had. She was 'plonked' in an American family and 'became Americanized a bit'. Others emphasized selectivity. AFS was many students from each country, 'the World Youth Forum is one', said Hiranthi (Ceylon 67) and Ronny (Indonesia 68).[35] The Forum was also free.

The Forum's internationalism was appealing, or so delegates claimed in their autobiographies. Duangtip (Thailand 62) thought it 'an excellent opportunity for me to exchange the ideas with the other young students from other countries and that will create the international understanding among the young people who in the future may handle the destiny of the world.' Yumiko (Japan 57) wanted 'to do something to contribute to the mutual understanding of nations and, if possible, to the peace of the world'.[36] They could sound a little like 'Miss World' contestants.

Many delegates entered the Forum competition without knowing much about it at all. They wrote the competition essay at school or were encouraged by a teacher. Maarten (Netherlands 61) entered because his classmates laughed at the idea that this young country boy from the far north of the Netherlands could fulfil the criteria for the Forum. He felt his resemblance at 17 to a young JFK assisted his selection! (The photograph on this book's cover shows there was a striking similarity.) Geneviève (France 56) was surprised to be selected: 'I knew much less than Catherine Marin [France 59] who would read *Le Monde* every day', she told me, but she had spent time in England and was clever at languages. Others were determined to go. Persistence rewarded John (UK 58) and Jorge (Mexico 65), who both tried twice, while sibling rivalry perhaps inspired Josephine (Australia 53) who succeeded where her brother had failed.[37]

A Nationwide Competition?

The *Tribune* emphasized the 'varied' social backgrounds of the delegates, reporting how Jawahir (Malaya 56) 'from a small fishing village where no English is heard or spoken' rubbed shoulders with Phuong (Vietnam), who had revealed to the judges ('after she had been selected', they claimed, perhaps to avoid accusations of nepotism) that her uncle was the Vietnamese Ambassador in Washington. Far from being a country bumpkin, however, Jawahir was at the Zainab School, which taught in English, and had not lived in the fishing village for more than half her life. She and Phuong perhaps found common ground despite the latter's illustrious relatives. Both had been forced to flee their homes during times of conflict.[38]

Competitiveness varied from country to country and over time. In 1949 Ferdinanda from Vienna and Gerhard from Linz saw off 4000 applicants from 167 schools. Much was made of Vangala (India 54) who had 'beaten 17,000 students'. Fifteen years later, Malverne High School's yearbook claimed their 1968 Forum delegate Mark (NZ) had bested 15,000 applicants, which feat he modestly called 'a stroke of luck'.[39] Other delegates, including in Australia and Germany, were only up against students in their state, as the competition rotated.

Not everyone was eligible. In 1949 teachers encouraged Ines Kirsimagi in Bregenz, Austria to enter and she came third in the essay competition. She was devastated when told that she was ineligible as an Estonian displaced person (DP), rather than an Austrian citizen. Ines told me she 'complained to the *Herald Tribune*!'. Forum staff upheld 'the decision of the Austrian authorities', but were sympathetic, perhaps regretting that they would not be able to have a DP's perspective at the Forum. When Ines immigrated to New York with her family a year later, 'penniless and without resources', Forum connections helped her apply for a college scholarship. The Forum publicized this 'success story' in the Forum newsletter. In 1969 in Israel, the 'very, very bright' Jonathan Kramer, a recent South African immigrant, who spoke superb English and was politically engaged, failed the three-year residency requirement for the competition—a lucky break for his friend Amos (Israel 69).[40]

Race could be another discriminator. In 1957, Susan (SA) told television viewers the competition was compulsory for 'every senior high school student' in South Africa. What she meant of course, was every *white* student, but neither she nor program moderator Helen Waller commented on this; then it was unexceptional. South African delegates were always white, and usually Afrikaans. Rhodesia, however, sent white delegates for two years, then a black delegate in 1962. Jeremy (61) claimed credit, having petitioned the education department 'about getting a Negro Rhodesian to be chosen', but Auxilia (Rhodesia 62)'s selection was indicative of broader national changes. Australian delegates were also white, while New Zealand sent one Māori delegate (Marama) in 1970. Alberto (Guatemala 63) thought it 'was a credit to the organizers that they chose me, the son of Chinese immigrants, to represent Guatemala'. Having said that, he admitted that indigenous Guatemalan would have been ineligible because of a lack of education. Jorge (Uruguay 53) was also an immigrant, with Jewish parents from Ukraine and Latvia. He said he was not a 'typical' Uruguayan, most of whom had Spanish or Italian Catholic ancestry. He felt that choosing Jewish delegates (in both 1953 and 1955) reflected well on Uruguayan society, 'the most laic Catholic country' in South America.[41] As in Guatemala and Australia, and several other South American countries, the notion of an indigenous delegate was beyond imagining.

Facility in English also disqualified some and benefited others. Louise (Belgium 49) was born in England and spoke English at home with her parents. Hameeda (Pakistan 52) was one of a few students who knew English at her school, so was a natural choice to write an essay. Her victory over the other three (all older boys) was particularly sweet because one was her brother, two years her senior; 'We were always competing with each other'. She thought that, being younger, she 'must have sounded more optimistic about the world we want than the others did'.[42]

Sometimes the competition was restricted to a few schools, especially where only a few elite schools taught English, often American, British, international, or missionary schools.[43] In Guatemala, country schools could not compete educationally with those in the capital. Other times it was perhaps convenience. Angeliki (Greece 58) commented acerbically in a Forum newsletter that in 1959 that 'for the first time, His Excellency the Minister of Education has decided ... to tell all of the schools about the Forum', rather than just 'two or three'. She declared, perhaps tongue-in-cheek given she had been a stand-out delegate, that 'I may suppose that this year you will have a good Greek for a change'. Minh (Vietnam 65) felt 'a little bit uneasy' years later, reflecting on the 'subtle bias' of his selection, coming from 'one of the feeder schools to the Forum'. Similarly, five of the seventeen Nigerian delegates came from Kings' College and three more from sister school, Queen's College. Jan (67), the sole Czech delegate, said his Prague school, The Economic School for Foreign Trade, was simply asked to supply a delegate. They chose Jan, who 'argued and asked difficult questions', he said, rather than 'risking a good Communist family' by sending a well-connected scion of the party bureaucracy into a potential political minefield.[44]

In the Forum's later years there was even less competition. Maarten (Netherlands 61) said only ten Dutch students 'had bothered' to enter. Pietro (Italy 70) told me the Forum program was 'not very well advertised' so 'the odds were in [his] favor', but perhaps he was just being modest. Michael (UK 72) said he was one of only two entrants. In Britain, unusually, the Ministry of Education outsourced the selection to the Council for Education in World Citizenship (CEWC), 'an organization of the United Nations Association'. CEWC was an ostentatiously politically neutral body 'appointed by national associations of local education authorities and teachers' to 'promote international understanding ... and the teaching of home and world affairs'. It provided citizenship education, organizing youth debates and conferences, including the *Daily Mail World Youth Forum* (1949–51). Perhaps competition was limited to the 600 affiliated 'schools of the Grammar school type' in the UK.[45]

Delegates often came from the same social circles and knew each other's families. There were even six pairs of siblings, and at least one set of cousins. Meliton and Araceli (Philippines 50, 53) almost made it a hat trick; younger sister Maria was runner-up in 1957, narrowly beaten by their friend Dennis (Philippines 57). 'Dennis is a worthy and brilliant chap,' wrote Araceli to the newsletter. She knew the others too: 'I sometimes see Roman [55] in Ateneo parties or in the activities where our schools are brought together. Raul [56], too, since we're both active members of Catholic Action'. Similarly, Ibrahim (Lebanon 58) was friendly with Thuraya (Lebanon 54), at the same school as Ziyad (Lebanon 57), and dated Mona (Lebanon 61), telling me, 'I was the one who encouraged her to apply for the Forum'. There were other connections. Patricia (UK 55) was a teacher at Alison (UK 60)'s school, while Gerry (Rhodesia 60) demonstrated Commonwealth networks: 'The new Rhodesian delegate [61] is terrific', she enthused, 'also the UK delegate [Zoe] goes to the school of my headmistress's sister in Birkenhead'.[46]

There were suggestions of nepotism. Interviewees often commented of some delegates, 'of course he was a prince in his country' or 'she was the daughter of a government minister'. 'Well-connected' was a common phrase. This does not mean that such delegates were not intelligent, well-educated, and deserving of a place at the Forum. Indeed, their very 'well-connectedness' was another qualification for selection. This was an elite program targeting individuals who were, commented Metropolitan School Study Council's Dr Guy Hilleboe, 'the best brains of their countries', destined to 'take their places in leadership in their own countries'.[47] We might expect then, that the sons and daughters of presidents, government ministers, ambassadors, and high-ranking civil servants would find their way to the Forum. The first Indonesian delegates in 1950 included Soesilo, son of Indonesian President Sukarno's personal physician. The other was Sabam, son of a Calvinist minister. Possibly less well connected than Soesilo in Indonesian government circles, he was a member of the USIS lending library in Batavia, and may have had influential friends. He was a worthy candidate: in later life he was *Jakarta Post* editor and Ambassador to Australia.

Salika (Thailand 52) was, according to a fellow delegate, 'outspoken' and 'impressive' with excellent English. She also had friends in very high places. Her name, she wrote in her autobiography 'was given to me by HRH Prince Narisa, a son of King Mongkut'. He sent it 'to my grandfather with a bracelet made of three noble metals: gold, silver and gold-copper alloy'. Her mother was 'brought up and trained in the Royal Palace' as 'a lady in waiting to one of King Chulalonkorn's daughters'. Her father was a scientist, 'widely traveled', and speaking 'half a dozen languages fluently'. Her grandfather was 'grand marshal of the Court in the reign of King Vajuravudh', and like most of her family he had studied abroad. Sanaa (Egypt 61) was born in Washington DC while her father was Egyptian ambassador. And, as Sanaa reminded organizers in her autobiography, her 'noteworthy' ancestors included her grandfather, Dean of the Faculty of Medicine and 'first pure Egyptian to get the title of Pasha', and her great-uncle, who had 'ruled the country during the Khedive's reign'. In contrast, Christian (Norway 49) kept quiet about his father's position as Norway's Foreign Minister until after he was selected, he told me, because he felt it would be a disadvantage.[48]

Iranian cousins Nasreen and Naila (Iran 53, 58) also moved in elite government circles. Nasreen's father, Dr Nazir Ahmed OBE, a physicist, was the first chair of the Pakistan Atomic Energy Commission, while his brother, Naila's father, was the highest-ranking civil servant in Pakistan and Ambassador to the US from March 1959. Marta (Argentina 69)'s father was a dentist but was also a friend of President Peron. Others were part of the business or cultural elite. The Orcel sisters, (France 57, 64) were the daughters of successful fashion entrepreneur Gilbert Orcel. Mona (Egypt 65) was (very glamorously!) the daughter of a film star.[49]

Not all delegates were elite or well connected. Rosa (Iceland 49) was the daughter of a Rejkavik plumber. Beryl (Australia 68) came from a farming family in rural South Australia. Luis (Cuba 47)'s divorced parents were poor and his town clubbed together to buy him clothing for his trip. Emmanuel (Ghana 68) was at a government boarding school in Tamale, while his widowed mother lived in a small village, struggling to make ends meet.[50]

'Of High School Age'

Delegates were mostly between 16 and 18, creating relatively cohesive groups. This was an ideal age, according to some, because their 'opinions, ideas, [and] habits are less crystallized than those of older people, and the acceptance of new ideas and customs is easier', while their 'emotional' response is 'more intense'.[51] Some countries ignored the guidelines. Records survive of ages for 799 of the 807 delegates. Eleven of the youngest were just 15 when they arrived, and another 167 were 16. At the other end of the scale there were forty-five 19-year-olds and fourteen delegates in their 20s, the oldest, Pablo (Uruguay 47), was 24. Most, (562, just over 70 per cent) were aged 17 and 18.

Thirteen of the delegates in their 20s were from Africa or South America. All except three were boys. Local selectors justified choosing Dwarika (Nepal 54), a 20-year-old, second-year university student at a local Kathmandu College: 'his age and school attainment by Nepal standards are somewhat above competition rules, but will probably not more than equal secondary school standards of the US'.[52] They also emphasized he was 'typically Nepalese' with 'a nice personality'.

The age distribution within years varied greatly. Except for 1947, which might be seen as an experimental anomaly, the greatest spread of ages was during the later Forums. The most extreme was in 1965. The youngest, Hawa (Sierra Leone 65) and Farouk (Pakistan 65), were just 15, while Peter (Kenya 65) was 22, although still a high school student. Peter may have felt disconnected from the group, with the next oldest delegate only 18. In contrast, while Thierry (Belgium 63) was nearly 21 when he arrived at the Forum, three other boys were 19, so he did not feel out of place, despite the presence of six 16-year-olds. He also speculated decades later that he shared in the 'naïvety' of the delegates more generally. 'During those years we didn't have access to so much information ... The older delegates were not necessarily more aware than their younger counterparts'.[53] Interestingly, too, when younger delegates commented on individuals in their year as being 'a lot older than us, of course', often those they were referring to were just very articulate 18-year-olds. As might be expected in a group of handpicked intelligent teens from diverse cultures, calendar years were not the only factors determining maturity.

A Boys' Club?

The advertisement for the first Australian delegates to the 1948 Forum was gender-specific—only boys need apply. Fortunately, when Australians were invited again in 1953, girls were eligible, and subsequent Australian delegates were split evenly between sexes. This was not the case everywhere. Of the 807 delegates who attended the Forum, there were 338 girls and 469 boys. Girls were 42 per cent of delegates overall. This compares favorably with broader statistics on foreign exchange students in the US, which averaged about 24 per cent female representation annually between 1955 and 1973. These latter figures primarily included older, college and university-aged students, who stayed for longer periods, perhaps partly explaining the wider gender disparity.[54]

Gender differences become significant when broken down by year and country as the tables in the appendix show. In only six of the twenty-five years were numbers of boys and girls even.⁵⁵ In another four years there were actually more girls than boys—the most was in 1952 when 63 per cent were female delegates. This was an anomaly. In the remaining fifteen years, boys dominated, usually significantly. The worst year was 1968, with twenty-eight boys and just seven girls.

One might have expected increasing numbers of girls in the 1960s. But no. Helen Waller presided over much more balanced Forums, with 46 per cent girls: (208 out of 449 delegates). Bob Huffman's Forums were just 37 per cent female (118 out of 321 delegates). Virginia Wieschhoff's Forum had only 30 per cent girls in 1962 (11 out of 37 delegates). There were two reasons. First, some countries had gendered selection policies. Second, Forum organizers took their eye off the gender ball after Helen Waller's death.

Of the fifty-eight countries which appeared four or more times at the Forum, Sudan, Jordan, and Bolivia only sent boys. Another ten countries had 75 per cent or more boys. Ceylon sent only two girls alongside twelve boy delegates. The Forum newsletter emphasized enthusiastically that Bizu in 1959 was 'the first girl delegate...from Ethiopia'. She was one of four girls out of fifteen Ethiopian delegates. One explanation for this is religion. Some Muslim countries would not send girls. Another is education, available at a higher level to boys than girls in many places. Girl delegates from countries that usually sent boys were often particularly excellent—perhaps because they had to be. After the boy-girl pairs in 1950 and 1952, India sent its first of just four girls in 1955, Usha, whose autobiography revealed her as thoughtful and willing to articulate her opinions. The second, Nalini (59), was smart and, by her own admission in her autobiography, 'very talkative', with the bonus of being an Indian classical dancer.⁵⁶ Both stood out in the televised debates.

The poor performance in gender equity by my own country New Zealand, which sent only three girls out of ten delegates, is just embarrassing, potentially a sign of persistent ingrained sexism. This, along with the predominance of male delegates from Sweden, the Netherlands, and Belgium, might also have surprised Forum organizers—the belief that Western democracies offered women more freedom and equality than other societies pervaded the Forum.

Only nineteen out of all eighty-four countries sent more girls than boys. Austria was the only European nation to have more than 65 per cent of their delegates female. The other countries with predominantly female delegates were Brazil, Burma, Lebanon, Thailand, and Japan, which had the highest ratio (16 out of 21). Some Japanese delegates, however, suggested that final year exams were considered more critical for boys than girls, so that their consistent female presence should not be interpreted as a feminist statement.[57] Japanese girls with their kimonos and cultural performances were also more decorative than Japanese boys, and clear envoys of peace.

'Please Choose a Girl!'

Forum organizers were conscious of the gender issue. It was played down in early years, with the *Tribune* reporting in 1948, that 'both girls and boys are expected to be represented among the winners, though no mathematical formula to assure this has been established'. It certainly had not, and the selection of five boys and one girl from Sweden, along with two boys and no girls from Australia skewed the balance that year to fourteen boys and eleven girls. While by no means the worst year, it raised eyebrows. In June 1949, Helen Waller implored the Public Affairs Officer at the US Embassy in Saigon: 'if it is at all possible, we urge you to choose a girl'. She added, 'Since some Arab states cannot be expected to send a girl, we hope that you can do so'. A penciled note in the margin of the filed copy of this letter directed that this instruction should also be included in the letters to 'Ceylon … Iran, Iraq, Lebanon, Malaya, Syria'. Only Lebanon obliged, although Iran sent both a girl and a boy. There was no list of the 'some Arab states' who would be expected to always send a boy, although Jordan, Afghanistan, Saudi Arabia, and Yemen were all invited (and in the end did not send any delegates at all).[58]

For 1955, after a year dominated by boy delegates (twenty-three boys and nine girls in 1954), selection instructions to countries were explicit: 'other considerations being equal, PLEASE CHOOSE A GIRL!'. The Forum 'inevitably' attracted more boys than girls and the program worked 'best when there is a fairly equal distribution'. This plea was repeated in subsequent years, resulting in more equitable gender distribution, and slightly more girls than boys in 1958, 1959, and 1961. Thenceforth, the instruction to 'please choose a girl' was not included in the instructions, despite Bob Huffman being aware of the issue. After the 1963 forum, in which eleven girls were faced with twenty-eight boys, he was delighted to report a 'much better ratio' for 1964 (twenty-one boys and seventeen girls).[59] He appeared concerned, but the ratio reverted in 1965 (twenty-five boys and just ten girls).

When asked about the comparative numbers of girls and boys years later, most delegates were sanguine. Many boys did not even notice. Kris (Ceylon 68), who was one of twenty-eight boys and seven girls, remembered 'marginally more boys than girls (60:40)'. It was actually 80:20. One 1965 male delegate expressed surprise when reminded that only ten of the thirty-five in his year were female: he suggested the girls were so smart, vocal, and articulate that they more than made up for their number. Similarly, another from 1962 had 'never noticed' the disparity, but when I revealed that there were only eleven girls in the group of thirty-seven delegates, he said, 'but what amazing girls—every one of them outstanding and lovely and I immediately remember each one of them'. (Teenage hormones?) But many girls also expected to be outnumbered. They accepted that was how the world was. One female delegate joked that being in a minority ensured instant popularity and increased choice in romantic dalliances. Another pointed out perceptively that all the boys were so different, being from different countries, that she did not feel like she was part of a minority. Cultural backgrounds trumped gender difference, and the girls were more than able to hold their own.[60]

A Home Crowd

American students were involved in the Forum both as hosts and as participants in panel discussions throughout the 1950s. From 1959 New York area students competed to be an official American delegate. The first, Cora (US 59), felt uninformed, answering 'I would have to think about that' to many questions. Later she asked the selection panel, who were all Forum alumni, why they had chosen her. 'You doubted', they said, 'We wanted an American who doubted'.[61] The composition of the selection panel was significant: an all-American panel might not have chosen a 'doubter' as the US representative.

Candidates from 160 schools competed to be the American delegate in 1961. The twelve finalists faced a demanding task, required to discuss

> an international, a national and a personal problem in terms of the concept illustrated at a sailboat race when one onlooker remarked of the lead boat, "How free she runs!" and another observed, "Free because she is perfectly attuned to those forces of wind and wave, which she must obey and cannot deny."[62]

By 1964 the competition had expanded, rebranded as the 'Greater Metropolitan Forum'. Schools within fifty miles of New York sent one senior class candidate to compete in panel discussions. Initial rounds were performed in school assemblies with the semi-finals and finals broadcast on New York local television. This development reflected the Forum's increasing interest in engaging and educating American teenagers, not just potential future international leaders. From 1959 there was an annual US delegate. In 1961 there were three, including Roberta from Hawaii, and in 1968 and 1971 the US delegates were African American.[63]

Representing Diversity

Deciding which countries to invite, issuing invitations, and negotiating with foreign government and US consular officials to ensure thirty teenagers turned up in New York was a huge task. Geopolitical considerations, gender balance, global distribution, and personal connections all fed into the process. Then it was in the hands of others. Countries selected their own delegates, following (or adapting) guidelines provided by the Forum, guidelines that shifted over time as priorities changed.

The Forum prided itself on bringing together teenagers with diverse opinions and experiences. Perhaps most striking was the difference between those who had experienced war firsthand, and those for whom international politics was at one remove. Evelyn (Nigeria 72) had lived through 'full-fledged civil war', determined to become a doctor 'after seeing a lot of physical suffering during the war', which had 'definitely killed a part of me'. In contrast, her fellow delegate Teresa (NZ 72) had 'been fortunate to be involved with people from many Asian Pacific countries as NZ representative to United Nations Conference for Young People in Australia and at United Nations conferences in New Zealand'.[64] For young people like Teresa, for whom conflict and revolution were at arm's length, meeting the likes of Evelyn, who had been in the thick of it, must have been an education.

Diversity in class was more difficult to achieve. Delegates often hailed from a small elite, particularly where English was not widely taught. And despite the declared shift towards less-privileged students after 1967, well-traveled delegates continued to appear. Nina (Brazil 72) had family in Greece, explaining to selectors that 'during my holidays in July I traveled to Europe by air and visited Paris, Rome and Athens—the city where my parents were born'. Donatella (Italy 72) and Randa (Lebanon 72) were similarly experienced travelers.[65]

In 1968 Sidney Green, commissioned to report on potential improvements to the Forum, suggested including delegates 'with contra-government views, especially within the third world of developing nations'.[66] Quite how this could be arranged, given the selection process is unclear. What government would choose a student with revolutionary tendencies? Sometimes a radical slipped through the cracks. Israeli officials were reportedly horrified by Snait (Israel 61)'s sympathy for Arab refugees, Susan (SA 57) was opposed to apartheid, and Mike (Australia 65) publicly opposed Australian involvement in Vietnam. Other later delegates were also vocal in their condemnation of the Vietnam War and American policies more generally, but whether this was the result of selecting more radical delegates or a broader tendency among young people at the time is unclear. Forum organizers encouraged delegates to express their opinions, and to represent what 'youth in their country' thought, but delegates were limited, sometimes by an understanding of potential consequences of speaking out, but more broadly by the selection process itself, which lent itself to choosing presentable, intelligent young people, but often from elite pro-government and pro-American circles.

Whether through a rigorous nationwide competition or blatant nepotism, the Forum ended up with an interesting and sometimes challenging Forum cohort of around thirty teenagers. Clutching airline tickets, and with suitcases full of (often unfamiliar) winter clothes, they fought back tears as they farewelled families and, with increasing excitement and some trepidation, climbed the airplane stairs. The adventure had begun.

Chapter 6

Coming to America
'"Getting to know you" over the kitchen sink'

Up, up and away

The first time 15-year-old Azer (Iran 56) went in an airplane was when he traveled to New York for the Forum late in 1955. His journey was more dramatic than most. He witnessed first one and then two more of the four plane engines fail halfway over the Atlantic Ocean. Escorted by a US Air Force jet, the plane eventually landed safely, leaving Azer with a healthy respect for the perils of flying and a story for his grandchildren.[1]

Air travel in this era was unusual. Flying for free—and sometimes in first class—was extraordinary. It was especially glamorous as a teenager, with attentive and attractive air hostesses at passengers' beck and call. Airplanes were smaller and less crammed with people than in the twenty-first century. Before jet travel was the norm, the planes hopped around the globe in short bursts, pausing to refuel in exotic capitals. Delegates' journeys to New York could be circuitous, depending upon Pan Am or TWA routes. It was not always comfortable. Jan (Sweden 48) had 'read all I could' about flying so he knew that air pockets were 'not really dangerous'. His plane flew into a 'terrible snowstorm over the Atlantic' and 'we fell and we fell but I knew we could not hit the ground'. Eva (Norway 48) remembered a 'terrible journey', everyone on the plane 'scared' and airsick as they bounced from Oslo to Copenhagen to Glasgow and landed at Goose Bay in Canada rather than New York because of atrocious weather. Eline (SA 54)'s plane had technical issues, abandoning take off several times before finally succeeding. Technical issues were not uncommon. Hameeda and Riaz (Pakistan 52) traveled together from Lahore, facing their first cross-cultural challenge with an unexpected delay in Brussels, where they were allocated a double hotel room. They 'didn't know how to cope', remembered Hameeda. 'How can I question this arrangement?'.

Perhaps this was normal in the West. But 'luckily for us, they did fix the technical fault, and we were able to fly off' within a few hours.[2]

For most, the trip was less dramatic, although memorable. Several delegates were seasoned travelers, particularly the Europeans, although previous forays were usually to neighboring countries or the UK, traveling by train and ferry rather than plane. A handful of privileged delegates had flown overseas with their parents. As a child, Eduardo (Argentina 47) spent a year in London, where his grandfather had an office; his family traveled frequently. But for most, this was their first flight and their first time away from home. It left an indelible impression. Seventeen-year-old Per (Norway 61) wrote a carefully constructed account in his diary on the experience of taking off; of 'sitting ... waiting; the lights are dimmed, and the propellers begin to turn with a purring sound ... suddenly the sound changes its tone, the body of the airplane begins to shiver, the sound increases to a roar, and the machine begins to move, the cabin begins to shake violently ... soon we are in the air'. He even recorded the flavor of the 'special SAS chocolate' he chose as they taxied down the runway—'the one with coconut'.[3] Others kept souvenirs—the inflight menu, a monogrammed paper napkin, the airline magazine, the ticket itself—squirreled away in boxes of Forum memorabilia produced for me to examine, decades later.

A lucky few traveled first class. Ibrahim (Lebanon 58) had a good night's sleep on what was 'almost like a bed' in Pan Am's first class cabin. Eeva (Finland 55) and Jack (Sweden 55) were the only passengers on the Boxing Day flight from Stockholm to Oslo, where Per (Norway 55) joined them in first class, along with some tourists in economy. Roger (Norway 59) was invited into the cockpit and saw Greenland glaciers in the moonlight. Ceridwen (UK 67) was thrilled to find British prima ballerina Margot Fonteyn was a fellow passenger. Ken (Australia 67), under the legal drinking age in Australia and the US, felt 'very naughty' because he 'ordered a glass of champagne'. By 1964, TWA still flew delegates first class, while Pan Am did not, although it allowed them first-class baggage allowance (sixty-six pounds) for the flight home.[4]

Students boarded alone, often unaware of fellow delegates on board. Some were proactive, approaching likely-looking teenagers during the flight, but others discovered each other only when met by the same Forum official in New York. When Marlene (SA 55) landed in Accra, the local Cultural Affairs Officer invited her to join Fifi (Ghana 55) and Minjiba (Nigeria) for a snack in the airport. Marlene and Minjiba later shared a room for Orientation week at Sarah Lawrence College. Similarly, Susan (SA 57) bonded with Amelia (Ghana 57) on their flight. Four years later, Grace (Ghana 61) and her aunt spent an afternoon in Accra entertaining Abimbola (Nigeria 61), but not the two white African delegates, Graham (SA 61) and Jeremy (Rhodesia 61). Grace told me they had not been allowed onto Ghanaian soil unless they 'signed some sort of document to say they were against apartheid', although Graham had no recollection of this. This is one of many persistent Forum stories that, true or not, are emblematic of the politics that enveloped the program.[5]

Imagining America

Delegates arrived with preconceived ideas about the United States. A few had visited or lived there previously. Rachel (Israel 64) spent two years in New York when her father was an agricultural attaché in 1957, acquiring an American accent, much to the disappointment of her Forum student hosts. Others had US-based relatives. During the Forum, Marco (Italy 49) visited his great-uncle in Pennsylvania, a younger brother of his American grandmother. Such family reunions became a problem. By 1961 the first 'Forum Rule' for delegates banned 'individual travel to visit friends or relatives in other parts of the nation'. In addition: 'Under no circumstances' could delegates 'extend your stay' in the US or 'change the routing of your return journey'.[6]

Delegates with siblings, cousins, or friends who had gone before knew more than most about America and the Forum. But all delegates were told to 'try to talk to or at least correspond' with their country's former delegates, who could 'best tell you what it is like to be a Forum delegate'. In 1961, a list of names and addresses was helpfully enclosed, and 'some had already been notified of your selection and may be getting in touch'. (Meanwhile Helen Waller sent alumni firm requests to seek out the new delegate, directing them to American consulates for address details.) Alison (UK 60) visited Sara (57), John (59) and John (58) in Oxford, finding them quite intimidating and sophisticated. Helen's assistant, Joan Lee Smith, reassured her after the Forum: 'What a terrific and lovely delegate you made. Be sure that bunch of alumni at Oxford would have been proud'. The first Austrian delegate, Annemarie (Austria 63), knew little about the Forum, and her mother was hesitant about letting her go: 'we were all scared of World War Three' with the 'Cuban Missile Crisis and all'. Fortunately, Kitty (Argentina 61), studying in Innsbruck, made a long train journey to reassure and advise Annemarie: she would have to talk about Austria to schools and should take a gift for the president.[7]

Delegates' preconceived ideas about the US mainly came from films, books and USIS propaganda. Helen Waller often invited them to share their more bizarre preconceptions in public, to demonstrate the power of the Forum program in dispelling such notions. Lee Hup Suan (Malaya 58) had thought the US 'a land of reckless people—irresponsible, indifferent, ambitious and too materialistic minded', that all Americans drove big cars at '100 miles an hour through the busiest streets' and 'don't care' if they knocked anyone over. Teenagers were too carefree 'having fun all day long', she said. Rafia (Pakistan 59) had a vision of 'a big, beautiful country' where everyone was a 'millionaire and they had oil in their backyards and all the members of the family had a car and … at least three televisions'. Teenagers 'were a bit wild … doing the rock and roll in the streets … the boys in jeans and carrying knives'. Her description is uncannily reminiscent of *West Side Story*, although the stage musical was barely two years old and the film would not be released until 1961. Minjiba (Nigeria 55) was also relieved to find New York streets 'were *not* full of cowboys and gangsters'. Yasar (Jordan 59) had five brothers, all of whom spoke 'cowboy English' and had 'Western aspirations based on … the films they saw in the cinema, the only entertainment available in a little town like Amman in the early 1950s'. Vangala (India 54) confirmed the association of the US with modernity when he told television audiences that, for an Indian, the US seemed like 'a young country … with remarkable progress in the technological sphere … with very high standards of living'. But, he added, 'material values rate over spiritual values' in the US, making a distinction between youthful, materialistic America and the ancient civilization of India. Trivo (Yugoslavia 58)'s opinion was understandably framed by anti-communist legislation in the US. Others did their research in USIS libraries.⁸

Some delegates knew little. Teklu (Ethiopia 60) told me he had 'no idea'. He 'knew where America was' but that was about it. Some were keen to learn more. Sven (Sweden 48), just 14 when he won his trip, impressed selectors by saying 'in school geography, we learn lots about square miles, numbers of inhabitants and cows and climate, but very little about people, how they live, work and think, so we need personal contact'. Jean-Claude (France 49) wrote of the stories 'going on in France about the US': 'people living all through the year in a 3 x 3 foot room on the 70th floor, couples divorcing every morning'.⁹ Delegates from later in the 1960s sometimes knew more, although often it was framed by their experience of American GIs, aid workers, or tourists. It was not always positive. The Forum aimed to counter ignorance and negative stereotypes of the US.

The Logistics of Arrival

Delegates would soon discover how true or false their imaginings of America were. They arrived in dribs and drabs, depending on airline schedules. Once the Orientation program was established in 1954, there was less variation, but some still turned up inconveniently early or arrived late, missing some activities. Jona (Iceland 60) was relieved to see people waving to her when she reached Idlewild airport, 'oh thank God, they really are here'. Bewilderment followed as she did not understand what anyone said—although she could read and write fluently, spoken American English was very different. During the Forum's heyday, most delegates were met by Forum staff at the airport and went directly to Sarah Lawrence College. Nuala (Ireland 63) described a sort of shuttle process. At Idlewild Airport she was met by 'a lady', who 'put me in a taxi, I presume to Grand Central', where Pan Am's Lorraine Kure was waiting. Nuala and one of the African boys 'were popped on a train to go Sarah Lawrence College', by themselves, as Nuala remembered it. They made it safely, although Nuala felt lost and self-conscious on the train as a white girl sitting with a black boy, who was also rather taciturn.¹⁰

Other times, especially early on and in the final years, delegates were met by host families, reducing Forum staff workloads. The Ball family wondered how they would identify Michael (UK 72) at the airport. 'I will wear a deerstalker hat', announced the British teenager, playing up to a stereotype. Even then Michael Portillo knew how to stand out, prefiguring his startlingly mismatched linen jackets and trousers in the later 'Great Railway Journeys' television series. If this was an attempt at sophistication, it was outdone by host mother Marie Ball, who picked him up in a Cadillac. They remained lifelong friends.[11]

Delegates who arrived unexpectedly early stayed with *Tribune* staff. Jona (Iceland 60) spent two nights with three other delegates on the floor of a Forum staff member's New York apartment before Orientation. Susan (SA 57) recalled her first 'American treat' while staying with Forum assistant Mary Warner—'cinnamon toast!'. Minh (Vietnam 65) was taken aback to see a table saw in the middle of his journalist host's apartment. 'He said he liked to do woodwork!', Minh remembered fifty years later, laughing, and 'that's all I remember ... a beautiful, fantastic table saw ... in New York ... on the twenty-fifth floor!' Forum secretary Sylvia Abraham not only hosted Brigitte (France 64) in her apartment, but also nursed Salah (Lebanon 64) who turned up with measles.[12] The Forum presented itself as a prestigious, well-oiled machine, but it was often improvised, relying on volunteers, keen Forum assistants, alumni, *Tribune* journalists and government functionaries, on willing host families and teachers.

'Orientation or Indoctrination?'

By 1954, Helen Waller realized the need for a formal Orientation program to make the group more cohesive. She co-opted the Nobel Peace Prize-winning American Friends Service Committee (AFSC), a Quaker organization with experience in internationalist youth programs, to run a five-day orientation program at Kober House at Sarah Lawrence College.[13]

It was not an altogether successful collaboration, judging from later reports by AFSC's Barbara Grant, who convened the program with 'house parents', Winni and Barry Barrett. Notably, some of their criticism prefigured later comments by Sarah Lawrence College staff. The organizations had different aims. The AFSC felt Helen Waller over-emphasized the benefits of American democracy and freedoms and tried to lead delegates by the nose. Helen was reportedly 'not terribly pleased' with guest speaker Max Wolff's presentation, which she called 'a good discussion of Marxist economic determinism'. She 'made it abundantly clear that... she wanted to talk about the benefits of "democratic liberalism"', which was 'the American way'. Grant was equally shocked by Helen's 'interrogation' of Nurit (Israel 54): 'As the questioning developed it became clear that Nurit was being "helped" to see and to say that the kibbutz, as an example of democratic liberalism, was a good thing'. Grant was relieved that Nurit was 'a very perceptive and modest person ... and far more cautious in her evaluation of the kibbutz'. Grant was 'somewhat bowled over' when Helen declared that she 'didn't know for certain' how many host families were African American. 'In America', Helen said, 'we don't ask about race or religion'. Grant thought this was deceitful. The delegates, 'by the time they leave, will know that this isn't true—but', she added, 'I think they will also be too polite to accuse Helen Waller of untruth'. Barbara Grant was not alone in her criticism. Her colleague Winni Barrett wondered if Helen 'really knows how far she falls short'. The AFSC did not run the Orientation program again.[14]

Helen's interventions in the discussion echoed the USIA advice pamphlet 'Americans Abroad', produced to enable Americans to counter criticism by non-Americans of US race relations and other controversial policies.[15] Delegates recalled Helen as a critic rather than an apologist; an internationalist rather than strident nationalist, but both here and in public appearances, she carefully kept to the official line, emphasizing the benefits of American democracy. The Forum relied on US State Department support.

Dishwashing Diplomacy

Orientation, thenceforth organized by Helen and Forum staff, continued at Kober House until the late 1960s, when it moved to Seabury House in Greenwich, Connecticut, an Episcopal Church conference center. It soon became a well-oiled machine. The delegates got to know each other through various activities, themed political discussions, informal chats, and by working together on the *Forum Tribune* (the delegates' annual circular). Guest speakers introduced them to aspects of the US. There were, as the 1960 cohort were told 'A Few Rules'.

- Delegates will make their own beds
- Delegates will clean their bathrooms daily
- Bedrooms must be kept <u>liveable</u>
- <u>Absolutely no smoking in the delegates' bedrooms</u>
- Each delegate is asked to have a bath or shower daily
- Please do not leave belongings downstairs at night
- When you leave Kober House please sign out on the bulletin board and sign in when you return.
- There will be no visitors at Kober House, unless with the permission of the resident leaders
- All delegates must be in their rooms by 10.30pm
- Relative silence is in order after that hour![16]

These rules remind us that they were, after all, teenagers and that many were away from home for the first time, with emphasis on liveable bedrooms and clean bathrooms. Some rules were clearly the result of experience (the request for daily showers, perhaps). And these rules were reasonable: only 'relative silence' was requested after 10.30 pm.

During this first week Forum organizers outlined the program for the coming three months, described American schools, family life, and what delegates should expect. While this was essential preparation, it was not always fascinating. One delegate wrote in her diary of 'Mr Huffman rambling on and on, sending you to sleep', talking about 'everything you shouldn't do and what bad delegates had done in the past … all most morbid and depressing'. The same delegate declared Sarah Lawrence College principal's lecture on education 'boring and hopeless'. He 'didn't know enough'. She found William Haddad's talk on the Peace Corps more interesting. By the end of the 1960s the 'week' had become four days at Seabury House and consisted of discussions preparing for television programs, with fewer guest speakers, although Huffman tried to keep up with the changing times. Just as Helen Waller introduced delegates to the likes of Pete Seeger, in 1969 Bob Huffman included John Parham of the National Urban League, which campaigned for civil rights. In 1970, activist Sam Brown, Coordinator of the Vietnam Moratorium Committee, spoke to the delegates. USIA chief Frank Shakespeare addressed the 1971 group, allegedly underestimating them as just 'a group of teenagers' to his cost.

Delegates recall his 'selective and simplistic' view of US twentieth-century policies being challenged by skeptical and well-informed delegates from Yugoslavia, India, Pakistan, Germany, and Italy.[17]

Orientation was also about introducing delegates to the expectations of American family life, which was central to the idealized image of egalitarian American democracy. Forum delegates, like other exchange students, would participate in 'such chores as washing up, making beds, etc', which were 'done by members of even relatively well-to-do families'.[18] Dishwashing was certainly a well-remembered feature of Orientation. Some delegates had never washed a dish in their lives; they had servants for that. A few boys declared it 'women's work', earning them swift rebukes from fiercely articulate female delegates.

But dishwashing had other benefits. In his evocatively titled article, '"Getting to know you" at the kitchen sink', for the *Straits Times*, budding journalist Peter (Singapore 57) described how delegates bonded as they washed dishes, becoming 'less and less reserved as they griped more and more about the society that required its guests to wash their own crockery after eating'. Karin (Germany 61) wrote that 'the first time I really felt that I belonged … was when I had to do the dishes'. Ashish (India 61) noticed the 'dishwashing ritual was the source of much leg-pulling' among the delegates, commenting (a little piously?) that he could not see why—it 'was but fair that we washed the dishes we ate on' and the duties 'were very evenly distributed'.[19]

Dishwashing was also a political strategy. 'Jordan and Israel were busy doing dishes together before either had fully realized the other's nationality', recorded Helen Waller in her 1955 report. Was this a watershed moment, as she realized the power of prioritizing domestic chores over 'representing one's country'? She noted that 'there was really no chance for the studiously hostile behavior between Arab and Israeli that has occurred in previous years', when delegates had behaved, she reported pointedly, 'in accordance with instructions from their governments' when they first met.[20] Although Helen was overly optimistic, for things were not always harmonious in later years, dishwashing broke down barriers, as team-building exercises focusing on practical, collaborative tasks often do.

Arabs and Israelis were not the only ones on opposite sides of long conflicts. And others had entrenched understandings about their fellow delegates, based on racial or religious beliefs, informed by popular culture, or resulting from a lack of exposure or simple ignorance. Meeting the array of teenagers could be a culture shock. It was 'the first time' Teklu (Ethiopia 60) had 'seen people from anywhere other than Ethiopia'. Irjaleena (Finland 57) had 'never seen so many colored people before'. Even in 1969, Jutta (Germany) had never met a black person. Tina (Spain 67) was shocked by the tribal markings on Jacob (Nigeria 67)'s face. This was not unexpected. The Forum explicitly aimed to break down barriers, to challenge these teenagers (and the American students they met) to move beyond stereotypes. And many of them did, although embedded cultural and racial pigeonholing was hard to eliminate completely. When Léon (Mexico 64) slept the day through at Sarah Lawrence College, after a long trip from home, he emerged to gentle ribbing from his cohort about 'the Mexican delegate having a long siesta'. Léon laughed when telling me this story nearly sixty years later; for him it was a benign one-off joke, but among the delegates there were cliques and hierarchies, often based on race or language. Writing in the alumni newsletter, *The Delegate,* in 1996, Difie (Ghana 67) recalled that she had felt she was in a room of strangers: 'I hung out with the delegates from Ethiopia, Kenya, Liberia, India etc, because basically we seemed to be one of a kind'. Others perhaps enjoyed the relief of not having to speak English all the time: Spanish and Portuguese speakers found common ground. One 1950s French delegate remembered gravitating towards the Europeans. She suggested that she and the other Europeans were 'not interested' in the Asian delegates. Perhaps she just had more to discuss with her near neighbors, with the European Economic Community high on the agenda. A European 'superiority complex' among delegates, however, was apparent in several years, as interviewees' portrayals of Asian delegates being there for 'exotic color' demonstrated. One 1960s English delegate wrote home that 'there is no Forum spirit: most say how happy they are in the host families and how much they dislike being together'. She described 'various cliques': 'the Asian group', 'the Coloured [sic] group' and the 'main group', into all of which she herself had 'entrée' because she was '"thoroughbred", English, white, a girl, and will do a great deal for devilment!'.[21]

English language ability was critical. Snait (Israel 61) noted that 'some of the people who are from entirely different cultures felt quite miserable, and the ones who didn't know English at all, (even less than I do) just tried to stay in their rooms'. She felt that whole group discussions did not work so well, dominated by four or five people. Smaller groups were better. Irjaleena (Finland 57) said something similar—it was difficult to contribute to a debate involving thirty-three teenagers! This would be true in any large group, but facility in English was significant. Christian (France 70) was top of his English class, but when he 'landed in the US' he 'did not understand half of what I was told!'. He was also 'used to being a leader in other circumstances'—the previous summer he had organized a group holiday for forty school friends—but he found himself 'crushed by those with louder voices in politics' at the Forum. British delegates felt special. Ceridwen (UK 67) advised that 'within the Forum group the UK delegate 'has a very important role ... helping those who have [adjustment difficulties], especially over language ... work[ing] closely with the US delegate who has the responsibility of being the host'. British girls remembered being hailed as 'Mother England' by African delegates when they arrived at the Forum.[22] Surely this was an ironic tag, I thought, but British delegates often took their country's role as head of the Commonwealth seriously.

Orientation week was not only work. In between lectures, formal discussions, preparation for TV programs, and the obligatory dishwashing, delegates had fun. Patsy (Philippines 58) taught Saroj (Thailand 58) how to dance. The 1964 Pakistani delegate read palms; in 1967 delegates from equatorial countries were inducted into the age-old pastime of snowball-throwing and snowman-building by their experienced northern European colleagues. Emmanuel (Ghana 68) remembered Amilcare (Italy 68) was 'like a comedian, so we got along pretty well until he got me infected with chicken pox'.[23] There was the inevitable New Year's Eve party. Pity the poor delegate whose flight arrived on January 1 and who tiptoed into an unnaturally silent Kober House early on New Year's Day, the occupants sleeping off the partying of the night before. This was not the result of excessive alcohol consumption, however—just high spirits and dancing into the wee hours. The delegates were under drinking age and official parties rarely included anything more lethal than soda, at least in the 1950s and early 1960s.

'Too Short'

The Orientation period was over in a flash. When asked to suggest improvements, 1961 delegates said, 'it was too short!'. Nevertheless, it began the important process of binding this disparate batch of teenagers into a cohesive group, introduced them to America and to their job as delegates and, importantly, allowing Forum staff to assess which delegates would make good television fodder, who would require 'mothering', and who were likely to go off the rails. Then it was time to say goodbye to newfound friends, leave the now-familiar surrounds of Kober House, take a deep breath, and venture out to 'real' America, to be 'walking textbooks' at the first of several host schools.

Chapter 7

'Walking Textbooks' at Host Schools

'The entertainment of foreign pupils in our schools and in the homes of our pupils has had real educational value',[1] pronounced the New York Board of Education in 1949, encouraging schools to participate in the two-year-old *Herald Tribune* Forum for High Schools. These host schools were central to the success of the program, initially established in partnership with the Metropolitan School Study Council and Board of Education (providing the Forum a useful entrée into local schools). By the early 1950s the catchment had expanded to include schools from New Jersey, New York State, Pennsylvania, and Connecticut. Throughout the twenty-five years of the program, delegates spent between two and three weeks at each of four or five different schools. These schools were responsible for entertaining the delegates, and for finding volunteer host families (who were then matched with delegates by Forum staff).

A major selling point of the Forum was its educative possibilities, addressing the recognized lack of global understanding among American students. Indoctrination operated in two directions. Delegates were introduced to the wonders of American education, illustrating the 'true democracy that flourishes in our schools', thereby 'having America "come alive"'. American teenagers were exposed to the best and the brightest of teenagers from other countries. The *Herald Tribune* waxed lyrical: 'It is hard to tell whether guest or host receives the greatest benefit'. The delegate 'will doubtless correct many of his old preconceptions about the United States', while for the high school student, who would not normally 'exchange ten words with a student from foreign lands', the visit may 'open even wider windows on the world and give significant direction to a whole future career'. The *Tribune* delighted in quoting the New York Board of Education's praise for the Forum's contribution to the creation of 'an enlightened citizenry ... interested in the problems, aspirations, and political objectives of all nations'.[2] The Forum's educational aims for American students continued to be important, outstripping the ambitious idea of influencing future international leaders by the late 1960s.

From 1953 there was also the promise of publicity: thirteen weekly half-hour television broadcasts. These would, Helen Waller suggested, 'feature different host schools and communities, and attempt to show how the guest student is integrated into the host student's school and home life'. Schools were invited to keep the Forum staff informed of activities that showed how their teaching programs were 'enriched by school-sponsored visits of students from abroad'.[3] In fact, only a few schools were ever named in the programs, although they were listed prominently in the finale's program and in *Tribune* reports.

Which Schools?

Many schools participated. Some hosted delegates once, others repeatedly. Analysis of the available lists for sixteen years between 1950 and 1969 revealed 263 schools, averaging 69 schools each year, although numbers varied widely. In 1954 and 1957, 81 schools hosted delegates, in 1964, 87 schools were hosts, but in 1961, only 47 schools were involved. Perhaps fewer schools volunteered. Most host schools were well within a 100-mile radius of New York, with a quarter within New York City, 16 per cent on Long Island, another quarter in New Jersey and about 12 per cent just north of New York city. Seventy-four of the 263 schools only participated once, and only 18 per cent of the schools hosted delegates for more than half the time. The top participating school was Dwight Morrow High School in Englewood, New Jersey, which hosted every year from 1952. Seven of the top nine schools were in New Jersey. In provincial New Jersey, Forum delegates would have been more exotic and potentially more attractive than in central New York.[4]

In early years, the Forum found public schools to host delegates, reflecting the involvement of the Metropolitan School Study Council. They wanted to introduce delegates to the wonders of free education, and to provide public school students with the benefits of interacting with delegates. Public schools remained dominant, but the range expanded quickly. Delegates were sent to immensely privileged schools on Long Island, small-town high schools in New Jersey, highly academic schools, private single-sex academies, Jewish schools, Catholic schools, and even boarding schools. Some had a predominantly white student body, others were more integrated, while a few delegates attended predominantly African American schools.

Ideally, delegates sampled a variety of schools. Some felt their placements had been carefully planned, as they went from being chauffeur-driven in limousines to impressive sandstone academies in extensive grounds to catching the subway in inner-city New York to a shabby multistorey on a pocket-handkerchief block, and then on to New Jersey, with its milkshakes, white picket fences, church attendance, and conservative values. How far the organizers curated each delegate's experience is unclear. There is some evidence that Forum staff paid attention to school allocation. Susan (SA 57) said she got the 'trifecta' of schools. She later asked Helen Waller if that was deliberate and remembered Helen's shrewd response: 'she didn't say yes or no but had this way of looking'. This was typical of Helen. Susan's placements were certainly not planned by Helen herself, who, by 1957, left mundane arrangements to assistants. Helen claimed in 1956 that two staff spent three weeks completing the 'particular puzzle' of matching '35 Forum delegates in a total of 90 schools and 140 families'. One of the six criteria they considered, she said, was 'a balanced total program so that each delegate will visit a variety of schools and communities (large city school, suburban school, small private school, etc.)' Admittedly, Helen provided this description of time-consuming diligence in defense of her staffing budget, which was under threat, but it suggests care was taken. Delegates often went in pairs or threes to the same school, but never in the same group to more than one school. This enabled delegates to get to know each other, as well as providing support. Many interviewees best remembered delegates at the same schools. Sometimes it led to a little (unspoken) competition. One delegate shared a school placement with a 'minute, beautiful' South American delegate, who 'could play the guitar'. The whole school 'fell madly in love with her' and the other delegate felt 'inferior', having no special talents. 'I was glad I could be good at talking', she said. In 1957, the Forum implemented changes recommended by a committee 'representing interested teachers and supervisors', reducing the five host periods to four, extending the first period from two to three weeks, and sending between two and four delegates to each school.[5]

Helen was more involved in selecting schools (and charming school officials) in the early years, although the only evidence suggests her interest was in convenience: A 1952 memo instructed colleagues to focus on 'upper Westchester schools, so that from my home base in Katonah I can have more personal after-school contact with them'.[6] Ultimately, the program relied on schools and families volunteering, and the main priority was ensuring delegates had places. All spent time in New York city, and New Jersey or New York State, and most found themselves in at least one predominantly Jewish school. Sometimes students also stayed briefly with host families during the group field trips.

In the 1960s school visits were coordinated so all delegates were grouped in the same area, allowing for mutual programming between schools and more interaction between delegates. In 1963, for example, delegates were sent first to Westchester, Long Island, and Connecticut. The second period was in New Jersey and Pennsylvania, and delegates enjoyed the delights of Greater Manhattan during the final period.[7]

'Thank Goodness for Mr Esser!'

Despite the variety of schools presented to delegates, interviewees sometimes found it hard to distinguish between them decades later. A few spoke of the provincialism of small-town schools, or the overwhelming privilege of private academies but for most it was the people—host families, school friends and individual teachers—that made a visit memorable or successful, rather than the location. One teacher in each school, often the counsellor, careers advisor, or world history teacher, liaised with Forum administration, recruited and advised families, and shepherded delegates through the host school period. The diligence and energy with which teachers performed these roles varied, as did individual delegates' need for their services. Particularly proactive teachers were valuable Forum assets, their schools receiving delegates annually. These schools often also hosted AFS students and had other internationalist and citizenship educational programs. Long-serving world history teacher, who taught between 1922 and 1969, Mrs Ione Eckerson of Englewood's Dwight Morrow High, wrote to the *Tribune* in 1952, 'I hope we can always be part of this worthwhile project', which was 'the most important' in which her school participated. She waxed lyrical about the 'beautiful English' spoken by the delegates, who were 'so mature'—a 'source of great wonderment to our students', proving 'that teenagers all over the world are much alike'. This school hosted delegates every year between 1952 and 1969. 'The sort of broadmindedness and generosity of spirit "Mrs. Eckie" exemplified were pretty unusual in the rather pinched atmosphere of the 1950s', remembered student Richard Cross (Class of 1958). Delegates also remembered her as 'most helpful and inspiring ... a wonderful person'.[8]

The importance of individual staff members cannot be overestimated. Woodmere Academy stopped hosting delegates after 1954, when Social Studies teacher Marie Underhill moved to newly established George W Hewlett High, which took over the Forum mantle, hosting delegates from 1956. Arnlaug (Norway 58) thought her 'fantastic' and learned 'a lot also about ways of teaching'. Similarly, Paul Biery Esser Jr was key to the Forum's success in Allentown, Pa, remaining faculty liaison for the school district when he moved from Allentown High to newly opened Louis E Dieruff High in 1960. Delegates followed. The local *Morning Call* reported Helen Waller's praise: 'The most important single American experience for the 1959 Argentine delegate was in Allentown', she wrote, when he 'interviewed new Puerto Rican residents'. This was just part of the varied program Paul Esser organized to ensure delegates met 'with representatives of management and labor, housewives and professional people, governmental representatives, and the man on the street'. Activities included athletics events, social programs, discussion groups, a union meeting, and visiting United Fund agencies. In 1963 Forum staff member Anne Counes briefed John Hay Whitney on Paul Esser and the school, which had 'always been most cooperative': they 'find excellent families and involve the whole community in the delegates' visit'. In fact, that year Annemarie (Austria 63)'s host family was a disaster; they 'did nothing together' and, although the father was a minister, did not even invite her to church. She envisaged watching lots of television in her bedroom, but Paul Esser involved her in school activities and took her out on weekends with his wife. 'Thank goodness for Mr Esser', Annemarie said. Later the Essers visited Annemarie in Europe and their friendship lasted until Esser's death in 1986. Esser also remained close to Minh (Vietnam 65), who recalled he 'even allowed me to go to see some of the poorer schools in the neighborhood', 'took me to one of the civil rights churches', and invited a Lehigh University professor to speak about a recent trip to Cuba. Minh was surprised to find someone so progressive at such a 'white bread' school. Other teachers also stood out. Judith (UK 56) remembered Charles Gorton High School counselor Denise Azzara, who epitomized 'how to be a school counselor'. Helen Brickell, Bronxville High counselor, who helped Direk (Thailand 53) with his Cornell application, was not the only teacher to facilitate university applications.[9]

'Walking Textbooks'

Forum publicity encouraged host schools to treat delegates as 'walking textbooks', invaluable for educating American teenagers about the wider world. Delegates, promised the *Tribune*, would provide social studies students with 'new and more personalized insights into problems of other people and cultures'. Forum administrators and the Board of Education briefed schools about appropriate activities and could be quite specific. For 1957, Helen Waller (based on the advice of her teachers' committee) suggested themes to be explored during visits. These included 'the federal system', 'foreign policy in the US', 'inter-racial problems', and 'economic development'. Between other speaking commitments, delegates should attend two regular classes daily. One should be world history, literature, comparative religion, or another class where delegates would 'make a unique contribution'. In reality, individual schools determined delegates' activities, and they varied, although delegates were usually kept busy. Suzanne (UK 62) recorded a non-stop whirlwind of talks, meetings, and new experiences, including visiting a Senior Citizens Center, a Youth Council meeting, and the local public library, where, 'as with everything else we were given a terrific reception'. She even had an interview with a police officer. Leevi (Finland 60) and Aloysius (Nigeria 60) had a 'nice program' at George W Hewlett High School. Leevi's host took him 'everywhere in the school and in the community', visiting school clubs and student councils. 'Different people take us to lunch everyday so that they have occasion to meet us and we can get to know each other', and they had 'discussions about education'. Susie (Brazil 58) and Arnlaug (Norway 58) took advantage of 'a box at the Met' held by Dwight School (a private girls school in Englewood New Jersey) and took themselves off to 'La Traviata', Susie's first experience of opera. Ceridwen (UK 67) found her first 'funny little private school—quite idiosyncratic' and 'very well-organized'; they 'obviously always had somebody, or very frequently' from the Forum. Her second school was Dwight Morrow High School, where she encountered the incomparable Ione Eckerson, disappointingly, few American students. 'The school did not arrange any of my social activities, [which] tended to be planned so that Foreign students and their hosts kept meeting'. Her third host school's faculty advisor, 'who was new to the Forum, did not fully understand the purpose of my visit'. She reported, 'I had to ask several times before I was able to give any speeches and people seemed surprised that I wanted to do it'.[10] One imagines that by the end of her visit school staff were well-apprised of their responsibilities.

What Do You Think of American Schools?

Delegates generally enjoyed American high schools, which were often very different from their own. Several interviewees still treasured local newspaper clippings and yearbooks featuring their visit. Teresa (NZ 72) remembered 'taking photos of the cars in the car park and kids not wearing school uniform', two aspects that were very different (then, at least) from Christchurch, New Zealand. Gerry (Rhodesia 60) also thought it 'strange' not to have uniforms, even more so 'to see the girls wearing make-up'. Michael (NZ 67) 'participated in their sports' and 'perhaps immodestly', he admitted later, 'enjoyed all the attention'. The school basketball team was 'lionized' and 'everyone went to the Friday night game'. On the other hand, Peter (Australia, 48) was critical that 'sport here seems to consist in sitting down and watching someone else play'. Patricia (UK 48) did just that and felt 'dizzy after seeing my first school basketball game', which she told reporters was 'fantastic, most undignified compared to cricket'.[11]

Several delegates were entranced by the range of subjects on offer—most notably driving lessons, with some taking full advantage. Raza (Pakistan 61) remembered the sketching and design classes; Emmanuel (Ghana 68) enjoyed 'jumping on the trampoline' in gym class; Geneviève (France 56) found it all quite different from a French lycée, which did not offer typewriting or driving lessons. She did not, however, like the way students went from one class to another. In France, the teachers moved about. One British delegate was intrigued that Massapequa High had a Russian language class and thought a chemistry teacher 'one of the best I have come across and that includes England too!' She was especially moved by the special needs teacher, John D Wool, 'the nearest thing to a saint I have ever met'. On the other hand, she thought one school psychologist 'a quack'.[12]

Delegates' enthusiasm for participating in class varied. Faculty advisor Mabel Tomb reported that Irjaleena (Finland 57) 'was the first *Herald Tribune* student delegate who willingly and eagerly did assignments' and 'in class responded voluntarily to any activity which was being conducted'. Serban (Bolivia 64) was also diligent, joining the Math Club at one school, and Emmanuel (Ghana 68) industriously did his homework. Marco (Italy 49) enjoyed the opportunity to show off in a Latin class: 'they were very surprised when I translated Caesar from Latin into English at first sight'. On the other hand, Susie (Brazil 58) remembered that during the second week of the stay at a 'boring' school, 'Arnlaug managed to get us off to the museums in New York'. She had 'such chutzpah', remembered Susie in admiration, adding, 'of course it was all very educational!' Host parent Shirley Streicker suggested in 1963 that delegates be 'given more work to do in school or the hosts should be given less'. She observed, 'delegates are bored in school because they have little to do, and it is difficult for the hosts to tend to their homework at night and do all the entertaining they would like to do for their guests'.[13]

Delegates accompanied their hosts and participated in lessons. As elite students in their own countries, many found themselves academically far in advance of the Americans. Some were disparaging about American educational standards, confident their own education systems were superior. Those familiar with strict 'teacher lecturing and students taking notes' regimes, typical in many Western European and some Asian classrooms, were astounded by the free-and-easy atmosphere in American schools, where students were encouraged to ask questions and express opinions (if sometimes not very well-informed ones). Marco (Italy 49) described American schools as 'not elite schools like in Italy, but democratic schools for everybody'. John (UK 59) became instantly unpopular by publicly deriding American education five minutes after he arrived, but by the end of his visit, he noted the democratic and inclusive nature of American education. He nevertheless remained adamant that more was needed for bright students. Another British delegate told of an English class, where she wasn't intending to speak, 'but when I heard the English teacher talking about "Bob" Burns, I nearly died!' She made her feelings clear (the very Scottish poet would *never* be called 'Bob') and 'he asked me to take over'. Patricia (UK 48) was disapproving of the 'lighthearted and carefree attitude' of female students, who 'don't take work seriously enough'. As she put it robustly, 'Nowadays a girl should be able to discuss the Palestine question, for instance, in as much detail as a boy'. Merete (Denmark 48) was similarly 'disappointed' that all American students could talk about was 'basketball, dates and the "new look"', in contrast to Danish students who discussed world affairs: 'After living through five years of foreign occupation, we know what it is like when totalitarianism begins to spread'. Yoriko (Japan 56) thought American students had 'not yet acquired an adequate understanding about things Japanese'. They were 'unaware of the Japanese suffering experiments of the atomic and hydrogen bombs'.[14]

On the other hand, Ken (Australia 67) was horrified to discover that although 'I'd done quite well at French at school ... I couldn't speak it, whereas their French classes were all conducted purely in French'. He used to go home at night and cram 'so that I wasn't letting the country down'. He was 'quite embarrassed'. Peter (Australia 48) thought Americans more interested in politics and world affairs than Australians. Casimir (Finland 48) put this down to the 'flourishing student organizations' in US schools, fostering interest in politics. Paolo (Italy 55) was also surprised by the important role of political and economic debates in American classrooms, along with the 'custom of reading newspapers at school and discussing the opinions expressed'. Paolo had to explain repeatedly that studies of history in Italian schools 'stopped at World War I, and newspapers were ignored'. On the other hand, he thought American education was 'too involved in the problems of the present time and lacking a historical perspective'. In later life, as an Italian high school teacher, he realized that while he had been 'sharply critical' of American schools, the Italian system of selective education that he had received was not ideal either.[15]

In their critique of American teenagers, delegates seldom remembered that Forum participants were an elite group; students they met in American high schools covered the full range of abilities. Similarly elite Americans sent to high schools in other parts of the world would likely be equally as disappointed in those students' lack of international awareness. Occasionally delegates were called to account. Rafia (Pakistan 59) pontificated forcefully in one television debate about how American students should 'study geography' after they suggested Pakistan was in Africa. Helen Waller then asked her, 'Where is Argentina?'. Rafia blushed, confessing that she had no idea. 'Maybe Europe?', she offered tentatively and then laughed, 'And here I was telling Americans they should study geography!' she exclaimed. This was one of the few times delegates showed an awareness that, as Helen Waller put it, 'no one has a monopoly on international ignorance'.[16]

'I Learned the Tricks'

Often delegates were pulled out of class to speak to other students or address an assembly. Sometimes they were paraded around other local schools or community groups. If any were unaccustomed to public speaking before they left home, they quickly became adept. Within twenty-four hours of landing in New York, a slightly bleary-eyed Jorge (Uruguay 53) accompanied his host family to a local show in Trenton, New Jersey. Much to his surprise, he heard over the loudspeaker 'and we have with us today, a *Herald Tribune* World Youth Forum delegate, Jorge Bargman from Uruguay, who is going to say a few words'. After the initial shock, Jorge, like many delegates, developed a standard patter, and became used to 'saying a few words' to assorted groups. 'I had no shame', he confessed, 'so I could wing it'. He was thankful that his English was competent. Some delegates struggled to find the vocabulary. Sergio (Brazil 53) remembered his first Millburn High School (NJ) assembly. A teacher beckoned him on stage, introduced him and whispered, 'Now you talk for half an hour about Brazil'. The 'stunned' Sergio 'gathered all my courage' and obliged. Ever since, 'I never felt uneasy' about public speaking, the retired ambassador said, although 'I prefer to use notes'. Theresa (NZ 72) went around thirty different classes at one school. Léon (Mexico 64) felt he 'had learned the tricks' of public speaking after listening to the adult speakers at Orientation. Sherille (Ceylon 71) had a slide presentation, which helped. Emmanuel (Ghana 68) 'felt like a big shot', but Diana (Italy 57), who was 'not a public speaker', found it 'agonizing', and Geneviève (France 56) hated going from 'one class to another and repeating' her spiel. Michael (UK 72) even suggested delegates were 'treated rather as a commodity, with some teachers inviting us to address their classes only because it saved them the effort of teaching for a few hours'.[17] Whether or not delegates felt exploited or excited, by the end of the three months they had certainly mastered the ability to speak in public, especially impressive when in their second language.

'Do You Ride Elephants to School?'

In her Forum Report's 'Information for Future Delegates', Ceridwen (UK 67) not only reminded delegates firmly that 'a short "thank-you" note is always appreciated and it is important to do these things', but gave helpful hints about speeches. 'Prepare a little beforehand', she advised, and 'ask for pamphlets and booklets' from the British Information Service in New York, (she gave the address). English pennies and pictures of the Royal Family were popular with children. British delegates should 'be able to talk on "Mod Fashions, Carnaby Street, Twiggy, and the Beatles" as well as our NHS, Educational System, Parliament and Monarchy, Economy, Commonwealth, and the UK's role in the world today'. She was right. Michael (UK 72) faced questions about 'the Beatles, the Queen, and peasouper fogs', with the occasional query about 'the worsening position in Northern Ireland', although he admitted that the interlocuter usually 'lost interest' in the answer 'after about five minutes'. Suzanne (UK 62) also listed topics in her Forum report, but importantly recommended being 'constructive in your criticism' and having patience with repetitive and 'stupid questions'. Most delegates found their counterparts in the US very ill-informed about the world. 'They were totally ignorant about anything outside America, and you spent a lot of time talking about very basic things'. But, as Rodel (Philippines 69) told me, 'you were the first person from your part of the world they had ever encountered'. America was very 'America-centric'. At the same time, American students took full advantage of the delegates, wanting to know about the world, asking anything and everything of these 'walking textbooks'. Helen Waller advised delegates to be patient. Annual instructions reminded them that 'as a recent delegate said "But don't you see, if they knew the answers, we wouldn't be here at all"'. That perennially 'recent' delegate was in fact Ines (Ecuador 47), whose words lived on in the welcome letter until at least 1962.[18]

Teklu (Ethiopia 60) was relieved American students knew nothing about Ethiopia. 'It made it easier for a half-baked kid like me to stand in front of them and talk about Ethiopia as if I knew a lot more than I did, and get away with it'. Geneviève (France 56) rolled her eyes as she recalled telling students she came from the Western part of France (rather than the expected Paris), to which they responded, 'oh yes, near the German border'. But she impressed the boys when she said her French school cafeteria served beer. Per (Norway 61) recalled most Americans 'thought it snowed all year round' in Norway. Erik (Denmark 55) had difficulty persuading Americans Copenhagen had no polar bears. Jona (Iceland 60) got 'lots of igloo questions'. Naila (Pakistan 58) was insulted when asked if she lived in a house. 'For goodness sake, we had servants!', she exploded, still exercised at the memory sixty years later. Questions like 'do you have running water' also made Carola (Chile 69) 'a bit mad'. Maarten (Netherlands 61) was most confused to be asked questions about the 'boy who stuck his finger in the dike' to stop it leaking.[19] He had never heard of Hans Brinker, who was the fictional creation of a nineteenth-century American children's author, Mary Mapes Dodge. It remains far more part of US culture than Dutch, although there are now several statues of the boy in the Netherlands, exploiting the American tourist market.

113

Some questions were so bizarre, one wonders whether the American students were always being serious, but perhaps they reflected the images and films the students had been exposed to. They were certainly direct. Hameeda (Pakistan 52) was taken aback when asked 'do you live up in trees?'. Sandra (Singapore 67) was asked the same question fifteen years later. Sudhir (India 66) was asked what was so holy about Indian cows. Manoli (Greece 62) was surprised by the enquiry, 'Do you wear pants in Greece?'. Emmanuel (Ghana 68) said the students were 'surprised' that there were no 'animals walking in the street' and that 'I never saw a lion or an elephant until my family here in America took me to the zoo'. Almost every Thai delegate was asked 'do you ride elephants to school?', as were several Indian delegates. For Michael (Jordan 58) it was camels, and Monika and Paul (Austria, 65 & 72) were puzzled to be asked about kangaroos in their country. Meanwhile, Beryl, who *was* Australian (rather than Austrian), admitted she felt guilty telling one group that she *did* ride kangaroos to school in 1968. She was in good company. Her predecessor Ken (Australia 67) convinced one group that 'we all had to wear magnets on our feet 'because we were on the other side of the earth'. It was not only the Australians pulling legs. Gustavo (Argentina 70), when asked 'how do you get dressed', immediately replied, 'We don't at all'.[20]

Sometimes Americans were in on the joke. *The American Girl* magazine described how 'gentle-mannered' Myrtle (India 52) 'could not resist poking a little fun at her American friends'. She told the magazine:

> 'I explained of course that we have taxicab elephants in India—two rupees for the first mile and one rupee for every additional quarter mile. The parking space is ten by eight, and we tie them to the parking meters by their tails. We dye them all colors to match our saris.'

The magazine ensured readers understood this was a joke: 'Even Myrtle had to burst into laughter at her tall story'. Two decades later, Sherille (Ceylon 71) told a fifth-grade class that 'instead of the school bus, I get on the school elephant and, you know, we stop at the grass station, not at the gas station; the elephant trumpets like this instead of blowing a horn'.[21]

American adults sometimes knew little more than their offspring. Susana (Ecuador 47) tried to be polite when Rotarians asked, 'Do

Ecuadorians wear feathers?' and 'Do you have clocks?'. Two decades later, Greg (NZ 69) was amused to be told, 'You speak such good English'. When asked by some wealthy New Jersey matrons, 'Do you have running water, toilets, cars?', Beryl (Australia 68) was mad, launching into dramatic stories of droving sheep, killing rabbits, and driving a farm truck at the age of 16. She added vivid descriptions of her family's 'dunny'—a drop toilet—'the details of which were a horror show for these women'. Later, when she told one class there was a bridge between Australia and New Zealand, the teacher asked, without a trace of irony, 'how long is it?'[22]

Alongside the ridiculous questions were the difficult ones, demanding much from delegates, who were just teenagers. British, Scandinavian, and Finnish delegates defended themselves against charges of socialism (because they had welfare states), while Yugoslavs constantly explained their communism was different from Russia's. Rina (SA 58) felt like the 'skunk of the world' as the question of apartheid came up again and again. Gerhard (Germany 54) was in a school with predominantly Jewish teachers, who, he felt, 'held me to be ... responsible' for the Holocaust, 'even though I was only 16'. He remembered Nurit (Israel 54) coming to his defense.[23] This was despite Nurit's instructions from her government 'not to get acquainted with the German delegate'. (Her passport was stamped with the words 'allowed to visit all countries except Germany'.) Vietnamese delegates had an increasingly tough time as American body bags began coming home from Saigon in the 1960s. As we shall see in a later chapter, delegates were expected to be conversant with international politics and able to explain their country's position on numerous issues.

Memorable?

High schools were sold the idea of hosting a delegate as a 'walking textbook' to educate American students. But what was the real impact of the delegates on the school communities? Some schools, particularly those beyond New York City, took full advantage of the foreign students and integrated them into their program. Of the thirteen schools involved in more than ten years of the program, eight were in New Jersey. In 1961, Anna Howell from Verona High School in New Jersey felt that the school's engagement with delegates 'had changed our student body from a provincial one into one with very definite feelings of the need for helping on a world scale'. She noted that several host students had 'gone on into international study and work'. Frank Updike of Burlington Senior High School said explicitly that the Forum 'had an influence far beyond the limited numbers of students who have been directly involved as delegates or hosts'. Long-time Forum associate Paul Esser at Louis E Dieruff High was equally enthusiastic in 1963: the school community felt 'fortunate to have a positive role' in the program. 'World problems classes are stimulated by the mere physical presence of the delegates', who brought 'a very personal viewpoint to problems that involve their countries'. Esser conceded that 'this contribution defies objective evaluation', but noted that 'even after the delegates have gone, their names and opinions are remembered'.[24]

Many American high school students themselves also enjoyed being shown 'that there are two sides to most of the world's crises...we are only told one'. They appreciated the personal contact, it was 'much easier to take an interest in someone than in an abstract, impersonal, far-away place or thing'. Comments like these were circulated by Helen Waller to *Tribune* bosses. Others comments about delegates, she buried. 'All they ever talked about is how much better their schools are than ours and we did not get a chance to answer them back', complained one student. Another dismissed them: 'They're a bunch of dirty reds'. These were a minority of comments, but show that, unsurprisingly, not everyone was impressed.[25]

A few schools beyond the eastern states were inspired. In 1950, after receiving the delegates' autobiographies and Forum material, seventy-nine East High School students in Denver, Colorado, made up a series of scrapbooks about themselves, their school, and their state to send to delegates. In other schools, however, delegates' presence barely registered, leaving no lasting impression beyond a yearbook photograph; sometimes not even that.[26] They appeared for a few weeks and were gone. Arguably AFS students, embedded in the school community for a year, were slightly more memorable. Even then, though, their impact beyond the hosts, personal friends, and year group, was minimal.

Schools also sent students to watch the grand finale, and Forum delegates participated in local forum discussions. The idea of a 'forum' of school students, discussing current issues, was not new, and different schools ran their own versions, often in conjunction with neighboring schools. The *Herald Tribune* Forum took this idea to another level, with international students, and it made those students available. In 1952, fourteen delegates attended the High School General Organizations and Press Association Convention at Abraham Lincoln High School. Here, they mingled with 850 representatives of New York area high schools, posed for a group photograph, and provided copy for the *Tribune* reporter: Riaz (Pakistan 52) 'beat all comers in games of tic-tat-toe—he called it Knocks and Crosses', another delegate read letters from home, while Hussein (Egypt 52) 'proudly exhibited his picture opposite that of Hedy Lemarr in a native newspaper', but 'would not divulge what the captions said'. A few days later all twenty-three delegates were rolled out again at the UNESCO conference for 1000 students at Julia Richman High School. In 1953 the visit of the *Herald Tribune* Forum delegates to Richmond sparked the inaugural Miller and Rhoads Virginia High School Forum, held at John Marshall High School in Richmond. Sponsored by the eponymous local department store, this initiative lasted into the 1960s. From 1958, however, local AFS exchange students rather than the Forum delegates provided the foreign component.[27]

In 1955 the Forum experimented with combined workshops with Sarah Lawrence College students, as we have seen. More successful were the weekly seminars during each host period, introduced in 1960. Three seminars took place concurrently, involving neighboring host schools. Ten delegates and ten American students discussed the chosen topic, under the watchful eye of an Alumni helper and school faculty advisors. This continued in 1961 with discussion workshops, along similar lines. Holy Trinity School in Hicksville not only hosted Ayzer (Turkey 61) and Denis (France 61), but also held three discussion panels on three consecutive Tuesdays. In all three panels delegates and American students discussed differences in their countries' education systems.[28]

These panels heralded an increased focus on the participation of American students, as the Forum's domestic educational aims became more important. The involvement of American students through the Greater Metropolitan Forum expanded from 1964 with the introduction of the Summer Forum, which invited hosts and semi-finalists from the Metropolitan Forum to participate in a 'reverse forum' to Europe. These initiatives meant that the Forum program became more than just the appearance of a foreign student in the school halls for three weeks each year. The Forum's engagement with American students became increasingly critical to its success in the 1960s, for all its 'future leaders of the world' ideal.

Host schools played a critical role in delegates' Forum experiences, but even more central to the aim of demonstrating American society and democracy were host families. And while delegates were publicly critical on television debates and newspaper interviews of American schools and education, they generally praised the families with whom they stayed. Between themselves however, it could be a different story.

Left: 1. 'The Icelandic delegate with an ice-cream sundae': Jona (1960) posed for the obligatory publicity shot on arrival. [PA]

Right: 2. Per (1961) described his free flights in his journal. [PA]

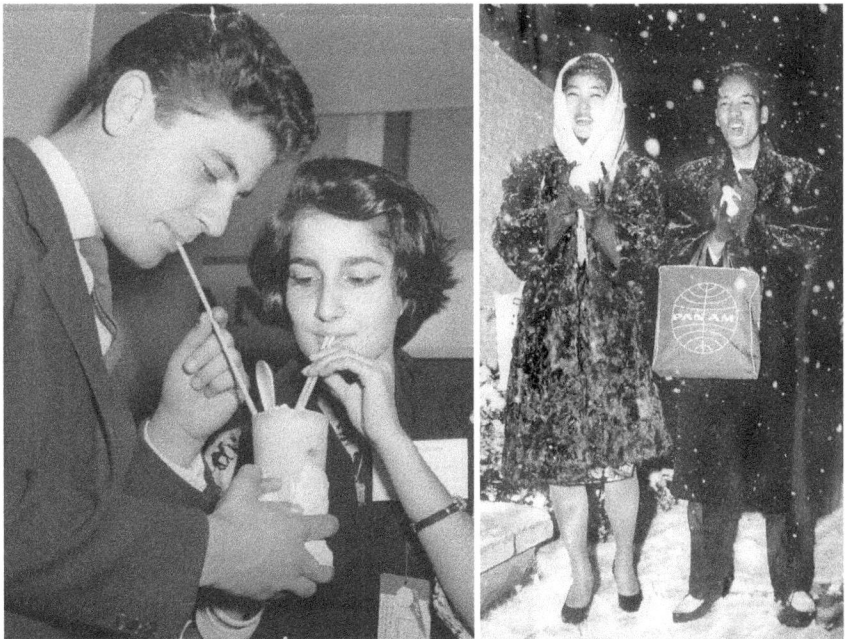

Left: 3. Ibrahim and Naila sharing a milkshake 'the way American teenagers do'.
PA *World Airways Teacher* April 1958, T-4

Right: 4. Snow and the cold made an impression: Dorothy & Thac (1962). PA

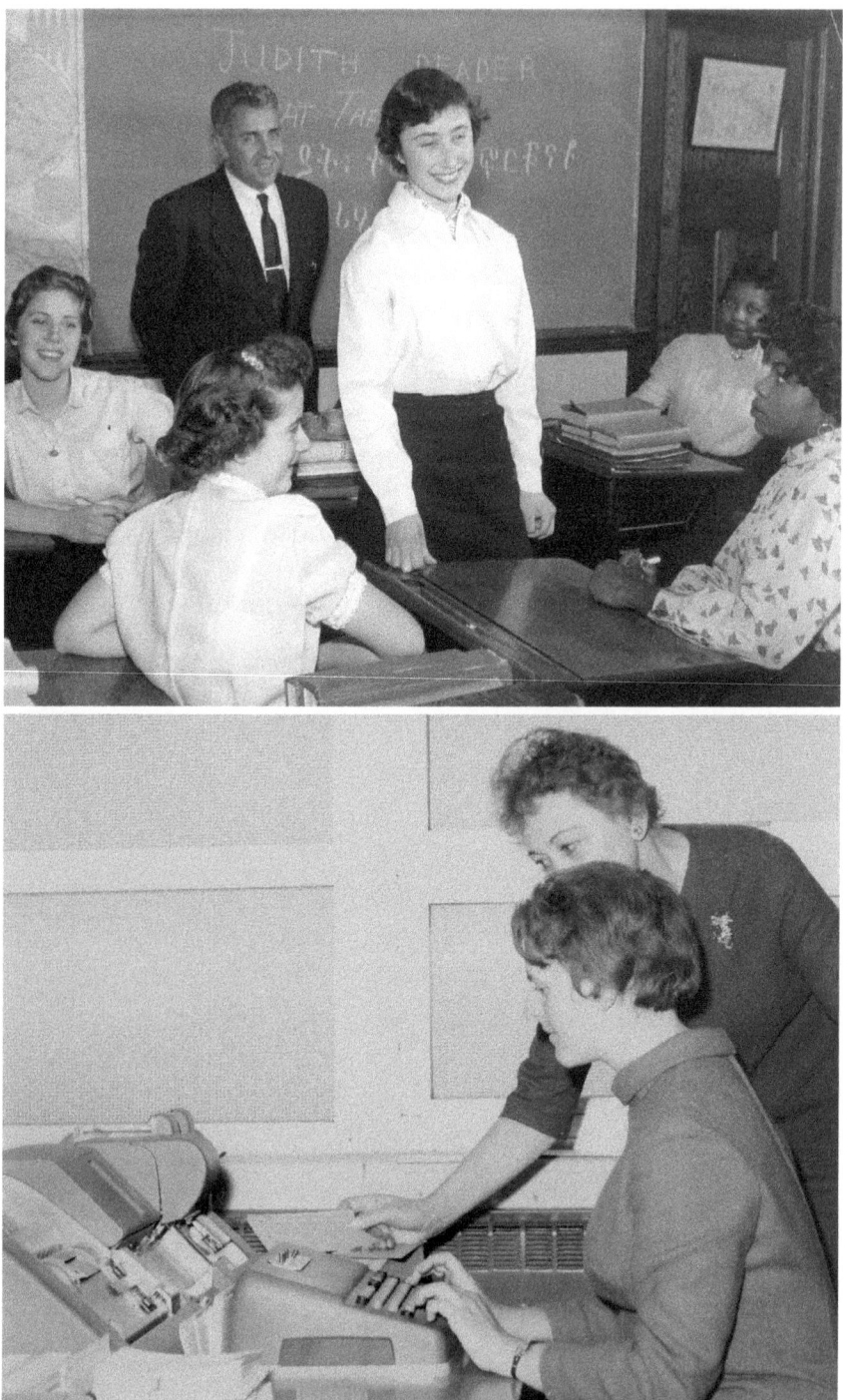

Top: 7. Introducing Hee Joon & Inge (1956) to US modernity – a dishwasher.
Guy Smiley

Right: 8. 'Do you ride elephants to school?' Tissa (1959) as 'walking textbook'.
Daily Mail Hagerstown or USIS

Opposite top: 5. Photographers followed delegates around. Judith (1956) Montclair High.
Opposite bottom: 6. Learning to type was a novelty for Monika (1965).

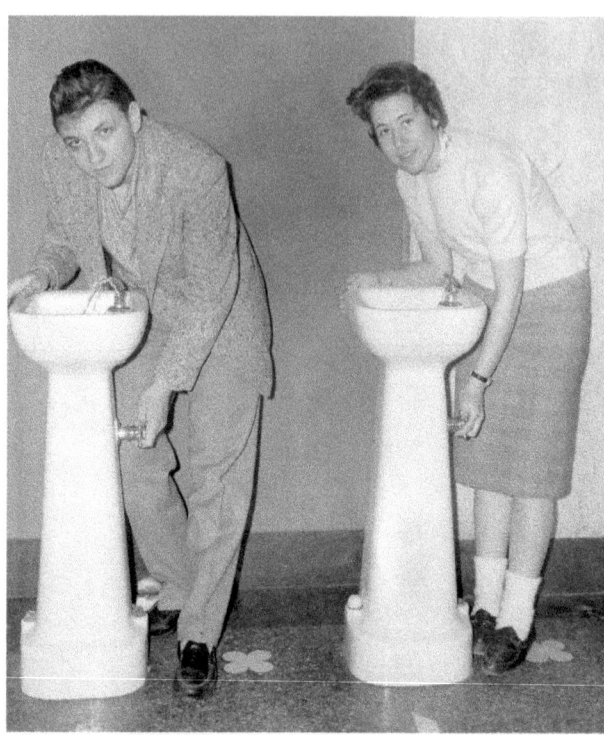

Left: 9. One of the more ridiculous poses: Gus & Ida (1959) at water bubblers.

Bottom: 10. Another school, another polite tea party. Charles Gorton High principal Thomas Kelly, teacher Denise Azzara, Johan & Judith (1956), hosts Joyce Meyer, Ed Kelly.

Top: 11. New experiences: teenagers & cars: Ibrahim & Vivian pretending to drive (1958).

Bottom: 12. New experiences Eddie (1965) shoveling snow for real. Teo

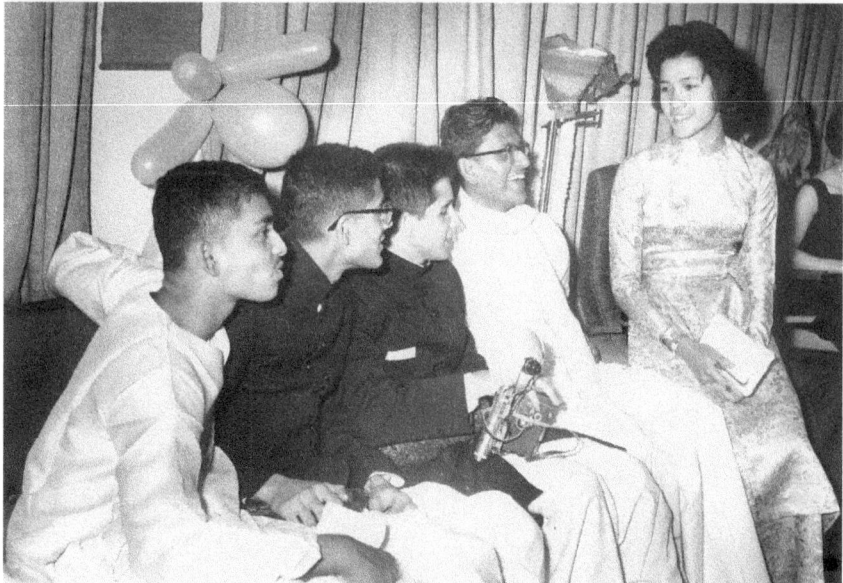

Top: 13. National costumes as visual symbols: Ismail, Sahadya, Liselotte, Chung Wha, Ahmed, Jose (1960).

Bottom: 14. Girls outnumbered: Ylang holds court with [L–R] Ashish, Raza, Jehangir & Gemunu (1961).

Opposite top: 15. Waldorf Astoria Finale (1956): delegates hear Marion B Folsom on 'Freedom: The Essence of American Education'. NYHT

Opposite bottom: 16. Michael (1967) 'played a Māori', like other white NZ boys at the finales. Vincent Parmentier

Top: 17. Santi (1952), like others, became adept at addressing school assemblies.
Bottom: 18. Performing in national costume began at Orientation: Saroj (1958).

Chapter 8

Part of the Family

'Long, Detailed, and Interesting Dinnertime Conversations'

In 1959 five male delegates descended upon Martin Van Buren High School in New York. Their hosts included Burt Brody, who was keen to volunteer. His mother, he remembered sixty years later, was 'delighted' and his father said, 'it would be okay with him if it was okay with her', recognizing where responsibility for hosting really lay. Burt corresponded with his allocated delegate, Ejvind (Denmark 59), before he arrived. The two boys hit it off, which was just as well, because Ejvind's next host family had chicken pox and he had an extended stay with the Brody family. They lived in a picture-perfect, two-story, square, brick home, complete with white painted timber shutters, on a corner block in Bellerose, a middle-class neighborhood in Queens. The boys enjoyed 'long, detailed, and interesting dinnertime conversations'. Both were interested in music, notably Tchaikovsky's Fifth. 'Together we bought the record and listened to it almost every day lying on the carpet downstairs with the record player at the upper end of the staircase', recalled Ejvind. They were 'eager students, avid to learn anything', and both loved maths and physics. Burt remembered Ejvind had 'an especially ambitious and outgoing personality'. One of the 'best parts' of the visit was that it was a 'great incentive for us to get away from where we lived', he said. On weekends, Burt's mother took the boys to 'the great monuments and sights' in New York City. 'We went everywhere—to museums, sights, shows—with my mother, places I would not have gone myself'. The boys' letters dropped off after the Forum as life got busy after 1959, until one day Burt saw Ejvind's name in an academic journal. In great excitement he wrote a postcard to the university: 'Ejvind, is this really you?'. It was. They had both become physicists. Their renewed friendship has lasted into old age.[1]

Ejvind's host family experience with the Brodys went exactly as intended. Across the twenty-five years of the Forum, over 3000 families hosted the 807 delegates, who each had three to five homestays during their three-month visit. Not all of them were as successful as Ejvind's, but they were at the heart of the Forum program. The choice of families, and the seriousness with which they took their responsibilities were crucial in the delegates' experiences of America?

'Nice' Families

In the Cold War era the 'family' became a political tool for the West, forged in opposition to the perception that on the other side of the 'Iron Curtain' loyalty to the state undermined 'the family'. As historian Sara Fieldston noted, '"American-style" child rearing was an emblem of the democratic way of life'. Staying with American families, therefore, just like their attendance at American high schools, was part of exposing delegates to American democracy at work and giving families an international outlook. Outsourcing responsibility to volunteer families was also an economically sensible solution to the problem of boarding and entertaining (and parenting) thirty teenagers for three months. Less cynically, it reflected the view of Experiment in International Living founder Donald Watt, as experienced by Helen Hiett Waller herself in Europe: 'you learn to live together by living together'.[2]

In interviews decades later, 'nice' was the most common adjective used by delegates to describe host families. 'Lovely' and 'welcoming' were others. This was not unexpected; a family that was not 'nice' or 'welcoming' would hardly volunteer to host an exchange student. For volunteers they were, recruited by the host schools, and allocated to delegates by Forum staff. Lucie (Norway 57) was 'amazed by the hospitality' of American families, willing to 'take a foreign and completely unknown person in their house, and to treat him or her like one of their own children'. Jona (Iceland 60) later worked for AFS and came to appreciate the difficulties in finding suitable host families, although it was easier for the Forum—three weeks was less of a commitment than a whole year. Most families were new to Forum hosting, although not all. Howard Liebman's parents Martin and Frances did two tours of duty—Howard hosted Jomo (Malaysia 70) and his sister Leslie was the host of Nina (Brazil 72). Some families also participated in other programs. Emmanuel (Ghana 68)'s first host family, the Mokovers, had previously hosted a French exchange student for a year.³

Forum organizers set out requirements: host families should be 'understanding, and able to cope with the special—and unpredictable—problems that inevitable [sic] arise'. Nevertheless, they depended on school faculty advisors to select suitable families. We do not know how many volunteering families were vetoed. One delegate felt uncomfortable in her family (who were 'very kind' but 'had no idea what a bath was') and the school faculty advisor was apologetic. The family had been so keen and supportive in past years and were desperate to host a delegate. The school 'understood that they were not ideal but they had to have a turn, and I was the "unlucky" one', she recalled.⁴

Families were given some guidance. A briefing session in December 1951 included talks from two Indian Embassy officials and a UN director. In December 1953, Tan Joon Kheng (Singapore 53), then at Princeton, addressed potential 1954 host parents. Forum staff provided instructions and by 1965 there was an official handbook on 'Receiving Your Forum Guest' with clear guidelines. Families signed an agreement to provide two- or three-weeks' hospitality. Host students should be at least 17 and the same sex as the delegate (there were rare exceptions). Delegates should have their own room if possible. If sharing, the delegate would have their own bed and 'ample space' for belongings. (At least once this instruction was apparently not followed. One boy delegate, just discovering his own sexuality, found it difficult when told to share a bed with his host brother.) Parents should treat the delegate as 'a member of the family, sharing household chores and subject to the same regulations' as their own children and provide 'proper chaperonage' at all times. The delegates should attend school regularly with the host student. Parents and school advisors dealt with any change from planned activities, such as visits to delegates' friends or relatives in New York.⁵

Learning from experience, Helen Waller advised 1953 hosts to ensure delegates, 'unused to the American tempo of life', got enough 'down time'. She warned against any activity that 'puts the delegate on display as a curiosity', instead suggesting delegates participate 'on an equal basis with

American students in their regular activities'. Down time was hard to come by. As we have seen, delegates had punishing schedules of school lessons, talks, parties, and extracurricular activities. Annemarie (Austria 63) described the strain of being 'on' all the time as the center of attention, coping in a foreign language. She remembered one host family's kindness, giving her an after school 'snack' of ice cream and canned peaches (for which she had confessed a fascination), and then packing her off for a much-appreciated afternoon siesta.[6] Annemarie was one of the few interviewees who admitted to exhaustion. Perhaps after sixty years, others only recalled the excitement, carried along by adrenalin.

Families were asked to give delegates money for 'carfares, lunches, and other incidentals', because it was 'not possible to ask delegates to bring a set amount of spending money'. Some delegates 'have far more money to spend than we would advise', confided Helen Waller, while others 'have no money at all', or were 'limited by their country's currency restrictions'. Later instructions to delegates recommended they bring a minimum of $50 in travelers checks for incidentals. Host parents gave Ronny (Indonesia 68) the same allowance as his host brother, '1 silver dollar' a day. School food was free, but he bought hot dogs for fifteen cents, burgers for a quarter, and French fries. He also used the allowance to go to movies and parties. Host parent in 1963, Shirley Streicker, felt the *Herald Tribune* could do more. 'Good will could certainly be engendered' among host families if the Forum provided them with 'student passes and student discounts for sightseeing and education events'. She pointed out that 'Everybody is going to want to go to the Empire State Building!'[7] Instead, the *Tribune* relied on families reaching into their own pockets, which was a drop in the ocean for some, but a stretch for others.

In 1948 instructions for chaperonage were gendered. 'The visiting girl student when away from school or the home to which she is assigned will always be accompanied by a local girl student'. It was more equitable later, with 'single dates' banned for both male and female delegates. Nevertheless, even in the 1960s, boys and girls were viewed differently. When host families in 1965 were warned 'not to stereotype' their delegates, the range of possible teenagers was described as 'a somewhat shy sixteen-year-old girl from somewhere women have not achieved the equality they have in the United States' to 'an extremely sophisticated young man from one of the major capital cities of the world'.[8] (As ever in the Forum, the United States and modernity were set as the ideal.)

A Variety of American Families

Forum organizers matched delegates with host students based on delegates' biographies and the small amount of information on the host families' application forms. Thus, as the *Tribune* reported in 1953, while 'unfortunately' the Forum could not place Niels, 'Denmark's amateur golf champion', in 'the homes of other amateur golf champions', they found 'golf conscious households'. (Funnily enough, sixty years later, Niels (Denmark 53) did not remember any being interested in golf!) Host family application forms requested the name, age, and sex of the host student, the ages of other children, home address, and school details. Interestingly, given many delegates later remembered religion as a significant factor in their placements, this was not a question. In the 1950s, two lines were provided for the host's hobbies and interests, but by 1961 host students had more space to write an 'autobiography' of sorts. Memorably in that year, 17-year-old Roger Kurland (Host 61) concluded his page of scrawling handwriting introducing his family—his father on the school board, his mother active in the PTA—describing his 12-year-old sibling, with typical fraternal condescension. 'Penny is, what I would think is, an average sister'.[9]

There were some attempts to give delegates a variety of experiences, but the most important thing was to provide (hopefully) amenable homes. Families were generally white and middle-class, the host students usually smart, friendly, outgoing, and engaged with the idea of the Forum. One American, who was not a host, said the two host students at his school 'were 'the type' to be hosts; 'they were sort of like "activists"', whereas I was more of a "goody-two-shoes" type of guy'.[10] This suggests that hosts often came from the 'popular' group, meaning delegates would have gained automatic entrée into the high school world of cheerleaders and football teams on the one hand, and class captains and debate team members on the other.

There were a few African Americans hosts, as well as families with a range of incomes, and of different religions. Notably, in his 1970 article about the Forum, Robert Huffman acknowledged that 'American families in poor areas—especially black families—seldom have the facilities or financial resources to host a foreign visitor even for 3 weeks'. Nevertheless, he suggested that the Forum had often been 'successful at bringing black and white together—sometimes through homestays, and other times through seminars or other activities not involving any expense'. This 'bridging the gap' was 'one of the greatest satisfactions of the Forum' he claimed.[11]

Inga (Denmark 54) was excited to stay with an African American family in New York, and was shocked when her host family in Richmond, Virginia, (who were of Danish heritage) expressed horror at the idea of her staying with a non-white family. Delegates themselves found it unremarkable—just another Forum experience. Judith (UK 56) enjoyed staying in Montclair, New Jersey with Dorothy Savoy, whose mother was active in civil rights.[12]

Ritva (Finland 58) stayed with Kate Clark, daughter of Drs Mamie and Kenneth Clark, psychologists famous for the 'doll test'. She got a front row seat, witnessing America's civil rights in action, when Minnijean Brown came to live with the Clark family while she was there. Minnijean was one of the Little Rock Nine, the first group of African American students to desegregate Central High School under the protection of troops. All nine promised they would not retaliate to any harassment. Minnijean was expelled because she responded to a white student bully by calling her 'white trash'. Her arrival in New York made headlines. The *Tribune* reported Minnijean had a scholarship at the prestigious New Lincoln School and would stay with the Clarks. 'The Clarks are Negroes', the paper reassured(?) its readers. Lincoln College was integrated but had only a small number of African American students, from influential middle-class families. Records show that Minnijean did not have a scholarship. The Clarks paid her tuition expenses. Unfortunately, we do not know what Finnish Ritva made of this first-hand encounter. Surely it had an impact, but, oddly, other delegates that year do not remember discussing it.[13]

Other delegates noted the various religious beliefs of their families, including Jewish, Catholic, Protestant, and Quaker. It could be an enriching experience to immerse oneself in different traditions. Mark (NZ

68) found accompanying Jewish families to Synagogue 'a wonderful breath of fresh air' after Christchurch High Church Anglicanism. An Australian delegate did not particularly warm to one wealthy kosher Jewish family who 'must've thought I came from the bush', she said, 'they asked me "Do you have toilets?"' She preferred her Long Island family, who were what she called (indicating her own preconceptions) 'stereotypically Jewish': 'a short little rotund watchmaker' and his family, who were 'very warm and inclusive'. The family she stayed with on a field trip in Virginia was more familiar, being Christian but 'very southern'.[14]

Families also varied considerably in wealth. Lucky delegates found themselves in Long Island mansions with not only their own bedrooms but their own bathrooms, being chauffeured to private schools by day and taken to Broadway shows or classical concerts by night. 'This family is rich', one English delegate wrote to her mother, 'They have everything, including 4 TVs! ... There are two cars, one a sports ... they have a deep freeze the size of our fridge. There is also a washing machine and spin drier, a dishwasher, a charcoal grill, a broiler, a spit, and a normal oven. The kitchen is any woman's dream'. But, she went on, 'my bedroom takes the biscuit', with 'a soft double bed, carpeted floor, TV, and lots of clothes space, plus a desk and lots of lights, soft or bright'. But the pièce de résistance? Her host sister, 'Louise and I share a bathroom and guess what? we have a sunken bath!'. Three weeks later, she moved to her second family, telling her mother, 'I seem to have hit the jack pot. They get richer and richer!' But it was different—'instead of 4 TVs [there were only 3] all the chairs in my room are covered with silk'. The house was 'crammed with real antiques', and she wrote, 'I believe I have a genuine Renoir on my bedroom wall!'. She contrasted this with another delegate's host family, whose home, she wrote, with the sort of disdain only a teenager can manage, 'reeks of interior decorators and is so pseudo it stinks'. She was particularly scornful of the way the 'typically nouveau-riche' mother and daughter copied the 'traditional' dress of their delegate.[15]

Tissa (Ceylon 59) remembered houses 'full of gadgetry: dishwashers, clothes washers and dryers and TV which was new to me ... One family even had a shirt ironing and folding machine'. Geneviève (France 56) never forgot the generosity of her second host family, who gave her the present of a three-minute international telephone call to her family. At the time, just having a telephone in France was unusual. Even after she married in 1963, Geneviève waited four years to get a phone. She was taken aback when her host sister Edith 'got her own telephone because she talked so much on the family phone'. The sheer size of homes was also noted. Liv (Norway 70) was impressed with the long dining table of her wealthy host family in Boston; 'the daughter and I sat one at each end, and there were servants!' Sandra (Singapore 67) stayed with architect Jacque Guiton and his wife Peggy, whose home, an 1899 townhouse, was three blocks from Central Park on New York's upper east side. She remembers each child had not just a separate bedroom but a separate *floor* of the five-story house, connected by elevators. She found refuge at the top of the house, where to her delight as a musician, she found a beautiful Steinway piano. This home was listed for sale in 2021 at $22,000,000. Ken (Australia 67) was overwhelmed by his first stay with a 'wealthy Jewish manufacturer with a black live-in maid'. Ken attended a private Jewish school. They 'were very nice and looked after me well', he said but it was 'all absolutely beyond me'. Teresa (NZ 72)'s host sister thought nothing of 'buying it and popping it on Daddy's account'. Carola (Chile 69) went skiing with one family and her host mother also took her to 'a beauty salon in Fifth avenue'. It 'must have been very expensive' Carola said.[16]

Hiranthi (Ceylon 67) found a different sort of wealth staying with Ruth and Bernard Belikove and their daughter Roseanne in Metuchen, New Jersey. Not only were they 'extremely' rich, with 'a whole collection of Indian art' and a Chagall painting (*'really* a Chagall') in their house, but host mother 'Ruth made it her mission to totally educate me on everything about American culture and everything... she took me to the Met, ... to the Guggenheim, to the New York Stock Exchange, to the Philharmonic Orchestra with ... a very famous conductor'. There were also 'all the little trips around, tea at the Waldorf, the Gotham, everywhere' and she 'had a lot of artist friends and writer friends and people like that'. Manoli (Greece 62) told one host mother that he 'wasn't a big fan' of opera. She had a box at the Metropolitan. 'Nonsense', she replied, 'It's a shame if you don't see it', and there began Manoli's lifelong appreciation. Arnold (Colombia 69) went with host father Robert Cowin to visit the printing presses of *Time Life*, where Robert was a senior executive. 'It was in Chicago!', Arnold remembered, 'we had to get up very early in the morning and fly to Chicago for the day'.[17]

Not all host families were as conspicuously wealthy, or even comfortable. Sometimes delegates experienced a less privileged America. Tan Wee Kiat (Singapore 61) went from 'visiting country clubs' with one family to the other extreme in Hagerstown, where the group stayed for a week while filming TV programs. That family was poor, he said, 'being helped by the state', and as part of that they 'had to take in foreign students'. What he remembered, however, was that they 'went out of their way to share and were generous'. The Ripatranzone family (Host 54), who lived in the Bronx, told Forum organizers they volunteered to be hosts precisely because 'we felt we are representative of millions of the lower income group and that our visiting friends would learn from us how contentedly we live, work and strive for more'. Lack of wealth did not mean a visit was any less rewarding. Dieter (Germany 62) found his most fascinating host family was a working-class Jewish family in the Bronx. Just seventeen years after WW2, this pairing was a potential disaster, but they discovered a shared interest in music.[18]

When Agung Came to Stay

Sometimes the boot was on the other foot when a middle class American family found themselves hosting foreign royalty. Roger Lang, budding violinist at the High School of Music and Art (in the days before it was immortalized in the film *Fame*), hosted Agung (Indonesia 67). Roger and his Hungarian immigrant parents lived in an eleven-room apartment (including a maid's room) in the now famous Apthorp Building. That was 'before it was fashionable', Roger hastened to add in our interview in 2022, by which time the Apthorp had become synonymous with extreme opulence and eyewatering real estate values. In his day the rent was $500/month and neighbors were 'arty/academic' types, including choreographer George Balanchine and writer Joseph Heller. Roger's parents both worked fulltime in their footwear importing business, Padrilles, and they had a housekeeper.

Roger read up about Indonesia so that he 'knew the difference between

Java and Borneo', but did not realize Agung was 'the Prince of Bali', until another Indonesian told him years later. Agung was circumspect in his Forum autobiography and did not reveal his royal status to his hosts. He stayed in the only spare bedroom in the apartment—the maid's room. If he felt he was slumming it, he did not say so to Roger.

Agung's visit had a profound impact on Roger. As the son of immigrants, Roger was already internationally minded, but orientated towards Europe. Agung's visit 'really broadened my mind' and 'expanded my horizons' to the rest of the world, he said. And there were unexpected bonuses. While a student later in Florence, Italy, working on a market stall selling leather bags to earn money, Roger was startled when a long limousine pulled up. Out jumped Agung's father, who 'scooped up a whole bunch of wallets and purses' as presents, before disappearing back into his car. It 'made a good impression on my boss', Roger smiled at the memory.

'I think Agung thought we were better off than we actually were', said Roger, for whom Agung operated in a whole other world of wealth, power, and international connections; 'a level of society that we get glimpses of once in a while from your nose pressed against the glass'.[19] This slightly surreal feeling of encountering different worlds was one shared more often by the delegates in American families than their hosts.

New Experiences & Cross-Cultural Collisions

Although 'nice' was the most common word used to describe host families, host stays varied enormously. The best were those like that of Agung and Roger or of Ejvind and Burt, when the students found shared interests and were introduced to new experiences. Some found themselves shoveling snow or ice skating, or having 'interesting discussions about politics, history, plays, and music', or found a host mother 'who let me drive her car when I wasn't supposed to'. One family gave Emmanuel (Ghana 68), who arrived totally unprepared for the cold, hand-me-down winter clothes, and also bought him an instant camera to record his experiences. Emma (Burma 62) exclaimed with delight over fifty years later that her second family 'gave me KFC with coconut flakes!'. Peter (Norway 69) had fond memories of long drives in station wagons, pancake syrup, and a particularly nice American girl. Tissa (Ceylon 59) never forgot accompanying one host father, a forensic pathologist, to see an autopsy. 'I had no idea what I was getting into. The sight of an obese cadaver being butchered with a mini stream of blood gushing out was more than I could stomach. Within minutes I rushed out of the autopsy room.' But he also had 'a warm memory of a young girl', aged about ten, in one host family. She had moved out of her bedroom for him. She bade him 'farewell with a warm hug and truthful words that perhaps only a child is capable of: "I am so happy that you stayed with us. I am so happy I am getting my room back."'[20]

In 1969 Forum staff member, Connie Walker, reminded delegates in her March newsletter that she was always available: 'Several of you have had questions or problems during this host period … you can call us if anything is bothering you'. Sometimes it was misunderstandings or cross-cultural collisions, stories that delegates could share with each other when they met as a group, bonding over the idiosyncrasies of American life and minor disasters. One delegate was startled when her second host family's solution to a broken dishwasher was to eat off paper plates rather than washing up by hand. Sherille (Ceylon 71) remembered a host mother 'put on her eyelids every morning and that really shocked me'. (Presumably these were false eyelashes?) Rodel (Philippines 69) was introduced to American football the night he arrived. His family 'were in a hurry to get home' from the airport because 'they wanted to watch a football game'. Rodel politely sat down with them, but 'they never explained how American football works and I didn't have any idea … I never even heard of American football'. He found it 'the most boring game ever' and 'fell asleep'. In the morning his family explained that he had slept through 'the greatest football game ever', the 1969 Superbowl.[21]

Jomo (Malaysia 70) was slightly bemused when one of his host families took him to the bathroom to show him how the toilet worked. Even when families did their homework there could be mistakes. On the one hand, Hameeda (Pakistan 52) had 'no issues with food' because her families had been told that Muslims 'don't eat pig'. But when hosts of Khin Aye (Burma 59) asked the Burmese Embassy what to feed her, 'pork, pork, pork', was the reply. Catherine (France 59) remembered Khin Aye found it 'a bit difficult' because she was unexpectedly Jewish 'and of course she didn't eat any pork'. Ibrahim (Lebanon 58) said his host families knew where Lebanon was, but he was surprised when one host 'mum took me in and said, "oh this is a refrigerator, this is the way we open it"'. The same mother went out of her way to prepare Lebanese food for him. 'This is great', said Ibrahim, 'I've never seen Mujadara done like this before'. She replied 'oh no, it's hummus'. In his embarrassment, Ibrahim knocked his wine glass all over the hand decorated tablecloth that he had just presented as a gift to the family. Myrtle (India 52) wrote home with great amusement: 'Mrs Rosenbaum even cooks rice for me but has no conception of what "curry" really is—she has some "curry" powder in a tin, and just sprinkles it over any preparation and calls that "curry"'. But when Myrtle cooked them 'rasam, prawns with masalai, as we do ... they liked it but thought it too hot'. On the other side, one host remembered being disconcerted by her very wealthy, 'extrovert', and 'assertive' delegate, who was 'a bit too inquisitive about my social life' and 'cozied up to me and made herself too familiar for a visitor'. She also 'showered' the family with expensive gifts, including 'two unexpected cashmere sweaters she'd bought locally at the fanciest ... shop'. This was completely overwhelming for the host, whose mother 'outfitted her girls' with an annual visit to 'Kleins Basement in NYC—cheap', and then 'shopped at thrift stores, cut out fancy labels and sewed them into our blouses' to fool the girls at school who always wanted to check 'where's it from'. This host felt her delegate's gifts, presumably expected behavior for the delegate herself, were 'way too much for a short visit'.[22]

Ahmed (Sudan 60)'s experience was cited at the final Forum as an example of cross-cultural misunderstanding and has joined the annals of Forum folklore. His host family, the Brysons, lived in a small Brooklyn apartment, and had a 'huge dog', which they washed in the bathtub. Soon the Brysons reported to Helen Waller that Ahmed was rarely about, 'every other day going to Manhattan'. When she tackled him about it, Ahmed explained that he was a Muslim and had been taught that dogs were unclean. 'I just couldn't take a shower in the same tub'. Instead, he 'took the subway to Manhattan', a 45-minute trip, to a 'friend at the United Nations', and he 'would go to his home and take a shower.'[23]

Some delegates found themselves renamed. Probal (India 53) temporarily became 'Pete'. The 1958 Ceylonese delegate left home as Mahipala and returned as 'Mike', a name which he adopted for the rest of his life. Shirley and Beverly Kaiser christened Iranian delegate Mahbonoo (Iran 52) 'Bonnie' during her stay, although 'Bonnie' taught them some Persian phrases including for 'good bye', which they tried out when they waved her off on the train to Toronto at the end of her visit with them.[24]

Occasionally problems were more serious. Delegates did not connect with their hosts, or the timing was off. In March 1967, the Rosenthal family were delighted to unexpectedly welcome their son Meyer home to New Jersey from his tour of duty in Vietnam, but it meant that Sandra (Singapore 67) 'felt I was in the way ... I remember staying in my room for most of the time'. One of (Chile 69) Carola's host sisters was distracted by a new boyfriend. Personality mismatches were possible. Saroj (Thailand 58) remembered one host brother as 'aloof'. Avri (Israel 68) described one host as a 'preppy character', who was 'not my type'. Another delegate told me the heartrending story of overhearing her host mother telling her daughter, 'Come on dear, it's only two weeks'. And the delegate had thought the visit had been going well! Sometimes the challenge of living the Forum's idea of bringing opposing views together was just too much. American Jewish host mother, Shirley Streicker, wrote a three-page letter to John Hay Whitney himself, entirely unimpressed with Muhammad (Jordan 63). She suggested the Forum might give host families pamphlets similar to those issued by the State Department to students going abroad, for 'dealing with answers to anti-American criticism', to prepare them for dealing with 'indoctrinated propagandists'. This was the only example I found of an Arab delegate and Jewish host family having difficulties, although perhaps that was the real reason behind Helen Waller's dissatisfaction with Arab delegates in 1952. Disappointed letters from host families are hard to find, with the Forum publicizing success stories, but this one demonstrated that it was not always smooth sailing. Occasionally delegates were moved to other families, but generally three weeks was short enough to for both parties to cope.[25]

All Change

There was some wisdom in sending a delegate to each family for only a short time, although it could be disconcerting. As Rodel (Philippines 69) said, 'just as you got to know one family and school off you go to the next one'. The changeover was often done at the *Tribune* offices in a sort of speed-dating scenario. Delegates would be deposited in one room by one set of host families, and after (sometimes) tearful farewells they were herded into the next room, where a whole new set of 'Moms and Pops' were waiting. These new families did not want to see downcast, teary teenagers, but bright and bubbly young people, eager for new adventure. It must have been emotionally exhausting. Suzanne (UK 62) was apprehensive about her families—worried that she might be unhappy with them. And initially she was 'overwhelmed' by the way families swamped her with 'affection and warmth', so that she complained to her mother that she 'never had a moment of solitude'. She soon grew to value the busyness and kindness, which offset the 'momentary feeling of aching lonliness [sic], like drowning in a sea of compliments'. And, she concluded, 'one of the most wonderful and moving things ... is to find that I can be taken into a family as if I belonged to it, and to feel as if I am leaving home when my three-week stay is over'. Geneviève (France 56) bonded so closely with her first family that while her second family was 'very nice', she 'spent all the three weeks trying to get together' with her first host sister: 'we would meet at the station'. Similarly, another European delegate found one family 'so "American"', making 'no effort to understand my culture', that in desperation she called her first host mother, begging to come back. This was not possible but that mother thoughtfully wrote letters so the delegate felt less bereft.[26]

In some years delegates had to choose which host family to return to for the final few days. This was a lovely chance to reconnect with favorite host families for some, cementing fledgling friendships. Others found it awkward, particularly as they had to decide during the final official host period. One delegate told me that she really wanted to go back to her first family but she stayed with the last family: 'It was too hard to pack up again'. Others feared offending the family they were already living with.[27]

Delegates were meant to take host family visits seriously. 'Living with the host family is an invaluable experience which should not be interrupted or shortened.'[28] Visits to or from their own family or friends in the US were not encouraged: family could visit only once during the three months and *never* during the first week of a host family stay. This was explicitly articulated in the 1962 'Instructions to Delegates', suggesting there had been issues in the past. Certainly, several delegates went interstate to family and friends. That so many already had relatives in the US was indicative of their privileged status and perhaps undercut one of the purposes of the Forum, which was to introduce teenagers to the wonders of America.

The host family program was not just an economical way to house delegates for three months. It was central to Forum aims. Immersing delegates in (hopefully a variety of) American families introduced them to American culture and values in a way that merely discussing it could not. The importance of 'living in' a country rather than just 'traveling through' was well established in internationalist circles, reflected in the large numbers of youth programs that adopted the 'homestay' strategy.

What's In It For Me?

Host family visits served another important purpose for the Forum, with delegates providing in-house learning experiences for Americans. While some were already familiar with other cultures, being first- or second-generation immigrants themselves, for others it was entirely new. Vivian (Argentina 58) wrote in a 1959 newsletter of an American boy she had met during her visit. She 'found his outlook very limited and rather uninteresting' but in his later correspondence with her, she said, he 'has acquired a much keener and objective attitude'. She thought 'the reason' was that 'he has been host to a Forum delegate'. She concluded, reaffirming the Forum philosophy, that 'words are nothing as compared to living under the same roof and sharing day-to-day experience with other people'.[29]

Host families and students had varied motives for volunteering. For some students it was a long-held dream, as they witnessed the visits of delegates to their school as freshmen, sophomores and juniors. Marion Lloyd of Great Neck High School (Host 56) had 'always wanted to be a

Forum hostess and was always eliminated because of age'. Her selection in December 1955 to host Yoriko (Japan 56) was 'a climax to three years of wishing'. She, like many others, enjoyed 'the experience of looking at the world literally through two pairs of eyes'. For some families it may have been a status symbol in the local community. Although families were warned not to use delegates as 'curiosity' pieces, at least one delegate felt like a 'prize exhibit', a status symbol to be shown off by his host brother.[30] Hosting a student also offered 'ordinary' Americans the chance to play a part either in idealistic internationalism or in the Cold War struggle for hearts and minds, demonstrating the 'American family' to the rest of the world.

A successful delegate visit provided tangible and intangible benefits. Marjorie Seiger, who hosted Daphna (Israel 57) in Mamaroneck, New York, found it a 'most enriching experience'. Kate Clark (Host 58) spoke at the final Forum in front of an audience of thousands. She was the ideal poster girl, a middle-class African American high achiever, who 'enjoys reading French and Russian literature'. She waxed lyrical about the delights of hosting a foreign student: 'We held many lengthy and wordy discussions ranging from discrimination and communism to serious music and rock 'n' roll', she told the Forum audience. Craig Scott, (Host 58) also spoke. Learning he was to host the Thai boy, he had read up on Thailand and 'had classified him, before he even arrived'. After meeting Saroj, however, 'how these ideas changed!'. It 'made us wake up to the fact that we cannot just pigeonhole people because of their customs, physical features, nationality, or religion'. The pair found things in common but also learned from each other. Craig told of a snowball fight. Not only had Saroj never seen snow, but he was horrified when Craig pitched the perfect snowball that knocked his mother's hat off. He explained to Craig that such 'disrespect' to a parent in Thailand would not be tolerated. Joan Kalina of Dwight Morrow High hosted Gladys (Lebanon 56) and got 'a survey of the East she never would have gotten otherwise'. Hameeda (Pakistan 52) thought it was the cumulative effect of small things that had an impact on her host families: 'the very fact that they had to change their eating habits, for instance', or the informal chats about things in Pakistan 'that they were not familiar with', and that 'would start a discussion about various things, and how girls behave, and how they dress and why, and so on'. She remembered having fun playing games with a 'younger brother, a very cocky young boy', in one house, and felt he would have learned a lot, 'having a different kind of person in the house ... Physically and otherwise I looked different'. Sudhir (India 66) noticed how his 'host parents were constantly reprimanding their offspring on how much neater I dressed (I always wore a tie) and how polite I was and more considerate than their offspring'. Recalling this years later he commented drily, 'I wondered why the Americans considered themselves superior'.[31]

Alice (Singapore 52) probably found her stay in Northport challenging. As her host mother Lillian Darling told Forum organizers, 'the older inhabitants of this village still look askance at so called "newcomers" even though such newcomers might be 100 per cent American and Republican in the bargain'. She continued frankly, 'You can imagine how they feel then about people of other races and nationalities'. She remarked on the enormous 'impact of Alice's visit' in a community: 'just a brief exposure to our guest's charm and sweetness, and you could almost see their prejudices crumbling'. One particularly vehement man who had 'no time for the Chinese' had been won over, Mrs Darling noting that, of course 'up to her visit, he had never talked to an intelligent Chinese in his life'. Northport was just over an hour from Manhattan but was still 'provincial'. Hugh Fullerton Jr, host father from Englewood, New Jersey, admitted that 'frankly I was rather doubtful of the success of the project before we met Pia' (Indonesia 52), but by the end of her stay he had 'a much better understanding of, and a more friendly feeling toward Asian people than I had before', and thought two weeks too short a time to keep Pia, 'our daughter from Indonesia'. Forum organizers seized upon such testimonies from successful host families as proof of the Forum's transformative effect to publicize the program as well as justify its existence to sponsors.[32]

Hosting a delegate was also simply good fun. Host students were included in some Forum excursions. They watched television recording sessions or accompanied their delegates to the UN. Roger Lang (Host 67) said that hosting Agung (Indonesia 67) was 'a great ticket to go and do what we wanted'. Roger told his teachers, 'I just *have* to show Agung Coney Island', and the following day they cut class and spent the day on the 'essential' mission of experiencing American fun park culture. Agung

135

was curious about New York, enjoying the 'wilder side'. They were 'two teenagers having fun', remembered Roger, visiting Time Square and Greenwich Village and hanging out in his friends' apartments. Agung had a slightly 'sardonic' view of America and Americans, jokingly calling Roger a 'greasy hamburger'. Roger Wollstadt (Host 54) remembered being served very spicy food at a Pakistani restaurant in New York when he visited with his delegate Rasul (Pakistan 54). Roger returned on another occasion and 'the food was less spicy'. He concluded 'they had "real" Pakistani food for nationals and the like, and a blander version for ordinary Americans'. Roger Kurland (yet another host brother called Roger) could not really say what his parents 'got out of' participating in 1961. He certainly enjoyed the experience of hosting Bruce (Canada), who 'had a wonderful sense of humor'. Roger's girlfriend had a friend who was 'sweet' on Bruce and they had a number of 'double dates'. He said that '"adults" really made more of the experience than we did ... we just had new friends'. He mused, 'in retrospect, I think that is the primary goal of exchange programs'. We 'realized there weren't any differences that matter', he said.[33]

For others, however, the experience could be profound. In 1966 Robert Koslow, a student at the predominantly Jewish private school, Woodmere Academy, hosted Mamud (Sierra Leone). Robert told me fifty years later, that Mamud was first black man he had ever spent time with. It 'blew my misconceptions out of the water'. He was 'brilliant and helped me through my senior year'. The Koslows treated Mamud like a son, although significantly, he was not allowed to date any friends' (white) daughters. On the other hand, Robert found himself dating black girls for the first time. Mamud and Robert remained in contact for a few years. Much later, Robert remembered that Mamud asked his parents for money, creating an 'awkward' situation, even though, as Robert acknowledged, the US was rich compared to Sierra Leone.[34]

Ongoing Relationships

Friendships between delegates and host families could last beyond the Forum, some for a few months or years, others for decades. Often delegates met members of their host families outside the US, repaying the hospitality they had received or meeting up in different cities. American host families could be keen travelers, especially to Europe. Marcella (Italy 58) met two host mothers over the summer of 1958: one at her home Torino and the other in Venice. Willy (Belgium 55) welcomed his Bronxville host, Charles Skinner. 'He is now a soldier in Germany and we are still very good friends', Willy told alumni in the newsletter. Annemarie's (Austria 63) reunion with host sister Lennie Liebermann in Europe in summer 1963 was bittersweet. Having lost her own father when she was four, Annemarie had basked in the affection of book publisher, Abe 'Daddy' Lieberman, who 'treated me like his daughter, brought home flowers in the middle of winter… took us out to dinner, made me feel special like never before in my life'. Tragically Abe Lieberman died of a heart attack that August, while Lennie was visiting Annemarie.[35]

Others found host families useful when they returned to the US to study. Mrs McKelvey (host mother) picked up Chit (India 56) from the airport in September 1956 and she and his host brother Don drove him up to Harvard. When Young-Koo (Korea 57) returned to the US to study in Detroit in 1959, he initially stayed with another delegate's host, Keith Cooper, who had recently moved to Detroit. The Gimpel family were a 'safety net' for Ronny (Indonesia 68) when he returned to the US. Irjaleena (Finland 57) and her new husband, who was studying at Columbia Law School, lived in her former host family's basement flat in Brooklyn for a few weeks in 1965 until they found long term accommodation.[36]

Like Ejvind and Burt, some delegates remained close for the rest of their lives. Valerie Hakam was still corresponding with her 'dear sister' Irjaleena in 2020. Saroj (Thailand 58) corresponded with his first host brother and sister for fifty years. Bill Reznikoff, one of Nii (Ghana 59)'s host brothers, was best man at his wedding in 1965. Ed (Philippines 63) and host brother Jay Shupe kept in touch through mail and email for fifty-four years before meeting again to talk 'about the good old days', in 2017, when Ed was writer in residence in Ledig House in Ghent, NY. Roger and Agung (Indonesia 67) kept in touch for years, even traveling around Mexico together in their twenties. At the end of that trip, Agung invited Roger to return to Jakarta, 'you could run my biscuit factory', he said. This was something of a 'Sliding Doors' moment for Roger. His decision to instead return to the US meant their friendship became more of an acquaintance, as their lives took different paths. [37]

Often it was host parents rather than the son or daughter who remained in touch. Avri (Israel, 68) told me he corresponded with the children and 'especially the mother' of his second host family, 'until her death in 1997'. Röggi (Iceland 62) wrote to his host mother Doris Fish until her death. He reflected, 'It's hard to say if I would have become something entirely different without ever meeting the Fishes. I probably wouldn't, but there is no doubt their influence was strong, lasting and for the better.' Hiranthi (Ceylon 67)'s daughters called her host mother, Ruth Belikove, 'Ruth archie' (Grandmother Ruth). She was 'really part of the family', visiting their home several times and even coming to one daughter's wedding in Australia. Michael (UK 72) bonded with the Ball family of Massepequa Long Island. There was the Cadillac in which the glamorous Marie Ball collected him from the airport, and a dinner 'in his honor' that night. Then Marie sat him down and said 'Now Michael, do you enjoy art galleries and museums, theatre, ballet, opera, fine restaurants? You do? Well, Michael I think we are going to get on fine!' It was, as Michael said fifty years later, the beginning of a friendship that lasted until Marie's death in 2016. When he was filming his 'Great American Rail Journeys' television series in the 2000s, he flew to North Carolina to visit Marie on his few days off.[38]

Host families rather than Forum administrators sometimes created the circumstances that changed a delegate's life. Whether through careful planning or just plain luck, some delegates found families with shared interests and connections. Jan (Czechoslovakia 67) stayed with SUNY academic Dr Jack Heller, who took him to a lecture by Professor Herbert Levine on 'Is Russia Going Capitalist'. Herbert and Jan maintained contact and in 1970 Herbert facilitated a student visa and scholarship for Jan to study Economics at Haverford College, Pennsylvania. Critical for Emmanuel (Ghana 68) were the Fieldsteels. Nina and Ira (helpfully an immigration judge) arranged for Emmanuel to return to finish high school, staying with them and another host family, before going on to university. Emmanuel truly became part of the family. 'We just fell in love with him', 93-year-old Nina told me in 2016. Her obituary a year later mentioned her 'son Emmanuel'; his children were her 'cherished grandchildren'. Emmanuel himself told me 'it's been wonderful—if you hear me say, "My mother", it's my American mother.'[39]

Part of the Family

Two or three weeks was not long to be part of a family, although it could seem interminable if delegates and hosts did not get on. Families were screened by their schools and matched with delegates relatively successfully. Schools and families continued to volunteer, with the occasional family double-dipping, indicating they saw benefits. The whole scheme relied on families providing support, entertainment, and care for the delegates. It was quite a responsibility, although delegates were told to 'fit in!', and few delegates misbehaved too badly. Both parties were keen to make it work and each gained from the experience. A few hosts and delegates had lifelong friendships that reached down into generations, others were introduced to a different culture or way of living. Ideally hosts opened their minds to the world beyond the US and delegates discovered the varieties of American family life.

The family home-stays were at the core of the Forum program, interspersed with field trips, allowing delegates to reconnect with each other, and exchange humorous anecdotes of 'the American family'. Throughout all, the delegates were also performing for the media and in person as 'adolescent ambassadors'.

Chapter 9

Adolescent Ambassadors

The Forum juggernaut was propelled by publicity as much as idealistic internationalism. The delegates were show ponies to be paraded around, not only in school assemblies, but also in newspapers, on radio, in Voice of America presentations, on television, and in the Forum's finale, in which they played out highlights of their debates and performed national dances and songs in front of a 3000-strong student audience. The Forum maximized opportunities for delegates' exposure, experimenting with different ideas over the years. This led to suggestions of exploitation by some observers, as we have seen, particularly in the hectic 1950s under Helen Waller's leadership.

Ideally, these foreign delegates looked the part. 'Be sure to bring your national costume if you have one', directed Helen Waller in her welcoming letter to 1957 delegates. Visually distinctive, national costumes provided a talking point, and identified delegates as exotic—useful for the publicity machine. For some delegates Helen's request was not a problem. Their 'national costume' was their daily clothing. Hameeda (Pakistan 52) wore her baggy trousers and sometimes a sari to school as she always did, although she got a shock being such a 'curiosity with everybody'. Nalini (India 59) said Americans were astounded that her sari contained six yards of material, although most teenagers were more intrigued by the bindi on her forehead. Some were fascinated, although others 'thought it was a blood clot or something!'. Malaival (Thailand 50), who was an accomplished Thai dancer, also had ready access to a 'national costume', which she wore when she danced, but Saroj (Thailand 58) had to buy one especially. Irini (Greece 63) borrowed one from a private collection. 'It was extremely heavy and took up most of my suitcase ... so difficult for me to carry around', she complained, and after all that, she was 'only asked to wear it once!' The American Friends Service Committee, co-opted to run the first Orientation in 1954, commented that national costumes were meaningless for most delegates—only half the delegates wore them and many of those had 'borrowed them from some elderly person who had stored them in a trunk'. They also noted that the *Tribune* photographer pushed some delegates aside in favor of those whose costumes would photograph well. Norbert (Germany 57) cleverly ignored the instruction about costumes, caught out when staff member Mary Warner visited him during her travels later that summer. 'He appeared in a wonderful pair of lederhosen which he'd neglected to bring to America' she reported. Tan Wee Kiat (Singapore 61) invented a costume; 'silk chinos with a sarong over the top'. One wonders what his fellow Singaporeans thought when they saw pictures of him. New Zealand boy delegates donned a piupiu (Māori flax skirt) to perform a Māori haka at the final Forum. Alan (NZ 63) showed initiative by approaching the Minister of Māori Affairs, who arranged for the leader of a local Māori concert party to teach him a haka. He was given a 'wooden carved mere and wore a grass skirt', and, as he put it, he 'played a Māori'. Such cultural appropriation by the Pākehā (white) boys was uncontroversial at the time.[1]

Performing for Media

We have already seen that free flights did not come cheap. Pan Am and TWA had their fair share of posed publicity photographs and inspiring stories about their delightful young international passengers. Local newspapers and Scholastic magazines also made the most of delegates, especially if they provided good photo opportunities (ideally in costume) or expressed controversial views. Josephine (Australia 53) found being 'a celebrity' was 'tiring' and was 'embarrassed' by journalists' questions such as 'do you have many dates at home?' and 'do Australian mothers approve of petting?'. She would prefer, she said firmly, to be asked about Australia's economy. *Herald Tribune* reporters and photographers were attached to the Forum group. Suzanne (UK 62) appreciated the talents of (later Pulitzer prize-winning) photographer Nat Wein; 'I come out looking quite good for a change', she told her mother. Her romance with 22-year-old *Tribune* journalist Philip D Carter, however, was frowned upon by the Forum director. (It was noticeable that Suzanne was the most often quoted delegate that year in *Tribune* coverage!) Philip left the paper shortly afterwards.²

Television was the modern medium of communication. In Hagerstown, Maryland, delegates were filmed in a variety of educational programs, including introducing American students to their countries and participating in mathematics classes. Telegenic delegates in the 1950s also made sporadic appearances on more popular television programs, such as 'Youth Wants to Know' and (less glamorously) in the New York City Board of Education's local series, 'The Living Blackboard', providing exotic appeal. The most popular and rewarding was 'Name That Tune'. John (UK 59) remembered participating with 'blonde bombshell' Kaarina (Finland 59), who, with 'only one second left to double our money', correctly identified a tune after a single chord: 'Autumn Leaves!'. They won $500 each, John said proudly, although they were neither the first nor the biggest Forum winners on 'Name That Tune'. In 1957 Norma (Brazil) and Mesfin (Ethiopia) appeared with American, Duane Carlson of Naperville, Illinois. After Mesfin fell at the first question, Norma suggested they team up. This was strategic, she told me later: there was 'all this noise about segregation versus integration' and it would have been 'too bad' to have only one delegate go through, and 'Mesfin was black'. After all, 'the Forum got very nice free publicity due to our presence', she said. The three contestants worked together winning an impressive $10,000. Norma spent her share on a long-wished-for piano and had lessons, adding an extra string to her bow as she forged a career as a film and stage actress. It was an extraordinary amount of money for any teenager, but particularly for Mesfin. His share was probably more than his father earned in a year as a teacher in Ethiopia.³

'They Really Used Us': American Propaganda Puppets

Jorge (Uruguay 53) had a scrapbook full of cuttings collected by his proud parents while he was in the US. The US embassy had 'at least one picture for every couple of weeks' he said, 'they really used us—the State Department'. The Forum worked hand-in-hand with the State Department, which benefited from delegates' participation in American government soft power propaganda programs aimed at international audiences. Every one of the delegates' published opinions about the US, whether positive or negative, underscored the fundamental tenet of American democracy—free speech. In addition, the presence of these grateful visitors learning about the modern new world emphasized the US's status as a global leader. Rafts of photographs and media releases were disseminated worldwide, 'intended to provide the 34 nations with a glimpse of American life seen through the eyes of one of their countrymen'.[4]

Delegates also made Voice of America (VOA) recordings in their own languages about their experiences. In 1952, in a particularly tasteless publicity stunt, Santi and Salika (Thailand 52) were dispatched to the hit Broadway production of *The King and I*. Their post-performance backstage chat with stars Yul Brynner and Gertrude Lawrence was broadcast by VOA to Thailand, where criticizing the monarch is a crime. Santi found the show excruciating. 'Seeing Yul Brynner portray one of the most revered kings of the current dynasty as a shirtless, head-shaven tyrant was difficult to take'. Other programs were less offensive. In 1953 an Indonesian studying media in New York interviewed 16-year-old Inajat (Indonesia 53), with testimony from her host mother Lela Pringle of Woodmere, Long Island about 'how her family and her community have enjoyed getting to know the Indonesian delegate'. Kikuko (Japan 53) was photographed, resplendent in her kimono, as she 'chatted' with VOA Commentator Shiro Nose at a supper party hosted by Pan Am at the 'Cloud Club', sixty-six floors above 42nd Street in New York's Chrysler Building. VOA extended its coverage in later years, making 'tape recordings of classroom discussions and interviews', along with the 'entire program in the Waldorf Astoria'.[5]

The students' adventures in the US also provided appealing film footage. In 1949, 16-millimeter US State Department propaganda films of the Forum group attracted audiences of more than 150,000,000 people at 375,000 performances across the globe. Encouraged by this success, the US government showcased the 1950 Forum group in what publicists called their American 'odyssey' in a 40-minute film. 460 prints were sent to 83 countries with commentary in 32 languages, in a variety of formats, 'many of them for 16-millimeter projection from portable jeep units in rural areas, others on 35-millimeter reels for theater projection'. The film showed not only the nonstop busyness of the Forum program, but its suitability for State Department publicity. Watching it, one can tick off the checklist of propaganda points: American modernity in the high rise buildings of Dallas; freedom of the press, as the delegates were filmed mounting the steps of the *Dallas Morning News* newspaper building while the camera scrolled upwards to the motto of the paper, emphasizing 'fairness and integrity' and the publishing of 'both sides of every important question'; benefits of American education in the images of classrooms, varied curricula, and canteens of a 'typical' American high school; superiority of American family and home life, with images of delegates eating dinner, playing records, and watching television en famille, while Nadira (Pakistan 50) enthused about her mischievous 'little brother' in her relaxed host family; technological advances through the Tennessee Valley Authority, and cultural life with the Library of Congress. Jack Connolly, chief of the newsreel and special events branch responsible for the film, told the *Herald Tribune* he expected it to be 'one of the most popular' films the State Department 'has ever sent abroad'.[6] The 1950 film was considered sufficient for the next few years, although surviving footage of the Forum's 1952 finale at the Hotel Astor suggests shorter films were made, possibly annually.

In 1958, Helen Waller announced with great excitement that 'the Motion Picture Division of the Department of State has started to make a full-length film of 1959 Forum activities'. Camera crews filmed delegates arriving at Kober House, the 'alumni crews in action', group discussions, the New Year's Eve Party, and meetings with first host families. The resulting 30-minute feature film was adapted into 12 languages, with more than 250 copies distributed in 41 countries in May 1959. USIS staff were impressed, one officer promising that 'this dramatic presentation of mutual understanding and friendship will be shown repeatedly throughout Jordan at every reasonable opportunity'. Bisidthisak (Thailand 59) did the Thai narration, which, he told fellow alumni, was 'a hard and careful job because in Thai you have to say a bit longer than in English' and he wanted to keep everything in the film 'alive in the Thai language'. He thought the film 'excellent indeed', although Jayantha (Ceylon 57) was less convinced. While it was a 'refreshing experience and evoked mildewed memories', he thought 'it was too much the story of one individual... the star, the Iranian girl... who had the luck to go to the States, her travels, and her feelings'. There was an 'inordinately long preamble' and 'the talk bordered on the mawkish at times'. Unfortunately, no copies appear to have survived. Whatever its limitations, the film was released for public educational use in the US in 1961 and was still circulating internationally in 1962, possibly later.[7] State Department enthusiasm waned in the 1960s with no further films recorded, indicative of declining interest in the Forum more generally.

The Finale

The three-month exchange trip culminated in a finale, a format based on the *Herald Tribune* Forum on Current Problems, in which eminent public figures and experts participated in panels and gave speeches in front of a large audience. The high school version was initially similar, including several adult experts, younger university-aged speakers, American high school student speech-competition winners, and a couple of panels featuring delegates, in a two-day extravaganza. It was played out in front of an audience of students from participating host schools, with host parents and representatives from high schools from further afield.

In 1949, the delegates gave prepared speeches and participated in panels, interspersed with adult experts, including Economic Cooperation Administration head Paul G Hoffman on European recovery, Maria Talkes of MIT, Richard L Meier of the Federation of American Scientists, the British Ambassador, congressmen, and senators. More delegates performed songs and dances, providing exotic cultural interludes, and the winners of the American high school speaking competition (both girls) spoke about 'The World We Want'. Young Rosemary Bristow's speech struck a chord with New York Senator Eugene Keogh, and it was printed in the Appendix to the Congressional Record, demonstrating that the Forum had some impact in the corridors of power, albeit when it was echoing the US government's own line. 'Ours is a weary world', she began, issuing a call to arms for Americans to assist in its rehabilitation through educating the youth of the world, honoring the ideals of the '300,000

American boys, whose dreams lie buried with them.'[8]

In 1950, with delegates solely from Arab and Asian countries, speakers included Carlos Romulo, President of the United Nations General Assembly, and American political scientist, Dr Ralph J Bunche. Later that year he would become the first African American to win the Nobel Peace Prize, for his mediation between Israel and the Arab states. Gordon Clapp, chairman of the Tennessee Valley Authority, which was touted as a world-leading exemplar for developing countries, spoke of the UN Economic Survey Mission to the Middle East. Democratic Senator Brien McMahon, known primarily as the architect of the Atomic Energy Act of 1946, opened his remarks with a resounding acclamation of democracy and free speech, his words resonant of contemporary US government propaganda. This kind of Forum, he said 'could happen only in a Democracy'; the audience had 'convened of its own free will', there was 'no official propagandist in charge of "spontaneous demonstrations"'. The audience 'may applaud or not as you choose', and 'No one has told me what to say'. His speech focused on the atomic arms race: it was six months since the Soviet Union had tested their first atomic bomb, seriously undermining American complacency. McMahon advocated instead for atomic energy's peaceful uses. The atomic arms race, and militarization of atomic development, was 'an insidious threat to freedom'. Quite how the threat could be avoided, he did not specify.[9]

Comedian Fred Allen provided light relief, and a reprieve from the otherwise male line-up came from Lilian Smith, author of *Strange Fruit*, a controversial bestselling novel about an interracial relationship that dealt with racism and lynching. Smith's speech was a powerful critique of racial segregation from a white woman who had grown up in the American South, linking Western racism to the spread of communism. In China, she said, she saw signs at the British park, 'Dogs and Chinese not Allowed'. 'Today,' she warned, 'communism, with its false promises, is finding it easier to win the Chinese because of that sign and the symbol it became in the minds of people who are not white, throughout the world'.[10]

Stephen Schwebel, who had spoken as a 17-year-old in that first high school Forum in 1946, returned in 1952 as one of the adult speakers: his topic, the International Student Movement for the United Nations.

Although only 23, he was a Harvard and Cambridge graduate, a published author, and UNESCO consultant. He told me he had 'pleasant' memories of the Forum, which had 'undemanding and congenial' organizers and an atmosphere 'celebratory of youthful international fellowship'. He recalled discussion as 'free flowing, though only a minority said anything'.[11] Adult speakers continued to dominate the High School Forum finale until 1955, when the balance began to tip increasingly in favor of delegates, perhaps in response to feedback.

'Quite Interested'

This grande finale was a key component in the Forum's aim of educating American high school students in world citizenship. Helen Waller took pride in circulating to her superiors the letters of praise and thanks received from those who attended. Reading these conjures up a vast hall chock full of teenagers gazing with rapt attention at the earnest delegates pontificating with the full confidence and arrogance of youth about issues of the day, and adults delving into the fascinating mysteries of topics such as, in 1949, 'The Social Responsibility of Science', 'Sun-heated Houses', and 'Books as Ambassadors'. The reality was a little different. Not all audience members were diligently attentive. In 1949, Flemington High School history teacher, Helen Scharrer, wrote a six-page epistle on her elegantly monogrammed, personal stationery to Whitelaw Reid. While praising the Forum program, she offered suggestions for improvement. She requested Forum staff to 'please ask Metropolitan schools to whom you give tickets to select their students more carefully'. She and her group were 'intensely annoyed by several groups of students who talked and laughed continually, despite requests to be quiet, and who paid no attention to the proceedings'. Instead they were 'reading magazines, doing cross-word puzzles, etc... just taking up space and ... not interested.' In contrast, her students from New Jersey were 'quite interested' and 'took copious notes' to report back to their classmates. They 'felt their responsibility as delegates', she said, emphasizing that she had not required notetaking, it was their own initiative. She enclosed a local newspaper article, in which her student Doris reported it was 'one of the most interesting days that she had ever spent'. Mrs Scharrer emphasized that Doris was also a 'high school senior with <u>less</u> than average ability', whom she had 'persuaded' to attend 'the entire meeting', partly 'as reward for excellent work (for her ability)', but also because she 'couldn't leave her at loose-ends for half a day in New York'. Her other students were 'better able to come and go unsupervised'. Poor Doris. One can only feel for the teenager whose 'reward' was to remain under the eagle eye of Mrs Scharrer, listening to worthy speeches, while her fellows were off enjoying New York for at least some of the time.

Helen Scharrer might have railed against inattentive 'metropolitan' students, but in the next breath (or on the next page) she criticized the dryness of 'some of the more technical speeches'. 'If you know much about youngsters, Mr Reid', she wrote, 'you must know that they soon get bored with being talked at'. The American system of education meant that 'they aren't conditioned to just listening to older people just talk'.[12]

One of Mrs Scharrer's more appealing proposed improvements was to include 'more informal talks' with the students, rather than speeches from worthy adults, and certainly future finales saw greater participation by delegates. Surviving 1952 film footage shows a stream of delegates, many resplendent in national costume, delivering set pieces at the microphone, and by 1955 the finale focused on delegates, with only two adult speakers. With the demise of the Forum for Current Problems in 1956, the *Tribune* attempted to frame the High School Forum as its replacement: 'High schools hold the key position in American education', so the High School Forum was 'trying to bring to the students some authoritative thinking on urgent national and international problems'. In reality, by 1958, adult experts and their 'authoritative thinking' had entirely disappeared. Probably a cost-cutting measure, it was also indicative of the very issue that Helen Scharrer had highlighted. American high school students wanted to hear from people their own age. So, in 1958, bookended by Forum director Helen Waller, who opened proceedings, and Ogden R Reid, *Tribune* editor, who closed the event, there were three panel discussions, two sessions, cryptically titled 'Our International Language' and 'Travel Tips for American Tourists', and two American high school student speakers, Kate Clark and Craig Scott. They spoke enthusiastically about their experience as student hosts, perhaps a recruitment exercise.

The finale was now all about the Forum exchange itself. 'Our International Language' was code for music. Minoo (Iran), Yukiko (Japan), Sangmie (Korea), Naila (Pakistan), and Saroj (Thailand) performed dances in their eye-catching national costumes. Saroj also played the Thai flute, while Vivian (Argentina) played the guitar and sang 'native songs'. Onder (Turkey), on the mandolin, accompanied a group of delegates singing his composition, 'The Forum Blues'. The 'travel tips' being offered for American tourists, however, were not reported.[13]

The finale continued to focus on youth. The 1964 program epitomized the pared down format. There were welcomes from John Hay Whitney, editor-in-chief of the *Herald Tribune*, and Robert Huffman, Forum director. The sole adult guest speaker underscored the close relationship between the Forum and the US government. Carl T Rowan, former diplomat and USIA director, spoke about 'the US and Revolution'. Then it was over to the delegates themselves. Eight gave profiles of 'Youth Around the World', then another eight formed a panel on 'A Generation Apart'. An interlude of 'national songs and dances', contributed by several delegates, was followed by nine more profiles of 'Changing Nations', and a last panel, 'Youth Looks Ahead', involving ten delegates. All thirty-seven delegates were represented. American history teacher (and former John Hay Whitney Fellow), Raymond A Antil, who drove 'four hours to the city' with Cobleskill Central School's International Relations Club representatives, expressed his 'sincerest thanks for allowing us all to share in the better international understanding which stems from your efforts'. Lynn Bitz from Tom's River High School, probably designated to write her school's thank you note, echoed Mrs Scharrer's comments fifteen years earlier: 'we learned a lot' but wanted 'more time to talk with' delegates.[14]

Three years later in 1967, there was no adult guest speaker at all. Frank Conniff, editor of the *World Journal Tribune*, and Robert Huffman were the only adults on the podium. In 1969, Ambassador James Roosevelt addressed the forum crowd in his role as president of the Forum's latest sponsor, the IOS Foundation. Reverend Martin Luther King Sr spoke in memory of his son in 1970, in what was the last of the big Forum gatherings at the Lincoln Center.[15] The finale had been the centerpiece of the Forum program—the climax for which the delegates prepared during their school debates, television programs and other performances. It harked back to the days of the prestigious Forum for Current Problems, from which the High School Forum had emerged. By 1971, however, financial constraints brought it to an end, a telling sign of the decline of the Forum program as whole.

'A Little Bit like Trained Seals'

Forum promotors often used the phrase 'walking textbooks' to describe the delegates; others could be less polite. The American Friends' Service Committee, who ran the initial orientation program for the Forum in 1954, were not the only critics of Helen's manipulation of the teenagers. Harold Taylor, president of Sarah Lawrence College and a supporter of the Forum, acknowledged in 1958 that 'there is still too much tendency to exploit the students for television and Forum purposes so that by the time they appear at the Waldorf they are a little bit like trained seals'. The Forum group were living breathing exemplars of international camaraderie. Helen Waller delighted in creating public visual demonstrations of their friendship, especially between Arab and Israeli delegates, or between white South Africans and the black Africans. She was adept at creating provocative encounters and discussions. She probably encouraged Wentworth 'Kiddy' (Ghana 54) to befriend Afrikaans Eline (SA 54), who commented decades later that before this she had never 'met a black man on equal footing', and certainly not one who was her intellectual superior. Jona (Iceland 60) felt stage-managed in the 1960 finale. Nani (Ghana 60) was asked if he had faced any racial problems in the US and Jona, as a 'very blonde girl, very Icelandic' was 'schooled by Mrs Waller to jump out of the ranks and shout "Well, how could anybody have a problem with Nani?"'[16]

Trained seals or not, the delegates were always on display. Whether on television or radio, delivering VOA propaganda pieces, starring in government documentaries, or performing live on stage, discussing, dancing, singing, or just *being*, decked out in their exotic national costumes, these delegates were the living embodiment of 'peace in our time'—the future of the world. Perhaps the most exciting of all their public appearances, however, were the regular weekly television shows, in which delegates appeared in panel discussions like those performed at the finale. The creation of these TV shows, many of which survive from the 1950s, illustrate the intersection of government, media, and internationalism, and the role delegates and Forum played as the *New York Herald Tribune* positioned itself as a national and international political media voice.

Chapter 10

Media Darlings

The Forum on TV

Delegates often noticed television as one of the marvels of modern America, particularly in the 1950s when it was not a global phenomenon, but also later. Emmanuel (Ghana 68) said television was a big deal in Ghana. 'The whole secondary school had, maybe, one. And it was in the auditorium and if there's a special show, you know, like, a soccer match between Ghana and Nigeria, we would all congregate and go and watch.'[1] And that was just *watching* television.

For many delegates the first time they *saw* television was when they were *on* television. The Forum had its own TV show from 1953. Delegates participated in panel discussions televised weekly, complementing their performances on high school stages and in live forums. Helen Waller told delegates the shows would 'let the widest possible audience get better acquainted with your country through you' and 'let the audience share your thinking about "The World We Want", especially ... any new insights, ideas, and understandings ... that may be connected with your Forum experience.'[2] Chaired and (often heavily) curated by Helen Waller and her successors, each program focused on a particular theme or issue, with contributions from groups of selected delegates.

The series was initially titled 'The World We Want', changing in 1959 to 'Young Worlds', when it moved from National Educational Television to CBS. It survived until 1972, unlike some other aspects of the Forum program, an indication of its centrality to the Forum concept and continuing interest from television stations. The format remained similar for the twenty years of its existence, although panel sizes increased and topics for discussion varied. Surviving films from 1954 to 1959, and a few sound recordings and lists of topics and participants from the 1960s, allow some insight into the continuities and changes. The 1950s programs opened with the strains of an orchestral version of 'Getting to Know You' from the Rodgers and Hammerstein 1951 musical *The King and I* that so annoyed Santi (Thailand 52). In 1959 delegates' lively chatter replaced music, and by 1965 there was a less recognizable piece, probably by Charles Williams. The initial simple picture of a rotating globe accompanying the titles was soon replaced with an image typical of both Soviet and American youth propaganda of the era and epitomizing the hope placed in youth globally. A group of multicultural youngsters gazed upwards towards a globe, with 'The World We Want' emblazoned above their heads (see illustration on front cover).[3] The staging also developed. In early years the delegates and Helen sat on the floor or on cushions, casually arranged in front of soft curtaining. By 1959 the setting was more businesslike. The students sat in a semicircle behind a curved table, or around a desk, Helen in the middle as moderator, as if in a board room or on a UN panel, emphasizing their apparent authority as experts.

The format of between three and six selected delegates discussing a specific topic, albeit often resulting in a wide-ranging conversation, persisted through the 1950s, as did many of the topics themselves. Each debate had its own dynamic, depending on panel participants and the topic under discussion. Some were stilted, perhaps because of the students' facility with English; others were unbalanced, with one delegate overshadowing the rest. Sometimes one delegate struggled to get a word in. With boys outnumbering girls in most years, it was often the female delegate struggling to be heard—although by no means always. British delegates, with English as a first language, frequently dominated their panels, posing questions to others as well as articulating their own views.

Television Stars

For delegates, being on television was both nerve-racking and a thrill—another of the many new experiences they shared. Arnold (Colombia 69) loved it—'there was the makeup room and you could see actors going by for other shows', he remembered. Fifty years later, he could still recall the advice he was given: 'Don't swivel on your chair' and 'don't wear a white shirt'. Such insider hints added to the feeling of being special. One of the other delegates 'froze' on screen, but he intervened to save the day, Arnold remembered proudly. And when he went to Macy's department store, he 'got them to change the channel of the televisions to the right one' so he and the others could watch themselves! Avri (Israel 68) reminded me that CBS was nationwide television and television 'mattered' then. There were 'only three networks, so you're on one of them, one third of the population is watching you'. (He may have been overstating a little.) Roger (UK 69) got a thrill when he was recognized on the subway by an American girl. 'I really didn't make the most of that opportunity', he remembered ruefully.[4]

Others found celebrity more difficult. Geneviève (France 56) said 'we were treated like little stars and we had to shake hands with 50 or 70 people we didn't know and I said if this is glory I am not really interested'. She felt 'there was so much I didn't know about' and she 'didn't deserve' to be on television. She was not alone. Jona (Iceland 60) thought she was 'the worst informed delegate' in the whole Forum: 'I sat there with my mouth closed, because I didn't know what the other delegates were talking about'. Teklu (Ethiopia 60) felt he had been very naïve, 'spouting stuff I would be ashamed to repeat' today.[5]

Choosing the Panel

Any successful television program requires a good cast, and Forum directors had markedly different approaches. Helen Waller announced to the 1953 delegates the new 'frankly experimental' initiative: 'an unrehearsed half-hour discussion program which *will feature each of you at least once* between now and the Forum on March 21, together with American students' (my emphasis). This proved to be not entirely correct. American students *were* represented in 1953, with at least fourteen Americans, including four who appeared more than once. They were chosen from among the host students. The foreign delegates, however, did *not* all appear 'at least once', as Helen had suggested. Inclusiveness was never her priority. Based on discussions she had with them, she invited delegates to write essays on program topics, and selected participants based on their essays (as well as who she thought would perform well). The first episode included just one delegate from that year, Maureen (UK 53), who appeared with alumni, Bhinda (Nepal 52) and Chung Wha (Korea 52), both of whom were studying in the US. Six of the thirty delegates did not appear at all in 1953. On the other hand, Keith (UK) and Probal (India) each appeared four times, and another seven delegates appeared three times each.[6]

This approach continued for the next decade. Helen Waller was all about the end product: providing interesting television. She limited panel numbers, enabling focused and in-depth discussions, carefully selecting her television stars, and making sure they were well-prepared. Between 1954 and 1961, Helen Waller curated about eleven programs a year, each featuring, on average, four delegates. The 402 individual appearances in 82 programs across the 8 years were spread unevenly among the 275 delegates, as shown in the Appendix 1. Forty delegates had no individual appearances, only participating in the annual 'whole group' program. The majority appeared just once or twice. A lucky eight delegates (four boys and four girls) appeared four times. Three particularly articulate young men, Johnny (Philippines 54), Vangala (India 54), and Nakchung (Korea 55), fronted up for five performances each. No girl appeared five times. The gender split in the programs was in line with the numbers of boys and girls at the Forum in the 1950s.[7]

The representation of countries among the forty-one delegates who appeared in three or more programs was notable. Some delegates appeared because they came from countries with controversial or topical political situations, or because their nationality qualified them to speak on the week's designated topic. Thus, 'The Future of Africa' featured African delegates; 'The Problems of Europe' included Europeans. Beyond that, it was all about competency. Articulate delegates with excellent English and something to say were rewarded with more than one appearance. English delegates appeared often. Judith (UK 56) remembered Helen Waller telling her 'I'm using you because you speak English and you are fluent so don't be surprised if you are on television every week'. (She appeared four times.) Other regular participants included the two Australian delegates and five of the eight Indian delegates, who also benefitted from an English language education. The articulate and well-informed Chit (India 56) was

155

on four TV shows. He, Johan (Norway 56), and Christoph (Germany 56) were the 'serious' group, he recalled, and enjoyed engaging in debates. He thought he was chosen for more debates because he had the best English among those representing the 'Asian point of view'. Christoph and Johan competed for the 'European' perspective, he said.[8] Also appearing in multiple programs were four South Africans and three Israelis (from 'controversial' countries), and three Norwegians.

In sharp contrast to Helen Waller's approach, her successor in 1962, Virginia Wieschhoff, ensured every delegate appeared at least once, and increased panel sizes from four to usually six delegates to enable this. And all ten Asian delegates were in the program on Asia: I wonder how much they each got to say in the half-hour show. Eight of the thirty-seven only appeared once, while seven appeared three times apiece. There were also two 'extra' Americans, runners-up in the competition for the American delegate. They appeared once each while the actual US delegate, Gus, represented the American point of view three times.

Robert Huffman followed Virginia Wieschhoff's lead. The 1963 Forum information brochure outlined fifteen weekly discussions involving six delegates in each episode. 'Each delegate will appear at least twice' he promised.[9] Over the next few years between four and six delegates were in each program and everyone appeared at least once, with most in two programs and a few in more. In 1969, there were fourteen programs featuring panels of six delegates. The eighty-four spots were divided between twenty-nine delegates fairly equitably, with most appearing three times. Four individuals were on four programs each, while another seven only showed up twice each. The partial information available for other years suggests that this was typical. This was fairer for delegates but arguably not such good television, with less time for each delegate to speak, and potentially less dynamic participants.

Topics of Conversation

So what did panelists discuss? Chapter 11 delves more deeply into some of the main issues that pervaded the Forum. Several of those were the focus of TV programs, either explicitly or within broader themes. Subjects ranged across politics, education, family, and religion. Some delegates remembered talking about their schools and about life as a young person in their country—it was not political but social and cultural, they insisted. Other delegates were more politicized, either by nature, or because of the country they represented. Discussions about race, prejudice, imperialism, and the UN were perennial, as were focused panels on geographical areas: Europe, Africa, South America, Asia. The panels were bookended with programs in which delegates revealed their impressions of America—first their preconceptions and last what they learned—ranging from serious to trivial. Michael (NZ 67) remembered (somewhat to his embarrassment several decades later) 'advising New Yorkers to institute better "do" control as the "droppings" on the streets were disgusting and a health hazard'. As he said, 'back then dogs knew their place in New Zealand'.[10]

In the 1950s prejudice was an underlying theme, often featuring in a series of two or three programs. In the early 1960s topics were less connected, although general themes continued. 'Youth and Art' (1964) and 'A Foreign Student's View of New England' (1964) were potentially the least compelling programs, both for viewers and participants, while 'Youth and Christianity' (1964) seemed to be an extraordinarily narrow choice for an international Forum, particularly when previous years had explored religion more broadly. In 1965 one program focused on what delegates admired about America, producing a rather dull litany of pro-American propaganda. The next program in the series (which sadly does not survive) asked another group to discuss what they did not like about the US. It was a pity the two programs were not combined, allowing for a less sycophantic and more energetic discussion. In 1968, a commissioned report into the Forum recommended that it return to its 'original format', in which each Forum's discussion was focused on a major world crisis. It even had some suggestions: student power, the changing nature of communist and democratic blocs, the search for world peace referencing the Middle East, Asia, and Africa, the Black community in the US and links to Africa, and urbanization as a world problem.[11] The Forum's theme the following year was urban living.

After the year of student protest in 1968, one 1969 program topic was 'Why Students Protest'. This would have been unlikely even ten years earlier, let alone when the Forum began, indicating just how youth had changed. In the 1950s many delegates saw the US as a positive force in the world. By 1969 Bob Huffman noticed 'the current unrest among students manifested itself on occasion, with a few delegates expressing the desire for "revolution", and tending to blame all the world's ills on the United States and the Soviet Union.' Recordings of later programs don't exist, but, judging from those that do from 1965, Huffman would have found this frustrating, although he put a positive spin on it: 'We welcome the questioning which young people are doing, and we are reassured that the Forum is in step with the times,' he told alumni in 1969.[12]

A Smash Hit?

The programs were so successful during the 1950s that they were repeated and syndicated, and then the idea was expanded.[13] In March 1959, after the regular series, a three-month program also called 'Young Worlds', featured assorted alumni who were living in the US. They were persuaded to perform on panel discussions moderated by Helen Waller. They ranged in age from 19-year-old Naila (Pakistan 58) to 28-year-old Peter (Switzerland 49). Alumni from all over the world were represented, their participation determined by their availability. Five alumni living in New York appeared on at least three programs each.[14] This innovation was not repeated, but from 1962 another twist on the theme was established. Dubbed the 'Greater Metropolitan Program', the semi-finals and finals of the competition for the American delegate were broadcast. Robert Huffman moderated the panels which showcased American students discussing topics such as 'Is America a Cultural Wasteland?', 'What Does the Bill of Rights Mean to You?', and, demonstrating a post-Waller shift to the right, perhaps, 'How Can Democracy Meet the Challenge of Communism?'.[15] Screened in the last months of the year, this series led into the Forum programs featuring foreign students. By the late 1960s even more programs were added, showcasing American Summer Forum participants reflecting on their experiences. These American programs competed head-to-head with Dorothy Gordon's *New York Times* Youth Forum.

Dorothy Gordon's Youth Forum presented five or six American high school students discussing an issue from the news with an adult expert.

Unlike the more relaxed style of the early *Herald Tribune* programs, Dorothy Gordon's panelists were seated formally from the outset. In one surviving 1956 film, Gordon emphasized that one panelist was originally from Kenya and another from the Philippines, perhaps trying to compete with the *Tribune*'s series, which had more exotic participants.[16] Both Forums followed a format that was familiar to American audiences, although similar programs involved adult panelists. In 'Youth Wants to Know', for example, young people posed questions, but the expert voices were adults—usually white and male.

Who exactly tuned in to watch a group of rather earnest international teenagers pontificating on topics about which they often knew very little? It seems an unlikely hit. And yet it was. High school students watched as part of their curriculum, but other Americans also enjoyed 'The World We Want'. During this period television was an innovation, and one of the few ways Americans could see and hear people from other countries.[17] It was not bad television. The teenagers were often serious, but could be entertaining and occasionally witty, while those in national dress were visually striking. Laughter was important and several delegates managed some repartee both in the programs and to media. Obviously, this was easiest for native English speakers, and the two British Johns (58 and 59) were known for their dry asides and clever quips, but other delegates also gave it a go. They enlivened their earnest seriousness with what the US Department of State's magazine, *The Record*, called 'a fine sense of humor, whetted by their experiences in intimate sharing of American family life'. Soesilo (Indonesia 50) reportedly commented on the 'complex' nature of American life. 'On the floor I saw a carpet, which makes you need a vacuum cleaner, and for this you need electricity, and for this you need a hydro, and for this you need the TVA, and for this you need capital, and part of this comes from taxes, but', he concluded slyly, 'you do not like to pay taxes'. Probal (India 53) 'quipped' to reporters, 'Although I do not have any outstanding memory about your country in my mind, I shall never forget the terrific rush of your lunch hour'. In the final 1958 TV program, when delegates showed off their American souvenirs, Françoise (France 58) described her visit to a bookstore: 'So many beautiful books!' she exclaimed, 'I wonder why they don't read them!', having a dig at

American teenage anti-intellectualism. Peter (Norway 69) on the other hand, 'was very successful at the rehearsal' when he tried to be witty, but in front of the camera he 'was so excited', he had 'a blockout and didn't say a word'. He laughed at his younger self, 'I lost my footing totally!'[18]

The real key to the program's popularity, however, was that the delegates sounded both intelligent and genuine. Catherine Saffron, wife of a CBS cameraman, was 'impressed with the honesty of the young people being interviewed' in 1964. Carlos Mautner, a young Uruguayan engineering student at Fairleigh Dickinson, was gratified that the program's students actually 'realize the problems other countries face'. In 1957, 'one of the executives at the Educational Television and Radio Center' thought it 'one of the most fascinating programs I have ever seen'. The students 'appear to give an intelligent presentation of their own nation's point of view on a mature level and, unimpaired by the inhibitions and responsibilities of adulthood, express themselves rather freely'. He felt that this 'immediacy and spontaneity' were unusual, 'not present in most commercial programs and rarely found in educational programs'. Forum organizers, collecting such praise to impress their sponsors, would have enjoyed New Yorker Ruth Hannah's favorable comparison with the rival *New York Times* Forum in 1960. Mrs Hannah found *Tribune* Forum students 'bright and very much aware of the world they live in and what's wrong with it'. She contrasted them with the 'dreary American high school students on another programme', who 'always give the "right" answers'. These other students had 'no real interest, no courage, just a parroting of Cold War slogans'. She added rather acidly, 'That's why they're ON the programme, I suppose'. Miss Elthaire Martin also drew direct comparisons, sending her feedback to both the *Tribune* and the *Times*, thanking the *Herald Tribune* 'for a wonderful experience in listening to its 12th annual High School Forum' and making 'a plea to the NYT to duplicate it so that twice as many young people may have such an opportunity'. New York square dance caller, Piute Pete, wrote to Robert Huffman that the 1964 television programs were 'terrific', although he was really touting for trade. He suggested that delegates be taught to square dance (!), to advertise the activity, which he claimed boasted 'an estimated six million' American participants, to the rest of the world.[19]

'Freewheeling and Entirely Uncensored'

Much was made of the fact that the television programs were unscripted, 'freewheeling and entirely uncensored', as the *Tribune* put it in 1962. Some alumni remembered them being 'live', but most were pre-recorded. According to the 1963 Forum pamphlet this was for programming flexibility, so that they could continue to be shown after the delegates had returned home. A careful dig into the archives, however, reveals another possible reason. At least one program was recorded but never screened. Filmed in 1956 as 'the opening program in our 1956 discussion series' was 'My Image of America', featuring Chit (India), one of the stars of the year, (on four programs), along with Hee Joon (Korea) and Francesco (Italy), who appeared in one more program each, and Jawahir (Malaya), who did not. Although surviving in the archive, the program never aired. Instead, the series opened with 'An Alternative to War', shown on January 8, featuring some of the more articulate delegates, with excellent English: Judith (UK), Elizabeth (Australia), Christoph (Germany), and Nebiat (Ethiopia). Helen Waller also introduced this episode as 'the opening program in our 1956 discussion series', so the decision to ditch 'My Image of America', seemingly an ideal topic to begin the year, must have been made immediately. The program notes in the archive suggest why: it lacked 'the pace and spontaneity of the remainder of the series'. Perhaps Forum organizers thought its stiltedness would put the audience off. Delegates' observations were delivered in a very deliberate and clearly practiced manner, with Helen Waller working hard to move things along. The contrast with 'An Alternative to War' and the rest of the series was palpable. Delegates became more fluent in English and more relaxed with each other as the Forum went on, most noticeably in the fourth 1956 program, 'Has Europe a Future'. The voluble Australian, German, and Swiss delegates talked over the top of each other amid much laughter as they argued various points.[20]

While Forum publicity insisted that the programs were 'unrehearsed, this did not mean that they were not carefully prepared. Among the photos and programs in Forum memorabilia folders held by alumni, I also found pages of notes on discussion topics. By the end of the 1950s they had to write 'a full and detailed essay' on 'at least <u>two</u> subjects' that interested them most. Virginia Wieschhoff admonished her group in 1962: 'A number of you who have been on television programs came virtually unprepared on the subject for discussion', and warned that 'this cannot be allowed to happen where the panel discussions for the final Forum are concerned'.[21]

Delegates also held preparatory group discussions during Orientation. Onder (Turkey 58) recalled Helen Waller 'would mentor us to defend the opposite view to prepare us for panel discussions on TV'. In 1955 Helen told television audiences that Lesley (Australia 55) was such a good debater that, after 'ardently' defending the admission of China into the UN in the first televised debate, she had been told to take the opposite position in a live Washington forum. She had achieved this 'with equal eloquence'. Nevertheless, although some delegates understood that the debates were shaped by the moderators, and that there was some preparation and manipulation involved, most were adamant, like Saroj (Thailand 58), that 'Mrs Waller never put any words into my mouth or in anybody else's'.[22] They had said what *they* wanted to say. Of course, given that freedom of speech was central to the values of American democracy promoted by the Forum, this is scarcely surprising. Any restrictions or inhibitions came not from the Forum but from their own governments or from their own understanding of the consequences back home of articulating particular views. Like Helen Waller, Robert Huffman held discussions during Orientation to identify potential panel members and enable a rehearsal of arguments. He also gave delegates discussion points to consider in advance of the filming. Some delegates remembered delivering set pieces to the camera in response to Huffman's questions, rather than freeform conversations.

An Appetite for Controversy

'Be as frank, uninhibited, undiplomatic and controversial as you want to be, or as thoughtful or reflective as you are capable of being', Helen Waller advised delegates. The 1954 advertisements for the forthcoming series promised 'topics ... will be controversial: vote for eighteen-year-olds, religion, dating, national defense, foreign economic aid and what the visitors think of home and school life in the United States'.[23]

Helen Waller was all about producing good television, 'as vibrant a product as she could', ensuring dramatic tension by stacking her panels, putting Israeli, Yugoslav, South African, and sometimes British delegates as isolated defenders of their countries' policies against groups of Arab, anti-communist, anti-apartheid, and anti-colonial delegates. The likes of Sanaa (Egypt 61), who not only came from a politically interesting part of the world, but was described by one delegate as 'outspoken, contentious, provocative, self-promoting, and a thorn in many sides', were well-utilized (she appeared four times). Occasionally Helen strayed from the format. In one 1957 program she introduced Yumiko (Japan 57), 'whose English isn't quite up to participation in a quick give-and-take discussion', to give a statement about the topic before throwing the question to the four panel participants. It was no coincidence that Yumiko was decked out in her eye-catching kimono, displaying diversity. The Japanese delegate's English improved, and six weeks later she was properly on the panel, showing she was more than just a visual symbol. She reminded Americans pointedly that 'despite assistance from American soldiers after the war', 'the memory of the atomic bomb attacks... were still strong among the Japanese people... I still think the damage is larger.'[24]

Huffman invited the first South African delegate since 1962, Louis (SA 67), to discuss 'Who is an African' alongside delegates from Ghana, Kenya, Nigeria, Sierra Leone, and Egypt. Unlike Waller, however, he did not usually stack the panels for controversial effect. For instance, Orit (Israel 67) was never on the same panel as both Norma (Egypt) and Wael (Jordan). Perhaps this missed the opportunity for dramatic television, but Haider (Pakistan 71) felt that the 1960s 'and especially 1971' Forums had 'more open and well-informed' debates than those from the deep Cold War period.[25] (Perhaps, as a 1971 delegate, he would say that!)

Huffman was also a much more (overtly) interventionist moderator than Helen Waller. The few surviving recordings from the 1960s suggest the programs were more stilted. There were more participants, so less depth, less appetite for controversy, and Huffman was prone to asking long, convoluted, and leading questions.[26] Helen Waller crafted (and prepared) her panels so that sometimes she barely made an appearance in the actual program, letting the conversations flow freely—intervening only to allow a less forceful voice to speak. Delegates asked each other questions, some of which are clearly prepared, but others came naturally out of the conversation. She did not tolerate sloppy thinking or lazy arguments, however, and at other times she openly curated the discussion. She pushed and challenged, particularly those whom she thought could take it. Partly this was in search of good television, or a gripping headline.

For Helen, there was nothing like a controversy or drama to massage the ratings. In 1957 Susan (SA 57) provided this by bursting into tears on one program. Decades later, other delegates said that Mrs Waller had put too much pressure on her to denounce apartheid. Daphna (Israel) said that Susan had 'wanted to forget the Forum'. After all, she had been 'forced to leave' South Africa by the secret police because of it.[27] This story of Susan's dramatic breakdown has entered alumni lore, told and retold at reunions, used to exemplify Helen Waller's crusade to get individual South African delegates to repent and recant, repudiating apartheid, in a catharsis of self-realization, proving the worth and impact of her Forum.

Susan's own version of events was startlingly different. She told me she had always been opposed to apartheid, but hoped the Forum might be her ticket out of South Africa, so said what South African selectors wanted to hear. Throughout the Forum she walked a tightrope, she remembered, trying to keep to the party line. She 'got pretty slick' but felt 'very uncomfortable'. She became close friends with Amelia (Ghana 57). Her breakdown on TV was the result of this stress of lying to the media. Far from loathing Helen Waller and being a victim of bullying, Susan was one of the favorites. She *was* questioned by South African officials upon her return from the Forum but had already arranged (thanks to the intervention of Mrs Reid, as we will see) to return to Barnard College. Rather than wanting to forget the Forum, she was keen to recall what had been a pivotal experience in her life.[28]

There are several ways to understand these different versions. Was Susan really acting a part when she defended South Africa's political systems at the age of 17? Or is this a narrative that fits better with her later life as a prominent feminist activist in the US? Her statements on the television panels, if genuine, would be embarrassing. On the other hand, an anti-apartheid stance fits with her later persona. Susan was an articulate, forthright, and intelligent teenager—a leader in the group, and clearly appreciated by Helen Waller. Her arguments in the televised debates appeared a heartfelt defense of apartheid, but that may have been a consummate performance. Susan, like many delegates, was a practiced debater, well able to present an argument with which she did not personally agree, particularly given the expected reaction of South African authorities. For Helen Waller and the Forum, however, it did not particularly matter: controversial opinions and topics were the order of the day.

Helen Waller might have wanted 'uninhibited' discussion, but the US government and other national governments did not necessarily approve. Susan's experience was not unique among South African delegates. Israeli and Arab delegates also had instructions from their governments, and embassy officials monitored their public utterances. Vu Huy Kim (Vietnam 50) told a Hastings High School audience that he had been 'asked by the American consul in his country not to discuss political affairs'. This may have been a general instruction to delegates from American embassies keen to avoid diplomatic incidents. But it was not just delegates from the epicenters of international conflict. Before attending an event at the UN, Richard (Australia 54) 'was briefed beforehand on how to discuss the White Australia Policy'. Another Australian, Mike (65), felt he had been silenced by his government after expressing forceful opinions on the issue of Australian and American involvement in Vietnam. He was noticeably articulate and well-informed in an early televised panel discussion about Asia, although his on-air performance was not notably controversial. He did interrupt and contradict Bob Huffman on screen, however, and the pair had stand up arguments over the Vietnam war off-screen. Mike did not appear in another program. Whether this was an Australian government directive, or Huffman's personal decision, is unknown. For others, the repercussions were delayed until their return home, as we shall see. In contrast, some delegates felt remarkably ill-prepared, regretting the lack of assistance from governments and embassies. Jona (Iceland 60) was completely thrown when Helen suddenly asked her, 'Well what about Iceland, why does Iceland not allow the US to bring in black soldiers to the bays?'. Jona told me in our interview, 'my first reaction was "Oh? We don't?" ... I had no preparation, absolute zip, from the Icelandic Embassy on this situation'.[29]

Exemplar Panels

When the panels worked, they really worked. One of my favorites was from 1959. The discussion took off; Helen Waller barely spoke a word. This was one year in which girls outnumbered boys (by one) at the Forum, so, unusually, there were two television panels with three girls and one boy. Unlike the other such panel, where John (UK) got a good share of the conversation, in this panel, Hasan (Turkey) barely managed to contribute. Instead, it was the three girls, from Egypt, Iran, and Israel, who lit up the screen, their words tumbling out over the top of each other. They were articulate, smart, and aggressive without being obnoxious. A memorable moment was when Nadia (Egypt) suggested that her country had been 'desperate' when it accepted 'arms from Russia ... because of the Israeli expansion'. Daniella (Israel) was surprised. 'There is no Israeli expansion', she announced. There was a burst of laughter from Nadia; Maryam (Iran) grinned broadly, and even Helen Waller could be heard reacting off camera. 'Hmmm', said Nadia (Egypt), 'Hmmm, well, I think there is', she said carefully. 'I think that there isn't, I am sure there isn't', insisted Daniella (Israel). Maryam (Iran) stepped in and smoothed things over, observing that nations see things from their own point of view, 'that's what makes nations different'. But Daniella (Israel) was not mollified: 'point of view' did not apply because she was talking about 'facts', she insisted. Nadia (Egypt) chipped in with 'well just one thing ... all the time jumping on Demarcation lines ...'; Daniella (Israel) interrupted with 'and who did that first?', and for a second it looked like Helen Waller would have to intervene. Then Nadia (Egypt) herself steered the conversation back into safer waters, after sneakily getting in the last word. 'Who was the first time? Well, I think it was Israel ... but anyway I don't think we are discussing that now'.[30] Helen must have been proud of all of them. She was almost superfluous.

The 'Are Women Really Superior' discussion in 1959 was similarly compelling. In the program, Edgar (Philippines 59) advocated polygamy because 'men are superior' and it taught women 'to cooperate with each other'. Watching it, I wanted to slap him, and I suspect Kaarina (Finland 59), sitting next to him, did too. He laughed at her anger, almost as if the debate itself was a joke, comfortable in his own sense of superiority. The other male delegate, Tissa (Ceylon) wanted women to 'be women' and not act like men, although he was less comfortable with polygamy. Kaarina was the most radical of them all, insisting on equal rights for women and suggesting women should be allowed to have careers. Yukiko (Japan 59) was less insistent, looking forward to 'having a family'. Decades later I revisited this debate in a documentary with three of them. Tissa was abashed at his conservatism, Yukiko had managed a family and a stellar academic career, while Kaarina was embarrassed by her stridency as a teen.[31]

These programs were designed to challenge American students' preconceptions, and that extended even to the belief in the democracy itself. In one memorable exchange between 1959 delegates, Rafia (Pakistan) declared that 'we had democracy and it didn't work', things were 'so much better' now the army was in control. Having faith in one man to rule the country was better than having corrupt politicians, who bribed their way into government. Dictatorship suited Pakistan now, she insisted, until the population became more literate and capable of understanding democratic processes. Kaarina (Finland) was inclined to agree, but Adolfo (Argentina) was skeptical that a dictator would step aside willingly once the population was 'ready' for democracy.[32] That was not his definition (or experience) of dictatorship. Nevertheless, the association of democracy with corruption would have been challenging for late 1950s American teenagers, more used to that slur being attached to communist or totalitarian regimes.

Creating Educational Television

The televised panels became an integral part of the Forum, setting it apart from other exchange programs, and inviting comparison with Dorothy Gordon's Americans-only versions. They were the very public face of the Forum, reaching into American classrooms and living rooms, and more recently across time on YouTube as we will see. Carefully curated and prepared, yet 'freewheeling and uncensored', they were a surprising hit. For many delegates, these appearances offered a momentary thrill of fame; for others, an opportunity to practice public speaking and debating on an international stage, in preparation for future political or diplomatic careers. Most felt free to express their own opinions, albeit sometimes within constraints dictated by their own countries. Some recognized the powerful guiding hand provided by the Forum directors, however subtly it might have been applied, but most took on board the intended take-home lesson: American democracy meant free speech. Teenage audiences could see youngsters like themselves being taken seriously. Adult audiences were exposed to diverse opinions, appealingly presented by young people from around the world, safely contained within a carefully curated debate. They were invited to understand these youngsters as representative of worldwide youth—a source of hope rather than concern. The discussions performed on screen were emblematic of the conversations that energized delegates throughout the Forum. Some of the issues canvassed are the focus of the next chapter.

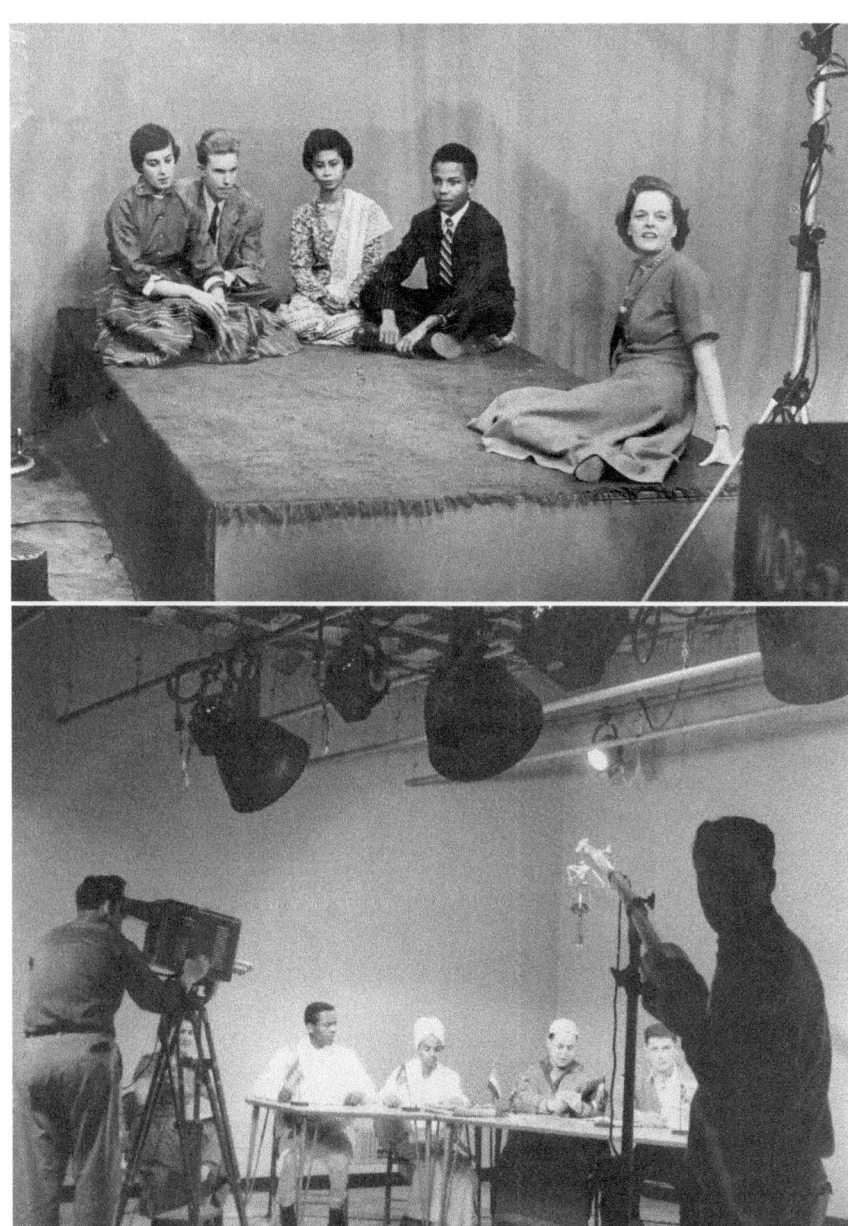

Top: 19. In 1955 TV debates were casually staged: Marlene, Erik, Tatty, Fifi, & Helen Waller. NET

Bottom: 20. Teklu, Ahmed, Tahir, Milan (1960) filming for a 5th grade Math class on educational TV in Hagerstown. USIS

Top: 21. Helen Waller sandwiched the Israeli between Arab delegates on the TV debates to create tension (1956). NET: IULMIA

Left: 22. Thrilled to be on TV, Sherille (1971) kept the evidence. Ismail

Opposite top: 23. The Arab League (1958), in Washington: Ahmed, Beshir, Michael, Omar, and Ibrahim in front. PA

Opposite bottom: 24. All friends at the Forum: Auxilia, Johannes, Bolaji, and Richard (1962). PA

Top: 25. Arriving in Berlin, a bonus field trip (1956). PA

Left: 26. 1949 Forum program cover, celebrating the group's jaunt across the US.
Ted Kell *NYHT*

Above: 27. Less glamorous bus travel in the US (1962). James Kavallines *NYHT*

Bottom: 28. Traveling light? Delegates on the road again (1962): Rudolfo, Sameh, Dieter, Manoli, Bolaji, Yosi, Suzanne, Lygia, Dorothy, Dureen, Emma. Ted Kell *NYHT*

Top: 29. Learning to pose: Omar, Mahipala, Onder, Marcella & Ibrahim arriving for Orientation at Sarah Lawrence College (1958). PA

Left: 30. Helen Waller counting heads and keeping calm in a busload of teenage delegates (1959). Bossi

Top: 31. Bob Huffman between John Warner (later Senator) and Emmanuel (1965) at the Capitol. Teo

Bottom Left: 32. Exchanging views was central to the Forum and the girls held their own. Vinod & Yvette (1969). Altuzurra

Bottom Right: 33. Posing for group photos was *de rigeur*, as were annual visits to the UN. (1954) James Kavallines, NYHT

Top: 34. 'Mini-UN' discussions (1965): Eddie with a Princeton student, and David in back row. Teo

Bottom: 35. Probal found meeting General Naguib in Egypt a highlight (1953).

Chapter 11

'Reds Under the Bed'...and Other Obsessions

'What were the main issues at your Forum', I asked in interviews with alumni. Most recalled little of the subjects or substance of debates. Of those who did, different delegates identified different issues, depending more on how close they were to a particular issue than on whether it dominated discussions. They had various responses: 'The Vietnam War', 'Civil Rights', 'Decolonization', 'Communism', 'The Middle East', 'International Aid', 'The United Nations'.

In previous chapters we have glimpsed some of the concerns that galvanized Forum participants as they were paraded across the country and sometimes further afield; of the preoccupations that provoked American students' questions and of the political milieu in which the Forum directors operated. There were shifts over time, although some things remained constant. The overarching theme of the Forum was prejudice, with delegates encouraged to explore its origins and ways of overcoming it as well as their own prejudices. Helen Waller told a story at the Forum finale in 1958 that perfectly encapsulated this approach. She announced that Saroj (Thailand 58) had 'mentioned casually that whenever people in Thailand talk about Westerners, they never refer to us as "he" or "she" but simply as "it"'. She continued, 'And the consequences slowly dawned on us: from the time they learn to talk, Siamese children absorb the idea that we are...neuter...something less than men and women...not quite as human as they'. Seventy years on, this statement has very different resonances as the idea of gender being binary is upended. But her point then was clear—prejudice seemed irrational. She had other examples: 'Björn from Iceland admitted that the only people he hated were the Turks, because his mother told him the Turks would take him if he didn't obey. In the Philippines, according to Patsy, it is the Indian Sikhs

169

that steal children who don't eat their vegetables.'[1]

These prejudices that seemed so ridiculous to Helen's audiences often had their basis in conflicts, both in the distant past and more recently. The drama of the Forum revolved around bringing youngsters from different sides of those conflicts together. Here we explore three pervasive themes: communism and the Cold War, with its proxies in the Korean and particularly the Vietnam War, along with decolonization; the Middle East conflict between Israel and its Arab neighbors, and racial discrimination, both abroad, notably in South Africa, and (much more discomfortingly for Americans) at home.

The Cold War

The centrality of the Cold War to the Forum was explicit in 1954, when the topics of the TV debates included 'How to meet the threat of Communist aggression' and 'Communism as a domestic problem'. Delegates from different parts of the world had different views of the immediacy and severity of the 'danger' and different ideas about solutions, but most agreed it was a danger. Later program titles were less overtly hostile; in 1957 delegates discussed 'What does Communism mean to you?', 1958 students talked of 'co-existence', and in 1959 they tried to decide 'what is the best form of government?' Delegates in 1961 wondered 'Is democracy the answer?' In 1962, a session on 'political systems, defined, defended and questioned' was followed by another on 'their relation to the concept of freedom'. In 1963, eighteen months after the Berlin Wall was erected, delegates thought about 'living in a divided world'. The Cold War was also the context in which other discussions, such as those around the atomic bomb and nuclear disarmament, played out.[2]

In the 1950s, the Forum took place in the shadow of McCarthyism. Helen framed communism as a threat in the discussions, but also encouraged delegates to express controversial views. Judith (UK 56) remembered receiving poison pen letters and having a bodyguard for a time after some remarks criticizing American democracy. She recalled that Helen was supportive but also 'amused': 'Don't be afraid …We are needling him!', she told Judith. Despite her bodyguard being a 'nice big handsome man', Judith found her experience 'a nasty whiff of what was going on beneath the surface'. She thought Helen 'very brave' to be 'sparring with' McCarthy.[3]

Communism was a hot topic more widely. Teenagers applying for the Forum were certainly aware of its significance. It would be fascinating to know how many railed against it in their selection essays. Only fifty mentioned communism, China or Russia directly in their autobiographies. Yugoslav delegates were notably silent on their brand of communism. Milan (Yugoslavia 60) came the closest, describing himself as 'a member of the Communist League', and his life as 'exciting because I live in a revolutionary country'. Most others who mentioned it were from countries for whom the 'cold war' was decidedly hot. Korean delegates wrote moving accounts of failing 'to evade the oncoming rapid invasion of the Communist army and suffered the merciless tortures of the red regime', of parents kidnapped and killed, with the only 'ray of hope' being 'liberated' by the UN. Minh (Vietnam 65) wrote that the communist Vietminhs found support amongst his countrymen 'supposedly in the fight "against French colonialists", but in fact for their own control over our land'. He found communism 'unsuitable to me in all respects … a negation of human nature, sentimentality and above all, the existence of the supernatural power: God'. Agung (Indonesia 67) was actively involved. He wrote of the 'abortive … communist … coup d'etat' in October 1965. 'Blood was spilled and feelings rose high' (something of an understatement for what was the mass killings of Communist Party supporters in a CIA-backed coup). He was proud to have participated in 'activities held against the communists', earning him the position as chairman of the youth movement, KAPPI, which 'arose from a firm conviction that society dominated by communism could not be tolerated any more'. It was a 'long ordeal that demanded many sacrifices' but which 'was worth it as communism was banned and outlawed'. Others were one step removed, but no less vehement. Rodolfo (Uruguay 62) declared that 'there is something I love—freedom, and something I hate with all my heart—dictatorship and communism'. He could not 'understand why good people, friends of mine, can have such mistaken ideas concerning the affair between Cuba and United States.' Edgar (Philippines, 59) declared 'Communism is the 20th century form of slavery … I will forever stick to Democracy'.[4]

Many delegates were politically aligned to the West, either directly through family, or indirectly because of their class and social grouping. Their passionate denunciations of communism and expressions of love for the US were genuine. It was personal for some. Nga (Vietnam 58) was 'enamored of the US from a young age': her father, head of the North Vietnam railroad, was murdered by communists when she was young. After the Forum, delegates continued to express their views in the Forum newsletter, their opinions probably influenced by their American experiences. Khin (Burma 53) welcomed the ascendence of General Win to leadership of her country in 1958, saying that she had feared 'communist insurgents were getting too much from the kind-hearted Prime Minister', and she wanted 'a strong government to deal squarely with things and guard our democratic rights'. She emphasized that this was 'not an army coup', but that the 'General was made a P.M. constitutionally'. This had 'put away the communist fear until the next generation', she concluded, 'perhaps till the university group grow up', explaining that the 'University is a stronghold of Communist insurgents'. Ahmed (Sudan 60) refused a scholarship to study in the USSR, which, he said, was just hoping 'to make a propaganda by them', but he did not feel the same about the Forum or about US scholarships, returning to Dartmouth College in 1962.[5]

Russians at the Forum

As America emerged from the depths of McCarthyism, a nationwide fascination with Russia and Russians developed alongside the fear of communists skulking in the shadows. In 1955 the Forum asked schools 'Where would you like an exchange student from?' The overwhelming response was 'from Russia'. This encouraged Helen Waller and the *Tribune* to push further. In 1956 Madame Ludmila Dubrovina, the Russian Deputy Minister of Education, spent two weeks in the US at the *Tribune*'s expense, speaking at the Forum finale about 'Education in the USSR'. Her talk was paired with the provocatively titled speech 'Freedom: The Essence of American Education', given by Mr Marion B Folson, Secretary of the US Department of Health, Education, and Welfare. Madame Dubrovina was, by all accounts, delighted to come to New York to inspect American educational institutions and to explain her own country's system. She told reporters that she considered it 'her mission to further the firm and sincere friendships between the Soviet and the American peoples, especially the young people', declining to confirm if she was a member of the Soviet Communist Party. The *Tribune* justified its invitation, pointing to previous exchanges 'by farm groups, doctors, and the like', suggesting that 'it is good for those who dwell in Communist countries to see the United States and know our thoughts and ways by personal contact'. It protected itself from any McCarthy-esque accusations by acknowledging 'the fundamental differences that divided a totalitarian from a free, democratic society', concluding strongly, 'Americans are resolutely opposed to Marxism-Leninism and the absolute state control, the liquidations, subversions, and desire of world conquest that is implied in this doctrine'. One reason for inviting Dubrovina was to pave the way for Russian delegates, but it was unsuccessful.[6] As we have seen, the Soviet government continued to refuse repeated invitations, as did most other Eastern bloc countries. Nevertheless, unsurprisingly, the only time the CIA showed any interest in the Forum was later in 1956.

Representing Socialism

As the presence of Madame Dubrovina and repeated invitations to Eastern bloc countries suggests, the Forum, particularly from the mid-1950s, was keen to include multiple perspectives. It demonstrated 'free speech' was a central tenet of American democracy, even if sometimes lost in the enthusiasm for the McCarthyist witch-hunts in the early 1950s, and was also part of educating American teenagers. The panic generated by the McCarthy era meant that American fears about communism translated into a distaste for any policies remotely approaching socialism and many American students conflated communism with socialism, and even with social welfare. Some Finnish delegates, who told me they had to sign declarations that they and their families were free from the taint of communism, found themselves repeatedly denying they lived behind the Iron Curtain. It was one thing to be a satellite state, which Finland was not, and quite another to live in harmony and avoid baiting the enormous bear right next door. Finland and the USSR shared a 1340 km border. Other Scandinavians, as well as the British and Australians, found, like Peter (UK 54), that 'very few Americans are able to differentiate between socialism and communism which makes it rather difficult for me as an Englishman coming from a welfare state'. Peter (Australia 48) also felt the average American 'can't grasp the idea that state control of essential industries and social services can also be supported by a democratic people'.[7]

Ideas about communism were ingrained and widespread, as Suzanne (UK 62) told her mother: there was not 'much anti-communist propaganda actually taught' in schools, but 'it comes much more from the home and the newspapers'. She 'had never met so many narrow-minded people in my life' and was 'subjected to the full blast of 14-year-old precocity' spouting 'rather dead than Red' views in a world history class. She was horrified that, even for teenagers, 'just the mention of the word "communism" makes them see scarlet'. Later, unable to 'resist a good argument', she 'agreed to defend Red China' in a Metuchen High School debate, in which she suggested that the State Department was not 'infallible'. She recorded wryly, 'I really should learn to keep my mouth shut'. The following day, 'Dirty Communist' was 'written in red chalk' on her school locker door. She certainly did her bit in challenging American students. It was not just Americans, however. Other countries also had exaggerated fears of communism. One Iranian delegate wrote in 1960 that 'few people are happy but few people say anything' in Iran. 'There is no communism here but ... people are afraid to say anything opposing because they may be stamped as communists'. She was concerned that 'this puts a good stop to new ideas'.[8]

There were no delegates from the Eastern bloc or China (apart from one Czech in 1967), but Yugoslav delegates appeared annually from 1955 (except in 1964). Here, at last, were voices from a socialist country 'striving towards communism', as Mirka (Yugoslavia 57) said. Although generally apolitical in their autobiographies, Yugoslavs were pushed hard in the televised debates. Mirka distinguished Yugoslavian communism from that of Russia in a heated debate with Young-Koo (Korea 57), who argued that communism and capitalism could not co-exist peacefully because of 'the very nature' of communism. Passions ran high. Young-Koo had 'experienced what communism is first hand' in 1950 in the Korean War.

Mirka was less impressed with his opinions when she elicited the fact that his family had escaped to the UN zone after just three months. Norbert (Germany 57) also weighed in, noting that the Yugoslavian regime was very different from East Germany. For Mirka, socialism and communism represented freedom, for Young-Koo, and to a lesser extent Norbert, communism was tyranny.[9] These televised discussions were at the heart of the Forum's agenda to encourage open debate and educate American student viewers, as well as the delegates themselves.

Communism was not just appealing to Yugoslav delegates. Saroj (Thailand 58) announced at the Forum finale in 1958 that he found American students 'too proud of themselves', thinking themselves 'the best in the world', yet with no idea about Thailand, even confusing it with Tunisia. He continued provocatively, 'I'm sure Russian education is far more advanced', telling of some Thai students who visited Russia and were surprised to be greeted in fluent Thai by Russian students, who learned the language at school. Mahmoud (Iran 52) returned to study in the US after the Forum but, unlike many delegates who returned, he was unconvinced by American democracy. He later became a socialist activist, published *Nationalism and Revolution in Iran* under a pseudonym in 1973, and returned to Iran to further the revolution in the 1970s, dubbed 'the father of Iranian Trotskyism'. Similarly, Phalla (Cambodia 60) went to university to study medicine in Moscow, seemingly the only delegate in the Forum's 25-year history to go to Russia to study.[10]

Decolonization and the UN

Engagement with the USSR was widespread in Asia and Africa, particularly as decolonization became more widespread. Americans and delegates from Europe and Australasia could be taken aback by some delegates' approach to the Cold War. When debating the role of the UN in the distribution of aid, Chit (India 56) disagreed with Johan (Norway 56), who felt that the UN should ensure aid was more equitably and less politically distributed. Instead, Chit took great delight in the competition between the USSR and the West, explaining that his country benefited greatly from the competitive enthusiasm of each power's attempts to gain influence in his country. Ironically, Chit's reliance on the 'market' of aid and influence revealed an underlying capitalist philosophy that would have been comforting for State Department viewers. On the other hand, Sanaa (Egypt 61) suggested US policy, in which 'it seems that the US was only willing to give aid in exchange for a ... pact which assured them we wouldn't go Communist' was a mistake. 'You cut off your aid from the Aswan Dam ... and practically forced us to accept the Russians to finance our high dam'. Tissa (Ceylon 59) was adamant that 'to remain free we need freedom from Russian and American interference. Please leave us alone.'[11]

In the 1960s, against the background of US engagement in Vietnam, the 'communist threat' became focused on 'Red China' within the United States. Robert Huffman made it clear where his sympathies lay, telling delegates on the 1965 Forum program 'Can There Be Stability in South East Asia' that 'the thing that an American audience is probably more interested in than anything else is the matter of China, communism, communist infiltration and this sort of thing'.[12]

Vietnam War

With growing recognition of the impact of Cold War politics on emerging independent nations, delegates became more critical of US imperialism in the later 1960s. Bahram (Iran 70) remembered US imperialism as a central focus of classroom discussions. His Forum took place against a background of 'the Vietnam War and overthrow of governments and replacement by US backed repressive dictators or sometimes by Soviet backed dictators'.[13]

American intervention in the Vietnam War, an extension of the Cold War itself, became an increasingly significant issue at the Forum during the 1960s, particularly after President Lyndon Johnson committed American troops in March 1965. Unlike the Korean War, the Vietnam War did not involve the UN. Instead, supporting Saigon were the United States and a mere handful of allies, including Australia, New Zealand, the Philippines, South Korea, and Thailand, all of whom sent delegates to the Forum. Vietnamese Forum delegates generally hailed from a privileged elite, and were chosen by South Vietnamese regimes in conjunction with American consular officials. For most of them, American intervention in Vietnam was a positive. They came under pressure from other delegates and from

American students, who were facing the prospect of being drafted. Anti-Vietnam War sentiment was widespread, even before the notorious draft 'lottery' from 1969. Ceridwen (UK 67) warned future delegates that 'in every question period Vietnam will come up'. Mike (Australia 65), who was in the US in March 1965, advocated the withdrawal of American and particularly Australian troops: 'We are losing in South Vietnam, we can't win the war and it would be better to give aid' elsewhere. He was even more vocal off air, having a virtual 'stand-up brawl' with Robert Huffman. 'They couldn't stop us—everyone was talking about Vietnam', he said. During a tour of the UN, he told Australian Ambassador Hayes, who Mike felt was trying to 'silence' him, that he was 'not there to represent the Australian government but Australian youth'. Minh (Vietnam 65), who had some robust exchanges with Mike over the Vietnam conflict, was more amazed at the ignorance of Americans about his country: They 'had no idea about Vietnam yet they were in a war there'.[14]

Emmanuel (Ghana 68) thought that the Vietnamese delegate 'had one of the hardest time ... because ... there was the resistance to the war'. He was 'peppered with questions'—and 'not very friendly' questions at that. Emmanuel thought it unfair because he 'didn't speak English' so well and 'people were blaming him ... and he was just a student about our age.' Joachim (Germany 71) found his third host family in the middle of a crisis, with their older son deciding whether to flee to Canada to dodge the draft. Some host families supported the war. 'I even pay for it with my own money', announced one host father proudly, thus 'putting an end to the discussion by taking out his wallet at pointing at the green dollars in there', recalled one late 1960s' delegate, who quickly changed the subject.[15]

Browsing 1969 delegates' scrapbooks, I found anti-war pamphlets from the Women Strike for Peace, encouraging readers to contact the government to tell them 'we've had enough ... 10000 American men died since peace talks began'. The delegates collected these from protesters outside the White House on February 21, when they took photographs of each other with the protesters' placards. They also had flyers about the Student Mobilization Committee to End the War in Vietnam Central Park demonstration on April 5, at which Black Panthers' Kathleen Cleaver was the headline speaker.[16] Although still in the country, no delegate was in the 20,000-strong crowd who gathered at the 'Be-In' that Easter Saturday, to protest the Vietnam War.

The eighth televised Forum discussion program in 1969, 'What Happens in Asia After Vietnam?', involved delegates from India, Japan, New Zealand, Philippines, Singapore, and Vietnam. Sadly, the program does not survive. Did they use it as an opportunity to express anti-war views, or did Huffman guide the discussion as he had in 1965? Ugi (Yugoslavia 69), coming from the European student protests of the summer of 1968, noticed 'different protest agendas' in the US. 'Vietnam and gender issues' were at the forefront, but he was 'surprised' that 'social equality, equal access to education, freedom of thought, bureaucracy', important issues in Europe, did not register highly in America.[17] In the US, race trumped class as an area of concern, along with the immediate threat of conscription to the Vietnam War.

Middle East Tensions

The situation between Israel and its Arab neighbors shifted throughout the Forum years. The state of Israel was proclaimed in 1948, prompting the 1948 Arab-Israeli conflict, at the end of which Jordan annexed the West Bank and Egypt occupied the Gaza Strip. Many Palestinians, including some who would become Forum delegates, left Israel. Tensions continued to simmer between Palestinians and Israelis until the Suez Crisis, in which Egypt nationalized the canal and Israel invaded Egypt with the UK and France. The crisis began just after the end of the 1956 Forum and lasted through the 1957 Forum. The Palestinian Liberation Organization was founded in 1964 and then in 1967 the Six-Day War brought matters to a head, leading to an Arab boycott of the Forum for the following years. Lebanon was the only Arab country to send delegates again—in 1971 and 1972.

It was easy for Forum organizers, themselves many miles away, to imagine that bringing teenagers from opposite sides of the conflict together would foster peace and understanding. But for delegates it was personal, and difficult. The autobiographies of the 1962 Israeli and Jordanian delegates demonstrate just how personal. The 'first memories' of Joseph (Yosi) (Israel 62) were as a 3-year-old in the 'Siege of Jerusalem' in 1948: 'I remember the explosion of a shell hitting our house. I remember the lack of food and water, but', he added carefully (and surely not from when he was three), 'I remember, too, the joy about the birth of the State of Israel'. Salah (Jordan 62) was on the other side of the Arab-Israeli conflict, from Deir Yassin: 'the picture of our calm and charming village is still imprinted on my memory'. His life changed 'when we heard for the first time the sound of shots … in a state of restless consternation amid the sound of grenades and rifles'. He escaped, but his two brothers were among the 'fifty young men of the village [who] stood against the tremendous number of Jews who were well armed' until 'they shot the last bullet they had'. Over 100 died in the Deir Yassin massacre. Salah and Yosi faced each other at the Forum in 1962. I asked Yosi what happened. 'We played ping pong', Yosi said, and avoided talking politics. This was not the first time 'ping pong diplomacy' was used at the Forum. In 1955 Gur (Israel) played ping pong with Akram (Jordan) and Rifaat (Egypt).[18] Such interactions were a lot to expect from teenagers.

Until 1964, Forums usually included one Israeli delegate along with three or more Arab delegates from neighboring nations. Most frequently these were Egypt, Lebanon, and Jordan, with the Jordanian delegates often displaced Palestinians. As Raja (Jordan 54) told me, 'I always consider myself as a proud Palestinian. Jordan was a British creation for its own Middle East agenda and a shield for Israel.'[19] The dynamics of delegates' interaction depended on personalities and politics, with gender also entering the equation. The Israeli delegate was always outnumbered in the Forum group, although a few other delegates might also be Jewish. Beyond the multinational Forum group, it was a different story. New York had a large Jewish population, and I wondered if Arab delegates ever felt isolated in host communities, after the comforting solidarity of being one of a trio in the Forum. No interviewee suggested this, although Muhammad (Jordan 63) certainly felt pressured, as we shall see.

Helen Waller put Arab and Israeli delegates together, particularly encouraging public displays of friendship and unity. Thus, the image of Israeli and Syrian boys shaking hands at the UNESCO Conference for 1000 high school students at Julia Richman High School in 1952 made local and international headlines. For Waller, the *Tribune,* and even the US government, such displays were gratifyingly emblematic of the Forum's role, but Middle Eastern countries on both sides of the conflict were not always so happy. This was a time when even personal communication between Israel and Arab nations was difficult. The Forum office acted as 'a transfer point for letters between Israeli and Arab delegates because, reported Waller, seemingly with some surprise (!) in 1952, 'there is apparently no direct mail service between their countries'. In 1954 Gerhard (Germany 54) also acted as messenger between Nurit (Israel 54) and the Arab delegates after the Forum.[20]

Arab and Israeli delegates often arrived with instructions to avoid each other. Governments monitored the televised debates, newspaper reports and images that circulated. Nurit (Israel 54) was 'scolded by the New York Israeli Embassy' after blaming 'our education' for the way she and Raja (Jordan 54) 'looked at the same fact in an entirely different way'. She 'shed many tears and felt almost like a "traitor"!' Similarly, Zohar (Israel 56), a fiercely intelligent and articulate 16-year-old, was 'scolded' by a 'supervisor from the Israeli foreign ministry' because she 'agreed too much with one of the Arab delegates about the state of the refugees'. According to her sister, 'she came back different', suffering some sort of mental crisis after her return to Israel. It was 'a trauma I bear with me', Zohar told her son many years later.[21] In 1961, Snait (Israel) was far more openminded about the Palestinian situation than her selectors understood. The friendship between Snait and Sanaa (Egypt 61) made gratifying headlines for the Forum but caused problems for Snait upon her return home as we shall see in Chapter 14.

As well as encouraging demonstrations of friendship, from 1956, Helen Waller made a point of sandwiching the Israeli between Arab delegates on television panels to discuss the Middle East. During the Suez crisis tensions were high. One delegate described the four Arab boys in 1957 as 'in your face', one of them 'a bundle of rage'. Sarah Lawrence College girls complained about the 'rather pointed and unpleasant propaganda from the Arab nations' left in their rooms.[22] Daphna (Israel 57) needed every inch of her six-foot height as she faced the boys from Jordan, Lebanon, Morocco, and Sudan, and an Egyptian girl. Hisham (Jordan 57) refused to talk to her. And there were other potential pitfalls.

In January 1957, the American Friends of the Middle East, 'an organization dedicated to the promotion of better relations between the United States and the Middle Eastern countries', invited Daphna to attend a reception 'in honor of you and your Middle Eastern colleagues'. Looking back in 2020, Daphna said 'I was so naïve... the Israeli embassy caught me in time and explained to me why I should not go'.[23] Helen Waller, who provided Daphna's contact details, probably hoped for gratifying headlines like 'Israeli girl builds bridges with pro-Arab organization'. Or perhaps all sides hoped to leverage the very 'naïvety' of delegates in an idealistic attempt to improve relations, on the grounds that teenage 'ambassadors' could get away with things that their more cautious elders could not.

On a personal level, despite political tensions, things improved between Daphna and some Arab delegates. Peter (Singapore 57) wrote of the 'most heartwarming sight of the Moroccan delegate Mohd Amine, who is much shorter than Daphna, dancing the rock 'n' roll with her and repeatedly swinging her over his shoulder' at the Forum farewell party. It was forty years, however, before Hisham and Daphna had a conversation.[24]

In 1958, the boys from Egypt, Jordan, Lebanon, Morocco, and Sudan dubbed themselves 'the Arab League'. They 'immediately clicked together', and were friendly with Naila (Pakistan). Ruth, a serious-looking, quietly-spoken 16-year-old girl from a farm just outside Tel Aviv, represented Israel. The Jordanian and Lebanese delegates told me they were 'polite' and 'avoided talking to' Ruth. It was nothing personal, but both felt politically that 'you had to be careful not to befriend an Israeli'. Ruth and others tell a different story. Naila and the 'Arab League' boys, with the exception of 16-year-old Ahmed (Egypt 58), did not just ignore Ruth, but actively sidelined her, playing childish pranks such as 'forgetting' to tell her she had a phone call. During one debate, when Ruth suggested Israel was 'compensating the Arabs that were sent out of their homes', Ibrahim reacted: 'Without waiting for her to finish, I stood up and shouted, "this is a lie, all we got is bullets in our chests"'. Ruth told me sixty years later that her Forum experience was 'traumatic'. There was 'no possibility to create a dialogue', instead 'only nasty remarks, attacking and lashing out'. She said Naila, although Pakistan did not border Israel, thought she had to 'attack on behalf of the entire Muslim world'.[25]

The boys and Naila may have been unaware of the personal pain they caused a 16-year-old girl while they were performing their solidarity. One cannot ignore the heady combination of hormones, new-found freedom, and sense of importance, as delegates found themselves away from home, politics, and responsibility. It was a tough gig to be the Israeli delegate within the Forum group, especially when the Arabs were a band of boys trying to impress a rather gorgeous Pakistani girl. The situation was not helped by Helen Waller's enthusiasm for drama and her encouragement of robust conversations on contentious issues. She did not intervene, although Ruth's distress was apparent to other delegates and at least one host family. Other years were less fraught; political disagreements were confined to the formal discussions and television programs.[26]

Robert Huffman's first year as Forum director in 1963 was also the last year there was a panel discussion specifically on the Middle East, and the last year a sole Israeli encountered an 'Arab League'. Gideon (Israel 63) felt outgunned. The announcement in early April of a tripartite Arab Federation between Egypt, Syria, and Iraq, caused great jubilation for Raouf (Egypt 63) and Rabih (Syria 63), who 'gloated about it', telling Gideon 'now we will beat you', implying 'it was likely the end of Israel'. Gideon remembered 'the Arabs gave me a miserable time' and was pleased that Raouf (Egypt 63) spent much of the Forum distracted by Nuala (Ireland 63), leaving him more often with just the Syrian and Jordanian delegates to deal with. (Was it Raouf, however, who persuaded Nuala to introduce Gideon at the Forum finale provocatively as 'from one of the world's most controversial countries'?)[27]

Muhammad (Jordan 63) was the real catalyst for the change in Forum policy about the balance of Arab and Israeli delegates. Tord (Norway 63) remembered Muhammad as a pleasant boy with a sense of humor, and they remained friendly after the Forum. Muhammad's first host family also enjoyed his visit. But over the next three months, Muhammad, according to Forum records, became increasingly unwilling to listen to others, instead 'using the Forum for his own purposes and as a platform for anti-Israeli propaganda'. He had a shouting match with Bob Huffman, accusing Americans of discriminating against him. It was Muhammad who inspired his American Jewish host mother, Shirley Streicker, to send her long letter of complaint and recommendations to Huffman. Muhammad had 'stated quite openly that he had told his Minister of Education only what the Minister wanted to hear and not what Muhammad believed himself' in his selection interview, 'felt nothing but contempt' for Huffman and the Forum, and showered the Streickers with anti-American insults from the first night he arrived. Delegates needed to have 'a genuine desire to understand [other] points of view', wrote Mrs Streicker pointedly: 'It often seemed to us that this Forum was a place where everybody talked and nobody listened'. Muhammad also disappeared for a week to visit his brother in Chicago, the only delegate to 'blatantly break the rules' banning private trips during the Forum that year.

Was Muhammad an arrogant propagandist with scant regard for the Forum? Or was this the story of an increasingly unhappy and isolated teenager, who genuinely felt alienated among New Yorkers? Did he escape to Chicago, not out of insolence but desperate homesickness? Huffman's 'delegate report' on Muhammad reveals more than he may have intended about the milieu in which the Arab delegates found themselves. This was not neutral territory. Huffman emphasized that 'Forum staff members, faculty advisors, and host families ... understood the deep feelings which the Arabs have toward Israel', and 'were prepared to go *considerably more than halfway* in listening to the Arab point of view ... The initial goodwill shown to the Arabs [is] even more genuine than that shown to delegates from *less controversial countries*'. (my emphasis) Huffman went on to compare Arab delegates with 'communist delegates ... who have realized that one's cause is furthered by *at least giving the impression* of being reasonable and a little open-minded'. He suggested that 'If the Arab countries would tell their delegates to soft-pedal their basic feelings even a little they would win many more friends for their countries'. The unspoken assumption was that Americans naturally supported the Israeli cause over that of the Arabs in the Middle East, just as they naturally supported democracy over communism. Huffman implied that communist (and Arab) delegates were disingenuous in 'giving the impression' of open-mindedness. Here is a clue to Arab delegates' frustration: perhaps some Americans themselves performed open-mindedness but were actually not listening at all.

Whatever the truth of the matter, 1963 was a turning point for Middle Eastern delegates. Huffman initially threatened to ban future Jordanian delegates, but, as we have seen, he was persuaded that this would be diplomatically counterproductive. The difference between Helen, a journalist looking for the dramatic headline and newsworthy soundbite by stacking a panel with several Arab delegates surrounding a lone Israeli, and Robert Huffman, who was more focused on education, was stark. Delegates did not feel manipulated, a term sometimes used in reference to Helen Waller, by Virginia Wieschhoff or Robert Huffman. John Hay Whitney was also more concerned with balance. As he told the US ambassador in Jordan, 'The mistake ... was having three Arab delegates and only one Israeli' in 1963. Was this a criticism of Helen Waller's approach? Whitney also made an intriguing distinction between the Arab countries themselves, noting that 'adding Jordan' to the list for 1964 would be fine, because the only other Arab country was Lebanon, which 'does not present quite the point of view as that of the pure Arabic countries'.[28]

Arab and Israeli delegates continued to appear together on panels (until 1968), but diluted as two of five or six panelists, and not specifically discussing the Middle East. Rachel (Israel 64) remembered being quite friendly with Gaby (Jordan 64), and that Salah (Lebanon 64) was 'a playboy not interested in politics'. When they explored 'the origins of wars' more generally, they concluded that the fault lay with 'the arms dealers'. Similarly, Minh (Vietnam 65) was impressed with the cordial relationship between the delegates in his year, commenting, 'if it's left to us there would be no war, you know'.[29]

Nevertheless, the Middle East remained a live issue. The Six-Day War of 1967 was a critical moment. Arab countries boycotted the Forum because of US involvement. Avri (Israel 68) arrived in a state of euphoria after his country's 'huge victory'. He described it as a 'great relief', because in May 1967 there had been 'the feeling that there's going to be a disaster ... everybody's going to get killed'. For 15-year-old Avri, it was a frightening time. 'Egypt was amassing troops ... broadcasting even in Hebrew that: "We're going to throw you into the ocean" ... as kids we were helping to dig mass graves and [fill] sacks of sand for protection'. Avri felt his responsibilities as a delegate keenly: 'I was there not to express my opinion but to represent young people in Israel's attitudes towards other young people'.[30]

Israeli and Arab delegates were under a great deal of pressure at the Forum: they had to represent and defend their countries' positions, deal with the expectations of their own governments, and perform friendship with youngsters from the other side of what were insoluble conflicts. That Helen Waller, in particular, continued to throw these delegates together demonstrated both admiral optimism in the power of youth, as well as somewhat irresponsible näivety, ignoring the consequences for the young people themselves. Among the delegates, probably only one other country's representative had as much pressure placed upon them at the Forum. That was the South African.

Apartheid

Racial prejudice was a perennial subject at the Forum. South African delegates (invariably white and frequently Afrikaans) were invited to defend their country's racially-based apartheid regime by articulate black Nigerian, Ghanaian, and Kenyan delegates, with Ethiopian delegates providing a fascinating twist on the debate. Meanwhile, segregation in the United States was also under the spotlight.

Black and white African delegates could be friendly. They often met on the plane, as we have seen. Marlene (SA 55) and Fifi (Ghana 55) shared a box of chocolates and had memorable adventures with Minjiba (Nigeria 55) during their Lisbon stopover. They talked of this on the relevant television panel discussion, exemplifying Forum magic at work. These were personal relationships, however, and Marlene emphasized that Fifi was 'very different from the Africans in our country', telling him in a beautifully clipped South African accent, '*you* are an educated young man'. Delegates discovered they had things in common. Louis (SA 67) was allocated a room at Sarah Lawrence College with Jacob (Nigeria 67) and recalled that the Nigerian 'had a wicked sense of humor, had sung the same hymns at school as I had ("O God, our help in ages past")', and, not only that, he 'wore the same brand of underpants as I did'. Nii (Ghana 59) was close friends with Marita (SA 59), who was remembered by her fellow delegates as 'wild and audacious', a 'total non-conformist'. Emmanuel

(Ghana 68) said of his South African delegate, Marilyn: 'She was very charming—she was white, and we used to tease her, "If you hang around us and go back home, you're going to get in trouble". He and the other African boys, Nurein (Nigeria), Joe (Kenya), and Mammo (Ethiopia), epitomized the Forum spirit by including her, saying '"Come join us, you're from Africa", and she was easy going and very playful, like, we really enjoyed her company.' In this case, it probably helped that she was both charming and female. Their teasing remarks however, had a serious side. As we have seen, Susan (SA 57) faced the security services upon her return home. Johannes (SA 62) was persuaded by a journalist to take a stroll down Broadway with the black delegate from Rhodesia, Auxilia (Rhodesia 62). The resulting photograph appeared in South African newspapers, under the headline 'Johannes still believes in apartheid' and with suggestions there was more to it than a simple walk. Johannes was annoyed, especially at his own naïvety—it was a reminder of the very public nature of the Forum.[31]

Auxilia was the first black Rhodesian delegate, her presence reflecting the changing dynamics of race and politics there. Previous white delegates Gerry (Rhodesia 60) and Jeremy (Rhodesia 61) had taken pains to distinguish their government's policies from those of their southern neighbor. Gerry was pleased to report upon her return from the Forum that 'Our country is jumping forward very quickly, developing into a multi-racial state very fast ... and what astounds everyone is, it works!'.[32]

Like Israeli delegates, white South African delegates were outnumbered at the Forum. Unlike Israeli delegates, there was little public support for their country's regime beyond the Forum, for all that the US had its own racial issues. They were under pressure, but all were articulate, well-educated, and well-briefed. The surviving films from the 1950s show South African delegates vigorously defending apartheid, insisting that it was not discriminatory but equitable. Not many went as far as Dicks (SA 56), who suggested that the Africans in South Africa were incapable, having not learned 'the Western idea of work', insisting 'the ANC were the aggressors'. Marlene (SA 55) was more typical, delivering a well-rehearsed propaganda prospectus extolling apartheid as separate development for 'natives' who were 'about 200 years behind us in civilization'. White South Africans were 'having a very hard time trying to get them on the same level as we are', gradually 'giving them more rights ... as they develop'. She concluded, rather piously, 'We South Africans feel it is our duty to help the less fortunate people in our country, and we are doing our very best for them'.

Helen Waller told Marlene that 'for a difficult position', she had made her case 'very effectively', but, never one to miss an opportunity, suggested Fifi (Ghana 55) might 'have a word with Marlene'. He obliged, asking her how it was that 'the African in South Africa is 200 years behind the European, but the African in West Africa is *so near* the European' (my emphasis).[33] Significantly, despite challenging the South African regime, Fifi appeared to accept a racial hierarchy with Europeans at the top. He was not alone.

Watching the television programs from a twenty-first-century perspective, one is struck by the pervasiveness of the loaded language of colonialism, which carried assumptions of hierarchies of 'modernity', 'progress' and 'development' that placed white nations at the top. This was an era of decolonization, but even non-white delegates appeared to subscribe to the rankings of states in terms of their 'development'. The US was modern and developed, Britain was less modern but highly developed, the rest of Europe sophisticated. White settler colonies, Australia, New Zealand, and South Africa, whose delegates were always white (except one New Zealander), were also 'developed' rather than 'developing', although, like the US they were 'new' nations, their histories perceived as beginning with colonization. Other places, especially those in Africa, striving for independence, were 'developing'. Kenya, announced the British delegate in 1959, was not 'ready' for independence. In another debate, rebutting Dicks' idea of African incapability, Alfred 'Nini' (Ghana 56) said his country had 'been able to develop everything ... themselves', but then added, that was only after British assistance. But then he doubled down: 'Everyone knows that Africa is for Africans and when we think of African we think of Blacks'.[34]

African politics was not just about Black vs White, although that issue dominated debates. Helen Waller was adept at bringing out some of the other points of contention. Mohammed (Nigeria 56) told of a religious divide: 'In northern Nigeria we often feel that Africa is for Muslims not for Christians'. Nebiat (Ethiopia 56) caused raised eyebrows when he announced that he 'never felt that I was a Negro until I came to the US'. His teachers had told him he was 'a sunburned Hebrew'. His successor in the Forum, Mesfin (Ethiopia 57), repeated this on the equivalent television program, much to the amusement of his fellow panelists. Amelia (Ghana 57) could not stop her mouth twitching into a smile, while open laughter was heard from Susan (SA 57) and Boniface (Nigeria 57), as Mesfin insisted that Ethiopians considered black Africans 'inferior', and that he came from the lost tribe of Israel. Amelia then said that Ghanaians considered 'Nigerians were mostly beggars', while Boniface was equally dismissive of Ghanaians as 'overly individualistic'.[35]

Bizuayehu (Ethiopia 59) was proud that Ethiopia had never been a colony. 'We don't want to marry with the white people' because white people might 'want to make Ethiopia a colony'. Teklu (Ethiopia 60) told me he 'had no idea about the racial situation' in South Africa and Rhodesia. 'Being Ethiopian is a strong national identity; the white/black problem was irrelevant'. He was impressed with the knowledge of his 'African sister in white skin', as he called Gerry (Rhodesia 60), but the Forum experience meant he began to expand his understanding of countries that comprised Africa, and introduced him to pan-Africanism.[36]

Focusing both on the extreme policy of apartheid in South Africa and probing intra-African divisions and prejudices was part of contextualizing American segregation. When self-described 'country bumpkin Afrikaner boy', Johannes (SA 62), was 'baited by questions on race relations in the US versus SA', he declared that 'the US seemed to have its race problems too'.[37] But white American students watching the programs in the 1950s and 1960s would be permitted to feel that the racism in their country was not so bad after all.

Having been a constant presence since 1954, South African delegates pretty much disappeared after 1962. There were only two further South African delegates, in 1967 and 1968. Perhaps this reflected the State Department's decreasing enthusiasm for the regime after the 1960 Sharpeville Massacre. In any case, the developing civil rights movement had brought discussions of race closer to home. Alberto (Guatemala 63) was not alone among delegates in the 1960s in identifying the civil rights as 'the issue of the moment'.[38]

In Our Own Backyard: Segregation

'Americans must realize that the majority of the people in the world are not white,' announced Mahipala (Mike) (Ceylon 58) on television. American racism and segregation were key issues for the Forum from the very first international Forum, hosting delegates from Canada and South and Central America. Planning the group's trip to Maryland, Helen hit a roadblock. What to do about Maurice (Haiti 47)? A frantic correspondence with the United Nations Association of Maryland ensued. Helen wanted to include Maurice in all activities *and* to find him a white host family. She reminded the UNA that delegates had been hitherto 'agreeably ... surprised to learn that in our schools here colored and white students work and play together on terms of equality', suggesting that this good 'report' taken back to their own countries would be affected if Maurice was not included. 'I realize that this would be impossible if he were a United States' Negro', Helen Waller continued, in a startling acknowledgement of racial policies in the American South. She felt, however, that the UNA, like the UN itself, would surely not 'discriminate against a colored person who is an official delegate of his own country'. She helpfully suggested Maurice might speak at 'one of your Negro high schools' while other delegates went to white schools and also included a list of another four delegates who would 'be willing to speak in Negro schools'.[39] Her approach worked, but her negotiations underscored a perennial problem for Forum delegates of color.

In public forums, Helen was decidedly less frank. She generally managed to successful contextualize segregation, following State Department guidelines, suggesting that America was 'not the only country with problems' and was 'doing better' than before. She was gratified when during the 1956 group's Berlin tour, Gerhard (Germany 54) who accompanied them, stepped up to defend the US from 'a sharp attack on the "overbearing" Americans', reminding Germans (rather naïvely?) that 'the American racial problem was only a hundred years old, and was decreasing, while the German prejudice against Jews was five hundred years old and hadn't been solved yet'.[40] In the 1960s, Robert Huffman had a harder job than Helen, as the civil rights movement gained momentum.

Delegates witnessed segregation, most often when they went south, although I was surprised how many (mostly white, male) delegates did not notice. Others were often shaken. Ibrahim (Lebanon 58) found it a 'shock ... when in Virginia we saw the blacks only and whites only bathrooms, public toilets'. He remembered that the 'very dark' Sudanese and Egyptian delegates 'really agonized over this, they didn't know which one to go to'. White-blonde Jona (Iceland 60) and Nani (Ghana 61) 'caused quite a stir' when they walked down the street together in Washington DC. Susana (Ecuador 47) saw the 'Whites Only' and 'Coloreds Only' signs as she traveled through Miami en route to New York, reflecting in 2011 that President Obama's election would have been unthinkable in 1947.[41]

The 1962 group visited Greensboro, North Carolina, where two years before students had successfully desegregated Woolworths lunch counters by staging a sit-in. Traveling through Virginia, however, delegates had difficulties finding places to eat as a mixed-race group. In one diner, where 'the atmosphere was not exactly warm', Suzanne (UK 62) remembered David (Kenya 62) 'sat next to me at a segregated lunch counter ... maintaining his dignity and controlling his fear'. Casey's Diner, near Richmond, was better, she recalled. The manager eventually agreed to serve them, 'risking a disturbance that [might] result in a loss of his licence [sic] and livelihood'. The 'untidy', 'but very cheerful and extremely hungry' group rushed in and filled up the tables, 'talking at the top of our voices', and playing 'Forum favourites' [sic] on the jukebox. Another customer (Suzanne labelled him a 'poor white') watched 'in amazement' but 'did not move away'. The manager told the story on local television that evening. Thenceforth, wrote Suzanne proudly, 'black and white may eat in Casey's Diner', concluding 'on the wall behind the counter hangs a picture of 37 faces, 37 smiles of hope and thanks from all over the world'.[42]

Whether or not the Forum singlehandedly desegregated Casey's Diner, the discrimination they faced in Southern states wase not unusual for foreign non-white visitors, even high-ranking ones (despite Helen Waller's suggestion in 1947). Like Forum delegates, diplomats representing newly independent African nations at the UN in the early 1960s were infamously refused service at cafés along Route 40 between New York and Washington DC, causing State Department officials to worry that such experiences of American racism would push African nations towards Russia and communism.[43]

Within this context, Forum staff, *Tribune* owners, and the State Department were all curious to know delegates' opinions about segregation. When Helen invited public commentary, however, she did so well-prepared. She asked Minoo (Iran 58) on television, 'wasn't it you that said you thought that the American government appointed committees to kill Negroes?' Minoo agreed that she had read this in newspapers at home, but 'couldn't see it here...I saw a little segregation, but not as much as' she expected. She neatly illustrated the inaccuracy of foreign propaganda, the benefits of the Forum itself *and* the idea that segregation was not as bad as suggested. Helen Waller had done well. Bizuayehu (Ethiopia 59) was similarly tactful in the alumni newsletter: 'few people believed' her in Ethiopia when she said segregation 'is not as bad as it was talked about'. Understandably, they thought that she 'was saying it just because the Americans were good to' her. She concluded more strongly that the world would 'not easily forgive the US unless what is going on, however little, *completely stops*' (my emphasis).[44]

In 1956 Helen invited African delegates to describe discrimiiiition they had experienced. Nebiat (Ethiopia 56) could not get a haircut in a 'strictly white residential New Jersey community' for about two weeks because 'the white man don't [sic] know how to cut this type of hair'. He felt this was discrimination: 'the United States is a business country and if they discourage their customers by their types of hair then they are defeating their own purpose'. Conversely, Nini (Ghana 56) went looking for segregation. But, he said 'they know I am a foreigner'. Even with an American haircut and American clothes, he stood out as different.[45] Racism, he seemed to be saying, was only targeted domestically, at least around New York.

Ten years later, American Robert Koslow (host of Mamud, Sierra Leone 66) also noted that 'American and foreign blacks were very different'. He suggested perceptively that African Americans suffered discrimination daily, while those from overseas were less exposed to it and had more confidence and a different perspective on the world. African Forum delegates were also an elite—the most intelligent, well-educated, and sometimes well-connected of their generation—so it was inevitable that they exuded more self-confidence than many of the American students they encountered.[46]

Delegates also made the distinction. Duangtip (Thailand 62) described the African delegates and the African Americans she met in Greenboro, North Carolina, as 'worlds apart'. The delegates were 'nice … gentle'. Dancing with African American undergraduates on a field trip, however, 'terrified' her. They were tall, large, and 'smelt of onions … and the way they pulled you in.' She escaped and hid in the bathroom. It was a 'horrible experience', she said. She was 'glad she met the delegates first'. Emmanuel (Ghana 68) found it 'very troublesome' that he 'couldn't get the accent' of 'American blacks' and 'when the American whites spoke I understood them better'. He had 'easier dealings' with whites, although perhaps he met more at his overwhelmingly white host schools.[47]

High schools in the north were not immune from segregation, although it could be informal. Ginger (Summer 64) admitted that her own Montclair High welcomed foreign students and the World Youth Forum, but except for sports teams and a few clubs, there was 'little mixing between black and white students'. She confessed later that 'I didn't know why, nor did I think about it much. The separation, the difference and distance, were things we just accepted.' Similarly, Erik (Denmark 55) remembered American white boys being 'embarrassed' when challenged by a European female delegate, who was staying with an African American host, about why they 'refused to dance with colored girls'. Erik's host explained that 'this community is not mature [enough] for intermarriage'. Minh (Vietnam 65) told me, 'I never saw a black person in any of the social gathering at all'. In January 1962, Suzanne (UK 62) recorded in her diary that the 'large coloured [sic] group' at her second host school, Metuchen High, seemed to 'keep together and not to mix with the other kids at mealtimes'. She thought this was because integration was 'a comparatively new thing', although she also suggested they might 'prefer their own company'. Not far away, she wrote, Dwight Morrow High School in Englewood was 'having a great problem with the integration of the coloured [sic] students, they are not being given equal rights'. African American parents and students 'were staging boycotts and protest marches'. As Suzanne said, 'it's unfortunate that the delegate from Tanganyka [sic], happens to be the visiting student just at this time'.[48] Sadly no record survives of his reaction.

Harlem, Black Power and Civil Rights

For many delegates, Harlem symbolized the civil rights movement and African American culture and activism. Gerhard (Germany 54) went to Harlem 'as a tourist', but later host families told delegates it was dangerous. School friends took Snait (Israel 61) 'unofficially'. Joachim (Germany 71) went on a 'sort of tour' with a 'priest who was active' there, attending a church service, but being told to 'lock the doors when you are traveling through Harlem by car'. Peter (UK 65) went to Harlem unintentionally, after making a mistake on the subway, going north instead of south. Realizing his error, he got off to change platforms but had to go up to street level. When he emerged from the station, he found himself in the center of Harlem; the only other white person in sight was the policeman directing traffic. The tension in the air was palpable—this was February 22, the morning after Malcolm X was shot. Peter made it home safely, recounting the tale to his 'horrified' host family.[49]

Unbeknownst to Peter, or to Forum staff, Malcolm X himself had a connection to the Forum. Ahmed (Sudan 60) delivered a eulogy at Malcolm X's funeral. He had met Malcolm on his own first visit to Harlem in 1963, while a student at Dartmouth College. The pair had become friends, Ahmed influential in Malcolm's later interpretations of Islam. There are echoes of the Forum, too, when Ahmed arranged Malcolm X's 1964 speech at Dartmouth College. 'The best hope for equality, he said, rested with the "youth of the world" and the "humans of the world working together"'.[50]

In 1964, European newspapers were full of 'images of rioting and fires in Harlem and other American cities'. German students asked Maria (Summer 64) 'about the "race riots" that were tearing up American cities that summer'. Maria remembered that 'We white high school kids were hard pressed to explain what was going on', because the civil rights movement was moving so rapidly. By the end of the 1960s it was in full swing. As Huffman explained to Forum alumni in 1969: 'The delegates also got a first-hand view of the problems in this country between the whites and the blacks, as many of you know from your reading, we are having serious problems in this respect.' They participated in a seminar on 'African Nationalism and Independence: Its Meaning to Black America', run by the World Affairs Council of Philadelphia and featuring African American writer Playthell Benjamin. Background notes were provided, but it is difficult to know whether the resulting seminar pushed beyond the academic and into activism.[51] It nevertheless gave Forum delegates insight into some of the issues galvanizing the protests they saw around them, if they were not already aware.

Some delegates, especially from 1965 onwards, 'got involved'. Michael (Australia 65) 'played pool with SNCC and CORE leaders in Harlem' and met Joan Baez and 'Martin Luther King Jr's white right-hand man', who invited him to attend the Selma–Montgomery marches in March 1965. Liv (Norway 70) and other young Forum radicals visited the Black Panthers in Harlem: 'we didn't understand that it could be dangerous'. One European delegate wanted to take his host brother to hear controversial African American feminist academic activist, Communist Party member, and Black Panthers affiliate, Angela Davis, but was told firmly by his host mother that it was 'out of the question'. She added, 'I am sure if you want to listen to Hitler-types, you can do that in your own country.'[52] Feelings ran high on both sides, and youth were on the front lines.

Beyond the US and Africa

Much of the race debate focus was on South Africa and segregation in the US, but sometimes other delegates were quizzed about their own countries. Evelyn (Brazil 59) was caught out after enthusing about the lack of racial prejudice in her country: 'Everyone intermarries... it is just wonderful... America could learn from this'. Helen Waller asked if she would marry a 'dark person'. She replied, 'No', but adroitly shifted the blame back to colonial powers: 'my family are recent immigrants from Europe and wouldn't approve'. One Australian delegate in the 1950s was surprised to be asked about Indigenous Australians. 'I didn't think there were racial prejudices in Australia until I came to America... our aborigines seemed to be a special case—interesting for scientists to study.'

She remembered talking about Aboriginal Australians as a 'dying race', a product of the education of her times. Australia was also attracting international censure for its White Australia policy, which all but banned non-white immigration to the country. Generally, Australian delegates got off lightly on this issue, although Eddie (Malaysia 65) remarked pointedly to Mike (Australia 65) on television that 'the Australians should associate themselves with the Asians more. But with the policy of the immigration law as it is I don't see how this can be possible', for once briefly silencing the voluble Australian panelist.[53]

A 'Baby UN'

Bringing together a group of young people from across the world in the name of international understanding was one thing, but the Forum went further. These teens were expected to discuss world issues, and to do so with competence. Huffman rightly called it a 'Baby UN'. Most delegates felt their views were taken seriously, by everyone, from American high school students to senators in Washington. The Forum was framed by the Cold War and there were some perennial issues, while others assumed greater importance as time went on. For some delegates the discussions were intensely personal—they had skin in the game—and the pressures spilled over into interpersonal relationships. There were real and immediate consequences. Most delegates did not radically shift in their opinions, but they were challenged to broaden their perspective and gain greater understanding of opposing views. By the end of the 1960s they were also caught up in the broader student protest movement as the Forum worked hard to remain relevant in a world in which young people were increasingly speaking on their own terms.

But the Forum was not all about serious discussions and solving the world's ills. There were privileges as a delegate, including seeing more of the US than just New York, and meeting a procession of political and creative celebrities. Field trips north, south and occasionally overseas, provided these opportunities.

Chapter 12
Beyond New York
Field Trips

The three-month Forum was punctuated with field trips, including, in very fortunate years, an extra international leg 'on the way home'. The extent, number, and glamor of field trips varied over time, depending on sponsorship, but they remained an important part of the Forum experience. Delegates discovered an America beyond New York and New Jersey, notably the center of political power, Washington DC. They saw the marvels of American modernity and industrialization in the steelworks and dam projects and were exposed to segregation in the American south. They often inspected university campuses. These trips were also opportunities to advertise the Forum, the *Herald Tribune*, and the US beyond New York, even internationally.

Delegates bonded during these trips, exchanging notes about host families, and (in some years) partying hard. Regine (France 62) had fond memories of all singing *La Vie En Rose* at the top of their voices on the bus trip to Washington. It was a heady time. Regine's roommate, Duangtip (Thailand), said to her one morning, 'Did you know that everything goes faster in America—even the sun rises faster!' Tord (Norway 63) diligently worked his way around the bus 'interviewing' delegates about their 'background, political and cultural aspects of their countries etc'. Meanwhile Catriona (UK 63), Ethel (US), Gideon (Israel), and Apichai (Thailand) were the core of that year's 'lighthearted "back-of-the-bus" gang', with Catriona composing many 'political-spoof lyrics' for their singing. Meanwhile Bob Huffman often had a busy time separating canoodling couples as the bus wended its way to its next destination. [1]

'Catapulting Across America'

The field trips were no leisurely holidays, but were packed with activities, discussions, sightseeing, meetings with dignitaries, and more host schools and families. Delegates were rolled out for photo opportunities and performances of their carefully prepared debates on various platforms, and were expected to mingle intelligently and sociably with a variety of people. It was non-stop.

Most trips were within the US. The most extensive was in 1949, when the fortunate 'Marshall Plan' delegates saw more of the US than most, traveling 6000 miles from coast to coast, pausing briefly in 'all ten major cities', reported the *Herald Tribune*. Sponsored and organized by the Civil Air Patrol (CAP), an auxiliary to the US Air Force, the group traveled in three Air Force passenger planes, escorted by the formidable Colonel Nancy Tier. It is unclear if this was a deliberate display of strong American womanhood or an understanding that babysitting a group of teenagers was women's work. Nashville, where warm southern hospitality contrasted with racial problems that were 'much worse' than expected, was followed by Dallas and Phoenix. In Los Angeles, delegates had the obligatory movie studio tour, 'traded mementoes with movie stars', and witnessed 'the shooting of ... a film' scene. They saw American Indian dances in Albuquerque, rode horses in Denver, and toured the Ford River Rouge plant in Detroit. Most were impressed, although one delegate was bemused by the 'catapulting across America visiting many states for one or two days at a time'. It was 'so tiring'. She later wondered 'what lasting purpose it served', while noting perceptively that, of course, 'one was aware that the organizers of the Forum wanted maximal exposure for the delegates'.[2]

This trans-American jaunt was never repeated to the same extent. The following year, CAP flew delegates south for a week in Dallas, then on to Chattanooga, and the delights of the Tennessee Valley Authority, before ending in Washington DC. With two CAP officials, two State Department press officers, two Voice of America broadcasters, and Helen Waller, they filled two C-47s. Local newspapers also followed them around, underscoring the exposure value of the tour. The *Dallas Morning News* had a story about 'Frisky Cyrus' (Iran 50). During the tour of newspaper headquarters, the 'mischevious [sic] 16-year-old' had managed to 'ask more questions about newspapering than several experts could answer', 'apply for a job as a research librarian and later as a reporter', 'step in front of an NBS television cameraman taking pictures of the presses running (but he smiled for the camera)', and 'get lost three times from the tour, protesting each time that he "was not lost only looking around for himself"'. Even more alarming, during the flight to Dallas Cyrus curiously turned a handle on the side of the aircraft. 'An escape hatch flew open' and he narrowly escaped being swept out 'through the hatch and to his death 10,000 feet below'.[3] Unsurprisingly, CAP did not volunteer again to fly the group of incorrigible teens around the country.

Later groups traveled by bus and train. Greyhound provided discounted buses, although Forum assistant Anne Counes complained to the company and to Jock Whitney in 1964 that 'Joe', their driver, 'was a bit too friendly shall we say', although she did not elaborate. He also often arrived late and, once, after he had 'made a big production of having been up since 4 a.m. checking over the bus', it broke down, causing a three-hour delay. Joe was replaced. (In Jock Whitney's formal thank you letter to Greyhound, this translated to tactful praise for 'your good offices in dealing with inevitable problems'.)[4]

After 1950, delegates only went as far south as Tennessee. The Tennessee Valley Authority (TVA) was a showpiece of American modernity and technology and a common destination for American and foreign student groups. The hydroelectricity project was innovative and potentially relevant to delegates from countries where water was a significant problem. As the *Tribune* reported in 1950, 'Safety and malaria-control work and other aspects of the project applicable to the students' native regions will be discussed in detail'. The TVA was a New Deal project, a successful example of a government-led economic project, with the hydroelectric dam as a centerpiece, supporting regional development programs. It became a global model, fundamental to US overseas programs. Its federal ownership was unusual in the US, which prided itself on private enterprise. This was not lost on 1962 delegates, who visited both the TVA and the Bethlehem Steel Company, a private industrial megalith. One delegate was surprised that both 'socialism' and 'capitalism' could exist in the same system. Supreme Court Justice William O Douglas felt in 1951 that the TVA might 'be utilized as one of the major influences to turn back the tide of communism which today threatens to engulf Asia'. His endorsement was a little ironic, given that TVA was controversially the target of McCarthy's anti-communist investigators in the early fifties.[5]

Regardless of destinations, the itineraries were packed. The 1952 and 1953 groups crossed the border north for a ten-day visit to Toronto, sponsored by the Toronto Branch of the United Nations Association (UNA) in Canada. They attended school, stayed with host families, participated in staged UNA forums, saw a hockey game, visited Niagara Falls, and danced with their hosts and friends at Toronto's 'castle', Casa Loma. Then it was straight off to Washington for a round of senators and sightseeing. The 1966 group left New York for Princeton University on a bus on a Sunday afternoon; their day included a two-hour bus trip, cocktail reception, and banquet (complete with Dean's welcome and a speech by Professor Fred Harbison on the economics of 'developing areas'). An 'informal mixer' at 10 pm rounded off the day. The following morning allowed for 'free time with hosts' and visits to classes, before a chemistry lecture, organized discussions with International Affairs Council Regional Committees, and, at 8 pm, a Model UN meeting on Rhodesia, in the wake of its 1965 Unilateral Declaration of Independence (despite there being no Rhodesian delegate that year).[6]

The benefit of the field trip was not just one way. Delegates were introduced to the US, but the US was also introduced to the Forum (and to the *Herald Tribune*). After the 1956 group performed 'the Forum' to great acclaim in Atlantic City, New Jersey, Helen toyed with grand plans to have 'five or six Forum projects operating simultaneously in as many US cities', starting with St Louis in 1958.[7] The 1958 group did visit St Louis, sponsored in part by local organizations, but there was neither the budget, the staff nor the desire to continue it so far beyond the reach of the *Tribune*'s readership.

'One Senator at Breakfast and Another at Lunch'

Delegates visited Washington DC every year, often sponsored by Scholastic Magazines. Teklu (Ethiopia 60) remembered Washington DC 'blew my mind'—it was 'so new and exciting'.[8] They were escorted around the principal monuments, visited the White House, the Pentagon, and Library of Congress, and met with State Department officials, congressmen and women, and senators.

Delegates were sometimes entertained at their own embassies, with varying degrees of enthusiasm. Saroj (Thailand 58) remembered being so acclimatized after two months in the US that he stuttered in Thai when dining with the Thai ambassador. 'I don't think he took me very seriously', said Saroj, 'he sat and had dinner and let his wife talk' to me. In later life, 'when I became a foreign ministry official, I never reminded him of our meeting!' Eline (SA 54) was chauffeur-driven in a long limousine to her embassy, a butler taking her coat and ushering her up a long flight of stairs to have 'a cocktail' with Ambassador Jooste and his wife. When offered a drink, she thought 'this occasion needs something special and, rather than requesting 'sweet wine', which would have been appropriate, she remembered the drink the American sitting next to her on the plane had repeatedly ordered: 'A Scotch, thank you, Mr Jooste', she said. This was 'without the slightest idea what a Scotch was', she admitted decades later, 'and it was horrible!' She was grateful the ambassador poured her a *very* small and *very* weak drink. The Pakistani embassy entertained all the delegates in the early 1960s—it could scarcely do otherwise as the Ambassador's daughter had been Pakistan's 1958 delegate.[9]

Maarten (Netherlands 61) summed up his Washington trip as 'one senator at breakfast and another at lunch'. Delegates enjoyed political discussions in which senators and officials spoke to them seriously, appearing to listen sincerely to their views. Emmanuel (Ghana 68) was delighted that the assistant secretary for Africa at the State Department actually 'knew about our countries—it was nice...impressive.' There were moments of light relief. Tissa (Ceylon 59) remembered that at a Congressional Hotel lunch a senator persuaded Nalini (India 59) to ask Lyndon Johnson if he had presidential ambitions while. 'This she did with the innocence of somebody who knew nothing of the intricacies of US politics'. It was 1959, barely a year before Johnson would make an unsuccessful run against Kennedy for the Democratic nomination. Johnson was suitably 'embarrassed' and there was much laughter.[10]

The availability of senators and political functionaries depended on the year: Senator Eugene McCarthy appeared in 1956, JFK's brother-in-law, Sargent Shriver of the Peace Corps, met delegates in 1961. Even when the Forum was on the wane, connections in Washington pulled strings. In 1969 delegates met the father of Forum assistant Connie Walker, US Secretary of Agriculture and ex-Governor of Minnesota, Orville Freeman. They also particularly remembered meeting Teddy Kennedy and the man Bob Huffman later called 'that idiot Spiro Agnew when he was Vice President'. In 1970 delegates visited the World Bank, lunched with a foreign service officer and, possibly most interestingly for them, met Vietnam Moratorium committee coordinator Sam Brown.[11]

'Shaking Hands with JFK' or Another President

Meeting the US president was a bonus. Early delegates met President Truman. Amongst the treasured memorabilia of Thor (Norway 48) is a souvenir Parker pen inscribed 'I Swiped This From HARRY S. TRUMAN', demonstrating a surprising sense of humor from the Oval Office. Between 1953 and 1957, President Eisenhower shook hands, posed for photographs, and accepted gifts. Kaarina (Finland 56) 'shook hands with him twice' outside the White House, while Judith (UK 56) found him 'charming'—he 'liked the British very much because his chauffeur in Europe had been a young Englishwoman'. Yoriko (Japan 56) not only shook hands with Eisenhower but remembered that 'Mrs Eisenhower winked at me'. Chotima (Thailand 57) gave the president a Thai khon giant hermit mask. 'Unbelievably it looked just like him', giggled one delegate, and indeed there was an uncanny resemblance! Did Eisenhower get bored with meeting teenagers? From 1958 to 1960 there was no presidential audience. 'He was out playing golf or something', Ibrahim (Lebanon 58) grumbled.[12] The reason for the president's loss of interest is unclear, although he did have health problems. It was certainly not due to the newspaper's change of ownership. John Hay Whitney was one of Eisenhower's major supporters and his ambassador to the UK.

In 1960 presidential aide Homer Guenther welcomed delegates to the Oval Office and accepted gifts on Eisenhower's behalf. Some were government gifts. Gerry (Rhodesia 60) presented two copper bowls from her prime minister. Tamar (Israel 60) came bearing a porcelain oil lamp dating back to the first century. Jona (Iceland 60) brought a replica Icelandic spinning wheel. Others were more local. Leevi (Finland 60) had a crystal bowl made in his home town. Onder (Turkey 58) had gone one step further, carving a chess set himself. It is unfortunate that having gone to such trouble he did not get to meet Eisenhower personally.[13]

The arrival of John F Kennedy in the White House saw meetings resumed. JFK was no stranger to the Forum. Naila (Pakistan 58) told a good story of sitting 'right next' to Senator Kennedy in 1958, when he came to speak to Forum delegates. 'His thigh was touching mine, and someone said, "he will be the next president", and I went "really?", … he looked like an older young person—very slim and charming'. Another delegate remembered wondering why on earth they had to go and listen to this unknown senator, Jack Kennedy.[14]

Three years later he was president, and many delegates from 1961 to 1963 have treasured photographs of their meetings with him. These meetings continued, even after Kennedy canceled his subscription to the unapologetically Republican-leaning *New York Herald Tribune* in the middle of 1962. The political furor surrounding 'the banning of the *Tribune* from the White House' did not seem to touch the Forum. The Kennedys, both JFK and his younger brothers, Robert and Teddy, as well as Sargent Shriver, brought real star power to the Forum. Katherine (Kit) (US 61) and her cohort became restless waiting to 'catch a glimpse' of JFK, and 'began to sing "He'll be comin' round the White House if he comes"', despite their advisors trying 'half-heartedly to quiet us'. Then the man of the moment appeared. 'He not only came into the room but actually spent some time with us asking questions and listening to our responses', recalled Kit, as clearly as if it were yesterday. 'He seemed so much more real and human than the figure seen on television'. Maarten (Netherlands 61) remembered Kennedy quipped, 'I guess you are all going to be prime ministers of your countries someday?', before turning to one of the delegates. 'Where are you from?' Of all the group he had singled out Mack (US 61), who was not from some exotic foreign realm, but from 'New York, Mr President!' The newly inaugurated president then spoke appropriately of his latest initiative, the Peace Corps, which had synergies with the ideals of the Forum. JFK paid particular attention to the pretty girls in the group, lingering over the gift from the tall, blonde Kirsten (Denmark 61) (See cover photo). 'We were all jealous!', one boy told me, although of JFK or Kirsten he didn't say. Two years later, Irini (Greece 63) was more impressed with Robert Kennedy. Jack, she felt 'held his office' very seriously. Robert, on the other hand, 'was like an ordinary citizen, very friendly, very open, he chatted with us'. She smiled, remembering that his very large formal carved desk had 'his children's drawings ... scotch taped on it'. Presidential encounters ended with JFK. Presidents Johnson and Nixon did not entertain visiting Forum delegates.[15]

Delegates also met politicians, ambassadors, and high-ranking civil servants beyond Washington. In New York they visited the UN. The finales were held there in 1954 and 1955, allowing delegates to imagine themselves as UN representatives in the future. And some were, even during Forum years: Helen Waller made much of Eddie (Malaya 50) and Vangala (India 54), both at the UN in the 1950s. Having connections was all important. *Tribune* reporter Darius Jhabvala, 'our man at the UN', was of 'immeasurable help' to Anne Counes, who told John Hay Whitney in 1964 that, 'besides helping me count heads for the tours, he secures speakers for us ... and gives a very interesting talk to the delegates about being a reporter at the UN'. The year before, Darius had recruited as a speaker, UK Ambassador to the UN Sir Patrick Dean, who 'enjoyed the question-and-answer session so much that he invited the Commonwealth delegates to his home for a dinner party'.[16]

Hobnobbing with Stars

'Having my picture taken with Ingrid Bergman', 'meeting Eleanor Roosevelt', and 'jamming with Pete Seeger' ranked high in delegates' memories. Harry Belafonte, 'a beautiful young man not much older than us ... just becoming famous', thrilled delegates in 1956 when he sang to them in 'a lovely flat overlooking the park'. Tissa (Ceylon 59) recalled that, alongside serious political heavyweights Thurgood Marshall, Senator Lyndon Johnson, and Congressmen Brooks Hays and Dalip Saund, he met Pete Seeger, Harry Belafonte, and Count Basie. The Forum provided unimagined opportunities for delegates to meet a cavalcade of celebrities and influential people. Helen Rogers Reid and John Hay Whitney both entertained the delegates at their homes, as did Pan Am boss Juan Trippe, who held a lavish cocktail party in his mansion on a private beach. Several lucky delegates arrived by private helicopter. British delegates John (58) and later Catriona (63) were most impressed when they visited the guest cloakroom during the fabulous annual party. 'There was a real Picasso hanging in the loo!' John commented on this marvel to his host, who allegedly remarked drily, 'Well of course, it is *only* a Picasso'.[17]

In 1948 Annelise and Johnny (both Denmark 48) met with Danish pianist Victor Borge, providing a photo opportunity with their American host students for the *Tribune*. Hazel (Ireland 48) from Belfast was a 'guest of honor' at the Ulster-Irish Society's annual dinner at the Waldorf Astoria, rubbing shoulders with Eleanor Roosevelt. Judith (UK 56) also met Eleanor Roosevelt, who had 'the most vivid blue eyes I think I have ever seen' and was 'the most memorable person' Judith met. 'Invited to afternoon tea in her cottage, I was overwhelmed by her kindness, modesty, and intelligence. She had made me a chocolate cake and before her other guests arrived, we had a delightful and easy chat about several things: her great love of England, the Royal Family, our literature, and the bond between our countries.' Judith had just come from a formal and rather stifling visit to the British Embassy, so was easily charmed by Eleanor, who 'opened her own front door and made the tea and served the cake' with 'no apparent servants or butler'.[18]

Sometimes the celebrity value was lost on delegates, at least at the time. Teklu (Ethiopia 60) enjoyed Pete Seeger's visit, but 'had no idea who he was'. It was 'a very happy occasion, but the importance of it was lost on me', he recalled, rather shamefacedly decades later. Cora (US 59) certainly knew who Pete Seeger was and had strong memories of sitting in a circle with him. 'He asked us to sing songs of our countries … when he didn't know the song, he learned it from singing it with us.' They also 'sang "Everyone Loves Saturday Night" in more than a dozen languages'. More amazingly, when she shyly approached him decades later at a People's Music Network gathering, Pete Seeger stopped her mid-introduction; 'Don't tell me—you're Cora Brooks, and you were with the Forum years ago'. John (UK 59) reflected that it said a lot about Helen Waller and the Forum, that 'the first person we were introduced to from the world outside' the Forum was Pete Seeger, 'so untypical of 1950s America', an activist who was an 'admitted communist' with 'progressive' views.[19]

The Reid and Whitney families were well-connected socially and politically. Helen Waller made the most of the connections, ensuring a network of the great and the good were on hand and that delegates had access to key figures. Robert Huffman was less adept at this, or perhaps he operated at a different level, especially after the *Tribune* folded. he had the support of the IOS Foundation's Ruth Bishop, who was ineffably elegant and internationally influential in UNA circles, and James Roosevelt (and forum assistant Connie Walker), but this did not translate into the sort of upper level political or showbiz clout of previous decades.

International Reach

Impressing foreign delegates with American star power and modernity was one thing, but the Forum had broader aims. As Richard Kluger noted, the extension of the Forum overseas 'carrying the HT flag', fitted Ogden Reid's ambition to make 'the Trib a political force and free-world voice'.[20] Ogden Reid was not alone. The *Tribune* had a European edition, and the Reids, Whitneys, and the Forum directors all had ambitions to enhance the *Tribune*'s influence beyond the US. This did not mean, however, they would pay for overseas jaunts. Just as the Toronto Branch of the UNA had chipped in for the Canadian excursions in 1952 and 1953, other backers were required for more extensive perambulations.

After border hops to Canada in 1952 and 1953, the next (and most ambitious) of the overseas trips was in 1955. The Forum and Sarah Lawrence College joined forces and applied for a Ford Foundation grant. The original proposal was that 'the majority of the delegates ... excluding South Americans and Africans, who depart ... in different directions', and including 'most of the Europeans and all of the Middle Easterners and Asians' would travel as a group and perform the Forum in Rome, Cairo, Beirut, Karachi, and New Delhi, thus allowing a 'large number of young people' internationally to 'share the "mind-stretching" experience which this Forum group never fails to provide for the American student audiences'. Joining the Forum students were two Sarah Lawrence College girls and staff member Ed Solomon. College Dean Esther

Raushenbush was skeptical about the educational value of the 'whizzing trip around Europe and Asia'. Despite being an 'entertaining stunt', and good publicity for both the *Herald Tribune* and the College, she told College president Harold Taylor: 'I should think it would give a student indigestion', with little to recommend it beyond 'the lark they would get out of a two-week round-trip of this kind and one-night stands in strange cities in odd places'.[21]

In the end, the trip included most of the delegates, along with two lucky College girls, Joy Reidel and Emily (Lee) Workum, who was also Helen Waller's neighbor. Lee later wrote a Columbia MA thesis about the Forum, using her privileged access to Helen's Forum records. The group went to London and Paris, then split in two. Half, along with Joy, and staff members Doris Wolff and Ed Solomon, went to Beirut. The other half went with Lee and Helen Waller to Cairo. The Cairo group joined the others in Beirut before they all moved on to Karachi and then New Delhi. The delegates 'performed' their Forum panels in front of audiences of school students and adults. In some places they stayed with host families, but were usually in hostels or student accommodation.

Reports of the trip from Helen Waller, Doris Wolff, and Ed Solomon indicate it was not an unqualified success. Much of Doris's time was spent chasing up airline tickets, rearranging unsatisfactory accommodation, or running after stray delegates, except when she fell ill in Beirut, and all the responsibility fell to Ed Solomon. He apparently acquitted himself superbly, with both Doris and Helen appreciative of his support. Helen admired 'his warm, friendly, and unusually sensitive relationship with the students'. She told Solomon's boss Harold Taylor that she had 'rarely known a human being who, intuitively, is so aware of which person in a group is self-conscious, lonely, ill-at-ease and who seeks them out and sets things right with such imperceptible grace'. One wonders what Ed Solomon (who was copied in) made of this, given his own opinion of the Forum, and more particularly of Helen herself. He had reported that 'the Foreign Forums were successful in light of their purpose'. Joy Riedel and Lee Workum had had 'an interesting and enlightening experience', but their position was 'ill-defined', as they were not identified as American Sarah Lawrence students. He conceded that 'no bad mistakes were made' and 'everyone wants the Forum back', but was less enthusiastic about Helen Waller, who, 'has a good deal of hostility toward the College and does not want any help (or interference as she would interpret it) from us', he told Harold Taylor, firmly. He concluded, 'That suits me.'[22]

The Politics of Taking the Forum to the Middle East

Gur (Israel 55) was one of those who left the group in London before Beirut and Cairo. Was he due home anyway, excluded by Lebanese and Egyptian authorities, or banned by Israel from going on? Decades later he could not remember anything significant about his departure. I asked another Israeli alumna, who was sanguine. 'To me it seems so natural that if group is invited to a country we have no relations with—we just don't go … we have been living like that since 1948'. In any case, not every delegate was included in the 1955 trip, so the Israeli's absence went unnoticed. Six years later, however, Helen Waller's attitude had shifted. In 1961 the Egyptian government invited 'the entire 1961 Forum group to visit Cairo for two weeks as guests of the Egyptian government "except the Israeli delegate"'. Helen told Jock Whitney, 'an invitation on those terms obviously cannot be accepted'. She then demonstrated her irrepressible, idealistic opportunism by suggesting to Jock that 'perhaps we should take advantage of this opening to explore, at a fairly high diplomatic level, the future possibility of a blanket group visa that would include the Israeli without calling attention to the fact. It could be a small, but nevertheless significant, contribution to relaxation of tensions in that area'. Given that the whole point of the Forum was maximum publicity, the presence of the Israeli delegate would surely have been noticed. Her suggestion was not taken up, thankfully for Snait (Israel 61) who, when I told her of this plan, was horrified. She did 'not want to even imagine what could have happened had the true identity of such a person been exposed while there'.[23] This incident typified Waller's approach, which as we have seen, at times bordered on irresponsible manipulation in search of a good headline.

The Importance of Europe

The trip to the Middle East was not repeated, and, while the Israeli-Arab situation was a popular topic at the Forum, the real interest was in Europe.

Helen Waller spoke three European languages, had spent time there during the war, and took family climbing holidays in the Swiss Alps. But it went beyond her personal predilections. The *Tribune* had a European edition based in Paris, and the reconstruction of post-war Europe along with the development of NATO were topical issues. In the 1950s several Western European countries had large communist political parties; for the US government, Europe was another front line in the Cold War. In 1956 the Forum accepted an invitation to visit Berlin from the Federal Ministry for All-German Affairs. The invitation came at the instigation of Eleanor Lansing Dulles of the USIS's Office of German Affairs. Eleanor, reputedly dubbed the 'Mother of Berlin' for her role in revitalizing culture and the economy in Berlin, was the sister of CIA director John Foster Dulles and US Secretary of State Allan Dulles. If there was ever any doubt that the Forum was working in lockstep with the US government, it was surely dispelled by now. Both Helen and the USIA were delighted with the week in Berlin.

Helen told Ogden Reid that the trip was 'successful beyond my wildest hopes ... infinitely surpassing in importance anything we did on the world trip last year.' By 'success' and 'importance', she meant publicity. 'All the Berlin morning newspapers carried extensive accounts and photographs' of the Forum and 'several front-paged it'. A 45-minute television program and radio broadcasts followed, and a newsreel was 'being shown in all the cinemas'. She emphasized that 'the *Herald Tribune* has been far more prominently featured than we would ourselves. Delegates were 'recognized and sought out ... everywhere in street cars and subways', while 'a large coterie of Berlin students, including a large number who have recently fled from the East Zone, has attached themselves to us'. She described how they 'all felt in the midst of a widening circle of enthusiasm'. Equally pleased, the USIS office also reported the Forum's foray to Berlin was 'truly successful', claiming credit for 'the suggestion of the Department's Office of German Affairs' for the visit. 'USIS Berlin cooperated extensively with the Berlin office of the Federal Ministry for All-German Affairs, the official host for the group'. Particularly pleasing was the reflected glory: the visit demonstrated 'the significance Americans attach to the Berlin situation' and 'active American dedication to furthering world peace and international understanding'. Finally (and most importantly?), 'having just spent three royal months in the US, the delegates were quite pro-American, and rather demonstratively so, and made no bones about it'.[24]

The Forum group returned to Berlin for the following two years, although plans to include an additional stop in Paris never eventuated. Helen Waller was always looking to expand the Forum's reach and visibility to ensure its survival and Paris, the base of the *Tribune*'s European edition, was an obvious choice, but Helen probably offended the paper's editor in her pitch. The paper 'will never take root as a European institution unless it consciously undertakes leadership in the direction Europe must grow', she wrote, envisaging the Forum as part and parcel of its rejuvenation.[25] Helen was not backward in providing advice to all and sundry whether requested or not. This must have made her a difficult colleague. The Paris idea was abandoned, and Germany's situation deteriorated, culminating in the building of the Berlin Wall in 1961. The 1959 group remained in the US, and the 1960 group went somewhere very different.

'Gone to ... Ghana!'

The title of Lynn's (US 60) account of the Forum's next jaunt emphasized her surprise that she was indeed 'Gone to ... Ghana!'. 'There I stood in my drip-dri dress with my wrinkle proof coat and crease-resistant hat, surrounded by weightless luggage, spilless bottles, collapsible toothbrushes, drinking cups, malaria pills, and Mother's last nervous contribution—a crackproof bottle of vitamin pills. Yet I still couldn't believe I was going to Ghana!'[26] Lynn might have slightly overpacked, but nothing could really prepare her for Ghana, where delegates received red-carpet treatment.

Rather than resulting from US government connections or editorial considerations, the 1960 Forum's trip to Ghana was the brainchild of alumnus Nii (Ghana 59), who elicited the invitation for the week-long visit from the Ghana Ministry of Education. New York University's School of Education co-sponsored the tour, having been 'instrumental in obtaining a gift of $22,100 from an anonymous donor' to cover some of the transportation costs. But the enthusiasm of Nii and other Ghana alumni, whom he co-opted to help, was central to ensuring its success. As Helen Waller wrote in the Forum newsletter: Nii 'followed through with single-minded devotion'.[27]

Delegates stayed in the University College, enjoying daily contact with Ghanaian students, and what Helen Waller described as 'the luxury of Ghana's enthusiastic hospitality that must be unique in the world'. An unexpected highlight was 'lunching on coconuts in the middle of the rain forest when the bus broke down halfway to Kumasi'. Attending the final session of the Positive Action Conference for Peace and Security in Africa and meeting Prime Minister Nkrumah and heads of the other African delegations had a profound impact. Some delegates 'saw the conference as a vast storehouse of energy to produce progress'. Others were less certain. 'I saw people jumping on chairs and shouting in Arabic, and this was so different from' Europe. 'Suddenly, a man from Liberia jumped up and began hysterically to deride colonialism', wrote one delegate. She felt 'the crowd swayed me back and forth like a huge angry sea, the waves of hatred rising higher and higher'. It was confronting: 'It was the first time in my life that I had ever felt "white"', she wrote, fearing that 'Africa wishes only to become a power equal or surpassing that of the United States and Russia', rather than, as she had hoped, 'an important link in the chain of international unity'.

Lynn (US 60) was underwhelmed by Prime Minister Nkrumah, who arrived late, which she felt was 'a deliberate attempt ... to build up expectation'. He gave a 'short, rather innocuous speech', during which he was loudly supported by two 'mammy traders', whom Lynn described as 'the market women who virtually control Ghana's wealth'. Another delegate was taken aback by Ghanaians' reactions to Nkrumah. 'It was like here is Christ coming, people threw themselves on the ground and kissed his hem'. She 'shook his hand', describing it jokingly decades later as 'my greatest claim to fame'.[28]

Ghana was at an important moment in its history. For the delegates, the contrast between the US and Ghana was extreme. Ghana was 'a nation moving (in the words of a Ghanaian student) "from the stone age to the jet age"', and delegates were astounded by 'the staggering progress made in just three years of independence (both the quantity and exuberant quality of it) with the quite different tempo and kind of development during the previous decades of colonialism'. Gerry (Rhodesia 60) described Accra as 'an overgrown village', compared to her own capital city of Salisbury. She enjoyed seeing 'a normal school', which was unlike the private school Nani (Ghana 60) attended. For Teklu (Ethiopia 60), the Forum as a whole, but especially the Ghana trip was mind-expanding. He had learned African geography in school, and could 'name all the rivers and mountains', but he 'didn't really know anything in depth'. This experience 'enlarged' his image of Africa and introduced him to the issues of pan-Africanism and independence that were prominent at the time: 'I was discovering Africa myself', he said. Gerry (Rhodesia 60) was inspired by the Ghana visit and reported in the September newsletter that Rhodesian Prime Minister Roy Welensky had 'promised to invite either the '62 or the '63 Forum' to Rhodesia, regretting that he could not invite the '61 because he was 'busy with constitutional talks'.[29] Sir Roy remained preoccupied with domestic politics for next few years as Rhodesia's racial politics intensified, and the visit never eventuated.

The 1960s

The Ghana trip was a one-off and the heyday of international jaunts seemed over by 1961, with delegates restricted to annual jaunts to Washington and Richmond for the next few years. In 1966 an additional nine-day tour to the north-east introduced delegates to the delights of Boston and Connecticut (plus relevant universities). This was dropped as purse strings tightened, but reintroduced in 1969, when delegates participated in a two-day Forum with the Massachusetts Junior World Affairs Council at the Fletcher School of Law and Diplomacy at Tufts University, thanks to Gus Nasmith, who studied there. Roger (UK 69) found it stimulating: 'in Boston we sat at the feet of Noam Chomsky, a leading anti-war intellectual', just 'months after the assassinations of Bobby Kennedy and Martin Luther King', and some delegates had 'participated in civil rights and anti-Vietnam war protests'.[30]

Investors Overseas Service Foundation (IOS) sponsorship in 1969 and 1970 allowed some delegates (those returning home via Europe) to spend four days in Geneva, hosted by the Foundation. They stayed with host families and visited the Red Cross, the World Health Organization, and the UN. They hopped over the French border to the Chateau de Pelly in Desingy, and had an afternoon seminar with various UN, ILO, and FAO officials. Only seventeen of the twenty-nine delegates in 1969 were involved, with South American, Asian, and New Zealand delegates missing out. The following year the trip was extended to all delegates, and lasted longer, giving participants free time as well as more lectures and discussions. Peter (Norway 69) found that last week in Geneva the highlight of the whole three months. His descriptions echo the feelings of earlier Forum delegates' experiences in the US, when the Forum was in its heyday. He 'lived in a wonderful house with a wonderful family' outside the city, 'in the green… very quiet, beautiful'. It was a time of reflection; he remembered having 'breakfast in the garden looking across the Geneva sea and the mountains'. And then he 'went with the others to a French castle for dinner—it was like of out of the world—so fantastic'.[31]

The field trips to Europe, Africa, and the Middle East were bonuses, relying on external sponsorship. They had a soft-power role, as delegates performed international friendship, enhancing the image of America as a global leader in cooperation. Forays to Berlin in the 1950s also provided copy for the *Herald Tribune*'s European edition, just as the field trips within the US advertised the newspaper to new audiences there. The Forum connected delegates, who were imagined as future international leaders, with current power-brokers and policy makers, within the US and around the world. For some delegates, the international field trips were the highlight of their experience, but for most, the US remained central. Forum organizers wanted to provide delegates with an enduring and positive impression of the US. The local field trips were designed to broaden delegates' experiences beyond the New York and New Jersey bubble, introducing them to the center of government in Washington DC, industrial advances in Tennessee, and sandstone educational institutions in Massachusetts. Certainly the delegates took home indelible impressions of America, but politics and industry had to compete with the more immediate delights of hamburgers, Bermuda shorts and rock 'n' roll.

Top: 36. Meeting the President (1952): Truman. Ira Rosenberg *NYHT*

Bottom: 37. Meeting the President (1957): Eisenhower [with the Thai Khon mask].
Ted Kell *NYHT*

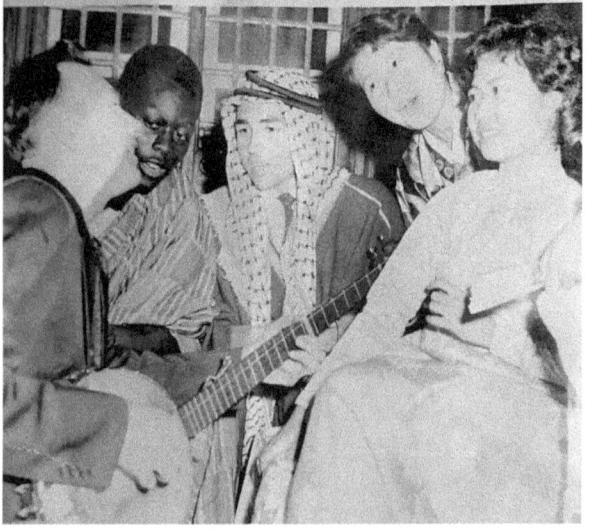

Top: 38. Some flew by helicopter to the annual dinner at Juan Trippe's mansion. On the lawn with the man and his chopper (1957). PA

Left: 39. Pete Seeger jamming with delegates: a highlight of Orientation. Here with Nii, Yasar, Esther and Lan (1959). USIS

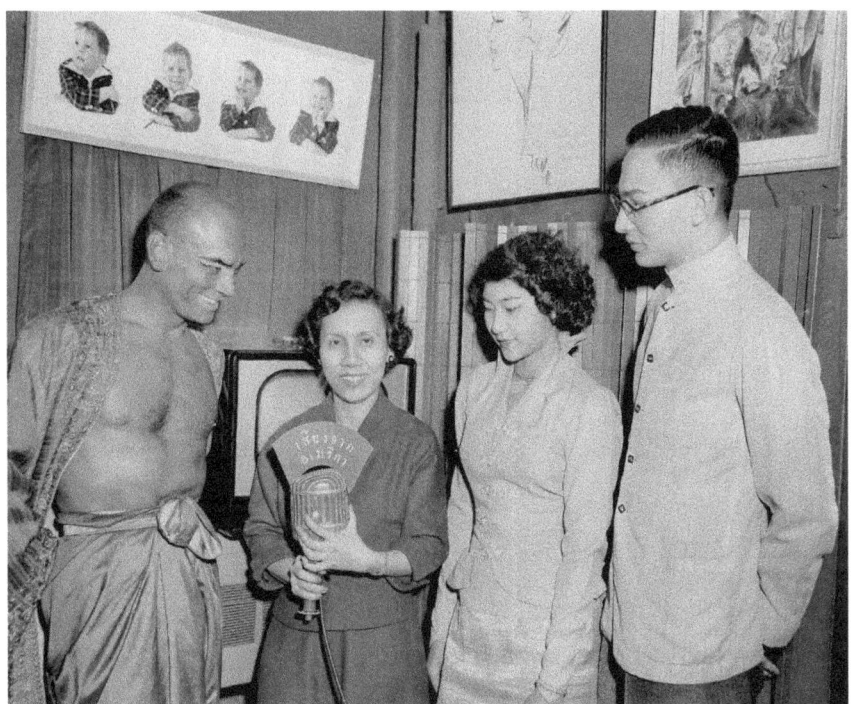

Top: 40. Santi had mixed feelings meeting *The King and I* stars, their encounter broadcast by VOA. Yul Brynner, VOA announcer, Salika and Santi (1952). USIS

Bottom: 41. More informal parties included dancing: Amos with a Forum host Esther Kurz (1969).

Top left: 42. Raimondo engaging with protesters outside the White House, 1969. Daoudi
Top right: 43. High jinks, Mike and Eddie in 1965. Teo
Bottom: 44. The cold not dampening spirits, Claudia, Nina, Keren, Jeanne, Teresa, Gloria, Donatella, & Sheila (1972) Penman

Top: 45. Rainer (Germany 1963) organized Summer 1964's Berlin activities. Seated (L–R): Gary, Stuart, Lew, Barbara, Jan, Nancy, Barbara, Glenn, Roger, Ginger, Victor, & Rainer. Standing (L–R): Ethel, Bob Huffman, Constance, Jay, Bernard Flicker, Orel, & Maria.

Right: 46. Maria (Summer 1964) sketched in the courtroom of the Frankfurt Auschwitz trials. Manhattan

Top: 47. A summer of train travel in Europe, 1964. Maria in Switzerland. Manhattan
Bottom: 48. The Forum relied on Alumni volunteers, here as Orientation kitchen staff in 1960. Andrea Cousins, Susan (1958), Jorge (1953), Judith (1953), Johan (1956), Raja (1954), Cora (1959). NYHT

Top: 49. Cora (1959) wearing one of the special '59ers' scarves presented by Nii (1959).
Bishop

Bottom: 50. One of the many Forum Alumni Reunions. Kapur

Top: 51. Interviewing Annemarie (1963) on Capri in 2018. Richard White

Bottom: 52. Nga (Vietnam 1958) watches her younger self on television in 2024. Joy Marini

Chapter 13

Hamburgers, Milkshakes, Sex, Drugs & Rock 'n' Roll

From the shock of the freezing cold of a mid-winter New York snowstorm to the delights of 'Awful Awfuls', hamburgers, pizza, and year-round ice cream, delegates became accustomed to a barrage of new experiences, whether in New Jersey schools, exploring Manhattan, or discovering the South. There was the modernity of the US itself with its skyscrapers, television, and drive-ins, plus indoctrination in the mysteries of the developing youth culture—doing the jitterbug and the twist, discovering rock 'n' roll, and the peculiar custom of 'going steady'. There is debate about the actual pervasiveness of American youth culture around the world in the 1950s and 60s, but there is no doubt that it was making inroads, with Coca Cola, jazz and rock 'n' roll leading the charge.[1] And delegates were bombarded by it all from the moment they arrived in the Big Apple.

Bigger and Better

The US represented modernity and the future for many delegates from what they themselves called the 'developing world', and from war-torn Europe. Teklu (Ethiopia 60) said it was 'like stepping into another world—into wonderland'. Per (Norway 61) was impressed even as they flew over to land in the dark. 'The city seemed endless, surrounding us everywhere, with innumerable flickering lights as far as the eye could see. A vision so gigantic and powerful that it almost felt scary'. Hiranthi (Ceylon 67) was 'just blown away by the buildings of New York'. Sherille (Ceylon 71) found New York 'eye-popping ... I had no idea of the scale of, you know, seeing eight lanes of traffic'. When I asked Ibrahim (Lebanon 58) why he had wanted to visit the US, he replied 'to see skyscrapers' (adding characteristically, 'and pretty girls'). Chit (India 56) was also 'flabbergasted' by the 'big huge skyscrapers' in New York, 'a city of wonder.'.

For him, the US was 'the leading superpower' who would 'dictate' the 'future of the world'. Indian students had gone to the UK in the colonial era, but Chit wanted 'to be part of the New World'.[2]

Emmanuel (Ghana 68)'s education in modernity began as he tried to leave the airport terminal—there was no door handle. A more confident passenger strode by and, as if by magic, the doors parted. The penny dropped. 'How amazing! An automatic door'. Tissa (Ceylon 59) was also fascinated by the airport's 'modern gadgetry'. The washrooms boasted dispensers for 'soap, combs, toothpaste, razors, and towels', and (the height of sophistication and convenience) 'there was even a machine that polished one's shoes!'. Probal (India 53) later regaled his daughters with stories of 'nattily dressed' New York taxi drivers, who wore shirts and ties. David (NZ 65) enjoyed 'all the action and buzz ... the doormen at the fancy apartment buildings with red carpet'. Terence (UK 48) commented that elevator operators were 'symbolic of all Americans ... They don't care where you've come from, they only want to know where you're going'. Television (and later color television) was a perennial novelty. Norma (Brazil 57) enjoyed 'American snow, milk, TV commercialism, and the glorious subway'. Ceridwen (UK 67) had to pinch herself as she discovered places she had only read about or seen in films. It was 'hard to believe I was actually seeing the Empire State Building or driving up Fifth Avenue'. Michael (NZ 67), a self-confessed 'impressionable youth from a provincial city' simply 'soaked it up': 'Imagine visiting the Met, Guggenheim and MOMA when your only previous exposure to art was the Dominion Museum' in Wellington, New Zealand.[3]

On the other hand, Philippe (France 69), whose idea of New York was Manhattan, was confused when his host family drove to Brooklyn. 'When will we get to New York?', he asked. The biggest shock for Michael (Jordan 58) was not the modern city but the wildlife at Sarah Lawrence College: 'I saw what I thought were big rats running around'. He had never met a squirrel. And Mahgoub (Sudan 57) had a new experience in a department store. He arrived with only a thin jacket and no sweater, so Helen Waller arranged for Mary Warner to take him shopping and put it on her account. Mahgoub couldn't believe it—woollen socks, an overcoat, and a sweater—'that'll be $85', said the assistant. Quick as a flash Mahgoub came back with, 'I'll give you $60'. Decades later, Susan (SA 57), who accompanied them, could still remember Mary explaining to Mahgoub that such bargaining was not part of American department store shopping.[4]

For Jan, arriving from Czechoslovakia in 1967, America's impact was immediate and profound. He was a good citizen of his communist state but, he said, 'it was clear to me almost as soon as I landed' that not only did Americans have a higher standard of living, but 'no one was worried about the consequences of free speech'.[5] The contrast with Prague was palpable. The Forum might be criticized for overemphasizing freedom of speech as a fundamental and perhaps exclusive tenet of Western democracy, but it for some delegates it was a genuine breath of fresh air.

'What Do You Think of America?'

Almost as soon as they arrived, delegates were bombarded with questions, notably 'What do you think of America?'. Delegates soon worked out how to get a reaction. Yukiko (Japan 59) told television viewers during one of her appearances that she quickly 'learned to answer "I love it"'. But she thought Americans were 'too easily satisfied' with her answer. In Japan, she said, 'they would never be satisfied with such a simple answer', nicely implying Japanese people were far more sophisticated than easily-placated Americans. The *Herald Tribune*, always on the lookout for appealing copy, reported delegates' candid comments. When asked what he liked best, Probal (India 53) replied 'American girls!', to roars of laughter. Terence (UK 48) said he was 'overwhelmed' by 'the urgency of the fairground' in New York. 'We met it the minute we crossed the Fifty-ninth Street Bridge, with traffic coming at us from five directions' and, he added mischievously to reporters, 'all on the wrong side of the street'. He knew how to get a headline. Newspaper reports reassured American readers that the United States was special and that delegates, particularly those from 'less developed' countries, were duly impressed. According to one *Tribune* report, Bhinda (Nepal 52) had 'a passion for vacuum cleaners ("Oh My!")', and for drinkable water, although 'bathing suits and abbreviated sun costumes... horrify her'. Eeva (Finland 48) was 'fascinated' by beautiful material in department stores. And Peter

(Australia 48), who the *Tribune* described (perhaps with some surprise) as 'an Australian who spoke cultured English', admired the tolerance of American adults for his host brother's speech in a local election. Young people were listened to, he felt. If he tried to give a political speech in Australia, he would be put in his place, 'told to go back to kindergarten'.[6]

Not all comments were positive. Eeva (Finland 48) was less complimentary about the 'contrasts' between the 'bright lights of Times Square and the slums that you see along the New York Central tracks'. Casimir (Finland 48) deplored Americans' propensity to resort to strikes rather than arbitration to settle labor disputes. Ulrik (Denmark 48) cut right to the chase, pointing out the hypocrisy of American students who saluted the flag, while pronouncing 'with liberty and justice for all', ignoring the 'race problem'. He said proudly, 'We know nothing about discrimination against Negroes at home', although he was forced to admit that 'we have only ten in all of Denmark'. The *Tribune* journalists had done their job, neatly neutralizing Ulrik's critique for American audiences.[7]

'Somewhat Ghastly'

Delegates arrived around New Year, and New York's winter weather made a big impression, especially on delegates from more temperate climates. Ashish (India 61) explained that while 26°F (-3.3°C) was not unusual for New Yorkers, for the three delegates from Burma, Ceylon, and India, it 'was not merely unusual; it was somewhat ghastly'. Leaving Kennedy Airport, Emmanuel (Ghana 68) said it was so cold that he 'felt like someone was boxing me in the ears'. He was concerned to see people with 'smoke coming out of their mouths and noses' and thought 'Oh dear, this is not good ... I don't think I'm going to like this place'. Jorge (Uruguay 53) saw snow for the first time and was impressed with the resilience of Probal (India 53), who wore traditional dhoti during the three months, despite the cold. (Probal's daughters laughed at this, their father being unusually impervious to the cold!) Beryl (Australia 68), resplendent in the red wool suit her fashion-plate mother had bought her, and with extra garments handknitted by her aunts, found it 'FREEZING!' at Oyster Bay: 'We were waist deep in snow'. Andreas (Ethiopia 61) was excited to see 'piles of snow on the pavement looking like piles of cotton wool' on the drive from the airport and 'eagerly wait[ed] for some snow to come'. He was rewarded: 'This morning I saw lovely droplets of snow tumbling down gracefully onto the trees ... creating a white cleanliness and beauty', he wrote in the Forum group's magazine. He was stunned that his roommate Mack (US 61), well accustomed to snow, calmly continued cleaning his teeth![8]

The 'Awful Awful' & Other Culinary Delights

The availability of ice cream all year round surprised many delegates, including 'sophisticated' Europeans, for whom it was an exclusively summer treat at home. Another novelty was the 'Awful Awful', described by Helen Waller on one television program as the 'most shattering' experience for Yuen Kum Chuen (Singapore 55). A milkshake made with ice milk instead of ice cream, it was apparently named after a customer called it (ungrammatically) 'awful big and awful good'. Johan (Norway 56) was reportedly the first foreign member of the 'Guzzlers' Club' of Bloomfield High School for consuming three in quick succession. Tissa (Ceylon 59) was also an 'instant convert'. It was, he declared enthusiastically sixty years later, 'no ordinary milkshake!' American food more generally was memorable. Toshio (Japan 67) found hamburgers and milkshakes 'fun'. For many, McDonalds, Mr Donut, and Dairy Queen were new experiences. Andreas (Norway 48) praised the bubble gum and candy, while Mark (NZ 68) discovered pumpkin pie and blueberry pie. 'OOOh very good doughnuts', sighed Geneviève (France 56), remembering those provided by her host father, a baker. Röggi (Iceland 62) recalled grapefruit served for breakfast—'unknown in Iceland'. To my surprise, Vincenzo (Italy 64) quite enjoyed American coffee, but, he added with a grin, only if he thought of it as an entirely different hot drink! Aysel (Turkey 64) also adjusted to 'Nescafe (instead of our fine Turkish coffee)', and 'tea-bags (instead of our loose-leaf tea)', and confessed that, although a Muslim, she tried scrambled eggs with bacon: 'God forgive me as I was in a foreign land ... but ... it *was* tasty!' When asked what they were taking home, several delegates declared 'a lot of extra weight'. One Iranian girl stayed out of sight when relatives visited her home after the Forum: 'my parents were so utterly ashamed of the dreadful figure I had come to possess'. And that was after she had lost eleven of the twenty-two pounds she had gained. 'I am stiff in every joint from exercising most of the time', she added.⁹

Others were less impressed. Emmanuel (Ghana 68) remembered good food on the plane(!) but was disappointed by the tastelessness of food in American school cafeterias. Anis (Pakistan 56) brought his own spices. Probal (India 54) also found the food 'bland'. Kris (Ceylon 68) was more resilient, although his comment, that he '*survived* without rice and curry for three months' suggests that it was not easy. Jorge (Uruguay 53) grimaced thinking of his first 'cherry cola'—'and I still don't like it!', he exclaimed.¹⁰

Sex, Drugs and Rock & Roll

As well as discovering high culture, often with host parents—seeing their first opera, hearing their first symphony live—delegates also immersed themselves in the music and culture of their generation. Helen Waller facilitated this in the 1950s, organizing evenings where delegates jammed with Pete Seeger, or were entertained by Harry Belafonte. They learned how to jitterbug, discovered rock 'n' roll, and bought records to take home. Forum assistant Dave Bromberg, later a professional musician, endeared himself to delegates by playing the guitar. Alan (NZ 63) remembered 'lots of singing' at the Forum and his first introduction to Joan Baez. Host Bob Durkees' father took Mike (Australia 65) to a New York nightclub to see famous jazz drummer Gene Krupa. Bruce (Canada 61) discovered Greenwich Village with one host brother and was 'thrilled' to hear Lawrence Ferlinghetti reading his poetry. 'There were still Beatniks in those days', he reminded me in our interview.¹¹

There were other rites of passage. One delegate remembered wearing nylon stockings and using lipstick and blusher for the first time in New York—much to the horror of her parents when she returned home—an external symbol of 'growing up'. Orit (Israel 67) noticed 'the noise of my heels clicking' when she walked along the pavements in New York, 'the first time I had worn heels'. It was, she recalled, in an evocative turn of phrase, 'a grown up sound'. Bermuda shorts were fashionable in the early 1950s. Hameeda (Pakistan 52) wore her own shalwar kameez most of the time but was persuaded to try on some Bermuda shorts, 'it didn't look bad at all'. Three years later Gudrún (Iceland 55) became 'the first girl in Iceland to wear them'.[12]

The American teenage social scene was a culture shock for many delegates. Columbia student Lee Workum studied the Forum for her MA thesis in 1961 and found that, of all the cultural differences they observed in the US, delegates from Asian and Middle Eastern countries commented particularly on family relationships, male-female interaction, and teenage independence. They were often accustomed to stronger parental controls, 'family unity', arranged marriages, and personal 'modesty'. Nalini (India 59) commented, 'problems of teenagers have never been considered as something important in India', but America was 'the cradle of teenage problems'. She deplored the 'little respect shown for elders'. Nakchung (Korea 55) 'was told that silence and modesty are not the signs of a healthy boy' in the US. Delegates from Europe, South America and Africa seemed less confronted. Nevertheless, this was the first time many had attended co-educational schools or socialized with the opposite sex. Being in classrooms alongside girls (or boys) was an eye-opener. Over fifty years later, some interviewees still smiled broadly when asked whether they appreciated this. When invited in the final TV program to say what he would like to take home, Mogens (Denmark 58) exclaimed excitedly, 'a cheerleader'.[13]

American teenagers drove, a novelty for many delegates. Mike (NZ 67) was amazed that 'kids drove to school in their parents' Pontiac!' Suzanne (UK 62) was impressed with one boy's white Cadillac convertible. Per (Norway 61) remembered going to bowling halls and basketball games, 'the boys drove and the girls were passengers'. Serban (Bolivia 64)'s principal memory of one wealthy New York family was of driving around with his host brother in his two-seater red Corvette. They would visit each of the boy's several girlfriends in turn, with Serban playing gooseberry (feeling a bit de trop) while his host was smooching. He had more fun when they piled three girls into the two-seater sports car and took a drive into Manhattan.[14]

The Forum's 'no single dates' rule, which banned a delegate going out alone on a 'date', was designed to protect delegates and avoid intense emotional entanglements. It was often ignored. In their final television appearance, the 1959 Forum group sang their own rendition of 'Oh Susannah', retitled 'Missus Waller'. Among the memorable couplets was:

'We've taken full advantage of the freedom in the States,
Despite your rigid Forum rules, we've all had single dates.'

'Dating' was a new experience. Some threw themselves into the game with gusto—at times with too much enthusiasm—while others observed from the sidelines the peculiar rituals of ring-wearing and 'going steady'. Nalini (India 59) was horrified that teenagers 'go out with anybody, anywhere, kiss all of them if they want, come back at any odd time in the night'. Geneviève was surprised at the public performance of teenage relationships. In France 'at 17 we would be in love with some French boy, but it was … a secret, but the American girls would carry a ring around their neck and "go steady"'. It was 'an institution'.[15]

Yasar's (Jordan 59) education started the moment he arrived. In an age before mandatory seatbelts, a group piled into the car at the airport to drive to Sarah Lawrence College. The boys took the seats and Yasar was startled when one of the girls sat in his lap. The first of many new experiences! Later Yasar's host brother was horrified to hear he had never been kissed. Sixty years later, Yasar mimed how at the next party the girls stood in a 'queue, with their chewing gum, you know', He explained that 'the first kiss went all right and the second, the third was really messy and, and the sixth and then I think I just passed out!' For Roger (UK 69) being UK's delegate was an amazing shot in the arm. 'I wasn't very sporty', he said, 'and shy, with freckles and ginger hair', but in the US he was suddenly a superstar. In a scenario reminiscent of a scene in the film *Love Actually*, 'girls would come up to me at the schools and say "Tawk"', and were interested in anything he said in his English accent.[16]

'Were there any love affairs between delegates?' was a standard question in my interviews with alumni. One common response was a flat denial: 'Oh no, of course not, we were hardly together as a group'. They got to know delegates who were in the same schools, but the rest of the group not so much. They dismissed any idea that delegates formed romantic attachments or 'hooked up'. The other common response was an immediate affirmation: 'Yes, of course, we were all quite cozy by the end, lots of snuggling up'. These interviewees remembered developing intense relationships with the other delegates. The group bonded during Orientation, and then later, comparing notes about their American school experiences during long bus journeys to Washington, Boston, and Tennessee.

Unsurprisingly, I sometimes got opposite answers from delegates in the same year group. Sometimes, perhaps, interviewees wanted to protect themselves and others from my impertinent question, while others might have wanted to impress with their modern outlook. Often, however, they were telling the truth as they saw it. As ever, in a group of thirty teenagers from vastly different backgrounds and ranging in age from 16 to 19 (and sometimes beyond), there was wide disparity in sexual and social maturity. While some might have been flirting with each other, others were oblivious, had more serious things to get on with, or had sweethearts at home. Boys like Yasar, from countries with more conservative approaches to sexual relationships, might have found the US liberating, but the girls were more circumspect. Korean and Japanese girls were often the focus of attention from Western boys. There was a disturbing hint of orientalist fantasy in their fascination with the petite, quiet, and apparently shy Asian girls. Years with disproportionately high numbers of boys meant that while there was a bit of a 'boys' club, the girls were prized entities. I was amused, when, fifty years on, almost all the male interviewees in one year instantly remembered the same girl delegate, and *all* felt they had shared something special with her.

The degree of friendly interaction also shifted over the twenty-five years of the Forum. Bob Huffman had a difficult task policing delegates' behavior in the 1960s, whether with each other or with Americans. Helen Waller's job in the 1950s was easier. Geneviève (France 56) wrote of learning to jitterbug and 'conversations in hotel rooms' late into the night on the field trip to Washington. Couples in 1960 were described as 'all very sedate', Jona (Iceland) and Nani (Ghana) making a striking pair. Alan (NZ 63) recalled that Apichai (Thailand 63) and Elba (Mexico 63) were a cute couple and he and Shahla (Iran 63) were close, but they were really 'quite an innocent bunch'. Suzanne (UK 62) had a wonderful time flirting—with American boys (including a Johnson and Johnson heir), with the young *Tribune* journalist, and with several delegates. When the Forum group visited a muddy farm, 'to prevent me from getting dirty the boys made a litter and carried me everywhere'. She acknowledged that 'the other girls weren't too impressed' musing, rather disingenuously, that 'I am the least cute and appealing of them all, yet I get the best treatment from the boys'.[17]

There were stories, however, of Mr Huffman separating overly friendly couples on buses by the mid-sixties. Sherille (Ceylon 71) remembered 'there was a lot of socializing—we went to parties all the time … there were a lot of romances and everyone fell in love with everybody else'. After all, he said, 'this was the '70s, so people were pretty experimental and open'. There was 'definitely' much more freedom than in Ceylon. One 1972 delegate told me, 'frankly, I think we were all a bit worried that one of the … girls had gone back pregnant', although she had probably just been overindulging in donuts and hamburgers.[18]

Few delegates went as far as Mike (Australia 65). Perhaps wanting to guarantee himself a place in this book, he announced during our interview that 'you know I had my first sexual experience in New York'. Somewhat taken aback, I prevaricated, 'But that wouldn't have been during the Forum', I suggested, wanting to get back to 1965, rather than hearing of other adventures. 'But it was', he told me. 'Some of the older male delegates' arranged for 18-year-old Mike to visit a prostitute for what was, he explained in graphic detail, a very brief encounter. The contrast with Yasar (Jordan 59)'s kissing experience epitomizes the changes in adolescent culture in the 1960s, although Mike's experience was unusual. The same year, Monika (Austria 65), who was only 16, remembered she and her roommates 'chatted all night through'—a far more wholesome and innocent image, indicative of how disparate a group could be. It is unsurprising that all the activity mentioned was heterosexual: throughout the period of the Forum, homosexuality was illegal in the US and most other places. Only one interviewee mentioned same-sex attraction, although others later came out as gay or lesbian.[19]

Amid the good fun and casual flirtations, there were occasionally darker moments. At the 1964 farewell party, one American girl accepted an invitation from a male delegate to 'see where we live', and found herself in a dorm room, fighting him off. On another occasion, a 20-year-old African male delegate tried to kiss a white female delegate as she was loading her suitcases onto the bus. There was no one else was around and she 'gave him an almighty shove and ran for my life', the incident shocking her, despite having 'escaped'.[20] Fortunately, such incidents appear to have been rare, although, like these two girls, victims may have been unwilling to report their assaults to Forum staff. It is not known if the male delegates involved tried it with anyone else.

Delegates' experiences of drinking, smoking, and drugs also shifted between the 1950s and 1970s. In 1950 Balakrishnan (India) took pains to inform selectors in his autobiography that he had 'never smoked a cigarette, nor have I taken a pinch of snuff', and 'I have never tasted intoxicating liquors'. Within ten years, cigarette smoking was common among some delegates. Lise-Lotte (Denmark 60) and Eric (France 60) reportedly 'smoked like chimneys'. Young Bimal (India 60), unused to seeing girls with cigarettes, thought Lise *very* sophisticated.[21] European delegates, well used to drinking wine, were also amused by Americans who snuck around, drinking beer 'under the local bridge' in secret, driving across state borders and getting very drunk.

Not until I interviewed delegates from 1969 did I hear any whisper of drugs. Mikko (Finland) remembered an American journalist sent him a joint in a letter; Stella (Italy) had her first joint with the friend of one of her host sisters; while Greg (NZ) and Rodel (Philippines) had a pot-infused adventure in San Francisco on the way home. By 1972, Paul (Austria 72) felt it important to emphasize in his autobiography that 'although I have got a modern attitude, I have a strong objection to those young people who build the so-called "progressive" groups and take narcotic drugs'. He reassured organizers that 'I know people who are taking drugs, and I am sufficiently informed about them so that I can abstain'. He concluded rather piously, 'I don't think that there can be any fulfilment in drugs.' Michael (UK 72) found 'marijuana in general use in some of the schools, but 'little evidence of hard-drug addiction', although a primary school principal had told him of 'pushers' targeting his seven-year-old pupils.[22]

Taking America to the World

Whatever new experiences delegates had enjoyed in the US, it was all too soon time to go home. The trip home was an event in itself. At the airport, the contrast between the arrival of apprehensive young delegates at the start of the Forum and their departure was stark. Lynn (US 60) described how they arrived at the airport with all their paraphernalia, 'en masse, some in national dress, some in newly acquired blue jeans, and all talking'. The men on the luggage scale 'paled and gave up trying to weigh such items as shopping bags filled with Pat Boone records, or a costume made with coconuts, or fan letters from girls who had seen the owner of the bag on television'. Similarly, Brigitte (France 64) turned on the charm (and tears), persuading TWA check in staff to give her an extra seat for a 'rather large stuffed giraffe'.[23]

There were hiccups. In 1964, four delegates were 'bumped' from their flights and 'had a high old time as TWA's overnight guests at Kennedy airport and ate up a storm'. Forum staff (and especially Anne Counes who offered to take them home with her if necessary (!)) were very grateful TWA provided accommodation for the teenagers, who were not even paying customers. Liz (Australia 56) became an Australian headline: 'Adelaide Girl Disappears Under Mysterious Circumstances'. She arrived in Singapore 'out of money', with 'nowhere to sleep' and 'no passage home (the booking office had not heard of me)', and with luggage '22 pounds overweight'. She turned down an offer of assistance from another passenger: 'He was just a strange man on a plane', and later 'kicked myself... when I found out who he was'—she had been seated next to the Governor General of Malaya. This incident might well sound alarm bells about Forum organization, with images of teenagers stranded around the world, but in fact, Forum administrators had provided all the delegates with a letter 'in case of emergency'. Liz, however, 'didn't want to use [it] as I felt a sense of loyalty towards the *Herald Tribune* and didn't want to be extra expense'. Instead, as one might expect from this group of teens, Liz used her own initiative and 'barged in on the Indonesian Consulate' with a the Indonesian delegate for a night, before staying with 'an English Major', whose wife worked in the Pan Am office. The Australian High Commission provided funds, and she had 'three terrific days in Singapore'.[24]

Stopovers, (planned or otherwise) clearly provided opportunities for fun as well as publicity. In 1957, Peter (Singapore), Le (Vietnam), and Nonna (Indonesia) were 'lionized in Manila' while staying briefly with Dennis

(Philippines). Having just come from cold Berlin they 'roasted in the Manila heat', but rallied to be whisked off to be interviewed by journalists, meet with youth organizations, and attend Dennis's welcome home parties.[25]

The highlight of the entire trip for Probal (India 53) was his weeklong stopover in Egypt as the guest of the Egyptian Education Ministry. His Forum selection essay, 'The greatest man in the world today' was about Egypt's revolutionary leader General Naguib. Newly independent India and Egypt made much of the publicity opportunity. Probal was photographed with Naguib, who presented Probal with a signed photograph of himself, writing 'To my dear son Probal Kumar Dutt, with my compliments and appreciation. Long live great India, forever the sister of Egypt'.[26]

Stopovers were not always such high-powered, formal events. In 1969 Rodel (Philippines) and Greg (NZ) made up their own, changing their tickets and stopping for a week in San Francisco, where Rodel's uncle lived. 'We left our luggage with my uncle, and that was the last we saw of him', remembered Rodel. They had a wild time enjoying a taste of the 'Summer of Love' in Haight Ashbury and Golden Gate Park. Their guide was teenage African American runaway, Shirley Winters, who took them around bars and clubs and to Fillmore West to see Chuck Berry. 'Who's Chuck Berry?' asked classical musician Greg from sleepy New Zealand. 'Everywhere, everyone was smoking grass', remembered Rodel, and told a wonderfully evocative story of having to hide a bag of weed down his trousers when Greg got arrested for fighting with the private detective on the trail of Shirley. 'I had to go and get him from the police precinct and there I was, standing in the precinct with a bag of grass in my pants!'. Greg remembered smuggling marijuana seeds back to New Zealand. They were growing nicely until his mother found them. Rodel took his share ('Greg kept most of it') back to Manila, where he enjoyed showing off to his friends, looking 'hip' smoking weed. 'I must have been the dumbest person in the world', he said in our interview, shaking his head. Their post-Forum American adventure 'upended the three months of ultra-positive education about the US that we had absorbed on the east coast'.[27]

Generally, however, delegates left in batches, flying together across the world, 'dropping off' delegates en route. On the plane, general chaos reigned. In 1960, they 'rearranged seats, tested safety exits and bathrooms and got ... friendly with the crew'. Lynn (US 60) thought the stewardesses 'were an especially hardy lot, who didn't even wince when Milan from Yugoslavia stripped off his undershirt in front of all the passengers'. Eddie (Malaya 50) also told of a party on wings with frequent refueling stops, starting with with snowball fights in Nova Scotia. Then they were 'telling tall tales, joking (with much loud laughter), and singing (???) songs, to the annoyance of the other passengers' across 'the gloomy, grumbling Atlantic', admiring 'old Nelson looking quite satisfied on his column' in London, enjoying views of the 'massive Bavarian Alps', and eating breakfast in Istanbul. Between Karachi and Calcutta, Kim (Vietnam 50) produced a cinema projector, put it 'into the plug for the shaver' and charmed the airline steward who 'ripped up a pillowcase to make a cinema screen'. After a few movies, they found a pack of cards and 'played "Bluff" right through the night'. In Bangkok, Malaival (Thailand 50)'s mother 'loaded all seven of us into her Buick Super 1965 model' for a 'fine four-hour sightseeing trip' concluding with a much-appreciated cup of 'real tea ... not the soppy stuff the US pretends is tea'. The journey was punctuated with tearful farewells as the delegates departed one-by-one, until there was just Eddie, on the last leg back to Malaya, 'sad at parting from 24 wonderful young people', but 'happy to be back to see the old faces, the old places' and 'happy to have helped a bit to get the World We Want'.[28]

These teens' version of 'the world we want' had been framed by their experiences in the US. They carried memories of friendships and romances, of peculiar cultural clashes and occasional moments of homesickness and disconnect. They had suitcases crammed full of records and books, American clothes like bathing suits and Bermuda shorts, and photographs, souvenirs, cards, and gifts from host families and friends. Some had drunk their first 'Awful-Awful', eaten their first hamburger, or had their first kiss. They had discussed and argued and laughed into the night. Their later nostalgia for the US pinpointed a surprising array of the concrete and ethereal. A year after his Forum experience, Nebiat (Ethiopia 56) wrote: 'I love your energy, your central heating system, your invention, your turnpikes, your virtue, your manners, and lastly your two-party system'. Anna Katrin (Iceland 56) confessed that: 'Before,

I just loved American clothes and shoes and so on, but now I love the American families and the people'. And while youth in different countries performed 'being a teenager' in various ways, the juggernaut of American cultural imperialism was hard to resist.[29] These Forum delegates were at the forefront of that juggernaut, as we shall see in the next chapter, as they became (usually) enthusiastic young ambassadors, bringing a little bit of the US home in their luggage, hearts, and minds.

Chapter 14

What a Delegate Did Next

'Under no circumstances will to be possible for you to extend your stay in the United States', delegates were informed firmly in underlined text in their Forum welcome letter. This was partly to avoid inconveniencing the airlines providing free flights, but, more importantly perhaps, to ensure delegates fulfilled their ambassadorial role—to 'return immediately to your own school to share accounts of your experiences here...and establish contact between your school and host schools'.[1] Neither was the Forum supposed to be an avenue for immigration or even an excuse to see friends and family, although a few (like Greg and Rodel) circumvented the rules, and more were back in the US at college within a few months. Most, however, returned home to take up their lives where they had left off. Some went on to fulfil Forum organizers' dreams by becoming diplomats, politicians, and global movers and shakers, although whether that created a network of pro-American internationalist leaders is dubious. Others had less obviously international careers, but were touched by the Forum experience nonetheless. Here we explore what delegates did next.

'How Could You Send Us Home?'

'How could you send us home?', wailed Lucie (Norway 57), who could 'hardly believe that everything which has happened during the last months really has happened, and that it is not only a wonderful dream'. Like many, she found it difficult to settle back into the routine of home and school, coping with that inevitable 'flat feeling' after an extraordinary three months, jampacked with new experiences, being treated as a teenage VIP. Some faced exams, like Farouk (Egypt 56), who was 'keeping his nose to the grindstone, so that I may make the work of seven months in one month'. Geneviève (France 56) was distracted: 'Reading about blood and germs and protection against them and suddenly I remembered Romano ... in Washington ... telling me how his father got wounded ... cutting himself with a dirty butcher's knife ... and I think about Washington, Williamsburg, rock 'n' roll and Dicks and Raul who jitterbugged so well, and our conversations in hotel rooms and so on and where is this poor biology?', she sighed.[2]

'Being only ordinary' again was hard. Judith (UK 56) joked that 'after three months of being treated as somewhat of a "celebrity" I was a little disconcerted to find myself treated as "bonne à tout faire"' in her summer job with a Parisian family. Niels (Denmark 57) wrote, 'If in my host schools in America I proposed something it was usually accepted. When here I open my mouth, I am told to "shut up and get into line"'. Some rebelled against the strictness of their schools after 'the free, democratic American schools', with 'everything at home ... so narrow and one-sided and intolerant'. When Irjaleena (Finland 57) challenged her teacher's evangelical Lutheranism, he 'stood and looked at me like a dumb fish!' She felt she had 'grown out of school'.[3]

Some also outgrew friends. Amelia (Ghana 57) had 'discovered the world' and was 'interested in news and recent history', but her friends thought her 'too loquacious and witty'. Nini (Ghana 56)'s friends 'would not understand my new mentality and ideas', although admitted he was 'a little bit dogmatic'. Nadia (Egypt 59) complained that 'people keep telling me the Forum is over—act naturally', but 'this is the first time in my life I'm really being myself'. She continued, 'the Forum gave me enough courage not to rebel against my own society and its traditions, but to question and accept what is good for me and reject what is not'.[4]

After being 'almost half frozen by the American winter', Amelia (Ghana 57) and Jawahir (Malaya 56) found the 'sun rather scorching' back home. For Jay (Ceylon 56) it was food: 'all the rice and curry I was longing for in the States' seemed now 'foreign and almost tasteless'. He felt like 'a foreigner here in my native place'. Lal (Ceylon 60) also felt 'Everything seems wrong or ugly', and, most concerningly for a teenage boy, he joked that 'even the Ceylonese girls don't appear pretty', although he was confident that 'of course this shouldn't exist for much longer'. Esther (Korea 59) worried she had forgotten how to behave, after the freedoms of the US: 'Will I remember to wait for the man to go first [through doors] when I get back home? Will I remember never to talk in a loud voice?'[5]

On the other hand, some found it only too easy to slot back in. Farouk (Jordan 56) 'said all I wanted to say about my trip to my family in three or four evenings'. It was 'really good to be home!', and he found that it was 'just what [Helen Waller] said: two or three days, a week at most, after our arrival, and everything will go on as usual'. The Forum seemed distant, 'like a beautiful dream', albeit with enduring 'lessons and experiences'. Jayantha (Ceylon 57)'s family noticed no difference in him other than that he had 'put on a couple of pounds' in the US: 'I have adapted myself so easily to life here that I am rather scared at the thought of slipping back into my old groove'. Minjiba (Nigeria 55) said her parents were 'relieved' she had not 'adopted an American accent nor pasted my face with makeup', but she found it 'amusing that most of my friends don't like the American style of dressing but they very much like my American dresses'.[6]

Being home meant the comfort of familiar people, places, customs, language, and food. Anna Katrin (Iceland 56) found 'it is wonderful to be home again and talk one's own language and get small potatoes with every meal'. Several Europeans told me that the American trip reinforced their sense of Europeanness. Rita (Germany 70) 'felt uncomfortable, foreign' in the US, but when her group arrived in Geneva, 'although I didn't speak any French, I felt at home (I felt European!)'[7]

Winning Hearts and Minds

For some, the hoop-la of the Forum continued as they arrived back to a hero's welcome, telling stories of America to fellow school students, members of local clubs, to journalists and government officials. Lesley (Australia 55) found it 'quite amazing how interested people have been'. Hee Joon (Korea 56) was kept 'very busy in telling and writing about my trip abroad for a complete two weeks'. He felt 'extremely lucky', he told Helen Waller smugly, to speak for twenty-five minutes ('even Korean Ministers seldom have twenty') with President Syngman Rhee, who was 'very interested' in his 'long journey to America and Germany' and in 'the activities of the *New York Herald Tribune*'. Hope (Nigeria 59) was 'besieged by newspaper reporters and radio commentators'. Nigerians had 'great admiration' for America but 'to many of them it is a fairyland', he said, feeling 'carefully scrutinized' because 'everybody expected me to become Americanized'.[8]

For the American government, returning delegates served as wonderful little pro-American mouthpieces. Mohamed (Morocco 57) gave radio talks and newspaper interviews, claiming proudly that 'ten million people in Morocco now know what the Forum is and many things about the USA'. Anis (Pakistan 56) did a month-long lecture tour from Rawalpindi through Lahore to Multan, 'under USIS auspices'. Ziyad (Lebanon 57) wrote a 'fine report' to his Ministry of Education, part of it earnestly titled: 'How the Americans Practice Democratic Life and Push Their Children to Bear Responsibilities, Face the Future, and Build Their Personality'. Krishnan (India 58) described the lack of class consciousness in the US as the 'best safeguard of capitalist America against the Marxian class-struggle. Most delegates agreed at the time that the US as a force for 'good'.

Romano (Switzerland 56) was condescending but appreciative of Americans who 'may be at times slow, clumsy, headstrong ... inconsistent, but more than anything else you are trying to do an honest and fine job'. Tomas (Argentina 57), a soldier in 1959, also thought 'the States is doing a fine job in South America.' Chile was 'Spanish in its customs and architecture, but you can see American influence in the economic life', he told fellow alumni approvingly: 'What a beautiful country!'. When NYU Education Professor F L Redefer traveled through India and South East Asia in 1960, he arranged to visit alumni. He was full of praise for Helen Waller and the Forum, found the delegates 'deeply affected' by their experiences, but was 'amazed that our Embassy officials made so little of the potentials of these young people on their return'.[9] Possibly he spoke to the wrong delegates, or perhaps by 1960, USIS enthusiasm was waning. Later delegates had less engagement with American embassies.

Gus (Netherlands 49)'s opportunity to promote the US came later than most, nearly five decades after his Forum experience. In 1997, he was invited to represent 'an ordinary Dutch citizen' at the Marshall Plan fiftieth anniversary celebrations. A White House factotum liked the synergy of one of the 'Marshall Plan' Forum delegates, who had met President Truman in 1949, encountering President Clinton in 1997. So Gus was once again a celebrity on the world stage, explaining how the US had saved his country with the Marshall Plan, noting that 'to meet one American president is an honor. To meet two presidents and the

American First Lady' was 'more than I could ever have imagined'.[10]

It was hardly surprising that delegates were (mostly) full of praise when they returned home 'deeply grateful for a valued experience'. As Avri (Israel 68) remarked, 'What is there not to like about a country that flies you (first class) for three months for an extremely interesting free tour, complete with meetings with various important people ... while the nation listens to your thoughts and ideas on coast-to-coast TV (not in prime time, yet)'.[11] And all at the impressionable age of 16 or 17.

An Unappreciative Audience

Vivian (Argentina 58), like several others, went straight to university, an exciting new adventure that mitigated the 'flat feeling'. But she felt she missed out, jealous of Pedro (Argentina 60), who was younger and had 'a whole year ahead of him in which to share his Forum awakening with his school friends'. But would they have been enthralled? Not everyone found willing audiences. Forum staff prepared delegates for a let-down. Diana (Italy 57) reported that she had started school again and, 'as you had told us, my friends were much less interested in the whole thing than I had expected'. Liz (Australia 56) was careful, making 'a point of not mentioning America or my trip unless asked, although I am just bursting to'. She also found herself defending America 'much to my amazement'. She confessed that she 'didn't realize how much I liked and enjoyed being in that country until I left'. Australians' criticisms of the US annoyed her ('most hadn't even been there!'), especially the claim that Americans had no culture: 'This is really ridiculous as Australia has even less!', she humphed. Khusrow (Iran 60) said 'the worst thing is that I can't talk about the Forum to anybody' because 'nobody is able to understand what the Forum really is'. Nalini (India 59) was frustrated that people thought she had gone 'on a sightseeing trip' and wondered why she had not seen Hollywood or Niagara Falls.[12]

Sometimes the apathy was cynicism. Jean-Claude (France 49) was 'at a loss to overcome ... the lack of interest in the listeners who think they have heard all this "baloney" before'. Leonor (Argentina 47) concluded that Argentina's youth were apathetic because they had 'not suffered at all', while 'in Europe, they have all suffered a war and they are eager to get together because they know that is the only way to avoid another'. A decade later Franca (Italy 60) found similar lethargy: 'I told you I was ready to change the world, but what can I do? I am alone with 48,000,000 population who seem asleep'. She despaired of asking them 'to be interested in the world of today and its problems when nobody cares about our own country'.[13]

Others had more immediate priorities. Hope (Nigeria 59) found that after initial interest, his friends found the Forum 'dull and uninteresting' because Africa was in a 'political ferment', and 'the fact is that we are indifferent to occurrences outside Africa'. Mohamed (Sudan 59) did a Forum exhibit in a nationwide schools exhibition, which pleased the American Ambassador, but did not cut through to Sudanese people, who, said Mohamed, 'have their bellies to worry about before thinking of an association' like the Forum. 'The word peace up here has a different meaning: food and shelter ... even among the students something like the Forum will be a mere distraction'. There was a fundamental difference between the US and Sudan: 'Right now ... everyone is spending all his time in a frantic trial to exist—exist not live as you are doing in America'.[14]

Nonna (Indonesia 57) got caught up in a civil war. She joined the women's corps of Permesta, a Sulawesi-based rebel movement, as an English language radio announcer. News of her reached the Forum via Soesilo (Indonesia 50), who was unimpressed that 'one of us has been unfortunate to get herself mixed up in a rebellion, which places us at this end in a rather unpopular picture'. A banker with ties to the government, he had 'connexions in the army', who told him Nonna had surrendered to government forces at Menado in 1959 and was 'being well taken care of'. Apparently forgetting Nonna's political activities, in the next breath Soesilo was disparaging about female Indonesian delegates who, he said, were uninformed about the 'quick and sometimes violent changes have happened in Indonesia during the past ten years' because they could not 'observe it from close range'. Nonna was certainly at 'close range', right in the thick of a rebellion that meant eventually she moved to New York to escape.[15]

Khanh (Vietnam 60) returned home 'ready to open my heart to the whole of humanity' but found her 'family nourishing hatred for half of it'. She gave a harrowing account of communists 'killing all the people who work for the government' using weapons 'from Cambodia'. They had 'kidnapped my uncle, who was only in his 20s ... You never come back when you are kidnapped by the Communists'. She felt 'very lucky to have known Phalla and Milan' the 1960 delegates from Cambodia and Yugoslavia, 'but I'm trying hard not to hate every other Cambodian or Communist'.[16]

Khanh's dilemma underscored how Forum idealism was divorced from the harsh realities many delegates faced. Eric (France 54) served in the French army in Algeria, where there was 'no place here for easy cynicism and a false intellectualism for surprise parties and winter sports. Life here is naked without comforts'. Even Ida (Italy 59), who, being in a more peaceful country, arguably had less reason to notice the disconnect, commented 'we were too theoretical in our speeches sometimes'; it was all words and no action. Henceforth, she 'prefer[ed] to live my ideas instead of spending time just talking'. And she did, later establishing a charity to build wells in Ethiopia. As delegates got older they also questioned the Forum's relevance, describing later delegates as 'idealistic and well-meaning young people but unfortunately far from the real ... and pressing ... problems of life'.[17]

Consequences

Alumni often told me 'they couldn't go home' story. In hushed tones they tell of the consequences for South African or Middle Eastern delegates, who spoke out or were too friendly with their country's 'enemy'.

> They came on stage and shook hands, and hugged each other, and said we must be friends. You know they didn't go back to their own country. They just stayed back because they were afraid of what would happen to them.[18]

Such tales have become part of Forum mythology. Sometimes told by fellow delegates, often the stories were second-hand, about another year, and seem to be exaggerated. I found no evidence of a delegate being 'unable to go home', because of the Forum, nor (conversely) of delegates being repatriated early because they became too friendly with an 'enemy' (the alternative version of the tale). Nevertheless, there could be significant consequences for delegates who overstepped in the eyes of their government. As we have seen, a couple of Israeli delegates were taken to task by government officials while they were in the US. After speaking out, one Vietnamese delegate had a telegram from her parents during the Forum telling her to mind what she said: 'remember you have family here'.[19]

This was not a new problem for delegates, and Helen Waller was certainly aware of the issue. In the very first Forum, she advised the United Nations Youth of Baltimore that Argentinian delegates should 'not be pressed' on 'how Peron's regime is accepted by the people of Argentina', because 'it is rather difficult for an Argentine citizen who wants to return to speak with complete frankness about the country's present Government'.[20] (Despite this, Helen continued to push boundaries with other delegates, ignoring potential repercussions.)

Some delegates did have uncomfortable homecomings. Perhaps the most surprising was Beryl (Australia 68), who thought she was being followed when she returned to sleepy, respectable Adelaide in South Australia. She told the Commonwealth Education Office official who had selected her as delegate, and she 'had the feeling he sort of knew ... and was mildly amused, as though he was surprised I picked up on it'. He told her he 'would "fix it"'. She 'thought it strange he would feel able to guarantee that immediately' and concluded that it must have been ASIO, Australia's equivalent of the CIA, who had been on her tail.[21] Why ASIO would have been interested in Beryl is unclear, unless she, like Mike (65), had drawn attention to herself with bold statements during the Forum. ASIO was more interested in travelers to and from communist countries than the US, although Mike, as an anti-Vietnam War activist was in their sights.

More explicit and alarming were the experiences of delegates from other parts of the world. Susan (SA 57) was questioned thoroughly by South African security service personnel. Eline (SA 54) returned home with a treasured photograph of her and Wentworth 'Kiddy' (Ghana 54). Invited to talk about her Forum experience to school audiences and adult groups, she rather naïvely told of her friendship with Kiddy and showed the photograph, the antithesis of apartheid. Her parents were horrified and told her of a young, white, female, anti-apartheid activist in a nearby town who had been imprisoned. Eline was suitably terrified into silence and retreated from political engagement, although not before she wrote a book, *In My Voortrekkerok Voor Die Wêreld*, telling of her Forum experiences.

Carefully mentored by her uncle, Afrikaans children's author Ben Conradie, Eline kept to the script in her book, producing an acceptable piece of propaganda which was distributed to South African high schools. She played down her contact with 'Kiddy' (Ghana 54), who 'always treated me with respect', and implied the US was similar to South Africa, describing Inga (Denmark 54)'s experience at an American high school when she wanted to demonstrate Danish folk dancing with Kiddy. A teacher stopped her 'The people here are conservative they won't like it'. She made much of her speech defending apartheid at the finale at the UN, after which, she remembered, Alan Paton, anti-apartheid author of *Cry the Beloved Country* told her he 'did not agree' but she had done 'a very good job'. Later William G Averitt of the Carnegie Endowment for International Peace wrote her a personal letter commending her 'explanation of apartheid' as 'the best I have yet heard'. The picture of Eline and Kiddy was not reproduced in the book. The ten images include Eline with white Americans and European, Japanese, or Arab delegates, with just one shot of the entire Forum group, chosen perhaps because their faces were indistinguishable.[22]

Israel also took a dim view of their delegates departing from the party line, as we have seen. Nurit (54) and Zohar (56) were reprimanded during the Forum, but Snait (Israel 61) faced the music at home. During a public appearance in the US, she 'said something about the vestiges of imperialism in the Middle East and … said it was up to Israel to work for peace'. Back in Israel, 'people at the foreign ministry had got the script and there was a scandal in the newspapers'. One *Haaretz* article announced that she was 'suspected of defamation' having 'spoken ill' of Israel and would be called before a special committee of the Ministry of Education and Culture. A ministry official quickly denied this, and Snait escaped personal interrogation.[23]

Help appeared from an unexpected quarter. Moshe Dayan, the charismatic Commander in Chief of the Israeli military, had coincidentally shared a TWA flight with Sanaa (Egypt 61) and Suheil (Jordan 61) from New York to Paris, and heard about the Forum and Snait. (The delegates were in first class!) Sanaa and Suheil have markedly different accounts of the meeting. Sanaa's 1987 autobiography, *Enemy in a Promised Land*, gave and account full of sexual frisson: Despite feeling 'a thrill of revulsion', she tapped Dayan on the shoulder. Invited to sit beside him she did, giggling nervously, 'her heart pounding with terror and delight'. He 'took my hand encouragingly in his', saying 'he was very fond of girls'. Later, hearing his voice on the radio 'would send the blood rushing through' her veins. Suheil was absent in her account, but he told me that he was the one who, recognizing Dayan by his distinctive eye patch, 'tapped the man on the shoulder … and introduced myself' as a boy from Birzeit in Jordan. 'Then we are neighbors', said Dayan. He moved the passenger in the neighboring seat and invited Suheil to sit next to him. They discussed the Palestinian Israeli dispute. Suheil was one of many Palestinians 'evicted from their homes' in Ramla and Lydda 'by Jewish fighters' in 1948. 'Naturally Mr Dayan stuck to the narrative that Palestinians … chose to leave their home under orders of the Arab armies', Suheil sighed, decades later. But Dayan also invited Suheil to visit him and meet his daughter, who was about the same age, in Jerusalem, 'if King Hussein of Jordan would give permission' for him to cross the border. 'To be honest I don't remember the part Sanaa' played in this encounter', Suheil concluded.[24]

Moshe Dayan's account to *Haaretz* was closer to Suheil's. More importantly, the encounter had implications for Snait in Israel. Both the Egyptian and Jordanian had engaged him in conversation, he said. He 'saw the dedication of Snait in Sanaa Hassan's diary—ordinary warm words—and was glad for this human contact'. He described Snait as 'a most wonderful young person' because, after meeting her, Sanaa 'now believed there was a possibility of peace with Israel'.[25]

Despite this support, Snait found herself a pariah. 'People at school stopped talking to me'. The 'main lesson' of this was that 'it made me not care what people think', she told me resolutely, decades later, 'It inoculated me for life'.[26] More broadly such incidents illustrated once again the dangerous game the Forum played with these teenagers, for whom the televised discussions and reported comments had real-life consequences.

The Forum also had an impact on Sanaa (Egypt 61), not just because of her meeting with Moshe Dayan. She became what the *Guardian* described as 'the Arab world's first, albeit unofficial and ostracized, peace envoy' to Israel in 1974, more than three years before Egypt's President Anwar Sadat's more famous peace mission. Surprisingly, Sanaa's 1987 autobiography of her experiences made no mention of either the Forum, or her good friend Snait, with whom she had no further contact. Perhaps this was because she shaved several years off her age, becoming a '23-year-old Harvard graduate student' when she traveled to Israel in 1974. She was actually 31. The fiction meant that she could not admit to being in the Forum cohort of 1961, instead playing up the (undated) meeting with Moshe Dayan.[27]

A Stepping Stone to an American Education

Other delegates used the Forum experience in different ways. The most common was as a stepping stone to an American college, often with a scholarship. Alice (Singapore 52) even framed educational opportunity as the primary object of the Forum, later telling historian Julia Horne that she had won a USIS-sponsored trip 'to visit a number of top academic schools that subsequently offered her scholarships and the possibility of going to Yale or Harvard'. Chotima (Thailand 57), who did postgraduate studies in the US after her medical degree, suggested that the Forum had made such 'excellent arrangements for us that … we nearly became spoiled children and that might be one of the reasons why most of the delegates want to go back to the States again'.[28]

It was not 'most', however. The Forum newsletter gives the impression an American education was a common outcome, but US-based delegates were, of course, its most regular correspondents. Of the 791 non-American delegates, I traced the further education of 480. Forty per cent of those had an American education: 63 delegates went to an American university but then returned home, and 129 delegates ended up living in the US, (most had also attended a US university). This includes those who did undergraduate degrees in their own countries and then won Fulbright and other scholarships for postgraduate studies. Arguably the Forum had less to do with this, although it had introduced them to 'irresistible' attractions of America. Some delegates reorientated their university ambitions from the UK to the US after the Forum experience, although others did not. Eighteen delegates went to university in the UK and then returned home, while thirty-one emigrated from Africa, Asia, the Middle East, or South America to the UK, Europe, or Australia. Some of those also attended UK universities.[29]

The Forum certainly offered an inside track and sometimes an introduction. Bhinda (Nepal 52) was unusual because she stayed in the US after the Forum. Rules about returning home were less stringent then. Bhinda told her granddaughter years later that at the Forum she 'met a lady in Voice of America who was from Barnard', the prestigious private women's liberal arts college at Columbia University. She organized Bhinda a scholarship to Barnard College and a job at Voice of America, translating scripts. The *Tribune* made much of Bhinda's success, including an illustrated fashion feature on her new American wardrobe, after Sterns buyer Lillian Harkow took her on a shopping spree. Bhinda was the first Nepalese woman to work for VOA and the first to graduate from Barnard College. She later returned home and continued to lead the way for Nepalese women as 'Nepal's premier woman diplomat' and the first female Nepalese ambassador, when she was posted to New Delhi.[30]

Susan (SA 57)'s path to Barnard college was also all about the Forum. Helen Rogers Reid, 'a tiny little woman with black dress and white pearls' was 'interested in me not in politics', recalled Susan, asking her 'had she ever thought about Barnard College?' Susan agreed it would be a lovely place to study, having not, she said later, thought much about it at all. Within the hour Susan was sent to 'have a look around' Barnard, and 'have a chat' with relevant people. She liked what she saw. Her application later that year was accepted, along with a full scholarship, much to her surprise, but not to those in the know. Helen Rogers Reid, Susan learned afterwards, was chair of the board of trustees of the college.[31]

Bhinda and Susan were Forum darlings, but not all those with ambitions to study in the US were so privileged. According to one delegate, Helen Waller refused to help Young-Koo (Korea 57) who was hellbent on getting back to the US for college. Perhaps she thought that was the only reason he had applied for the Forum, or possibly did not rate him. Already 19 when he came to the Forum, his education had been interrupted by the Korean War. Young-Koo found another pathway, joining the US Army and returning to the US the following year to attend Elgin Academy. Azer (Iran 56) was too young for college but strategically applied to transfer to Tehran's American Community School, which was, he said 'a co-ed school meant primarily for Americans living in Iran, but the Forum had made me famous!' so he was accepted, providing a pathway to a US college.[32]

College visits were part of the field trips in later years, especially in the 1960s. Arnold (Colombia 69) visited MIT during his Forum and successfully applied two years later, using Robert Huffman as a referee. American colleges were interested in this group of smart 'future world leaders'. Sarah Lawrence College's engagement with the Forum was designed to attract students, by showing them 'the image of an American college which is progressive, liberal, and intellectually interesting'. Williams College also made the most of the Forum talent, recruiting a slew of delegates in the early 1960s.[33]

For some, getting into an American college was lifesaving as well as life-changing. Vuong (Vietnam 68) said 'Vietnam in 1968 was a nasty place for a young man at the right age for conscription, or for a student whose family had neither fortune or influence, and no connections'. The Forum was like 'being lifted out of a nasty melee in the valley and deposited on a green peaceful hill side'. During the Forum, on a whim, he took the SAT with a host brother. Another host introduced him to Thomas Snyder, admissions officer at Washington University in St Louis. Thomas offered 'admission with a full-tuition scholarship', helped Vuong get a part-time job at the Olin Library, and organized a live-in au pair position with Michael and Nancy Edlin. As Vuong remembered, he owed his 'rescue' from Vietnam to these people, who 'changed my life completely'.[34]

For others, personal circumstances limited their options. In 1958 Salih (Turkey 56) explained why he was not one of the 'many' who were in a US college. Although he 'strived in every nerve to return to the States' and was offered full tuition scholarships from Columbia, Cornell, and Fairleigh Dickinson, it was impossible because of 'the shortage of appropriations granted by the Ministry of Education to those who wish to study abroad'. Phuong (Vietnam 56) was excited to win a scholarship to Vassar College and was all set to return to the US but, 'my mother does not want me to leave home for such a long time (4 years) especially when it's not safe these days'. Instead, she stayed in Vietnam and married young. 'Now Mrs Ta Ngoc Diep', she told Forum newsletter readers in 1958 that she was 'very happy with my married life', noting that 'although I study my law, I don't forget to study the role of good wife either'. Diep (Vietnam 55) wanted to stay in the US for her PhD after completing a Masters in 1959, but instead applied for a job with the Ministry of Foreign Affairs in Saigon. A PhD was too expensive, and she was 'anxious to go home to do something for my family and my country'. She thanked the Forum for giving her 'a terrific start' for 'you see I am just an ambitious little girl'. Despite this, she was still in New York in 1960, working for the Belgian Information Center.[35]

Irjaleena (Finland 57) would have loved a scholarship to the US, but less than a year after the Forum, her father had left, her mother had died, and she had sole responsibility for her brother, who was two years younger. 'There was no way I could leave him', she said. Instead, she went to Helsinki Business School, married at 21 and had a long career in the Finnish film and television industry. In any case, as she pointed out, an American education was an indulgence for Europeans: 'We had the university system here'.[36] Some Europeans went to the US, but few emigrated permanently. Three 1949 delegates escaped the rubble of post-war Europe, and later, others earned Fulbrights and other fellowships for postgraduate studies, or became academics and enjoyed American as well as other international postings. It was different for delegates from poorer countries with no or few universities at home. Studying overseas was the only option for Ghanaians Alfred (56) and Nii (59) because Ghana had no medical school.

Student life in the US was not easy. No longer were they privileged 'adolescent ambassadors' but ordinary mortals. For Avri (Israel 68), 'graduate school at Cornell provided a well-needed dose of reality'. There was 'no more national TV or UN Secretary general, only very hard work, cramped graduate student quarters, and K-mart'. It could be lonely. Direk (Thailand 55) was away from home for all five years of his engineering degree. His cure was the Forum connection: 'Once in a while I go to NY, and the customary thing to do is to see Mrs Waller and Freddie and pick up news about' other delegates. Saroj (Thailand 58) also found a (very tentative) Forum connection when feeling homesick at university in Wisconsin. Jenny (Netherlands 49) had just moved to Madison with her husband and kindly invited him to visit. Jenny admitted Saroj was the first alumnus she had met, having lost track of her cohort. Auxilia (Rhodesia 62) found it too difficult, returning home after just one year of study at Western College for Women in Ohio.[37]

Brain Drain?

Helen Waller was greeted by 'a chorus of "No!"' when she asked 1955 delegates, 'If you had the choice would you stay in the United States?' reported the *Tribune*. The newspaper was possibly allaying any concerns of delegates overstaying their welcome, but generally, delegates wanted to go home. Peter (Kenya 65) was 22 when he came to the Forum. He studied journalism at Ohio University and worked for the *Sandusky Register* in Ohio and the *Saginaw News* in Michigan. Despite any ties he formed, the pull of home was too strong. He returned to Kenya, where he reverted to his Kenyan name, Chege Mbitiru, and became a highly respected and influential journalist and eventually the East Africa correspondent for Associated Press.[38] For Chege Mbitiru, the Forum and an American education were positive experiences but did not lead to emigration.

For some delegates emigration to the US was not even attractive. In the 1990s Kris (Ceylon 68), a mid-career university academic, won a WHO fellowship to Maryland. He was scathing of the US Visa officer in Colombo who assumed all Ceylonese were hoping to sneak into the US permanently and initially refused his visa application. With an established life in his own country, why would he move, only to start again at the bottom? Neither did emigration guarantee success. John (Ghana 72) ended up at a New York soup kitchen in his later years, having lost his job as a financial consultant in the city in 2009.[39]

Forum alumni have debated the issue of whether the Forum (and similar exchange programs) caused a 'brain drain' from less wealthy countries, which could ill-afford to lose talented individuals, to the US. In 2005, John (UK 59) opened a discussion in the alumni's newsletter *The Delegate* about Forum impacts. He pointed to the fact that '59 out of the 130 delegates we have traced from poorer developing countries, now live abroad, nearly all in the US or Europe' and only 7 of the 21 African delegates had remained in Africa. More recent research suggests the picture is not quite so 'bleak'. John's sample, based on delegates traced by the Alumni Association (which is dominated by US-based and European delegates), exaggerated the extent of emigration. Of the 791 non-US delegates, 96 have been impossible to locate. Some of these may well have emigrated to the US, losing contact with compatriots, but generally US-based alumni have been easier to trace, as US records are more extensive and accessible than many in Asia and Africa.[40]

Of the 695 delegates who have been traced, only 129, or 18.6 per cent, settled in the US. As the table in the appendix shows, this figure was not consistent across continents. Europeans, Brits, Israelis, South Africans, Australasians, and Canadians generally returned home. Just over three-quarters of those South and Central Americans who were traced also went home, but there are 20 per cent about whom nothing is known. Most Asians and Africans also returned home. Almost all African emigrants were from Ghana and Ethiopia. Only 4 of the 42 remaining African delegates emigrated permanently, although at least 11 studied in the US. Delegates from Arab countries were most likely to emigrate, with nearly half of those traced relocating to the US. This figure is skewed, like that for Latin America, because 23 per cent of Arab delegates were untraceable.

How much of the brain drain was due to the Forum is difficult to assess. There were other factors at play, notably turmoil within their own countries. As Chit (India 56) said, 'I was lucky that I could return to my country—it didn't have the sort of revolutions that some places did meaning people had to leave'. Hanne (Denmark 49) could see the attraction of the US: 'I am so selfish as to think that it would be better to live in America in case of a new war'. Years after he made America his home, Raja (Jordan 54) contrasted the US with Jordan, where 'about half of my classmates lived in refugee tents, with no water or electricity—victims of the 1948 war with resulting non-voluntary exodus of the Palestinian people'. He felt that 'the Forum lifted me out of that grim reality into a world I never thought existed'. He was grateful that the experience gave him the courage to emigrate so that he could 'now contemplate the harsh realities from a "safe" distance'.[41]

Political coups, civil wars, and regime changes made some delegates, whose families were often part of the ousted political elite, persona non grata in their home countries. Some Ghanaians emigrated after the downfall of Nkrumah in 1966, Vietnamese fled in the 1970s, Iranians made tracks after the fall of the Shah. Forum connections were useful. Le (Vietnam 57)'s host parents in Sayre, Pennsylvannia, sent him 'papers and sponsored my wife and two children when came to US in 1975'. Forum administrators pulled strings to facilitate Jan (Czechoslovakia 67)'s defection a few years after the Forum, in a boys' own adventure involving one group of American Summer delegates, as we shall see. Haider (Pakistan 71) never went home from the Forum at all. He was due to fly via Karachi in mid-March, but the Bengali liberation war was brewing. His family was prominent in the Liberation movement, and Robert Huffman kept him in the US. 'In some ways he may have saved my life', reflected Haider. Ten days later, on March 25 the Pakistani Army massacred students at Dhaka University. Haider remained in the US with his final host family, the Huttos, who became his American 'Mom and Pop'.[42]

Others had less dramatic and more personal reasons for moving to the US. Academics found their careers developing in the US university system. Anani (Ghana 60) was professor of Afro-Brazilian studies at Brown University, playing a critical role in the development of Black Studies. Job opportunities also beckoned for recent graduates; others developed personal networks during their university days, finding friends and spouses. Nii (Ghana 59) told of the group of twelve would-be doctors from his school—all except one ended up living overseas. 'Many married in the countries where they had spent eight to ten impressionable years', studying medicine, which was not available in Ghana.[43]

Some delegates bounced between countries for several years. Nii, like Alfred (Ghana 56), 'tried to return home as an idealistic young medical doctor ... only to find himself frustrated at every turn by incompetence and poor organization'. Nii settled in Canada, where he had studied, while Alfred went to New York. Bharat (Nepal 64)'s Nepalese friends and family were astonished when he announced he would return home after university. 'Why would you do that?' they asked, 'you could have a better life in the US'. Bharat was torn, but in the end chose America, hoping that he could do more for his country by sending money back.⁴⁴

David (Kenya 62) declared in his Forum autobiography that he intended to study abroad 'in East Africa, England or USA', and then return to Kenya, 'not to indulge in politics, but be an ordinary school teacher', to address the 'lack of good teachers'. He graduated with an MA from Dartmouth in '66 but remained in the US, teaching in high schools for several years before becoming Professor of African and African American Studies at New Jersey City State University.⁴⁵ David might have left Kenya anyway, even without the Forum experience, but he was part of the broader 'brain drain'.

The Forum opened delegates' eyes to opportunities beyond their own shores, if they were not already aware, and sometime provided opportunities for college scholarships. Being a high school program, the Forum could not require, as some other university-level programs did, that delegates return to their countries to live and serve for *several years*, one solution to the 'brain drain' problem. Overall, however, Forum delegates tended not to migrate to the US permanently. Even if we assumed that untraced delegates did in fact emigrate to America, still only 28 per cent of delegates may have become American. The picture changes when looking at the 453 delegates from Africa, Asia, South America, and the Middle East. Potentially up to 40 per cent of them went to the US, if we include the 'untraceable' delegates.⁴⁶ Even this, however, was more about regional political instability or personal connections. Forum organizers, while encouraging delegates to get an American college education, did not want them to remain. Instead, they hoped delegates would return home to become influential leaders, retaining both a sense of gratitude to the US and an internationalist outlook fostered by the network of Forum alumni.

Future Leaders?

Forum delegates were encouraged to think big. Helen Waller opened her October 1957 newsletter: 'Remember how often you've day-dreamed about the future when you'd meet again here as UN Delegates?', explaining that she had just seen Eddie Hogan-Shaidali (Malaya 50) in the delegation of the newly-independent Malaya at the UN General Assembly, and was entertaining Vangala Jaya Ram (India 54), 'now a member of the UN Secretariat', to lunch. Bob Huffman similarly treated delegates like 'a baby UN'.[47]

The Forum's ambition, especially in the 1950s, to bring together future world leaders was apparent in the selection criteria, designed to identify those with potential to go far, whether through natural ability or the right family connections. The poster boys of the Forum, invariably mentioned by interviewees as exemplifying the ideal Forum Alumnus career, were Johan Holst (Norway 56) and Jayantha Dhanapala (Ceylon 57). Johan was a Norwegian cabinet minister and credited with shaping the Oslo Accord as part of the Israeli Arab peace process in the 1990s. Jayantha was Under-Secretary-General at the UN and stood for the position of Secretary General in 2006, his bid scuppered by Sri Lanka's civil war.

How many others went on to become prime ministers or international leaders, or had an impact on the world stage? The later careers of only about two-thirds of the 807 delegates are traceable—even with the wonders of various internet search engines and the growing digitization of archives—but it is reasonable to assume that if a delegate reached a significant position in political leadership, they would be discoverable. A rough check found about 90, or just over 10 per cent of all the delegates had become significant 'world leaders', high ranking civil servants, politicians, diplomats, or senior bureaucrats at the UN or the World Bank.

In addition, over 100 were academics, in a wide variety of disciplines. Some of these were also advisors to governments or international organizations. There were at least 45 doctors or psychologists and 25 lawyers or judges, including two Chief Justices. Others were in business, for themselves or climbing the corporate ladder, in tea, oil, aviation, and chemicals. There were delegates in banking, engineering, journalism, teaching; there were filmmakers, translators, musicians, writers, engineers, architects, accountants, administrators, even a fire chief, and a missionary. Some worked as activists, charity workers, philanthropists, and as housewives and mothers.

Considering delegates' careers through a gendered lens gives both unsurprising and surprising results. Most politicians and diplomats, business and corporate leaders were male. For example, John Goulden (UK 59) was a career diplomat, finishing up as Britain's Ambassador to

NATO in 1995. Michael Portillo (UK 72) was a cabinet minister and prominent member of the Conservative Party, standing unsuccessfully for its leadership. Amos Sawyer (Liberia 63), who declared on a Forum television program that he would 'be leader of his country', was Liberian president from 1990 to 1994. His compatriot Emmanuel Shaw (Liberia 65) achieved notoriety as President Charles Taylor's Minister of Finance, and has more recently reappeared as an influential figure behind the current President Charles Weah. Erkki Liikanen (Finland 68), in the Finnish parliament by the age of 21, has been a Minister of Finance, Head of the Finnish Mission to the European Union, Governor of the Bank of Finland and a frontrunner to be president of the European Central Bank in 2019. Christoph Bertram (Germany 1956) headed the German Institute for Security and International Affairs. Like Jayantha Dhanapala (Ceylon 57), others were in the UN, including economist Jomo Kwame Sundaram (Malaysia 70), who was assistant director-general of the Food and Agricultural Association and Krisantha Weerasuriya (Ceylon 68), a 'swashbuckler for Essential Medicines' at the WHO.[48] Diplomat Sergio Duarte (Brazil 53) was the UN High Representative for Disarmament Affairs, while Ugi Zvekic (Yugoslavia 69) was deputy director of the United Nations Interregional Crime and Justice Research Institute and Chair of the UN Economic Commission for Europe.

The girls at the Forum were smart and ambitious, just like their male counterparts, and some managed to navigate (or avoid) marriage and children, to play significant roles in foreign affairs, politics, business, and academia. They included Difie Agyarko Kuis (Ghana 67), Bhinda Malla (Nepal 52), and Melpomeni Korneti (Yugoslavia 70), who all held ambassadorial posts. Maryam Daftari (Iran 59) climbed the ranks of the Iranian foreign service until the gendered policies of the incumbent regime limited her ambitions. Human rights activist and chair of Philippines Commission on Human Rights, Purificacion Valera (Philippines 52), and Judge Cecilia Medina Quiroga (Chile 53) were both members of the UN Human Rights Council; Kustijah Prodjolalito (Indonesia 59) and Bemma Donkah (Ghana 71) also represented their countries at the UN. Orit Gadeish (Israel 67) became chair of global management consulting firm Bain and Company and was the ninety-fifth most powerful woman in the world in the 2005 Forbes list. Mona Zulficar (Egypt 65) became a lawyer and human rights activist, serving on the UNHRC and the advisory board of the World Bank. She also made a Forbes list—of powerful businesswomen in the Arab world in 2021. Dorothy Chen (Malaya 62) is a management consultant and consummate corporate board member, whose international networks would make Ruth Bishop or Helen Waller gasp. Law professor Alice Erh-Soon Tay (Singapore 52) was president of Australia's Human Rights and Equal Opportunity Commission. Sahadya Prabhavat (Thailand 60) became an Air Marshall in the Thai Airforce. Gudrún Erlendsdóttir (Iceland 55) was the first female judge in Iceland, and Hawa Tejan-Jallah (Sierra Leone 65) was Chief Justice of Sierra Leone. Lucie Falck (Norway 57), Chrysy Karydi (Greece 70), and Melpomeni Korneti (Yugoslavia 70) were all politicians. Chrysy also ran the family business, Ikaros Publications, with her sister. Sonja Liht (Yugoslavia 66) and Monika Kalista (Austria 65) rose to the top of their respective civil services. I interviewed Monika when we were both in Milan—although retired from her position as Austrian Head of the Department of Culture, she still had clout, charmingly delegating the cultural attaché, who was showing her around Expo 2015, to store my bags for the day in his office at the Austrian Consulate in Milan—quite the superior left-luggage repository for my scruffy suitcase!

Fascinating, to me at least, was the fact that the women who cut through the glass ceiling were predominantly not from the Anglosphere. Coming from New Zealand, where we pride ourselves on being the first country in the world to give women the vote, I have grown up naïvely assuming that New Zealand, along with Australia, Britain, and the US, had been leading in female emancipation more generally. In fact, neither the boys or girls from New Zealand and Australia distinguished themselves in politics or in international diplomacy. British female delegates included teachers, high-ranking civil servants, academics, and a university administrator. Maureen Cleave (53) was a journalist, whose claim to fame was her association with the Beatles in the 1960s.[49]

The girl delegates with the most conventionally 'influential' careers were predominantly from Asia and Africa. Class, money, and connections often trumped gender. This was brought home to me when I spoke with

Hiranthi Walpola (Ceylon 67). She had qualified as a doctor and had a career—children were no barrier in Sri Lanka. But, she told me, as one of her daughters pointed out, her career depended on cheap child care from other women, exploited and underpaid. A career was more difficult after she emigrated to Australia, where not only were her qualifications (from London) unrecognized, but childcare was expensive (albeit still exploited and underpaid).[50] I should not have been so surprised, however, by the predominance of non-Anglosphere highfliers among both boys and girls. The selection process for the Forum limited candidates to English-speakers. The pool was further limited in many places to elite schools or politically well-connected young people, who were predestined for greatness, with or without the Forum.

Beyond Politicians and Diplomats

Some of the more than 100 academics, in history, law and social science, as well as in medicine, and engineering, have had international impact, notably human rights activists Hameeda Hossain (Pakistan 52) and Priyanthi Fernando (Ceylon 70). Gus Nasmith (US 62, assistant director) studied at the Fletcher School of Diplomacy, with prospects of a promising foreign service career. When his homosexuality made that impossible in the late 1960s, he took an alternative path, working for the Forum and then with international NGOs and as special advisor to the president of the UN General Assembly in 1988, leaving 'a legacy of dedication and commitment to world peace, human rights, gay rights and international HIV/AIDS work'.[51]

Other delegates made an international impact in less exalted circles, but it was no less meaningful. Barbara Church (NZ 64) reinvented herself completely as Barbara Dawson, opening a Kiwi Café in Vietnam engaging with the local community. (I was particularly proud of tracing her story, given 'Church' was frustrating to google, and Dawson a name she picked out of the air!) Mike Jones (Australia 65) founded student activist group Students for a Democratic Society (SDS) in Australia, and later established an Australia-China Chamber of Commerce. Ida Bossi (Italy 59) started a charity to build wells in Ethiopia. Catherine Marin (France 59) worked in

Brussels for the European Commission's Leonardo da Vinci Programme, facilitating exchanges in vocational training. Gerry Bray (Rhodesia 60) and Jona Burgess (Iceland 60) also worked in student exchange.

On the other hand, Nasreen (Pakistan 55) was frustrated, telling fellow alumni in 1960 that 'although I would like a full-time job, nobody seems to take this seriously'. Nevertheless, she had 'not been altogether idle dabbling in several pursuits', including 'upholding women's rights and ensuring their protection by seriously doing some social work'. Jenny (Netherlands 49) apologized to newsletter readers for her 'rather poor' news, 'but since you asked for news from all of us, even housewives', she wrote anyway.[52]

Some delegates were skeptical about the ambitions of the Forum to create an international network of world leaders. As two 1960s alumni told me, most delegates were 'ordinary', and even though '90 per cent said they wanted to be politicians', most took other paths.[53] Sometimes political or diplomatic ambitions were thwarted by a change of regime or by more personal circumstances—life (or for women, children) got in the way. Nevertheless, the list of Forum alumni includes a good sprinkling of impressive global movers and shakers, with even more in careers reflecting the Forum's internationalist philosophy.

After the Forum

Immediately after the Forum, delegates settled back into the rigors of home and school, continued their performances as little ambassadors, or planned their escape to an American college. Some encountered uncomfortable consequences of their outspokenness at the Forum, an unintended but disturbing impact of the program for delegates from less tolerant regimes. The Forum did not cause a 'brain drain' of delegates to the US by itself, but was part of the larger movement of people, often caused by political and economic catastrophes. For some, the Forum opened doors to an international career; others were at the Forum because they were already destined for one. Still more were never global household names, but nevertheless had careers reflecting the internationalism of the Forum.

Meanwhile, by the 1960s, American students were wanting a taste of the same international experience that delegates enjoyed, and from 1964 a 'Forum in Reverse' was developed.

Chapter 15

Americans Abroad

A 'Forum-in-Reverse'

The *Herald Tribune* Forum's new initiative in 1964, a 'Forum-in-reverse' was 'another major step in our effort to increase understanding among the peoples of the world', said newspaper owner Jock Whitney, proudly. 'The top students' from the Metropolitan competition to choose the American delegate to the International Forum would have 'a seven-week educational experience in Europe during July and August'. He was 'enthusiastic about our young Ambassadors', telling parents of the first lucky cohort that 'as a former Ambassador myself, I can think of no better representatives of our country abroad than a specially selected group of young people, each of whom has earned the opportunity because of personal excellence'. The value of the experience was incalculable: 'Just as we anticipate there will be certain noticeable but, we hope, temporary changes in our group—such as berets, beards and Bardot hairdos—so we are certain that this summer abroad will bring about deep and worthwhile changes in each member of the group'.[1]

Where the idea of a European tour for American teenagers originated is not clear. It fitted with Whitney's interests, both his foundation's educational focus, and the *Tribune*'s European edition. A group of intellectually engaged American teenagers gallivanting around Europe was good copy. It was probably also a response to high school students lobbying for a larger piece of the Forum pie. In his first Forum job, Bob Huffman had organized the local high school competitions. He was aware New York high schools were home to a bevy of bright young things who would benefit from a Forum-like experience. Organizers were also beginning to shift the balance of the Forum's focus even more towards its educational benefits for American students rather than dreaming of creating a cohort of future international leaders. In 1964 Bob Huffman was reconstituting the Forum as an independent, non-profit, educational program governed by its own Board of Trustees. The new program, variously called the Summer Forum or European Forum, was part of expanding and futureproofing the Forum organization. Unlike the foreign delegates, American students paid for their trip, with the intention that this new initiative would subsidize the New York Forum.

Perhaps the most obvious question to ask about this 'Forum-in-reverse' is why Europe? A true Forum-in-reverse would have encompassed a broader range of countries. A more exotic (and potentially cheaper option) would have been Africa or Asia. But the *Tribune* had no African edition. Europe also had the largest concentration of Forum alumni who could be conscripted to assist. It was easily traversable by train, with multiple countries within reach, and was probably the most desirable travel destination for 1960s American teenagers (although by the 1970s Pamela Jacklin, who led three trips, said that her groups were keen to go further). A European Summer Forum also underscored the way the Forum, for all its internationalism, was intensely European. During Helen Waller's tenure, the Forum group had traveled to London, Paris, and twice to Berlin, with one foray to the Middle East with Sarah Lawrence College, and one trip to Ghana, initiated by Ghanaian delegates. Helen Waller's connections were in Europe, as were those of the *Herald Tribune*. Bob Huffman did not appear to introduce new connections himself, relying instead on those established and reinvigorated by new crops of delegates.

In 1964, sixteen students aged between 16 and 18 were selected from the Metropolitan competition between 150 New York schools. They included two former American delegates, Lew (US 64) and Ethel (US 63), and were evenly split between boys and girls. They visited Britain and continental Europe for seven weeks in the American summer. Forum publicity announced that the lucky group would be 'living with European families and talking part in seminars and discussions with student and adult leaders'. Ginger (Summer 64) described it as 'a kind of social science tour of Europe', during which they were expected to participate thoughtfully and intelligently. The tour was a success and expanded in 1965 with two groups crisscrossing Europe. By 1971 the European Program had its own brochure and offered five itineraries, each lasting about seven weeks, with smaller group sizes.[2]

The Young American Ambassadors

Delegates were initially drawn from those who had participated in the original Forum program. Priority was given to runners-up in the New York Metropolitan competition, then to host students, followed by a few places reserved for juniors nominated by their schools as likely to be American delegates to the Forum the following year. This ensured the European trip was well integrated into the broader Forum program. Most summer delegates were smart, articulate youngsters, primarily from the New York area. In 1970 the selection process shifted. Freed from the New York-focused sponsorship of the *Tribune*, the World Youth Forum tried to broaden its appeal beyond the eastern states. Along with two groups of East Coast high school students, drawn from schools that participated in the Forum, there was a 'Communication Group'. Four of its seven students came from California, Oregon, and Missouri, and all seven were sponsored by media outlets. This group followed a program focusing on the role of mass media, including a 'total immersion' week in Leeds with Yorkshire Television. They even lived with the company's executives. By 1971 this was the only selective summer Forum program. The others were no longer competitive, open to all high school seniors and juniors across America, with 'a sincere interest in the purposes of the program and the ability to contribute to its success'. It was still advertised as 'not just another student tour', but one in which 'the excitement of travel' was combined with 'an opportunity to learn about other people's problems and to discuss contemporary issues with them'. The broadening of the selection meant that this ideal was not always met. Of the three groups Pamela Jacklin conducted, two had deep divisions between those interested in discussions and those intent on partying. The middle group, in 1970, stood out in her memory. With only thirteen students, the group gelled, and all were politically and intellectually engaged.[3]

The 1971 brochure declared the groups would contain 'fellow Americans from a variety of backgrounds'. This was optimistic. Delegates were also usually solidly middle-class, sometimes affluent, predominantly white, and some had been to Europe before. After all, the trip was not free. Delegates paid $925 in 1967, rising to $1050 in 1971. This was $300–$400 lower than for 'most programs of comparable length' because administration costs were low, being absorbed by the larger program, and European alumni volunteers helped plan activities. Nevertheless, organizers acknowledged it was 'a formidable obstacle for many people', providing a few scholarships of $100 for those who demonstrated hardship, and offering suggestions for fundraising options. As the Forum program explored other avenues of sponsorship more generally after the death of the *Tribune*, the Summer Forum also benefitted, broadening its cohort. WCAU-TV sponsored Lorna Prince, from Archbishop Prendergast High school in Philadelphia in 1970, after a competition in which student speakers faced questions on 'America's priorities' and world opinion in the '70s'.[4] She had also hosted a 1970 delegate to the New York Forum.

Lorna was not the first African American to join the European Forum. Red Bank High School teacher Charlotte McCane was a leader in 1965, in charge of nine white boys and six white girls. In 1968 Craig (US 68) was in Eileen Gallagher's group. Brothers Bill 'BC' and Alvin 'AC' (Summer 69, 70) also traveled, part of a growing African American elite, their father a successful real estate investor and entrepreneur and one of the original founders of the Freedom National Bank in New York. Pennsylvanian Linda Watson traveled in 1969 as did Geoffrey Canada, from the South Bronx, at the predominantly African American Wyandanch High School, where his teacher Gary Walker was a Summer Forum leader. Gary and Connie Walker worked hard to raise sponsorship for less wealthy African American students.

In 1973 CBS sponsored Harlem Prep students Dawn Mitchell and Clifford Jacobs. Traveling through England, France, Belgium, Switzerland, and Italy was life-changing for 18-year-old Clifford. 'My world was turned upside down', he told me, but it was not the tourist sites that did it. 'In Europe I was accepted as a person, a human being, my ethnicity and country of origin were insignificant'. And in words that illuminate the stark and depressing reality of life as an African American teenager in the 1970s, he said, 'I had never, ever had such a feeling nor did I think such a thing was possible'. Nearly forty years later, he still felt the impact of that revelation.[5]

Leading the Charge

The Summer Forum was not a luxury program. It relied on badly paid leaders and volunteers, especially alumni. Bob Huffman led the first tour, with assistance from Stuyvesant High School teacher Bernard Flicker. Joint leadership was the norm in subsequent years, although Huffman did not repeat his experience. Instead, he traveled separately, his European jaunt a 'perk' of his job, doing preliminary organization and checking in with leaders occasionally. Leaders were schoolteachers and graduate students, usually with a 'junior leader', often a Summer Forum alumnus. Young high school teacher Eileen Gallagher did two tours of duty in 1967 and 1968. Gus Nasmith, assistant Forum director, and Ginger da Silva (Summer 64) oversaw Group B in 1967. Later Gus recruited leaders from among his fellow graduate students at the Fletcher School of Law and Diplomacy. This included Gary Walker and his wife Connie Freeman, who was on Forum staff. Others were Bill Hellart and his wife Pamela Jacklin. She had been a MacJannet Fellow with Gus in Geneva in 1967. Richard Kessler led the final group in 1973. He was a last-minute replacement. 'Bob Huffman interviewed me by phone' and was 'probably a little desperate', Richard said; the first and only time they met was at the airport on the way out.[6]

Leaders were not well paid. Gus was on the Forum payroll, and Eileen got an honorarium of $150 as a teacher leader. Pamela and Bill received $250 each in 1972, allowing them to remain in Europe for a few months afterwards. Assistant leaders were generally unpaid, but flights, accommodation, and living expenses were included. For Ginger (Assistant 67), it was 'a fabulous opportunity for a free, educational & fun trip to Europe'. Michael L Michael (Assistant 68) used his trip to visit sites of his mother's youth in Hamburg before she escaped the Holocaust. Eileen (Leader 68) remembered 'he took his quest seriously', tracking down his mother's old dancing school and relatives.[7]

A Place to Stay

Delegates stayed in youth hostels and student accommodation with a few homestays. Lynn (Summer 67) found her time with families in Berlin,

Stockholm, and Prague were 'the most enjoyable and beneficial' parts of the trip. Group B that year missed out on homestays, which Ginger (Assistant 67) regretted: 'a homestay is worth any effort necessary to arrange it', she insisted. Host families could be a bit of a lottery, however. Orel (Summer 64) was over-awed by the grand residence of her Milan homestay family but underwhelmed by their welcome. They gave her a silk scarf (decorated with Alfa Romeo cars!), but then grilled her about her family and connections, looking askance at this unfashionably dressed American girl. Dinner was at a long table, served by two silent servants. The saving grace for Orel was escaping to the terrace with the son of the house, Forum alumnus Marco (Italy 62), for teenage chat. The following morning the family apologetically disappeared to their country house on a prearranged trip, leaving Orel alone. She dined in solitary splendor, the two servants refusing to sit with her, instead hovering expectantly. In something of an opposite experience, Maria (Summer 64) was taken aback when her German host family in Berlin offered her an evening meal of blood sausage and hard cheese, rather than 'a meal my mother would have made—pasta, chicken or a roast'. She then asked to have a bath, 'an ordinary request' for an American teenager, but one that she later realized was 'a luxury', her host mother having to heat 'lots of water' to provide one.[8]

One of the youth hostels was also unexpectedly challenging. Ginger (Assistant 67) reported sardonically that 'though the Jugendherberge did serve to demonstrate the mettle of our group, bring them closer together and give them a lot of anecdotes for the rest of the trip, it must go'. At the top of a hill, and with a 9.45 pm curfew (lights out at 10!), it also offered 'ice water showers, rock-hard lumpy bunk beds, and watery sweet coffee for breakfast'—'a bit too much' for the first stop on the tour, 'especially in Nuremburg, which didn't offer a great deal to compensate'. Despite this, two years later, Connie (Leader 69)'s group were still visiting what had become 'the infamous hostel'. It was even more crowded than usual and the host, Wilhelm Tietz 'views himself as a dictator and perpetrates the idea of Germany as a continuously fascist country', reported Connie firmly. Perhaps Forum organizers saw this as an opportunity for the group to bond in the face of adversity. Other places were less criticized, although Ginger noted ruefully of their Belgrade hotel: 'Tea bad, but breakfast o.k. if you like prunes'. Alan (Summer 65) remembered that the most unusual place they stayed was in the grand, beautiful Der Kellerske Institution, a psychiatric hospital in Denmark, thanks to the parents of Joergen (Denmark 65) who were doctors there.[9] Five star it was not, but the accommodation was always interesting.

Relying on the Alumni

Forum alumni were the backbone of the Summer Program. Vincent 'Skip' (Summer 67) recalled years later 'the many smiling loyal Forum alumni who greeted us, toasted us, fed us, translated for us, and ... introduced us to their local dignitaries while engaging us in intriguing political and social discourse'. These young people variously arranged sightseeing excursions and accommodation; some were more diligent and appreciated than others. It was a tough gig. Riccardo (Italy 67) told leaders Ginger and Gus bluntly, 'he couldn't understand why anyone would want to come to Milan in the first place', especially in the summer, when everything closed and residents departed to mountains and coast to escape the heat. Sometimes, a younger alumnus guide became a 'rather frivolous member of the group', partying with their fellow teens, providing further headaches for the group leaders, themselves not much older. Young Peter (Germany 67) misunderstood his brief, merely offering 'suggestions of places to visit' when he met them at Nuremburg Station in 1967. Ginger efficiently commandeered 'Frau Hahn' at the Rathaus Office of School and Culture, recommending she should be used for future trips. Perhaps relying on teenagers to arrange itineraries was not a great idea. In contrast, Monika (Austria 65), although also only 18 when she led her first group, 'did an excellent job', managing to strike the right balance with a well-prepared program in Salzburg, inviting several Austrian students as guides, and making 'an effort to get to know the kids'. She became a mainstay of the Summer Forum. Perhaps unsurprisingly, Monika later became Austria's Director General of Cultural Policy in the Ministry of Foreign Affairs in Vienna. Joachim (Germany 71) provided a contrast for 1971 delegates, who were mostly 'running around seeing university students and art galleries', by organizing a tour of the VW factory where his father worked. They reportedly found it 'really interesting to see blue collar workers in Germany'.[10]

Professional guides and speakers were also a mixed bag, according to Forum leaders' reports. One in Geneva in 1967 was 'disorganized and rather a windbag', but it 'wouldn't be wise to alienate the [embassy], so send him a thank you'. Another guide in 1969 was 'snobby and flippant', refusing to answer questions, providing 'the worst and least interesting activity during the trip up to that point'. One Zagreb guide was 'delightful' but was merely 'a Belgrade student who happened to be visiting … during his vacation' and 'knew little about Zagreb'. One American embassy official should 'be thanked only as a matter of form: 'the briefing' was 'an insult to the intelligence of every member of the group. We were told nothing we didn't know already and our speaker refused to answer most of the questions'. On the other hand, most were like International Labour Organization's Snowden T Herrick, who 'was excellent and should get a nice letter'.[11]

Organization and Lack Thereof

Itineraries varied each year, with groups following different paths, but all involved a combination of educational and tourist experiences. Although described as a 'Forum-in-reverse', there were few opportunities for delegates to have the debates and discussions that characterized the New York Forum. After all, they were all Americans. They engaged with a few groups of European students, although this was limited by the timing of the trip—European schools, like American ones, were on their summer vacation. In Frankfurt the 1964 group participated in a three-day seminar with German high school students and American students of US Army and Airforce schools. They discussed the political integration of Europe, problems of the EEC, the German economy, and education. Forum alumni also facilitated contact with other young people, co-opting their student friends as guides. In Florence the 1964 group attended the Sarah Lawrence College Summer school and a four-day reunion of Forum alumni.

The 1964 itinerary included visits to UNESCO in Paris (as well as a tour of the *Herald Tribune* plant and dinner with staff of the European edition), with day trips to Chartres and Versailles. Like Forum delegates in America, these Summer Forum delegates had a window into the privileged existence enjoyed by some. Maria (Summer 64) found Europeans 'sophisticated', the Florentine men very 'stylish ... with their jackets over their shoulders'. She enjoyed the party in a former French delegate's Parisian home, where (in a story reminiscent of Forum delegates seeing a Picasso in New York) there was a 'Bonnard in the bathroom'. In Strasbourg they visited the Council of Europe and attended a Free Europe Committee Summer Session on 'The Philosophical Doctrine of Karl Marx'. In Milan they had homestays, met the Mayor and visited a bizarre combination of the Milan Stock Exchange, the famed Autodromo of Monza motor racing track, the Motta confectionery factory, and the Institute for International Political Studies. Such eclectic programming was not unusual, with some choices more successful than others. In 1967, a tour of a motor factory in Nuremberg was given the thumbs up by most, although one girl apparently suggested that a similar tour of a fashion designing house might 'round out the program' for those 'less interested in electrical equipment', or so Ginger reported to Bob Huffman, perhaps translating the student's actual words into more tactful language.[12]

Most 'sightseeing' was done in delegates' free time, although the 1964 group visited historic Pavia, and spent time at the Bavarian lakes and in museums, as well as a sobering morning at Dachau. Nearly sixty years later, Maria could still recall that, in contrast to their bubbly chatter while sightseeing, at Dachau 'all of a sudden we had nothing to say'. They drove through the town next to the camp in silence. 'Didn't they know?', Maria wondered. At Frankfurt she sketched the Auschwitz trials. 'You could hear a pin drop.' Even without understanding the language, the 'emotion of the testimony' was palpable. Nearly half of Maria's group were Jewish.[13]

They flew to Berlin from Munich and had another home stay, along with 'daily discussion programs on political economic and cultural life' of the city, and a visit to East Berlin, organized partly by German alumni. The 1964 group enjoyed a free day in Amsterdam before the final days in England, organized by Catriona (UK 63), whose family lived near Shrewsbury at Attingham Park. A string quartet was hired to play for an afternoon reception and there were lovely paintings on the walls. This was a world away from Maria's life at home. It was also a new rural experience for many of these New York teens. Maria had 'never seen a sheep in my life!'.[14] Their last night was at a central London hotel looking onto Bloomsbury Square. They had barely twenty-four hours in the capital before flying home.

'Best Laid Plans' and All That

There was 'a sense of wonder', said Maria about traveling in Europe in 1964. Arrangements were made by letter rather than by email or mobile phones. There was no 'plethora of tourist information' instantly available, and English was less widely spoken. 'Much of southern Europe shut down in the summer, and tourist attractions were less well signposted'. Ginger and Gus (Leaders 67) rustled up makeshift programs in Nuremburg, Milan, Dubrovnik, Venice, and Geneva: it was 'grossly unfair to the kids to spend more than three days without anything organized or intellectual', reported Ginger, although perhaps the 'kids' relished their freedom.[15] In later years Gus traveled around beforehand, visiting alumni and setting up the summer's activities, which became easier as time went on.

Things did not always go to plan, even with the best made of them. Among the lists of successful activities and rewarding experiences, leaders' reports contain catalogues of mishaps—missed trains, failures in communication, broken fingers, cut elbows, strange illnesses, underwhelming speakers, bad planning, and improvised itineraries. These reports were 'warts and all', so that the Forum could keep the best and ditch the disasters in following years. They demonstrate tour leaders working hard to keep the show on the road, with opportunities for derailment ever present.

Sometimes the most successful ventures were those concocted on the fly. In Milan in 1967 Gus sent groups of three students to neighboring towns with a list of tasks: getting proof of their visit signed by a city official, discovering something about the town, engaging in conversation with either a student, housewife, worker, shopkeeper, clergyman or an old man, and returning with a memento of the visit. It was a huge success 'the kids loved it', reported Ginger. One group 'came back laden with Communist propaganda', another charmed the local water commissioner, and one group 'brought back an Italian ex-AFS student as their memento

[sic]'. Connie (Leader 69) copied the idea in Prague in 1969, sending the group off in pairs to 'find someone who was not American but spoke English' to invite to lunch. Although initially 'skeptical', the students were all successful and 'most enthusiastic', enjoying a pleasant lunch.[16]

A highlight in 1967 was 'the day of our Great Adventure', as delegates later dubbed it, when the train from Salzburg to Zagreb pulled out with only half the group on board, leaving Ginger, five boys and most of the luggage on the platform. After some kerfuffle, they managed to reconvene at the next station. The next train stopped officially for only one minute. With military precision Gus and Ginger spaced small groups of delegates along the platform and they all leapt on the train as quickly as possible, spending the next nine hours perched on their luggage in the crowded Orient Express. Arriving at Zagreb at 3 am, the group were not at its 'most alert' at the 11 am talk by a government official on secondary education, but Ginger was proud that they 'nonetheless came through with questions'.[17]

Then there were the medical emergencies. 'Skip' (Summer 67) remembered starting an impromptu soccer game in a hotel lobby, managing to put his elbow through the glass pane of the fire hose box. 'Blood and glass everywhere', with Gus and Ginger, 'ever attentive and never condemning or indignant', going into full 'crisis mode' and dealing with the situation. 'My how they must have aged that summer', he reflected. Ginger's own report of the incident was remarkably matter of fact, merely noting the hospital visits to insert and then remove the required stitches. The hospital also gave Polly (Summer 67) medicine for a throat infection. By the time they reached Venice the following week, Polly's tongue was a startling brown (apparently an over prescription of antibiotics) and others had developed sore throats. Ginger worried about a contagious outbreak, but, as she noted drily in her report 'it seemed everybody developed unique diseases of their own'.[18]

Shepherding a group of teenagers around Europe held other minefields. Raging hormones, a first taste of independence, and exciting new surrounds were a heady mix. In week three, Connie and Gary (Leaders 69) dealt with 'some of the inevitable frictions' arising from 'personality conflicts as well as the waxing and waning of crushes' by taking three girls 'who we suspected might be slightly discontented' on a special excursion on the cable car above Dubrovnik and then out to dinner. As Connie had noticed 'romances blooming' during the Orientation days before the group left the US, such problems were unsurprising. Internal group tensions continued in this group throughout the tour, not helped, said Connie, by the exhaustion caused by the propensity of many to 'stay up all night'.[19]

Going East

Possibly the most interesting experiences, and those which had enduring impact, were those in Eastern Europe. Maria (Summer 64) found the visit to East Berlin, like those to Dachau and Nuremburg, 'serious stuff'. Aged 17, she had never come so close to World War II and the reality of a divided Europe. 'As an American tourist, I could go into East Berlin, but my host family, the Buskies, could not.' Upon their request, she telephoned their relatives when she was there, but 'was nervous' and 'didn't really know what to say'. She felt 'queasy' as she came out of the telephone box, worried about the consequences. The Buskies told of their only previous visit to relatives during a Christmas amnesty. They had 'scoured Berlin for the smelliest fish they could find and wrapped it in newspaper to take as a present'. At the checkpoint the guards got one whiff of the fish and waved them through. Maria was confused. 'Why take rotting fish?'. But 'we weren't bringing them the fish' the family explained. 'We were bringing *newspapers*'.[20]

Yugoslavia was also a revelation for the American students, who reportedly found it far 'more foreign' than the rest of Europe and were 'reluctant to go out on their own', finding that 'the difference in language was a bit scary', relying heavily on Branka (Yugoslavia 62) and others for translation. Branka even enlisted her parents, who spontaneously entertained one entire group of twenty-two Americans plus several Yugoslavs at their apartment one evening when other plans fell through. Sonja (Yugoslavia 66) organized an equally impressive program in Belgrade, including cultural and politically themed excursions. Ginger found the talk by a political officer at the American Embassy was particularly useful towards the end of the visit, 'it was interesting to hear a very well-informed, perceptive, and sensible foreign service officer discuss Yugoslavian problems', serving 'to tie together some of the loose ends left by disparate opinions and impressions we had received from Yugoslavians'. Perhaps the US official's 'sensible' views contrasted with the Yugoslavians' 'disparate' opinions and were simply more palatable for Americans. Nevertheless, as Ginger noted, 'it certainly helped the kids' impression of the Foreign Service'.[21]

Engaging with locals was rewarding, especially in Yugoslavia staying at an international youth camp also used by communist groups outside Dubrovnik. In 1970, the young Americans held long discussions about ideals, ambitions, democracy, and socialism with communist 'youth' (who could be up to 30-years-old) from throughout the Eastern bloc, including the USSR. William (Summer 70) remembered the delegates were singing folksongs, including 'Those Were the Days', when they were joined by Russians, singing the same song in Russian. They later retired to share 'Russian vodka and hot pepper brandy'. Encountering young people with different political views but often similar ideals was exactly what the Forum was about.[22]

The Prague Spring

Eileen (Leader 67, 68) led her group to Prague two years running. She remembered the 'annoying heavy-handedness' of Czech communist officials in 1967 but found 'the whole mood of the city had changed' when they arrived for a six-day visit on 31 July 1968. Hope was in the air, with crowds of Czech students in Jan Hus square day and night, daily parades supporting Czech President Dubček during his negotiations with USSR President Brezhnev, and locals 'talked openly about giving socialism "a new face", one facing west'. On one trip with delegates, 'Czech students sang folk songs long banned by the Czech Communists under Russian control'. The 'students assured us the Russians would never stifle the Prague Spring. "They are our comrades," one of them said'.

But it was an unsettled time. The delegates attended a student rally and, 'quiet Vivian Bakal from Paterson New Jersey' had her pocketbook stolen. When she reported it to the police she was unexpectedly arrested, released only after much negotiation. On the same night, another two girls stayed out late with students they met at the rally and could not understand why Eileen (leader) 'could barely speak to them' when they finally returned. She had worried they too had been arrested. Another day, one of their guides, 'quietly dragging on a cigarette, almost whispered, "The Russians will come. They came in 1948, and they will come again."'

She was right. Two weeks after the Forum group left Prague, Russian tanks rolled in. Eileen read the news in a Paris paper and they prayed for their Czech hosts at Notre Dame. Staff at the Czech embassy was 'stricken', but Eileen was shocked that an American Embassy official's attitude was 'laconic, bordering on indifference'. He said 'the Czech people had a spot of freedom, and it was up to them to make it grow'. Arriving home in New York at the airport, delegates carried placards deploring the invasion and sang 'We Shall Overcome' in solidarity.[23]

The return of the Russians to Prague did not stop Forum groups visiting. One 1971 summer delegate described beautiful old buildings but 'felt the constraints of the regime'—it was 'grey' the unhappiness of people 'palpable'. Jan (Czechoslovakia 67) was heavily involved with Forum visitors, arranging meetings with interesting people in 1969 as they all tried to evade the official Cedok guide. Eileen recalled that Jan 'did a great job … at considerable difficulty and risk to himself' as most people were 'unwilling to speak to any group'.[24]

Aiding and Abetting a Defection

In 1970 Pamela (Leader 70)'s group were at the center of the action when Jan defected to the US. Bob Huffman and Gus Nasmith sorted out an American college scholarship, accommodation, airline tickets, and relevant visas. Pamela and Bill (Leaders 70) were the couriers, dropping off documents and instructions with mutual friends at the Belgrade American consulate. In Prague they met Jan and his parents. Jan's move to the United States had ramifications for his family who remained behind. and had to be shown to be non-complicit. They concocted a plan. Pamela took charge of Jan's suitcase, with his clothes and belongings. 'It was a 1930s straw contraption', she said. For an American to be carrying such a case invited suspicion, but there was no time to change it. Meanwhile, Jan left to go to the very same 'youth camp' in Yugoslavia that the Forum had used. He telephoned his mother, declaring loudly that he 'disowned them all', for the benefit of any authorities listening in. There were a few hiccups as he crossed Europe from Belgrade to Paris, where he met Pamela again. She took the old-fashioned straw suitcase as her own, to draw attention away from Jan himself, they all held their breaths, and smuggled Jan onto their flight home, as 'just another American delegate'. Some of the Forum group doubtless felt a thrill of excitement, being on the fringes of a daring escape, but for Jan it was much more. For him, the Forum was his key to freedom—it utterly changed his life.[25]

Impact

Few summer delegates had quite such dramatic experiences, although Corey (Summer 73) had a moment going through French immigration on the way home. His mother had carefully labelled his belongings, including a pocketknife, with his initials, 'CRS', which was also the abbreviation for the French police reserves. This was just a few years after 1968, and officials thought he was making a political statement. Fortunately, group leader Rick Kessler quickly produced Corey's passport and an explanation. 'It was pretty funny', Rick remembered, 'but they weren't laughing'.[26]

Even without such dramas, most delegates found the trip significant. Although not as prestigious, nor, eventually, as selective as the New York Forum, the Summer Forum filled a gap in the market and had enduring impacts on participants. For many it was their first encounter with communism, and with the effects of World War II and the Holocaust. Some had never traveled before. They met government officials, intellectuals, and radicals, and contemporaries with very different life experiences. Their access to significant individuals—Venice-based art collector Peggy Guggenheim, prominent Yugoslav dissident Milovan Djilas, and Czech choreographer Ladislov Fialka, to name a few—was beyond what a regular tourist, or even a student tour group could hope for. Orel (Summer 64) felt the experience induced 'a new curiosity in our own country', while being Americans abroad 'tested their diplomacy'. Maria (Summer 64) found it 'truly awesome' to have had the opportunity to travel in Europe as a youngster, before it became crowded, to 'have walked through the Ufizzi (hot and unairconditioned) before crowds became the norm', to have stood 'alone in front of "Nightwatch" in Amsterdam', and to have discovered the Van Gogh museum, which 'was not a big deal at the time'. Gary (Summer 64) recalled Bob Huffman urging them to have a 'European' experience, not just 'an American experience in Europe'. Gary reflected that it was difficult for a bunch of teens, hormones raging and newly liberated from parental supervision, to always focus on the 'meetings with government, corporate, and cultural mandarins', the 'cathedrals, museums, and concerts', and the 'lectures by economists, government officials, factory managers, and scholars of cultural matters'. But it did place America in a new context, 'inducing a new curiosity in our own country', as well as teaching him a lifelong English habit of keeping 'the fork in my left hand, tines down … while eating'.[27]

Despite this enthusiasm, by 1972, Summer Forum applications were 'a disaster', with decreasing interest from students. 'From a high point of 67 participants in 1968, we are down to only 22 this year', Huffman confessed.[28] By this time independent student travel was increasingly affordable. Chaperones escorting teens around art museums and lecture halls on an educational tour were becoming old hat. This was yet another nail in the coffin for the Forum, which since the death of the *Tribune* had been struggling, despite Huffman's efforts to reinvent it, as we shall see in the next chapter.

Chapter 16

'An Exercise in Futility?'
After the Death of the *Tribune*

When Robert Huffman took over as director of the Forum in 1963, he likely saw the writing on the wall. He took steps. In 1964 the Forum was chartered by the Board of Regents of the State of New York as an independent, non-profit, educational organization, 'The World Youth Forum'. This was the start of futureproofing the Forum separately from the *Herald Tribune*. Jock Whitney was not losing interest in the Forum, although some of his management and financial team, as we have seen, were not enamored of the project. The *Tribune* also had bigger problems, not least the 114-day newspaper strike from December 1962 to March 1963, ensuing labor disputes, and stiff competition from the *New York Times*. The paper folded in August 1966. A new *World Journal Tribune* was salvaged from the ashes but barely survived a year. Europe's *International Herald Tribune* continued as a partnership between Whitney, the *New York Times,* and *Washington Post.* The Forum was now without its primary sponsor and its main marketing tool—no more *Tribune* journalists trailing in the wake of the delegates, ready to capture 'candid' snaps and 'unfiltered' soundbites.

The *World Journal Tribune* 'reluctantly' took over Forum funding (of $50,000) for a year. Bob Huffman also considered approaching the *New York Times* for support, particularly to publicize the Forum, but nothing eventuated. In 1967, WCBS-TV assumed responsibility, providing TV broadcasts and over $10,000 worth of staff, office, and postage costs. Just a year later, the network pulled back, limiting its support to making the TV programs, and contributing to accounting, legal, and postage costs.[1]

The Oram Report

The Forum was running out of steam both organizationally and financially. It was no longer as relevant or significant as in its heyday in the 1950s. Enthusiasm for and faith in internationalism was no longer the driving force it had been. Within the US there was a growing push for isolationism, as frustration with the Vietnam War, disenchantment with the UN, and economic woes developed. It was time for a rethink, and in 1968 the World Youth Forum trustees commissioned a report from Sidney W Green of the specialist fundraising and public relations firm, Oram Associates. Green provided a hard-hitting, clear-sighted analysis of how the Forum could build an 'independent fund-raising constituency'. His interim report was based on interviews with twelve people, including board members, potential sponsors, media, and foreign relations experts. Ten more interviews were planned, but his final report is not in the archive. Perhaps the interim report provided enough guidance, with its five suggestions, although they were not implemented successfully.

Green described the Forum's 'unique' problem: underwritten by the *Tribune* since its inception, it had never been forced to attract major external sponsorship, meaning that, unlike other organizations, it had never been 'sensitive to the current' of the philanthropic community. The Forum had remained 'static', unresponsive to the 'new forces shaping the world of youth'. It was time to re-evaluate 'the Forum's relevance as an educational medium'. His emphasis was significant and illustrated a shift away from the idealized aims of early Forum years—to produce peace through bringing potential future world leaders together—towards a focus on education for American students. Always part of the Forum's agenda, with delegates as 'walking textbooks', now became central. The program was 'too small' to have any 'appreciable influence' on world politics, Green said bluntly. The lack of continued contact with alumni meant that there was 'no lasting influence' on delegates' 'thinking or decision-making'. He criticized the program for its elitism, the selection process eliminating delegates 'whose participation would strongly enhance the program', including non-middle-class delegates, and those 'with contra-government views, especially within the third world of developing nations'. Green's five options for the Forum's future were: (1) phasing it out, (2) finding a new media sponsor (such as *The New York Times*), (3) merging with an existing organization such as AFS, or reconstructing the program to make it (4) 'more relatable to philanthropic priorities' or (5) 'a significant asset to a corporate sponsor'. Such reconstruction was not cheap, requiring the reconceptualization of the program, including greater focus on relevant issues in more depth, and engaging an audience beyond New York. One recommendation indicated how the Forum had drifted. Green advocated a return to what he called its 'original format', in which each Forum's discussion focused on a major world crisis.[2]

Bob Huffman paid some attention to the report, although he clung to the notion that delegates were 'future world leaders'. Nevertheless, the focus of the Forum shifted strongly towards educating American students, rather than positioning itself as a player in international politics.

Who was Paying?

In late 1968 the Forum was saved by Bernie Cornfeld and his Investors Overseas Service (IOS) Foundation, which stumped up $86,200 over the following three years, providing 80 per cent of Forum funding. IOS, an investment company selling mutual funds, collapsed spectacularly in 1970, with Cornfeld convicted of fraud in Switzerland. It was a corrupt organization, but Ambassador James Roosevelt, also on the Forum's Board of Trustees, was a key figure. Ruth Bishop, head of IOS in the US, was crucial to the Forum. Only the 'personal efforts' of Ruth Bishop 'made it possible for us to continue next year', Bob Huffman told Gus confidentially in July 1969. She had more sophistication in her little finger than Bob Huffman did in his entire body, and 'she knew everybody', said Haider (Pakistan 71), who remembered her as 'one of the most cultured ladies I've ever met', a 'very practical ... socialite with a good heart and a good head', and 'very good taste'. She had a 'well-appointed New York apartment', and 'her own blue monogrammed writing paper and envelopes'. She was also pragmatic. According to Forum deputy director, Gus Nasmith, Ruth 'really loved the Forum', and did not care if the IOS money was 'dirty', she would 'put it to good use'. The Forum's financial situation became more precarious in 1971 after IOS's demise. Bob Huffman wrote drily to friends in 1973, 'Ah for the good old days of the IOS. Bernie, where are you when we need you most (I know, in jail in Geneva!)'.[3]

Huffman's begging letters to alumni began in 1968, with some success. He amassed $20,600 in 'miscellaneous contributions (alumni, host families, schools, small Family foundations, friends)' over the next three years. 1969 also saw a one-time grant of $25,000 from the Foundation for Education and Social Development, a Boston-based philanthropic organization, perhaps with links to Richard B Gamble, Proctor and Gamble heir and family planning pioneer. On the Forum Board, Gamble also gave personal donations in 1968 and later in 1975. Huffman spent a lot of time schmoozing potential contributors, with varying degrees of success. Donald and Charlotte MacJannet, who established their own Foundation in 1968 to support global citizenship education, hosted summer groups and a reunion at the Macjannet Camp at Annecy in France, and gave modest annual donations of $500, 'regretting it could not be more'.[4] Jock Whitney, perhaps feeling responsible, gave $5000 a year from 1968 until at least 1973.

As Huffman told the alumni in his begging letters, large foundations like Ford and Rockefeller supported new activities aimed at domestic audiences. Of the one per cent of funds that all US foundations dedicated to international exchanges, scarcely any went to teenagers. For many too, like the Rockefeller Foundation, there was 'a general reluctance to move into public education activities because the cost is generally high, priorities are very difficult to establish, and results are not easily evaluated'. In any case their own 'priorities lay elsewhere'. They were certainly not interested in the relatively privileged international students at the Forum. 'New York corporations are very interested in helping the poor blacks and Puerto Ricans of the city', Huffman explained to the Forum Board in 1972. He reflected that 'the same corporation which would not give us a cent for our general administration might give us assistance if we were making our resource is available in certain ways to inner-city students', rationalizing this as 'a logical extension of our traditional activities and one definitely in keeping with our program philosophy'.[5] This was so far removed from the elite, internationally focused origins of the Forum, it is unsurprising these ideas did not come to fruition.

Huffman stepped up the campaign with the alumni. In January 1971 two former delegates and now Board members, Anis (Pakistan 56) and Gerhard (Austria 49), gently appealed to delegates' shared memories of 'the excitement of flying off to New York to meet a group of strangers who quickly became our friends, the fun of... new places... endless discussions... and more than anything... the ways in which each of us grew as a more complete person through this experience which we were so fortunate as to be given'. This softly-softly approach was followed up by Huffman in July with 'a frank statement to our alumni concerning the Forum's financial situation'. He was not subtle. 'Our most expensive program—the one in which you took part—has not charged a fee', noting that AFS students paid, on average, $500. He suggested alumni could 'repay' the cost of their experience, by each sending $20. In a reminder of the gendered economy, he told alumni that 'some of our most generous gifts have come from ... husbands on behalf of their wives who were delegates'. Ignoring that the Forum continued to be a PR exercise for American power, he took a swipe at 'other affluent nations': 'Why should the Forum always be supported by Americans?', he asked: 'Even the poorest nation has wealthy people, some of whom have [been] delegates', an unusual acknowledgement that while the Forum advertised the rigorous selection of delegates on merit, sometimes money and power were deciding factors.[6]

For the first time, the Forum sought government funding. The US State Department provided 'emergency grants' of $15,000 in 1970 and 1971, paying 30 per cent of expenses. This was not a permanent arrangement. Unlike some other teenage exchange programs (AFS, Experiment in International Living, International Christian Youth Exchange), the Forum was not contracted to the US State Department. Significantly, Huffman did not necessarily want it to be. As he told alumni, 'there are reasons why a permanent grant from the US government might not be desirable'. But needs must. He got $25,000 for 1974, on the proviso that 'future support will depend upon our coming up with new ideas and programs which they feel are worthy of support'.[7]

Belt Tightening and Staff Cuts

Another way of surviving was cutting costs. The annual expenditure of $63,800 in 1969 and $77,300 in 1970 plummeted to $46,800 in 1971, a drop of 39 per cent. There were savings across the board and no overseas jaunt. The 1972 budget dropped a further 32 per cent, to $27,950. This was a low point, although expenses for 1973 and 1974 remained below $40,000. By then, the Forum program was radically different, as we shall see.

Salaries made up most of the budget and the Forum really tightened its belt in the 1970s. In 1969 Bob Huffman had persuaded Gus Nasmith to become assistant director, telling him, 'You can certainly earn a living wage with the Forum or other organizations in this field, even if you're married'. He said, 'I have no outside income and have to live on my salary, and even though I'll never make $40,000, I'm not starving'. Not only that, he added, 'there are nice fringe benefits, like the 11 free trips I've had to Europe in the past seven years'. He reasoned, 'Of course, I've done a bit of work to pay for them, but it's better than selling insurance'. Gus took the job and Huffman also employed Linda Reed, who, he told Gus, was well qualified and, in language that underscored the blatant sexism of the time, 'a terrific girl … smart as hell, vivacious, miniskirted, and as attractive as anyone could want'. He thought Ginger 'might be more your type', but 'this Linda Reed would knock your eyes out'. (Huffman was clearly unaware that Gus was questioning his own sexuality at about this time.) [8]

Two years later, Bob was singing a different tune. The position of assistant director was unaffordable by 1971, but so was other paid assistance. 'It was nip and tuck all summer … we were within a few weeks of closing … I'm delaying hiring the secretary as long as possible, as each week I save her salary is money beyond March'. Huffman was the only paid employee, assisted by 'two alumni mothers', including Katherine Andrews, (mother of Lew, US 64), who volunteered one day a week. In August 1971 another volunteer arrived—this time with experience. Joan Layton was Huffman's assistant between 1965 and 1967 and led a summer group in 1966. After leaving to get married, by 1971 she had two small daughters and was keen to get 'out of her apartment' to give time to 'a worthwhile cause'.

Volunteers were all very well, but Bob was also worried about his own job: 'this state of affairs can't continue forever, and finding something appropriate at my age would take a bit of time'. By the start of 1972 he was 'quite frankly just keeping my head above water'. In the absence of assistants, he suddenly realized the 'incredible amount of detail surrounding the presence of the delegates'. Small pockets of funding allowed for some part-timers, but by May 1974 Huffman was 'again holding down the office alone'.[9]

'Radical Change'

After the closure of IOS, Huffman realized that depending on philanthropic contributions and government grants was unsustainable; the Forum needed to 'generate more income for the services we provide'. The American teenagers on the summer program had always paid for the privilege, but interest was waning, with only twenty-two students paying to travel in 1972, from a high of sixty-seven in 1968. The program was suspended after a final bijoux group of eleven traveled in 1973. Huffman was disappointed, but not just about the loss of income. A principal perk of the job, jaunts to Europe, were unjustifiable by 1972. As he told the MacJannets that July, 'for the first time in my ten years with the Forum—I won't be getting to Europe at all this year—there was neither the time nor the money this spring for my usual organizational trip for the summer program, and I have done the entire thing by mail'. He admitted 'I miss seeing Europe and all my old friends!'[10]

With the summer program no longer an income stream, alternative money-making schemes were required, and the winter Forum had to adapt and start paying for itself. 'The world of the '70s is vastly different from that of the time of our founding in 1946', wrote Huffman. We need 'new activities which would relate the Forum more to the educational needs of the present day'.[11] Here again, the emphasis was on American education.

The first step was introducing an 'enrollment fee' of $60 for schools' participation in the Metropolitan Forum to select the US delegate, and for host school activities. Huffman reported happily in September 1971 that seventy-one schools had enrolled for the selection of the 1972 delegate. In 1971, the Forum also launched a series of six seminars for schools in the New York metropolitan area to hear 'knowledgeable people in the fields of international political, economic, and cultural matters' and 'hold discussions' with them and with other students, including international

Forum delegates. The first seminar, held at the Carnegie International Center, boasted an impressive line-up of nine experts from the UN and its agencies, and the series attracted seventy-seven takers at $70 a time, garnering $4600 profit.[12] This success showed Huffman that 'people are willing to pay a fee for service intelligently rendered'. He planned to tap into the 'schools-without-walls' concept that was gaining popularity at the time, with ambitious plans to extend the seminar program overseas, broadening conceptions of 'youth' and potentially becoming self-supporting. He also considered 'Forum-produced audio-visual materials as a classroom aid'. None of these programs were ill-considered, but, as he acknowledged, the Forum needed to survive long enough to test them.

The Last Forum?

The Forum did survive, but not in a recognizable form. The last proper forum was in 1972. There were just twenty delegates, reduced because 'it was absolutely necessary for me to cut back on the workload', Huffman told the Board. This last Forum was a pale shadow of those of the late 1950s—there were no meetings with the president, no grand finale, no jamming with Pete Seeger, or hobnobbing with Harry Belafonte or the Kennedys. There was no longer the same hoop-la of publicity that delegates had enjoyed (or endured) in the 1950s, because the newspaper was long gone. There were still television panels, but otherwise it was just an exchange student program, like so many that had entered the market, albeit a highly selective one.[13]

The 1972 Forum was decreed successful, but Huffman concluded that the 'incoming' program had 'outlived its usefulness'. It had, in fact, become 'our Achilles Heel', no longer serving its 'original purpose' of 'enrich[ing] the lives of American students in the schools of the New York area'. This was partly due to the 'proliferation of similar programs', but also the 'growth of international travel'. He said 'no one is going to fund, in the amount necessary, the continuation of a worthwhile but rather amorphous program for a group of teenagers from abroad'. There was no mention of the original Forum ambition to create a network of world leaders nor of expanding the Forum's reach across the US. Huffman was doubling down on the benefits of focusing on the local. 'We have recognized (really for the first time in certain ways) that the <u>real source of our strength lies in our reputation and contacts in the New York area</u>', he told Board members in October 1972.[14]

'Hardly Reads Like a "Who's Who"'

The Forum's Board was formed in 1964 but only in later years had they been called upon to act. In 1972 there were thirteen members, including two alumni, and others from business and media and politics. Ruth Bishop of IOS was the only woman. Huffman's long overdue report to the Board in October 1972 was brutally frank. 'Let us be completely honest', he wrote, 'haven't we all wondered … whether this was an exercise in futility—whether we shouldn't have let the Forum die in 1968?'. He had felt a 'personal toll', but 'I hate to give up at this point', he insisted, before turning on the Board itself. Although they had joined the Board 'at my personal request' and he had 'appreciated' their help, he regretted that 'our Board hardly reads like a "Who's Who", nor does it include people whose names will instantly extract funds from the business community, people who can personally tide us over a $7000 anticipated deficit, etc'. He was not exactly buttering them up for his next suggestion: that 'each Board member could make a personal contribution to the Forum', identify potential donors among their contacts, and 'help us beef up our Board by adding to it people who really could be of help to us'. Those people would be New Yorkers: not 'your good friend who just loves foreign students or young people in general, but well-known, hard-headed people who might see some merit in this organization and what it is trying to accomplish'.

Huffman was desperate—on a personal crusade to save the Forum. 'The past two years have been traumatic for me personally, and perhaps you wonder why I haven't let the thing die'. He mused, 'I wonder sometimes myself', but then pulled himself together, reflecting on the 'goldmine of goodwill' that the Forum enjoyed. 'It wouldn't be a tragedy if the Forum disappeared from the face of the earth, but I'm not going to let that happen without one final gasp', he declared.[15] He felt sure his new programs were the way to go.

Local and Collaborative

The local seminar program that he trialled in New York high schools in 1971–1972 was expanded the following year. The 1972–1973 'World Youth Forum Course in International Relations' was advertised to run for twenty weeks from October to May, using 'the Forum's wide contacts in field such as diplomacy, print and broadcast media, finance, education, labor, culture, etc' with the prospectus 'worked out with the advice of high school faculty and other educators'. It was 'integrated with the Forum's television schedule' and 'audio tapes of sessions' were given to school classes. It involved American students, invited experts, and '165 students from 48 countries'. With 33 enrolments by July 1972 ('income $6600!', reported Huffman excitedly), things were looking up.[16]

This seminar program with paying customers was the way forward, with an important role played by international students. But these were not the specially selected national representatives flown in by Pan Am or TWA. Instead, three groups of about twenty International Christian Youth Exchange (ICYE), American Field Service (AFS), and Youth for Understanding (YFU) students, already in the US, but not near New York, were brought to the metropolis for three weeks each between January and April. Each group included one student from each country: they stayed with families, attended schools, and participated in the seminar series.[17] When announcing the revised Forum to alumni, Huffman stressed the students selected were 'of excellent quality—well worthy of carrying on the tradition of the Forum'. Nevertheless, they were a different cohort from the essay-writing, national-competition-winning, adolescent ambassadors who had starred on television and sometimes met the president. It is likely fewer alumni were persuaded to donate funds to this new Forum, which was unrecognizable in its narrowed focus on engaging American students in international affairs with a sprinkling of foreign glamor.

The idea of supplementing exchange students' programs with a visit to New York *and* engagement with other foreign students was not a bad one. Huffman touted the 'brand-new idea' as 'a new kind of service to some of our sister organizations', whose students often clamored to visit the Big Apple. It solved the problem of flying in students now that airlines no longer offered free international flights to exchange students. Administration duties were shared among the organizations, who were also facing financial constraints. By the early 1970s, American exchanges were losing their glamor. After the revelations about covert CIA funding of the World Youth Assembly and other organizations, young people were less trusting of exchange programs with strong relationships with the State Department. US involvement in Vietnam and more 'discreet' intervention in regime changes in other countries had not enhanced its reputation in an era of decolonisation and independence.[18] With the election of Richard Nixon as president, the US itself shifted further to the right, away from the optimism of the 'golden' era of JFK. It was no coincidence that 1971 was also the year that the AFS broadened its scope, exchanging students between other countries, rather than just to and from the US.

Huffman was optimistic. 'This new direction for us seems to have caught on very well, and if we can produce good programs for these students, I see no reason why this program can't continue and expand (continuing upon further help from the State Department, of course)'. The program relied, as ever, on high schools, several of which jumped on board. In 1973 Tappan Zee High's Exchange Club organized an 'International Weekend', involving their own two year-long exchange students as well as the visiting Forum delegates, during the three-week program.[19]

John Whitaker, a New Zealand AFS student from Pennsylvania participated in 1973 and was underwhelmed. He remembered having discussions with other delegates in a large room 'somewhere in New York', but the highlight was staying with a Kosher Jewish family. Nevertheless, Huffman persevered, reporting that the program was a 'a solid success', ensuring 'an extension of our State Department grant'. There was another grant of $25,000 for 1975, but, as Huffman reminded alumni, 'with the clear understanding that State will not be able to continue to help us unless we can show major success during the coming months in attracting new money from the private sector'.[20] The future looked bleak.

The Three Roberts of New Jersey

In 1975 Bob Huffman spent twenty-one weeks living on New York State unemployment benefit of $95 a week, until new State Department funding arrived. This funding dried up completely in 1976. At this point, the three Roberts of New Jersey stepped in. World History and Social Studies teachers, Robert Esik at Pompton Lakes High, Robert Bliss of Saddle Brook High, and Robert Meylan from Tappan Zee, had been hosting Forum delegates in their respective high schools for several years. They decided to continue the program in its new form. Each school hosted a third of the students, who were responsible for their own airfares from their host towns in the US. Robert Esik remembered the effort they put into fashioning activities. For each visit, he organized a focused module of work for discussion. One year he took students on a trip to New York City to see the different extremes of American life. After visiting Fifth Avenue, Macy's, Tiffany's, St Patrick's Cathedral, and the Rockefeller Center, they went to Chinatown, followed by the Bowery, then the 'Skid Row' of New York, and lastly Ellis Island, which was at that time pretty much a ruin. These New Jersey schools continued to run their programs for several years. In 1981 Saddle Brook High School advertised a film night about China 'for the benefit of the World Youth Forum which hosts exchange students of high school age from free-world countries in suburban and metropolitan New York'. Local New Jersey newspaper *The Shopper* went on to explain that the 'International Youth Forum was entering its seventh year at Saddle Brook High', obviously a remnant of the *Herald Tribune*'s original initiative.[21]

The Last Gasp

The decline of the Forum coincided with the breakdown of Bob Huffman's marriage. Perhaps it contributed. By February 1976, when his ex-wife Hilda was preparing to remarry John Mortimer of the *New York Times*, Huffman admitted to the MacJannets that he seemed 'to have little personal life other than trying to get the Forum back on the map'. He was 'happy for Hilda', and relieved to have no more alimony payments. But he still needed an income.

Huffman came up with new schemes, including a closer collaboration with Youth For Understanding, who wanted a foothold in New York, a film on multinational corporations as seen through the critical eyes of students from various countries (for an ex-employee of Board Member George Dessart's), and a plan to engage with university students to study how 'global education' could be advanced at high school level. All came to nothing. But one initiative in early 1976 looked promising. The television programs were long gone, but Huffman switched media, with a new radio series on WNYC in New York, hoping it would be a 'springboard for something bigger and better'.[22]

The series was called 'A World at Stake'. The press release promised it would 'explore complex problems facing people and nations in today's interdependent world'. America's role in the world, leadership crises, the status of women, the place of religion, nationalism, and 'the perils of international conflict' would be discussed by 'people of many nations' who were experts in various fields, 'often' joined by 'American and foreign students who will give their views on questions of future world order'. The first program on 'interdependence' featured former Assistant Secretary of State and Ambassador to NATO, Harlan Cleveland, who was the father-in-law of Jan Kalicki, Forum host, runner-up for 1964 US delegate, and Summer group leader in 1965–1966. Not for nothing had Robert Huffman kept in touch. Another program, 'Preparing Youth for the World Ahead', featured two AFS students and the president of AFS itself.[23]

Huffman scheduled discussions with National Public Radio and others, and sought funding to expand his program to other cities. He spoke at the annual convention of the '700 member stations of the Intercollegiate Broadcasting System' in Philadelphia. But, while 'he was the first person to actually get something off the ground' about the increasingly popular 'concept of interdependence on the part of government, foundations, and corporations', Huffman was certainly not in the inner circle. He lacked the connections of the Whitneys, Reids, and even Helen Waller. For example, when the Johnson Foundation held a conference on 'the media and world understanding' in December 1975, Huffman was not on the guest list. He joked that the conference organizers were 'unaware of my stellar efforts(!)', but it was a sign. A disgruntled Huffman told the MacJannets ruefully that '"my man at the State Department"—Fred Hartley—was there, along with loads of others whom I have been or will be talking to'.[24]

The radio series did not expand, nor even last out the year, and in

October 1976 the Forum Trustees (now numbering only seven) agreed to merge with another organization, but nothing eventuated. The last records I found of the Forum were the minutes of another Board meeting three years later in 1979. The Board consisted of Robert Huffman, Gus Nasmith, Ruth Bishop, Richard H Nolte, George Dessart of CBS, and Ralph Daniels, only four of whom were present. A skeleton committee was elected: Dessart, Bishop, and Huffman. The final agenda item suggested that they were not taking the survival of the Forum too seriously:

> Mr Nolte, informal chairman of the ad hoc Committee on Outer Space, led a fascinating discussion of ways in which the Forum could program for students interested in extra-terrestrial activities. On this interesting note, the meeting was adjourned.[25]

The Forum had finally breathed its last, having outlived its relevance for either the American government or for young people, both domestically and on the international stage. It slipped quietly into the dustbin of history without so much as a whimper. It seemed to have been forgotten, except as a pleasant interlude in individual lives. Bob Huffman went on to consultancies in broadcasting and worked for Save the Children. He died, aged only 65, in 1991, just a few short years before the Forum spirit rose like a phoenix from the ashes, as Alumni rediscovered each other around the globe.[26]

Chapter 17

A Forum Phoenix
The Alumni Association

The young Israeli waiter was at a loss. A large, lively, greying and white-haired group settled themselves at a long table in the middle of the restaurant. His confusion was understandable, for the table was reserved for the 'World *Youth* Forum'. He apologized to the guide who had booked the table, 'Shall I send them away?', he asked, but the guide just laughed. 'They *are* the World Youth Forum', he explained. 'This is their reunion ... and, believe it or not, these people are much younger in mind and spirit than many half their age!'.[1] (He might also have commented, as delegates' spouses often do, that alumni reverted to their 17-year-old selves at reunions.) The waiter retreated, relieved that a bunch of teenagers claiming to the real 'World Youth Forum' were not about to turn up. The 2012 gathering in Israel was just one of several 'reunions' of delegates after the 1994 'Corfu 1' experience, described at the start of this book. The 'reunion' was organized by the Alumni Association, officially formed in 1995. Why did it take nearly half a century after the first Forum for such an Association to appear, and what connections had persisted?

A Forum 'Family'

One of the 1968 Oram Report's major criticisms of the Forum was 'the lack of any organized approach to maintain the past delegates as an alumni group ... which could carry on a continuing dialogue among former delegates'. In 1968 this was certainly true: Arnold (Colombia 69) wished there had been 'more structured meetings for alumni a few years after the Forum' so they could keep in touch.[2] Under Helen Waller, it had been different. She clung to the idea of creating an influential network.

Waller worked hard to maintain the Forum's global connections. Central were the quarterly newsletters, which made Rasul (Pakistan

54) 'feel that I am still a member of the big friendly Forum family ... an inseparable part'. Opening with a brief message from Helen and news of the latest Forum activities, the remainder was alumni news: excerpts from their letters to Helen, updates on where they were living and who had US scholarships, and of careers, marriages, and growing families, along with commentary on their countries' political situations. By 1959 the newsletter was sixteen pages. Per (Norway 55) noticed perceptively in the same year that 'judging by the number of letters from former delegates, the interest in the forum decreases proportionately with the number of years which have passed since we were delegates'. He regretted the loss of 'the youthful eagerness displayed by us at the Forum' but suggested delegates became 'more realistic'. Nevertheless, there were still eleven delegates from 1953 writing in at the end of the decade, and even as the Forum grew more distant in delegates' memories, the newsletter was an ongoing reminder, turning up in letterboxes around the world every four months.[3]

These rich, collaborative newsletters barely survived Helen's death in August 1961. After an 'in memorium' issue in September, the November newsletter introduced Virginia Wieschhoff and included accounts of a reunion in Greece in July that year, even more poignant because Helen Waller had been there, full of enthusiasm and Forum plans. Subsequent newsletters, few of which survive, were from Forum staff, describing the latest Forum groups or activities, but with fewer alumni contributions. The newsletter's decline was one of the starkest illustrations of the disruption caused by Helen's death. Without her, and with Forum office staff constantly changing, there was no individual with whom fourteen years of delegates could correspond. Helen was the lynchpin that tied the alumni of the 1940s and 1950s together, but the threads were so slender that without her, the bond was broken. The closest equivalent to Helen Waller in later years was Gus Nasmith. The American delegate in 1962, he then worked for the Forum, becoming assistant director, and was central to the European summer program. He linked delegates, alumni, and staff.

Helen Waller, however, was very much the 'dear Mutti', as some delegates addressed her in their correspondence. The Forum office was always open to alumni, many of whom 'dropped in' when in New York. Christine (Greece 53) even landed herself a job as Forum assistant when popping in to show off her new baby. And Helen issued a general invitation to delegates to join her annual summer vacation, hiking and climbing in the European Alps: 'Visitors (especially mountaineers and Forum delegates) are most welcome'. Several took her up on it. This generous inclusion of Forum delegates in her own personal family circle went beyond her job description, but a visiting group of doting Forum acolytes probably boosted her ego. Being purely en famille with Ted may have been a strain, particularly later in their marriage. Playing happy families was easier with an audience.

With Helen also began the idea that being a delegate was entrée into a special club of remarkable individuals across the globe, offering friendly faces and hospitality when traveling abroad. Waller actively encouraged them, hoping that 'in your travels you see as much of each other as possible', reminding them that 'the cultural affairs officers of the US Embassy in any one of the 70 Forum countries you may visit will have the names and addresses of former Forum delegates on file'. The newsletter was full of informal meetings and planned reunions. European delegates had an advantage—with contiguous countries and an avalanche of delegates each year, their summer travels, whether immediately post-Forum or later, often included visiting other delegates. Eeva (Finland 55), for instance, spent the whole summer in 'the home of Madame Dantzenberg, who is the sister of Sabine' (France 55). She 'felt so much at home', with Sabine's mother, 'Madame Ewald ... like a mother to me'. The tradition continued with the production of an annual Forum directory listing contact details of Forum alumni from all years. Léon (Mexico 64) showed me his well-thumbed copy, which he used 'whenever I traveled'. He was 'always welcomed by Forum delegates', when he called them out of the blue. It was 'common practice' among delegates, he said, describing his first meeting with Orit (Israel 67) in the summer of 1968. The delegate from his year, Rachel (Israel 64), was not home when he arrived on her doorstep, so out came his trusty directory. It was not long before he was drinking tea with Orit in her family's apartment, no longer strangers.[4]

Other delegates repaid US hospitality entertaining host brothers, sisters, and parents, Forum staff, and even host school teachers. Helen's assistant, Mary Warner, reported meeting up with Norbert (Germany 57), 'minus his characteristic cigarette', during her European travels in 1957. When Guy (Switzerland 55) went climbing in the Alps in the summer after the Forum, 'his guest was Mr [George W] Briggs, faculty advisor of Harrison High School', where Guy had spent two weeks. Nii (Ghana 59) 'attempted to "repay" the immense hospitality I received in the US' by guiding a group of Connecticut high school students around Accra in June 1959. He had connected with them through the USIS and Afro-American Institute.[5] European alumni were also essential to the Summer Forum program as we have seen.

Some alumni met up again at university. 'Forum veterans at Oxford' gathered 'occasionally for a bout of gossip'. Hameeda (Pakistan 52) bonded with Alice (Singapore 52), Bhinda (Nepal 52), and Purificacion (Philippines 52), at university in the US, as did the bevy of boys at Williams College, Massachusetts. The American University of Beirut also boasted a cohort of delegates from Lebanon and Jordan. Sometimes it was just a nodding acquaintance. One Ghanaian was excited to spot the American delegate from her year while at Harvard. 'You could have heard our screams from there to the tip of Florida! But we never got together again because basically, we were strangers'.[6]

Delegates kept in touch for a while with their year group and/or with host families, but later, life often got in the way. University, marriages, families, and careers took over and serendipitous encounters were the main occasions of reconnection. Catherine (France 59) was delighted that, when 'getting off the bus at the St Lazare Station, which is worse than Times Square in rush hour, I bumped into Joan Lee Smith, Forum Secretary'. A long lunch with much conversation at the famous Paris restaurant Procop followed. Purificacion (Philippines 52) recognized Hameeda (Pakistan 52) in a hotel lift in Dhaka; others met at conferences, sometimes discovering their mutual Forum connection while chatting. Christina (Summer 66) accidentally found a delegate en route to the first Corfu reunion. As arranged, her (Pakistani) husband's friend, Pakistan's Ambassador to Greece, collected her from the airport. But when she started explaining the Forum, he stopped her. No need to explain—he was Amin (Pakistan 57)! Sergio (Brazil 53) was recognized by 'his host's sweetheart' when he visited an Ontario antiques store, forty years after the

Forum. Perhaps the most delightful surprise was when the son of Léon (Mexico 64), Pablo, found that his university girlfriend Yvette was the daughter of Vicente (Mexico 67). The two older men had met in 1966 when Vicente was selected as a delegate.[7]

But it was not just the next generation who fell in love. Alongside the sporadic and serendipitous reconnections were lifelong friendships, love affairs, and marriages.

Forum Couples

Bring together a group of thirty teenage boys and girls and sparks are bound to fly. Snatched kisses and snuggling in the backseat of the bus on Forum tours were not unknown, and some went further (although few will admit it and I am sworn to secrecy with the rest). There were crushes, temporary liaisons, and passionate friendships, some of which outlasted the Forum. Gerhard (Germany 54) had it bad for Inga (Denmark 54). After he returned home to Hamburg, he visited her in Skaerbaeck, 220 kilometers to the north. His parents were 'not about to pay for a train ticket' so he cycled. 'The fanciest bicycle you could get was a 3-speed bicycle... I think I did it two days', he remembered, decades later, 'which seems miraculous!' he added. Despite that display of devotion, the romance between Gerhard and Inga petered out after a couple of years, although they remained good friends. Decades later, Inga did not recall the epic bicycle journey: 'I thought he came by train!', she said.[8]

There were several more long-lasting relationships or 'Forum couples', although not all marriages lasted lifetimes. For some, the Forum was coincidental rather than pivotal. Kiko (Japan 53) married Minoru (Ben) Makihara in 1957. He was not a delegate but was in New York at the same time. 'I have known him for more than 10 years but this would not have happened had I not gone to the US for the Forum', Kiko said, although perhaps it was always their parents' plan.[9] Minoru was the son of a Mitsubishi executive, and Kikuko the daughter of the founding family of the company: Minoru later became president of Mitsubishi. Similarly, the marriages of Richard (Burma 50) and Sophie (Burma 52) and of Riaz (Pakistan 52) and Nasreen (Pakistan 55) were probably not really 'Forum matches', but more evidence of their intersecting social circles. Neither were Ulrik (Denmark 48), who has been dubbed 'playboy architect of the Eastern world', and Tamar (Israel 60) a classic Forum couple, as their common Forum experience, over a decade apart, had little to do with their meeting.

But several relationships were intrinsically linked to the Forum. Twenty-two-year-old American, Michael Kovalsky, saw a picture of Jenny (Netherlands 49) posing with President Truman in the *Tribune* and was instantly smitten. They married two years later. John (UK 58) and Angeliki (Greece 58) met at the Forum and married a few years later. Although they then divorced, they reconnected in later life. Judith (Canada 53) was an alumni helper in 1956 when she met Johan (Norway 56). They chose to sneak away and get married in 1960 while on a Forum excursion as alumni staff. Often remembered as the ultimate 'Forum couple', their marriage also ended.

More happily, Serban (Bolivia 64) could still tell me in 2021 what dress Orel (host/Summer 64) was wearing at a Forum party in March 1964, although it was not until a year later that his university friend and fellow Forum delegate Lew (US 64) set them up on a blind date. 'You were the girl in the pink and orange dress dancing the Highlife with the African delegates', Serban greeted Orel in 1965. She was suitably impressed, and they are still together. So too are Tommy (Sweden 63) and Umbereen, the younger sister of Naila (Pakistan 58). They first met when Naila's father, then Pakistani Ambassador to the US, entertained Forum delegates at their embassy in Washington. A case of mistaken identity led to Clifford (host Ceylon 69) marrying Ilona (Austria 69). Ilona was looking for another American host at a 1969 Forum beach party and found Cliff instead. 'Honestly, I fell in love with her', remembered Cliff, and after a long-distance relationship, they married in 1974. Unlike many delegates, whose marriages took them back to the US, in this case Cliff moved to Vienna. In 1970, Pamela (Leader 70) appointed one of her students, Howard (host/Summer 70) to 'distract' the young female official Czech guide, while Jan (Czechoslovakia 67) acted in an unofficial capacity and told them the real story of Prague. Howard obviously distracted her well: a few years later they married.[10]

Phoenix from the Ashes

Personal relationships were one thing, but what of 'the organized approach to maintain the past delegates as an alumni group' that the 1968 Oram report recommended? Alumni made sporadic attempts to create a connected group beyond the newsletter and the Forum directory. In 1957, Dennis (Philippines 57)'s mother reported enthusiastically that 'the Filipino delegates, the Salazars, Junior and Raul and Dennis are all set to organize an organization called the '*New York Herald Tribune* Alumni'. They will keep you posted ... and will play host to any Forum delegate who may come this way.' Nothing came of that initiative, but there was a more concerted effort at the 1959 Forum. Decades later, John (UK 59) remembered with amusement how the '59ers, during their last days at Kober House, 'produced a pompous nine-page manifesto, with detailed plans for a set of regional alumnus organizations, linked by an HQ in New York, an archivist, and a magazine (Forum Heritage)'. Pompous it might have been, but this went beyond the '59ers, involving several US-based alumni. The December newsletter announced the election of Johan (Norway 56) as president of the 'World Youth Forum Association' at its 'annual conference' in September. Other officeholders included Judith (Canada 53), Naila (Pakistan 58), Cora (US 59), and Hernan (Nicaragua 47). Cyrus (Iran 50) was the 'Legal Counsellor', assisting with incorporation plans. Catherine (France 59) announced a gathering of 'the French National Association', and an 'Association of the Ceylon Delegates' formed in June 1961. This was just before the first Forum Reunion in Athens for two weeks in July. Those who attended the reunion were predominantly from the 1958–1961 Forums, but included delegates from Europe, the US, and the Middle East, and others studying in Europe. Any impetus this reunion created in the development of a World Forum Association was cut short by Helen Waller's sudden death three weeks later. A reunion tentatively planned for Oslo in 1962 did not eventuate.[11]

The next 'reunion' was in August 1968, when Gus Nasmith organized a gathering at the MacJannet's summer camp on the shores of Lake Annecy in the French Alps. About twenty-five delegates (from 1964, 1966, 1967, and 1968) gathered. They were mainly Europeans, with a few others conveniently in the vicinity—Orit (Israel 67), Norma (Egypt 67), and Léon (Mexico 64).[12] It was a one-off. The money worries facing the Forum probably meant there was little energy for organizing official alumni gatherings.

The death of the Forum proper in 1972, and the slow demise of its spin offs removed a last focal point for any alumni. By the early 1990s, pockets of linked alumni existed across the world but there was no central organization. Then the Alumni Association was born. It became an independent phenomenon, connected to the Forum, but with a life and meaning of its own. Tales of its genesis grew in the telling, and, as we saw at the beginning of this book, 'Corfu 1' or the first reunion, assumed mythological proportions as a foundation story. But the credit really belongs in the first instance to Gerry (Rhodesia 60).

Just as people had individual motivations for joining the Alumni Association, so too those who founded it had various understandings of what it was intended to be. Given that the Forum tried to select future leaders, one interpretation of the alumni is of a network of powerful individuals, along with those seeking to exploit connections to further their own careers. In November 1995, in *The Delegate*, the Alumni Association's newsletter, Gerry (Rhodesia 60) described how the idea of an Alumni Association actually emerged. In September 1992 she met with Stanford University president Gerhard Casper (Germany 54), who had been an alumni fellow in her year. He apparently mused that 'it was a shame that there was no means of keeping us all in touch … Some of us were in very important jobs, and anyway, we all should be able to network and help each other'.[13] Gerry took the bait. In 1993, she charmed the editor of the *International Herald Tribune*, which ran her advertisements seeking former delegates. Gerry also penned the first issue of *The Delegate* in May that year and the small groups of connected delegates began to coalesce, Jordan (Greece 60) issued a blanket invitation to a 'reunion' in Corfu, mailing letters to every delegate, using the decades-old addresses in the last Forum directory, and the first glimmerings of the Alumni Association appeared.

It was officially formed in 1995, with members paying an annual subscription of $40. Accumulated funds meant that membership became free in 2010. Membership was for former delegates but extended to include 'Forum friends': host family members, Forum staff, and members' partners and children. Inclusivity was important to ensure the Association's survival. It was formed under French law because many of the movers and shakers were in Europe. An Association Board was responsible for the newsletter and later the website and online directory. It helped organize major reunions, collected archives, and facilitated delegate tracing. It was elected approximately every three years until 2013. There have been no elections since then. Ideally it included both men and women, representing different years and different parts of the world. The first chair was Gerry herself, then Ginger (Summer 64) in 1997. Dorothy (Malaya 62) took over in 2004, and Catherine (France 59) became chair in 2013. Between 1995 and 2024, twenty-three people were on the Board. Long-serving members included Roger (Norway 59) (twenty years), Rita (Germany 70) (seventeen years), Catherine (France 59) (fourteen years), and Dorothy (Malaya 62) (twelve years). The Board was only part of the Association's core. Curt (Austria 70 and Forum Archivist), along with Catherine (France 59) and Ginger (Summer 64), editors of *The Delegate*, were integral to the Forum from its inception. Ida (Italy 59) and Sudhir (India 66) were Board members, and hosted two reunions each, no small undertaking.

According to Alumni Association statutes, its purpose was 'to further contacts and communication among the persons who participated, from 1947 to 1972, in an educational exchange programme called "The *New York Herald Tribune* International Youth Forum" (and its successor, "The World Youth Forum") and who wish to promote international understanding and peace through various activities geared to this end'. There were those who, as Catherine (France 59) put it, 'felt a strong desire to give the Association a purpose in line with the idealism that inspired their original Forum experience'.[14] Suggestions included starting a new international student program. There was much heated debate. Some members were concerned that any such program would push individual political agendas, reflecting the interests of a few powerful alumni. And it would not be truly international, these members argued. Their concerns had validity, for many of the active members of the Association were based in Western Europe and North America. Nevertheless, it was perhaps naïve to think that any international student exchange program was without an agenda. Consider the Forum itself. In the end the idea was scrapped, requiring more time commitment (and funding) that members were able to give, in what was already a crowded market, with numerous existing exchange programs.

Another idea was that Association support charities or worthwhile projects, although agreeing on which projects were prioritized was problematic. Ultimately, the Association limited itself to informing members about charitable projects, particularly those run by Forum alumni. The Association's purpose was described as 'increasing communication' among delegates, which would 'give rise to other meaningful ideas and projects'.[15]

The principal means of communication was the quarterly newsletter, *The Delegate*, started by Gerry (Rhodesia 60) in 1993. She was delighted when journalist Ginger (Summer 64) offered to co-edit in 1996. Gerry retired, leaving her to it in 2000, with Catherine (France 59) assisting. *The Delegate* appeared quarterly, and lasted twenty-seven years, issue 49 appearing in 2020. Starting in print, by the 2010s it was arriving by email. It was a platform for issue-based articles and opinion pieces, sometimes answering a particular question. Along with pieces about climate change, AIDS, poverty, and war, there was, most poignantly in 2001, an article by Suheil (Jordan 61) which began joyfully, 'As I write … the Taliban regime in Afghanistan has all but collapsed'. Presciently, however, he suggested that 'the seeds are being sown for another Afghani civil war'. He was critical of the US: 'once its "surgical" bombing campaign achieves its limited objective with minimum loss of American life, the US withdraws again into its own shell … shy[ing] away from [its] responsibilities' as a world superpower.[16] As I was writing this book in the 2020s, the Taliban were again in control in Afghanistan, the US and its allies having departed, defeated, watching on as the country disintegrated, as the burqa became mandatory, women were barred from public places without a male escort, and girls were banned from education.

As at the Forum itself, *The Delegate* contained multiple and opposing views. In 2017 Graham (SA 61) deplored that the world seemed to have 'abandoned civilized standards of debate and discussion'. 'If one points out something positive about President Trump, friendly faces turn into a snarl', he wrote, 'There is no debate, only prejudice.' In the same issue Maarten (Netherlands 61) called for a 'stronger and more effective Europe: 'Putin, Erdogan, and Trump give us no other choice'.[17]

Interspersed with serious political debates were lighter pieces. One suggested that, given food was a highlight of many mini reunions, perhaps they should call themselves the 'World Culinary Forum', with delegates invited to pen new essays on 'The Meal We Want'. New alumni were 'found' and enthusiastically welcomed to the fold in the pages of *The Delegate*. Old alumni provided updates on travels, books they had enjoyed, and self-confessed obsessions. (Dorothy (Malaya 62) contributed eight pages on growing orchids in 2005.) *The Delegate* was also where the Alumni Association Board communicated decisions and where candidates for Board elections introduced themselves. Probably the biggest part, however, was taken up with reunions—both the 'official' and 'unofficial'.[18]

'Reunions'—of people who have never met before

Explaining Alumni Association reunions to outsiders often resulted in bemused looks. 'So, this was a "reunion", but they were strangers?', they ask, 'and they bonded over a "shared" experience, even though they had quite different experiences often decades apart?'. Perhaps the best comparison is with a multi-year high school reunion, but with a greater sense of exclusivity. Inclusion was via participation in the Forum, whether as delegates, hosts, or staff (along with their family members and a few friends). The reunions changed over the years from 1994, most significantly after the 2020 Covid pandemic, but remained central to the Association. As Ginger (Summer 64) wrote in 2010, 'although there have been many ideas for more vaulted purposes for the Alumni Association, the enduring goal has been expanding and holding onto connections'. This was why, she said, so many 'look forward to the next big reunion' and 'seek each other out when we travel'.[19]

An initial flurry of reunion activity included Corfu 1 (1994), Washington (April 1995), Austria (August 1995), Corfu 2 (1996), and then the 'big' one, back where it all began—in New York—in 1997, celebrating fifty years since the first international Forum. Catherine Marin (France 59) told me much later that the Association had not planned to hold any more reunions—the New York one was it. On the last day, however, Sudhir (India 66) 'jumped up and invited everyone' to India in 1999; Graham (SA 61) followed him immediately: 'you took the words out of my mouth', he said, proposing a reunion in South Africa after the India gathering. Reunion locations depended upon the willingness of local alumni to organize them. Sudhir entertained thirty delegates with twenty associated family and friends in India in 1999 and two years later South African delegates welcomed a group of thirty-two to Cape Town. In 2004 it was the Italians' turn, with fifty-six people going to Rome. A group of Francesco's (Italy 63) philosophy students from La Sapienza University and Liceo Torquato Tasso high school English students attended some of the meetings, joining in 'after a short period of shyness'. The high school students were impressed that the older delegates were 'full of passion' expressing their diverse ideas, but that the 'feeling of anger usually present' in such discussions 'never appeared'. Although from all over the world, 'you talk as if you had always lived together'.[20]

In 2007 a group of sixty-seven, including forty-two delegates from twenty-six countries, representing seventeen years, met in Boston. A reunion was planned for Thailand in 2010, but at the last minute the political situation was deemed too dangerous, and it was canceled. Instead, Sudhir stepped up again to host a group in India later that year. In 2013, sixty-two people visited Berlin. There was a reunion in South Africa in 2016, another in Italy in 2018, and one in Singapore and Malaysia in 2019.[21] Fewer people participated in these later years. Forum reunion trips were not cheap and some enthusiastic participants of earlier years were less able to travel.

One unusual characteristic of a formal reunion, setting it apart from being 'just a tour group', was the programming of lectures and discussions. This continued the tradition of the Forum itself, where delegates were more than just exchange students. At the reunions, they mused on 'the world we wanted' as well as 'the world we want'. The difference with the alumni of course, was that in addition to external lecturers, many of the alumni themselves were now acknowledged experts. The authoritative speeches of diplomat John Goulden (UK 59) and foreign policy journalist Christoph Bertram (Germany 56) on 'The World We Face' at the 2007 Boston Reunion were reproduced in *The Delegate*. In 2001, alumni discussed global warming, the need for 'clean' technologies and the lack of political will to address the issue: 'we need a paradigm shift in our thinking and in the minds of politicians'.[22] Twenty years later, the world was still debating and we were just starting to see that shift emerging.

Alumni on these reunion tours also had special access to places and people, thanks to the network of local delegates, who were dragooned (usually willingly) into putting on a display of the best of their homeland. The 2001 alumni group visiting South Africa went to a concert celebrating the seventieth birthday of Archbishop Desmond Tutu 'and some of us had the thrill of speaking with Archbishop Tutu and his wife Leah' during the intermission. When I joined the alumni group for the Singapore leg of their 2019 reunion, we had a VIP visit to Gardens by the Bay, the hugely successful initiative of Tan Wee Kiat (Singapore 61). Not only was the boss himself on hand as a guide, so too were his top assistants. We were shepherded past the long line of waiting tourists to the elevators that took us to the spectacular sky walk. So *this* was what it felt like to be a delegate, I thought, feeling a little undeserving as we swanned into the elevators, not a ticket or wallet in sight. Tan Wee Kiat told me that he felt 'a deep sense of obligation' to host the reunion group, because the Forum experience had opened doors in his life. He probably would not attend other reunions, however.[23]

The reunions consisted of a strong core of regular participants, which meant that over time they became real 'reunions'—not to reminisce about the Forum itself, but to remember the previous reunion, to explore a new part of the world, and to discuss ideas. The core was dominated by the '59ers, who became legendary among delegates. At one reunion, Nii (Ghana 59) presented each of his cohort with a special scarf, identifying them as one of the chosen. The first thing I saw, when visiting Cora (US 59) two decades later, was her scarf, hanging in pride of place on her kitchen door. But the 1959ers were not exclusive and the core also included delegates from other years. And they were a welcoming bunch, keen to meet other delegates recently 'found' and particularly thoughtful of the wives, husbands, children, and friends (and Forum researcher and partner), who accompanied delegates. Nevertheless, other people at reunions acknowledged the '59ers' special bond, occasionally with an affectionate eyeroll.

Alongside these bigger meetings, 'mini-reunions' of delegates continued, as well as get-togethers of national groups—The Israelis announced their second reunion in 1995 and Thai delegates began meeting together regularly in 2000. They were still doing so twenty years later. Such reunions were more informal. They often revolved around one year group or were less structured. For instance, in 1999 Catherine (France 59) planned a reunion in Burgundy for '59ers, but 'in the end other years and lots of kids joined us', she remembered in delight. In 2005 a Board meeting in Oslo sparked an informal reunion, Roger (Norway 59) opening his mountain cottage and co-opting neighbors into providing accommodation. 'Fiftieth' reunions for year groups were common: Susie (Brazil 58) said her group 'immediately reverted to adolescence' in Iceland in 2008. Along with sightseeing, they 'remembered old stories, jokes, adventures and misadventures ... we sang old Forum songs; we giggled about who had had a crush on whom; we laughed and were silly and forgot that life was moving on'. The '59ers met in Japan in 2009, prompting 'the great footsie scandal' (resulting from a photograph of delegates' feet under the low Japanese table). Tragedy struck in 2010 when Leevi (Finland 60) died on the eve of the fiftieth anniversary reunion of his year—a celebration he had helped organize.[24]

A 2012 reunion in Israel caused controversy. Arab delegates were unable to attend and some other alumni boycotted the reunion on principle. Generally, however, reunions have been inclusive. In 2014, Manoli (Greece 62) was unable to attend the reunion in Shanghai, but his wife went anyway. Smaller gatherings were also reported in *The Delegate*: Gustavo (Argentina 70)'s sixtieth birthday in 2013 saw five alumni from 1970 and one from 1965 celebrating in style with a boat trip on the Seine in Paris, where Gustavo lived. The 'grand finale' was them all singing the 'signature tune' of the 1970 Forum, 'Leaving on a Jet Plane'.[25]

My presence at recent reunions produced more reminiscing about the

Forum itself, as I took out my notebook and tape recorder over breakfasts and on bus trips, fitting interviews between excursions. Perhaps the most interesting was the 50-year-reunion of the 1969 group. This was one of the informal get-togethers initiated by individuals. Amos (Israel) who lived in London, co-opted Ugi (Yugoslavia) and Stella (Italy), who lived in Rome, and they organized a weekend in Italy's capital. They spent months planning and tracking down delegates (with help from one enthusiastic, self-appointed Forum historian keen to find potential interview subjects). In the end, out of the twenty-five surviving delegates, twelve gathered for the weekend. In the process we traced five others, who were unable to attend, although two enjoyed a Zoom call with those gathered in Rome over the weekend. Unsurprisingly, given its location, the reunion was dominated by European delegates. They were joined by the Philippino and Colombian delegates (now based in the US and Spain) and Carola from Chile. Neither the organizers nor I managed to contact the delegates from Ethiopia, India, Japan, Kenya, Nigeria, Ceylon, Turkey, or Vietnam. We found leads for some—perhaps the Turk was now a doctor in Germany; an obituary in Canada several months later provided a sadder clue for the delegate from Ceylon—but others proved impossible.

Being a fly-on-the-wall at this reunion was a privilege. I watched a group of people reconnect, most having not seen each other for fifty years, getting to know the teenagers they vaguely remembered as fully-fledged adults. Politely tiptoeing around contentious issues, feeling their way towards renewed friendship on the first evening, seventy-two hours later they were engaged in free-flowing debate, with a few old tensions resurfacing. At this reunion, as at the larger ones, the delegates found that they were older, with greying (or balding) heads, they moved more slowly perhaps, some had modified or developed their opinions, but essentially 'they were still the same people'.[26]

Why join?

The Alumni Association meant different things to different people. For some, perhaps it *was* strategic networking—the opportunity to move beyond the thirty individuals from their own year group to harness the power and influence of the wider cohort of 807 former delegates.

For others, nostalgia and the affective power of shared experience was key. The Association became an important part of some delegates' lives. They were seduced by the magic of 'Corfu 1' and the way that just being a delegate provided a point of connection and commonality even if decades apart. Their experiences of the Association became linked but separate from their teenage Forum experiences, and equally as significant. Other delegates were less seduced, seeing reunions simply as easy-plan holidays in congenial company, especially in retirement. And several alumni found the appeal of the Association minimal, even unfathomable. Their lives were full and they had little desire to reconnect with people they met over fifty years ago, and the idea of spending days with complete strangers, with whom the only tenuous link was a Forum experience in different years, was unappealing. Some also felt their own careers insufficiently glamorous. One delegate traced a few delegates from her country but felt their lives had taken such disparate paths that even being the same nationality and a delegate was not enough to justify a gathering. Instead, she, like many others, maintained contact with friends from her Forum year.[27]

Occasionally delegates found reunions and the Association particularly difficult. It was one thing to gather as a group of teenagers in New York—on a level playing field—but quite another to meet as grownups, particularly when some might be in positions of power and influence, some might be on opposite sides of international disputes, and now with significant roles. One delegate, four decades after her exhilarating experience at the Forum, wrote in *The Delegate* that the 'delegates turned middle-aged have become real bourgeois who are more interested in food and idly dozing in the sun than in the challenging discussion of the difficult issues which confront us today'. She missed Helen Waller's 'well-informed' moderation that had 'empathy with conflicting views'. Further, she felt that some in the group were 'striving to manipulate our ignorance on world events'. The Alumni Association also 'had no set objective', she complained, which was 'extremely dangerous'. The ensuing brouhaha was played out in the pages of *The Delegate* resulting in a group of delegates leaving the Association.[28] It was a salutary and sad reminder of the diversity of Forum delegates and the naïvety, perhaps, of Forum aims.

One African delegate had doubts about attending a reunion. Her last memory of the Forum was hearing the South African delegate declare 'as a justification for the situation … in his country, that the black man was the white man's burden and would continue to be'. At that point, she 'knew for certain that basically, we were parting as strangers'. But decades years later, after meeting Jordan (Greece 60) and reading about the Corfu reunion, she went to a small reunion at a European delegate's home. Her African friends and family asked her, point blank, 'Don't you feel awkward keeping company with all these white people? … Black is black, white is white, and ne'er the twain shall meet'. But she was comfortable: 'I knew I was likely to be the only African there, but that was ok too.'[29]

Others found the Alumni Association inspirational—a point of calm in an otherwise chaotic world. Marita (SA 59) wrote that the 'times spent together had become a sort of world we want inside the world we have'. One Iranian alumna, returning to her home in the US after a reunion in Italy, astounded airport staff when she explained she had been with former delegates, *including* Israelis and Jordanians, and they 'had fun'. For Johannes (SA 62), 'the excitement' of the Forum and alumni reunions was personal: 'a few insignificant folks can share their thoughts and feelings in a way that they feel close to some of the edges of history, and go home enriched and to a degree even inspired.' Alumni were realistic about the impact their Association might have on the world but felt they did have a role. Gustav (Argentina 70) was 'not sure that we can change the world, but I'm convinced that we can help enlarge an international dialog that I believe can't be limited to politicians and businessmen'.[30]

The personal remained important. The Alumni Association facilitated re-connections between delegates, as well as useful onward introductions. Scattered Vietnamese delegates found each other again through the Association. John (UK 59) found it 'one of the most enriching experiences of my life: more important in many ways than the Forum itself'. He and his wife retired to central London 'to be sure of seeing the many delegates who pass through Heathrow'. In 2003, Geneviève (France 56) wrote in *The Delegate* about the treasured enamel bracelet given to her by Azer (Iran) at the Forum. She had tried to find him but failed; 'His name was Azer Kahnemooiypur and I would like to thank him again.' Sixteen years later, I tracked Azer down and reconnected him with Geneviève through the Alumni Association. 'There is simply no end to the Forum adventure', observed a delighted Geneviève.[31]

Connections extended beyond delegates to family, friends, neighbors, and colleagues. One of Gus Nasmith's friends in Nepal got project funding through a contact of Ginger's (Summer 64) in the Netherlands. Rita's (Germany 70) neighbor's son went to study in Canada, where Rita's fellow Forum delegate Bahram (Iran 70) provided a home away from home and even a job. Daphna (Israel 57) ('matching people's interests is one of my hobbies') thought carefully about activities for participants in the Israel Reunion. 'And so Manoli [(Greece 62)] and Pat were hosted by the Dean of the Medical School at Tel Aviv University, accompanied by Gur [(Israel 55)], who is a professor at this school; Johannes [(SA 62)] spent some time with a top person from the Finance world in Israel; and Sudhir [(India 66)] and Graham [(SA 61)] were invited to the Agritek—the Agricultural world exhibition which took place right here at the time—escorted by an old friend of mine'.[32]

The Future of the Alumni Association

There was a reunion planned for early 2020 in San Francisco. The global Covid pandemic forced its cancellation. As the pandemic stretched on, Daphna (Israel 57) introduced online meetings. One of the few positive outcomes of the pandemic was increased technical literacy. Octogenarians found themselves conversant with Zoom, and suddenly alumni of all ages could connect. The first Forum Zoom reunion was a hit, with around sixty participants in January 2021. An alumni committee organized a program of 'ZoomUnions', as Ginger named them, which refocused 'the Reunion' on discussion, debate, and learning about 'the world we want'.[33] Speakers were drawn from Forum ranks or their associates. Leading economist Jomo Sandaram (Malaysia 70) and executive director of the International Women's Rights Action Watch-Asia Pacific, Priyanthi Fernando (Ceylon 70), led a discussion 'navigating our brave new world', in which issues of climate change and global economic inequalities were to the fore. As Russian tanks rolled into the Ukraine in 2022, the focus shifted to Europe, with ex-politician and Bank of Finland governor, Erkki Liikanan

(Finland 68), and ex-director of the German Institute for International and Security Affairs and *Die Zeit* diplomatic correspondent Christoph Bertram (Germany 56) discussing the European Union. Later former NATO Ambassador, John Goulden (UK 59), and former Italian Defence Chief of Staff, General Vincenzo Camporini (Italy 64), talked about military implications. The ZoomUnions were more inclusive because they did not require money, time, and health to travel. Time zones were an issue, but some heavily caffeinated enthusiasts managed to prop their eyes open with matchsticks and participate in the wee small hours. This alternative way to connect came when many core Reunion attendees were getting older and less able to travel anyway. Such discussions do not appeal to everyone, but they continued have continued into 2024, with topics including migration and the rise of AI.

The heyday of the Alumni Association and reunions, like the Forum itself, is in the past. Ironically, the beginning of the end coincided with my discovery of the Forum in 2012. There have been no Board elections since 2013, the last issue of *The Delegate* landed in email in-boxes in 2020, the website has not been regularly updated since 2021, and the last reunions might be in New York and London, to celebrate the launch of this history. Or perhaps the phoenix will rise again, with later generations of alumni stepping up to stand for election, attend reunions, and take the Association forward. Perhaps though, just as it evolved organically, rather than being imposed by the Forum organization, the Association will gradually fade, having served its purpose of global reconnection.

Chapter 18

Changing the World
One Teen at a Time

> [The Forum] was kind of a deluding experience … we were exposed to all this idealism and it was so obvious that we should be friends with all those wonderful people with whom we were brought together. But … I don't think it is just as obvious that Eisenhower and Khrushchev should sit down and be good friends. They hold vested interests, and they represent powerful decisions, and they can't just be friends like ordinary people.
>
> Johan (Norway 56)[1]

An elite program involving just 807 teenagers over 25 years might be expected to have had little impact beyond the delegates themselves. And certainly, the main lasting impact of the Forum has been on that small group. They were, however, specially selected young people from around the world, meaning that the Forum's links, albeit tenuous, had global reach. Different people had competing and complementary aims for the Forum. For Helen Waller and Helen Rogers Reid, who initiated it, the Forum idealistically (and ambitiously) aimed to gather 'future leaders' and introduce them to each other, to create mutual understanding that would contribute to world peace. For the *Herald Tribune*, the Forum provided good copy and a claim to a serious political voice. For the US government, the Forum was a Cold War hearts-and-minds program, promoting in these hopefully-soon-to-be-influential teenagers democratic values and admiration for American modernity and power. For high school educators, the Forum offered a slew of international 'walking textbooks', broadening the minds of local students and creating globally-minded American citizens. For others, the Forum aimed to give youth a voice, but within 'sensible' constraints. How far did the Forum fulfil these ambitions and what *was* its impact and legacy?

A Network of Leaders?

About ten per cent of delegates became global leaders, as presidents and ministers, high ranking civil servants and diplomats, with more engaged in international activities, as academics, in business, or UN administration. The aim of creating a network of future leaders working towards a more peaceful world, however, was always idealistic. It was clear by the late 1960s that there was no global community of Forum alumni world leaders communicating regularly. The Forum connection popped up occasionally, often by accident. For example, Sergio Duarte (Brazil 53) met Jayantha Dhanapola (Ceylon 57) in Geneva in the mid-1980s while they were representing their countries at a Conference on Disarmament. Their friendship was well established by the time they discovered they had both been Forum delegates.[2] Nevertheless, while the Forum itself was not responsible for connecting them, it was not necessarily coincidence that both Duarte and Dhanapola were working for disarmament?

The Forum certainly worked on a personal level for individual delegates, enhancing their understanding of the world and sense of community. As Cora (US 59) put it, 'if there's an earthquake someplace, I think of a person I know there'. Sherille (Ceylon 71) also found 'it shrunk the globe in an amazing way ... Everything that happens I personalize it'.[3] Delegates, hosts, and Forum staff acquired extended personal networks stretching around the world and occasionally intergenerationally. In the 1990s, the Alumni Association reinvigorated connections, some of which had lain dormant for decades.

Hearts and Minds

Delegates were divided about the American government's influence in the Forum. Hiranthi (Ceylon 67) was adamant that they 'were not politically compromised or indoctrinated' and that it was 'not a Cold War hearts and minds' exercise. Gus Nasmith rightly rejected out of hand any CIA interference, but there did not have to be as the USIA was heavily involved. The Forum and State Department were essentially on the same page. Other delegates were sanguine. Any government involvement was a soft sell, promoted peace and understanding and was internationalist.

They felt that even if peace and goodwill were on American terms, it was better than war (or the alternative represented by USSR).[4]

The State Department certainly saw the Forum as a soft power weapon in the Cold War. For the US government, if ten percent of its delegates became politically significant and if they retained positive feelings towards the US, it was a worthwhile enterprise. Targeting potentially influential individuals was key to American soft diplomacy. What one USIS official said of a Ceylonese Fulbright scholar might have been applied to any number of Forum delegates: 'we achieved with one grant more than we could have with a whole year's program of media operations'. This was exemplified by Sonja (Yugoslavia 66), who 'proudly wore the red scarf of a Pioneer' and gave 'lectures condemning capitalism' in the US, but returned home 'increasingly critical' of her country's political dogma, joining the dissident group Prakis at university.[5] Having said that, for most delegates who rose to positions of influence, their genuine gratitude to the Forum organizers, the *Tribune*, the US government, the schools, and the families that hosted them did not translate automatically into a devotion to all the United States stood for. Once alumni were in positions of power, it is hard to see their decisions being directly shaped by the Forum experience. Nevertheless, soft power is subtle, and the Forum introduced delegates to ways of thinking about the world that potentially had some enduring impact.

But delegates were not just an audience for the State Department: they were also ammunition in the cultural Cold War, particularly in the 1950s. Their faces were plastered on magazine covers, their debates broadcast, their words printed in newspapers and government-sponsored newsletters around the world. The USIS distributed multiple copies of the Forum films around its offices, to be shown in cinemas and village halls or projected from the back of trucks onto draped bedsheets. The films presented the marvels of the US through the eyes of these remarkably articulate teenage ambassadors, with whom audiences might identify. Upon their return home some of these ambassadors became live exhibits, giving interviews and delivering speeches about their experiences in America. By the end of the 1960s, however, few returning delegates found themselves being feted by media or the USIS, beyond the odd article in a local newspaper or talk to a Rotary club. By then American soft power diplomacy had been framed as underhand, the scandal of CIA secret funding of other youth organizations taking its toll. Nevertheless, for much of its life, the Forum was, to use Professor Redefer's telling phrase, an 'arm of our State Department in spreading understanding among our young people'.[6]

The Forum also engaged with the 250 schools involved in hosting students, and the thousands of students attending the Forum's finale each year. Each year around 120 students were hosts. Some were also directly involved in Forums and television programs in the 1950s, and more from 1962, when they competed in televised discussion panels to become the American delegate. The Summer Forum provided further opportunities for American students, who encountered Forum alumni in Europe. We have seen that some hosts and delegates formed lifelong friendships. Schools themselves saw value in the program, repeatedly hosting delegates as 'walking textbooks', but did American students learn anything other than that Australians did not ride kangaroos to school, and there were no polar bears roaming the streets of Copenhagen? Forum archives from the 1950s are full of glowing testimonials from students and teachers, who had hosted students or attended the finale. They were carefully collected by Helen Waller and her staff to prove the Forum's impact to *Tribune* bosses. Less positive testimony was not circulated. The television programs engaged with a wider audience, as did delegates when they went further afield. Educationalists were also interested: as far away as Miami the Florida Education Association requested a Forum performance at their annual convention in 1957.[7] The enduring effect of the Forum beyond host schools, however, remains less certain.

Containment

Giving young people a platform to express their views was an important part of the Forum agenda. Delegates reported that senators and government bureaucrats listened and took them seriously, interested in understanding what young people thought. But there was another side. The Forum was also a performance to reassure young people more broadly that their voices were being heard. Commentators in the late 1940s were increasingly concerned about juvenile delinquency and the Forum was firstly a way to demonstrate teenagers were not all dangerous delinquents—they could be the 'hope of the future'—and secondly a way to give teenagers a means of expression that put the brakes on any disruptive tendencies. It gave a special few, chosen by their governments, the opportunity to speak in discussions that were carefully curated by adults. By broadcasting them, it seemed to be saying '*This* is what the world's smartest young people are thinking and *this* is where they can be heard'.

As the sixties wore on, the moral panic shifted from being about the delinquency of youth to their radicalism. Young people increasingly organized their own platforms to protest against wars, social and economic inequalities, and governments. The 1968 Oram report assessing the Forum's future noted the 'sense of alienation' felt by young people who were 'determined to be heard'. The Forum was not immune from these forces. Robert Huffman reported that the 1969 Forum had been in general a 'great success', but 'the current unrest among students manifested itself on occasion, with a few delegates expressing the desire for "revolution" and tending to blame all the world's ills on the United States and the Soviet Union'.[8] The Forum's usefulness as a containment strategy diminished, perhaps one reason it became less attractive for sponsors.

Impact

Rolf (Denmark 68) like many delegates, thought the Forum 'was good for me personally' but he 'didn't understand why it was worthwhile'.[9] The Forum certainly did not change the world, and it was only small arms in the Cold War 'long game' of capturing hearts and minds both for internationalism and for 'democracy'. That it survived for twenty-five years, however, suggests that the US government, the *Herald Tribune*, and American high schools found it an appealing and useful program. Nevertheless, the real impact of the Forum remained on the 807 delegates.

Almost all delegates described the Forum as having broadened their perspective and opened their minds to a world beyond their national borders. It began before television, let alone the internet, brought the world into our living rooms. Any teenager would have been amazed to fly halfway around the globe to the richest country on earth and become friends with teenagers from thirty different countries, some of which they might not even have heard of. Nordic delegates saw Black Africans for the first time; small-town New Zealanders experienced bustling New York; sheltered Pakistani daughters discovered how to be an American teenager; there were unexpected friendships among delegates whose countries were at war; they starred on television, were recognized on New York streets, and met senators, presidents, and icons of popular culture.

Of course, being a delegate did not make one immune from prejudice, as Helen Waller so expertly encouraged them to realize during some of the television discussions. The white female delegate who was forcibly kissed by an African delegate while loading the bus was explicit about her distaste: 'Quite apart from the colour of his skin, the idea of his touching me, let alone kissing me, of all things revolts me', she wrote home. The incident occurred on the way back from what she called the 'squalid' South, where she did not 'like being surrounded by so many blacks ... and felt oppressed by them'. She expressed her feelings in a private letter home, but it does suggest that beneath the surface of Forum camaraderie, prejudice could remain. By the end of the three months, delegates had had opportunities to question their assumptions. Occasionally, ingrained perspectives proved too strong for the Forum magic, as I found in a handful of interviews in the 2010s. Antisemitism survived: one delegate described a host family as 'stingy', adding 'maybe because they were Jews', and blamed Israel for all the world's ills. Racial stereotypes still permeated some conversations. Some Europeans dismissed Asian delegates as just there to dance and sing (although, to be fair, 'exotic' costumes and cultural performances were valued highly, particularly in the 1950s). Local rivalries persisted, even beyond the very real issues in the Middle East and Africa. I asked Argentinians about Brazilians or vice-versa at my peril. 'I did not take a national costume but the Brazilian delegate turned up in what was really Argentinian clothes', harrumphed one delegate from Buenos Aires. The Argentinian girls were 'too flirty', sniffed some Brazilian girls.[10] There were only a few delegates whose subsequent careers did not exactly embody the Forum spirit—a notoriously corrupt politician and an ambassador disgraced by a financial scandal.

Most delegates left the Forum more internationally minded and more tolerant, although many already had an international outlook. It had prompted them to apply for the Forum in the first place. Beyond that, the impact varied. For many, the Forum was a pleasant interlude, one of many privileged experiences that would characterize their lives. They came home, went to university, married, had children, and pursued successful careers without thinking much about the Forum. There was the occasional letter (or later email) from a former delegate, or a distant memory of having known someone from that exotic place. The Forum was mentioned in only a few resumés, obituaries or—the modern equivalent—Wikipedia entries. Several delegates' children and grandchildren whom I contacted while tracking down delegates knew nothing of the Forum.

But then there were those for the whom the Forum was genuinely life-changing, a pivotal moment that upended their lives completely, perhaps providing a path to immigrate to the US, or smoothing the way for an American college education leading to a significant career back home. It changed university plans, altered intended careers, and opened doors.[11] Forum connections enabled Jan (Czechoslovakia 67), Vuong (Vietnam 68), and Haider (Pakistan 71) to escape wars and revolutions. It quite possibly literally saved their lives.

For most, the impact was somewhere in between. Most delegates acknowledged that the experience of being selected as their country's representative, of traveling to the US, of making international friendships, of performing on stage and on television, of having their views sought, listened to, and respected—all as an impressionable teen—had, in sometimes undefinable ways, left an indelible impression. If nothing else, the Forum experience opened the eyes of delegates to some of the difficulties facing other parts of the globe. (At least one delegate knew nothing of the Vietnam War until arriving in the US.) Some gained extensive friendship networks, through the alumni or personal contacts. For most delegates, the Forum could legitimately claim to have shaped, if unconsciously, at least some of their future decisions and thinking.

Not Always Positive

For most delegates, the Forum was a wonderful experience. Some acknowledged that it was exhausting at times, they were always busy, always 'on show', and were sometimes homesick. A few dismissed any suggestion of tiredness or unhappiness, caught up on the adrenalin-fueled roller coaster of new people and new experiences. But for a handful of the 807 delegates, as one would expect, the Forum was a difficult experience. Host families might be a bad fit, although no one told me of anything more alarming than a personality clash. Teacher Robert Esik remembered having to move one delegate because he would not follow a family's (quite reasonable) rules. More significantly, Erica (Canada 47) was disastrously hospitalized with pneumonia for much of the Forum. Thelma (Liberia 53) went home early, apparently because she could not stand the cold. (She returned to live in the US in later life so perhaps homesickness made the cold worse.) One delegate developed an eating disorder. Another found the whole experience so overwhelming that she began cutting herself. Her father was flown in by the Forum, but she did not go home. Instead, she went to family friends to recuperate, able to rejoin the group for the Forum finale. She had not spoken about her time at the Forum to anybody until I contacted her decades later.

For others the negative impact hit after they returned home. Some Israeli delegates were reprimanded by government officials, with Snait (Israel 61) being pilloried in the media as well, 'inoculating her for life' against fearing other people's opinions, she told me. Similarly, Susan (SA 57) was hauled over the coals by South African officials, altough the Forum also provided her an escape route back to Barnard College. But sometimes it was personal. One delegate compared the Forum to the situation of young sports stars, who are given the world while too young, only to fall flat when their moment of fame ends. Imagining a diplomatic career before the Forum, she retreated upon her return home: 'After an intense three months being treated as a VIP', with celebrities coming and talking to you, you 'almost feel as though you have done it—where do you go then?'[12]

Some delegates died too young, in accidents or through illness. Bisidthisak (Thailand 59) committed suicide in 1963 while at Cambridge, the pressure too much, underscoring the immense expectations placed upon some delegates. Possibly the most tragic story is that of a European delegate, who was excited to visit a Latin American from his Forum about ten years later. Arriving at a modest house, he found his friend's mother and sister, dressed in black. His friend had committed suicide a week earlier. Since then, the visiting delegate has carried the burden of wondering whether his impending visit was part of the cause. During the Forum his friend had described a fantasy upbringing of privilege, wealth, and connections. Could he simply not face the reality of a small house and ordinary family being exposed?[13]

An Unexpected Legacy

The television programs were moderately successful at the time. A few delegates remembered being recognized in the street, and some series were repeated. But surprisingly, the television programs made potentially even greater impact fifty years after the final program aired. And that impact was international. In 2020, after I identified many of the 1950s programs in the Indiana University Library Moving Image Archive, they kindly digitized and put their collection online, from where they have migrated to YouTube. Since then, they have attracted millions of views from around the world, engaging a new generation of young people, alternately impressed by the articulate intelligence of the delegates on screen and appalled by some of their out-dated views. The programs attracting most notice have been those on prejudice, particularly with African delegates. 'These kids are more mature than most adults and university graduates', was one comment about a 1957 program, while another viewer was 'a proud Nigerian just watching this'. The 1958 Brazilian delegate impressed too: 'Susie crushed that debate. What an intelligent, articulate ambassador'. Many viewers wondered 'what happened to these teenagers', inspiring Danny Buenventura to film his reminiscences of his grandfather Johnny (Philippines 54) and upload them. Other YouTubers have reposted the films with information about delegates. One person has even (ahistorically) colorized them.[14]

Comments on YouTube are rarely subtle, particularly in an age of 'Me Too' and 'Black Lives Matter', when calling out sexism and racism. Yilma Tadesse (Ethiopia 57), later Ethiopian Ambassador to the African Union, suffered most. He was one of at least two Ethiopian delegates who declared 'We are not Africans at all. We don't have any race relationship with Africans,' reflecting a strand of Ethiopian identity in the 1950s. Some on social media called for Ambassador Tadesse to be 'deported to

Saudi Arabia or Yemen.' I had to scroll halfway down the page before someone sensibly pointed out that 'he was young and naïve and just a high schooler with limited knowledge of issues at his time', concluding 'leave the man alone'.[15]

The idea that something you said when aged sixteen (and Yilma was 'sixteen years and one month' when he went to the Forum) could come back and haunt you nearly seventy years later is horrifying. The criticism ignored both the fraught historical context of the original remark, and the likelihood a teenager might have matured in the intervening fifty years. But it underscores how very public the Forum was, with sometimes unanticipated and far-reaching consequences.

The World We Want

Founded in the aftermath of war, with an ascendent and increasingly outward-looking US, the Forum became a small cog in the Cold War being fought to capture hearts-and-minds, before fading towards irrelevance as young people changed, not least in their view of US imperialism. It exemplified the long-game approach to the cultural Cold War: each individual mattered, but especially those who might wield influence in the future. Media, business, and government were like-minded allies in the Forum project. The Forum was genuinely trying to be internationalist, emerging in a cosmopolitan era in which 'world citizenship' and ideas of 'one world' were popular, especially in sophisticated liberal Republican circles, and surviving even after that idealism waned in the early 1950s. It was always framed around an understanding that a better world should be shaped around a dominant US, with young people the key. Background political machinations notwithstanding, a program that encouraged young people from across the world to talk to each other in the interests of peace must have been at least a modest force for good.[16]

The Forum also provides a unique opportunity to examine the ways gender and culture operated and the way teenage experiences varied across the world over the third quarter of the twentieth century. Powerful women in the US media used the Forum to flex their muscles on the international stage. Female delegates were usually outnumbered but, reflecting their times, they expected to be. Delegates discovered American youth culture and its creation 'the teenager'. Young people changed from conservative-looking 'mini-adults' to long-haired, casually dressed teenagers. As they changed so did the world. As Robert Huffman told alumni in 1969 in a newsletter:

> When the Forum began it was a sort of 'model U.N' but this idea no longer grips the imagination as it once did, and advances in transportation and communications have changed the world beyond belief. We will be on the moon a few weeks after you receive this letter, but the real job which remains to be done is the one here on earth... With the rich nations moving farther and farther away from the poor nations, and with young people demanding to be heard as never before, the Forum believes that its challenge is greater today than ever before.[17]

Five years later, as the Forum was breathing its last, things had not improved; 'the world is struck with blow after blow', wrote Huffman, outlining a catalogue of economic and political crises, 'poverty... assassination, torture and terrorism'. But he still had hope in young people: 'the students in many countries are saying that things must change ... working ... to try to bring peace to warring nations, and to try to change governments and other sources of entrenched power.'[18]

Robert Huffman's remarks would not be out of place half a century later. The further advances in transportation and communication have exploded beyond even Huffman's wildest imaginings, and as I am writing this, space is being opened to private tourism, and the potential of AI just being realized. The divide between rich and poor remains, exacerbated by a global pandemic. Issues that dominated the Forum between 1947 and 1972 remain central to global debates in the twenty-first century. Tensions remain between Russia and the US, with a new Cold War-proxy conflict in Ukraine. China threatens to replace the US as the dominant world power. The Middle East remains in turmoil, closer than ever to erupting. Feminists continue to fight for gender equality, with contemporary discussions around sexuality and gender identity shifting the conversation forward. Apartheid has gone, but racism remains a global issue. 'American democracy', promoted so assiduously by the Forum, is becoming almost unrecognizable, with populist nationalism on the rise globally. On the other hand, 'Model UN' activities have reappeared, student exchanges persist, and teenagers are making themselves heard. 'Underdevelopment' was at the forefront of Forum delegates' debates; now climate change is a more pressing issue on the agenda, thanks, in part, to a 15-year-old Swedish schoolgirl.[19] The voices of young people are again at the forefront, desperately trying to imagine there might be a chance for 'the world we want'.

Appendix 1: Tables

Table 1: Gender Split of Delegates at the Forum By Year

Year	Girls	Boys	Total	% of Girls
1947 HHW	11	22	33	33
1948 HHW	11	18	29	38
1949 HHW	17	17	34	50
1950 HHW	9	16	25	36
1952 HHW	15	9	24	63
1953 HHW	16	15	31	52
1954 HHW	9	23	32	28
1955 HHW	16	18	34	47
1956 HHW	15	18	33	46
1957 HHW	16	17	33	49
1958 HHW	18	16	34	53
1959 HHW	19	16	35	54
1960 HHW	16	19	35	46
1961 HHW	20	17	37	54
Total HHW	**208**	**241**	**449**	**46%**
1962 VW	11	26	37	30%
1963 RH	11	28	39	28
1964 RH	16	21	37	44
1965 RH	10	25	35	29
1966 RH	14	17	31	45
1967 RH	12	22	34	35
1968 RH	7	28	34	20
1969 RH	10	19	29	35
1970 RH	16	13	29	55
1971 RH	12	20	32	38
1972 RH	10	10	20	50
Total RH	**118**	**203**	**321**	**37%**
Totals	**337**	**470**	**807**	**42%**

Table 2: Gender Split of Delegates at the Forum By Country

Country	Girls	Boys	Total	% of Girls
Hong Kong	0	1	1	0%
Ryukyus	0	1	1	0%
Ivory Coast	0	2	2	0%
Sudan	0	4	4	0%
Tanganyika	0	1	1	0%
Cuba	0	1	1	0%
Dominican Rep.	0	3	3	0%
El Salvador	0	1	1	0%
Haiti	0	1	1	0%
Honduras	0	1	1	0%
Nicaragua	0	2	2	0%
Puerto Rico	0	2	2	0%
Czechoslovakia	0	1	1	0%
Jordan	0	11	11	0%
Morocco	0	2	2	0%
Syria	0	3	3	0%
Bolivia	0	6	6	0%
Paraguay	0	1	1	0%
Venezuela	0	1	1	0%
Afghanistan	0	2	2	0%
Iraq	0	3	3	0%
Ceylon	2	12	14	14.30%
Netherlands	1	6	7	14.30%
Peru	1	6	7	14.30%
Uruguay	1	6	7	14.30%
Nepal	1	5	6	16.70%
Kenya	2	9	11	18.20%
Mexico	2	7	9	22.20%
Belgium	2	7	9	22.20%
Sierra Leone	1	3	4	25%
Guatemala	1	3	4	25%
Ethiopia	4	11	15	26.70%

Sweden	4	11	15	26.70%
India	6	15	21	28.60%
Ghana	4	10	14	28.60%
New Zealand	3	7	10	30%
Pakistan	6	13	19	31.60%
Nigeria	6	12	18	33.30%
Norway	8	15	23	34.80%
Philippines	6	11	17	35.30%
Spain	3	5	8	37.50%
Italy	8	13	21	38.10%
Germany	9	14	23	39.10%
Malaya/sia	4	6	10	40%
Liberia	2	3	5	40%
Costa Rica	2	3	5	40%
Iceland	4	6	10	40%
Australia	4	6	10	40%
Denmark	9	12	21	42.90%
Switzerland	3	4	7	42.90%
Argentina	6	8	14	42.90%
Colombia	3	4	7	42.90%
USA	7	9	16	43.80%
Singapore	4	5	9	44.40%
Turkey	8	10	18	44.40%
Egypt	8	10	18	44.40%
Korea	7	8	15	46.70%
Vietnam	8	9	17	47.10%
Greece	8	9	17	47.10%
Yugoslavia	8	9	17	47.10%
Iran	8	9	17	47.10%
France	10	11	21	47.60%
Panama	2	2	4	50%
Luxembourg	1	1	2	50%
Portugal	1	1	2	50%
Finland	7	6	13	53.80%

Canada	5	4	9	55.60%
South Africa	6	4	10	60%
Chile	8	5	13	61.50%
UK	18	11	29	62.10%
Indonesia	10	6	16	62.50%
Israel	15	9	24	62.50%
Thailand	12	6	18	66.70%
Rhodesia	2	1	3	66.70%
Austria	6	3	9	66.70%
Ireland	2	1	3	66.70%
Brazil	10	5	15	66.70%
Ecuador	2	1	3	66.70%
Lebanon	9	4	13	69.20%
Burma	7	3	10	70%
Japan	16	5	21	76.20%
Cambodia	1	0	1	100%
Trinidad & Tobago	2	0	2	100%
Cyprus	1	0	1	100%

Table 3: Number of Television Appearances per Delegate between 1954 and 1961

No. of Appearances	Boys	Girls	Total	% of Total
0 (only group)	19	21	40	14.5%
1	67	56	123	44.7%
2	38	33	71	25.8%
3	16	14	30	10.9%
4	4	4	8	2.9%
5	3	0	3	1.1%
Total	147	128	275	

Table 4: 'Brain Drain': How many delegates returned home

Continent/ Country	Returned		In US		Elsewhere	Untraced	Total
	%	No.	%	No.			
Europe	93%	240	7%	18	0	17	275
Canada/ Aus/NZ/SA	87.2%	34	5.1%	2	3	0	39
Israel	79.2%	19	12.5%	3	2	0	24
Latin America	75.9%	66	20.7%	18	3	24	111
Africa (not SA)	69.6%	48	27.5%	19	2	10	79
Asia	62.5%	105	27.4%	46	17	30	198
Arab Middle East	46%	23	46%	23	4	15	65
Total	77%	535	18.6%	129	31	96	791

Appendix 2: List of Delegates

(Interviews, Conversations, Emails)

Key: Delegates were known by the first name unless indicated by a name in quotation marks. Women's married names are in brackets. Mr/Ms denotes sex. I interview; SI Skype Interview; ZI Zoom Interview; PI Phone Interview; C Conversation; ZC Zoom Conversation; PC Phone Conversation; E Email; d daughter; s son; sis sister; bro brother.

1947

Argentina	Mr Eduardo Braun Cantillo SI Apr 24, 2017
Argentina	Mr Luis Siri
Argentina	Ms Leonor Escudero (De Lechenet)
Bolivia	Mr Luis Beltran
Bolivia	Mr Ronald Arellano
Brazil	Ms America de Oliveira (Campbell)
Brazil	Ms Carmen Calheiros (Gomes)
Canada	Mr Alcide Lafortune
Canada	Mr David Ellis SI Apr 27, 2018
Canada	Ms Barbara Ann White (Green)
Canada	Ms Erica Mitchell (Prescesky)
Chile	Mr Carlos Montoya Aguilar
Chile	Ms Celinda Fabres (Garces)
Colombia	Mr Rafael Moreno Castro
Costa Rica	Ms Kitty Morales (de Traque)
Cuba	Mr Luis Calvo ZI d Nilda Cravens, Jan 3, 2019
Dominican Rep.	Mr Rafael Oller Castro
Ecuador	Ms Susana Donoso (Ashton)
Ecuador	Ms Ines Utreras (Eichler)
El Salvador	Mr Jose Antonio Rodriguez
Guatemala	Mr Julio Caballeros
Haiti	Mr Maurice Kerby
Honduras	Mr Fernando Humberto Gomez
Mexico	Mr Luis Perez Maldonado
Nicaragua	Mr Hernan Arostegui
Panama	Ms Armonia Oses
Paraguay	Mr Luis Heraclio Segovia Nerhot
Peru	Mr Alfredo Larranaga (did not attend)
Peru	Mr Jose Luis Bustamente Rivera
Peru	Mr Oscar Castenada Bocanegro

Uruguay	Mr Juan Antonio Rodriguez Nery
Uruguay	Mr Pablo Fernandez Saez
Uruguay	Ms Beatrice Monestier Lopez
Venezuela	Mr Leopoldo Figarella

1948

Australia	Mr Donald Peter Ewing
Australia	Mr Norman G Curry
Denmark	Mr Jonny Christensen
Denmark	Mr Niels Jorgen Skydsgaard
Denmark	Mr Ulrik Plesner
Denmark	Ms Annelise Hansen
Denmark	Ms Hanne Nielsen
Denmark	Ms Merete Bjorn Hanssen
Finland	Mr Casimir Ehrnrooth
Finland	Mr Martti Kristian Soisalo
Finland	Ms Eeva Rhea Tilus
Norway	Mr Andreas Jorgensen
Norway	Mr Brynjulf Otnes
Norway	Mr Thor Hjort Johansen I d Grete Hjort Johansen, Mar 16, 2019
Norway	Ms Anne Pernille Vogt
Norway	Ms Eve Kristina Paasche I May 3, 2019
Norway	Ms Hilder Ve
Sweden	Mr Jan Carlestam I Apr 29, 2019
Sweden	Mr Lars Ake Ameus
Sweden	Mr Leif Erland Yngve Moller
Sweden	Mr Sten Stromholm
Sweden	Mr Sven Ingemar During
Sweden	Ms Carin Eyvor Qvarnström (Ygberg)
UK	Ms Hazel Barbara Corry (Mackenzie)
UK	Mr Calvin Fraser Hider
UK	Mr Colin Meredith
UK	Mr Terence Nelson
UK	Ms Isabella Tweddle PC sister Cathy Donaldson 2017
UK	Ms Patricia Fender (Bensted-Smith)

1949

Austria	Mr Gerhard Andlinger
Austria	Ms Wera 'Ferdinanda' Popper (Aigner)
Belgium	Mr Roger Debecker
Belgium	Ms Louise La Boulle (Bird) E
Denmark	Mr Torsten Hvidt

Denmark	Ms Hanne Thomsen (Mundt)
France	Mr Jean-Claude Salle
France	Ms Jacqueline 'Kiki' Landre (Jamot)
Germany	Mr Georg Albrechtskirchinger
Germany	Ms Elfriede Kapp
Greece	Mr Antony Demetriades E
Greece	Ms Zoe Dragoumis (Mazaraki)
Iceland	Mr Elnar Benediktsson
Iceland	Ms Rosa Thorbjornsdottir
Ireland	Mr David Hegerty
Ireland	Ms Rosemary Nugent (Walsh)
Italy	Mr Marco Bacciagaluppi I Jun 6, 2018
Italy	Ms Gabriella Gisci (Bullington)
Luxemburg	Mr Jean Roeder
Luxemburg	Ms Mady Weisgerber (Peters)
Netherlands	Mr Gustav Albert Sedee
Netherlands	Ms Jenny Ellen Van Reyen (Kovalsky)
Norway	Mr Christian Lange I May 9, 2019
Sweden	Ms Lena Kihlmann (Ekman)
Norway	Ms Solvi Bauge (Sogner)
Portugal	Mr Miguel Maria Paixao d'Oliveira
Portugal	Ms Maria Manuela Guerreire Rebeca (Viana)
Sweden	Mr Esbjorn Esbjornsen
Switzerland	Mr Peter S Burgi E s Michael Burgi
Switzerland	Ms Verena Haefeli (Ehrich-Haefeli)
Turkey	Mr Fuat Tekce
Turkey	Ms Jale Ergunkan
UK	Mr John Williams
UK	Ms Anne Mueller

1950

Burma	Mr Richard W Htun Nyunt
Burma	Ms Yadana Nat Mai (Postiglione) (June Bellamy) E s Michele Postiglione
Ceylon	Mr Chitranjan F Amersinghe
Egypt	Mr Hamed Mansour Attia
Egypt	Ms Berlanta Morsy Ali
India	Mr P. Balakrishnan Nair
India	Ms Usha Roy (Franklin)
Indonesia	Mr Sabam P Siagian
Indonesia	Mr Soesilo Sardadi
Iran	Mr Cyrus Ansary I May 31, 2016
Iran	Ms Mahine Pishdad

Iraq	Mr Farouq Said Huwaidi
Israel	Ms Ada Kleinman (Zamir)
Israel	Mr Avigdor Ziv
Lebanon	Ms Latifie Ameon Saad
Malaya	Mr Syed Adam Edward 'Eddie' Hogan-Shaidali
Nepal	Mr Tarani Prasad Pradhan
Pakistan	Mr Jehingir Farhad Mirza
Pakistan	Ms Nadira Aziz
Philippines	Ms Emma Laureno Garcia
Philippines	Mr Meliton Valerio Salazar E Salazar children
Syria	Mr Abdul Cader Shishakli
Thailand	Mr Supri Prakob-Santisukh
Thailand	Ms Malaival Mojdara (Bunyaratavej) I Mar 2, 2019
Vietnam	Mr Vu Huy 'Kim'

1952

Burma	Ms Sophie Cho (Nyunt)
Egypt	Ms Omaima Nour El-Din
Egypt	Mr Hussein Mohamed Ga'afer
India	Mr Rajendra Nath Bara
India	Ms Myrtle Dorai Raj
Indonesia	Ms Supia Latifah 'Pia' Soerjomihardjo (Alisjahbana)
Indonesia	Ms Latifah Sabarudin (Huthudi)
Iran	Mr Mahmoud Seyrafi-Zadeh/Sayrafizadeh
Iran	Ms Mahbonoo Payvar (Farhang)
Iraq	Mr Ma'moon Ibrahim Hilmi
Israel	Ms Tamar Aschner (Stoler)
Israel	Mr Ami Tal
Japan	Ms Kayoko Saito (Kodoma)
Korea	Ms Chung-Wha Lee (Iyengar) E
Lebanon	Ms Viola Nowfel (Chakkour)
Nepal	Ms Bhinda Malla (Shah) E s Anil Shah
Pakistan	Mr Riaz Mahmood
Pakistan,	Ms Hameeda Akhund (Hossain) SI Jun 19, 2017
Philippines	Mr Nemesio Gomez
Philippines	Ms Purificacion Cenabre Valera (Quisumbing)
Singapore	Ms Alice Tay (Kamenka)
Syria	Mr Marwan Sadat
Thailand	Mr Santi Vibulmonkol (Vibul) SI Nov 25, 2018
Thailand	Ms Salika Supol

1953

Australia	Ms Josephine Glen-Doepel (Spratt) C s Erle Spratt Mar 16, 2022

Belgium	Mr Bernard Mamet
Brazil	Mr Sergio de Queiroz Duarte E
Burma	Ms Khin Ohn Thant (Mrs Maung Myo Nyunt)
Canada	Ms Judith Perry (Holst)
Chile	Ms Cecilia Medina Quiroga ZI Aug 5, 2020
Denmark	Mr Niels Thygesen ZI Apr 23, 2022
Egypt	Mr Mohammed Khattab Rushdy
France	Mr Jean-Pierre Lugan
Germany	Ms Marian Wasielewski Gallis (Quednau)
Germany	Mr Rainer Dietrich
Greece & staff	Ms Christine Sifneou (Dodson) I Jun 11, 2016
India	Mr Probal Kumar Dutt Z C d Dutt sisters Apr 7, 2022
Indonesia	Ms Inajat Hanum
Iran	Ms Zohreh Sarmad E niece Moujan Morton
Israel	Ms Thelma Hirshson (Shocat) E d Yael Shocat
Japan	Ms Kikuko Iwasaki (Makihara)
Korea	Mr Chung-Hyun Kim
Lebanon	Ms Joumana Beydoun (Fakhoury)
Liberia	Ms Thelma Goll (Reeves)
Netherlands	Mr Hakeem van Lohuizen
Norway	Mr Tor Svendsen
Pakistan	Mr K A 'Abdul' Aziz Khan
Philippines	Ms Araceli Salazar E family Chito, Isa, Bong Salazar
Singapore	Mr Tan 'Joon Kheng'
Sweden	Mr Uno Hagelberg
Thailand	Mr Direk Charoenphol I Mar 3, 2019
Turkey	Ms Gulsen Cimilli
UK	Ms Maureen Cleave E d Dora Nichols
UK	Mr Keith Hopkins
Uruguay	Mr Jorge Bargman Z I Apr 9, 2022

1954

Australia	Mr Richard Walter Jahn PC Jan, 2016
Belgium	Mr Jean-Pierre Jeukenne
Burma	Mr David Tin
Chile	Ms Tila Hormazabal (Hancock)
Denmark	Ms Inga Wolfsberg (Wiehl) E
Egypt	Mr Nabil Mohamed Yousri
France	Mr Eric Laffont
Germany	Mr Gerhard Casper I Aug 23, 2018
Ghana	Mr Wentworth Bosman 'Kiddy' Ofuatey-Kodjoe
Greece	Mr Demetrios Papageorgis
India	Mr Vangala Jaya Ram

Iran	Mr Bagher Ghodsi E
Iraq	Mr Mahdi Abbas El-Baghdadi
Israel	Ms Nurit Auerbach (Duchin)
Italy	Ms Maria Pia Guasti (Foglia)
Japan	Ms Kimiko Fujii (Tsuchiya)
Jordan	Mr Raja 'Roger' Mafouz Ajluni E
Korea	Mr Chin-Tai Kim
Lebanon	Ms Thouraya Lababidy (Fischer)
Nepal	Mr Dwarika Ram Bhagat
Norway	Mr Gunnar Aasland
Pakistan	Mr O Rasul Nizam
Peru	Mr Ernesto de Losada
Philippine	Mr Johnny B Antillon E grandson Daniel Buenventura
Ryukyu	Mr Satoshi Kawamitzu
South Africa	Ms Eline Louw (Loubser) I May 7–10, 2018
Spain	Mr Sergio Santiago Paez
Switzerland	Mr Philippe de Vargas
Thailand	Ms Mattanee Mojdara (Rutnin) I Mar 2, 2019
Turkey	Ms Esin Epcel (Bursa)
UK	Mr Peter Anthony Hudson
Uruguay	Mr Carlos Bazzano

1955

Australia	Ms Lesley Scholes (Crutchfield) I Dec 3, 2016
Belgium	Mr Willy Widar
Brazil	Ms Leila Moraes (Knight)
Burma	Mr Sai Sang Toom
Ceylon	Mr Samuel H L Fernando
Denmark	Mr Erik Stig Jorgensen
Egypt,	Mr Mohamed 'Rifaat' El-Far
Finland	Ms Eeva Kaarina Lehtinen (Winter) I May 7, 2019
France	Ms Sabine Ewald (Frouin)
Germany	Ms Sabine Specht
Ghana	Mr Lebrecht Wilhelm Hesse
Iceland	Ms Gudrún Erlendsdóttir
India	Ms Usha Thadani (Kinnon) E husb. George Kinnon
Indonesia	Ms Tatti Larasati Soekandar
Iran	Mr Majid Tehranian
Israel	Mr Gur Ben Ari
Italy	Mr Paolo Filippini E
Japan	Ms Hisako Shimazu (Hirose)
Jordan	Mr Akram Z Barakat
Korea	Mr Nakchung Paik

Lebanon	Ms Saniya Yusuf Lababidi (Nahas)
Nigeria	Ms Minjiba Felicia Karibo (Ateli) E d Amie Georgwill
Norway	Mr Per Friis Rusten
Pakistan	Ms Nasreen Nazir Ahmed (Mahmood)
Philippines,	Mr Roman A Cruz Jr
Singapore	Mr Yuen Kum 'Chuen'
South Africa	Ms Marlene Roodt (Martin)
Sweden	Mr Jack Ramstroem
Switzerland	Mr Guy Waldvogel
Thailand	Mr M L Tuang Snidvongs
UK	Ms Patricia Sandford
Uruguay	Mr Daniel Orsuj
Vietnam	Ms Nguyen Ngoc 'Diep' (Dang)
Yugoslavia	Mr George Kocetkov

1956

Australia	Ms Elizabeth Ann 'Liz' Woodgate (Alpers) I Nov 17, 2016
Ceylon	Mr Joseph 'Jay' Jansen
Denmark	Ms Inge Stoustrup (Lind) E
Egypt	Mr Farouk Ezzat Mahmoud
Ethiopia	Mr Nebiat Taferi E s Haddis Taferi
Finland	Ms Marja 'Kaarina' Mantyla (Noble) I Jun 24, 2017
France	Ms Geneviève Martineau (Cimaz) I May 29, 2019
Germany	Mr Christoph Bertram ZI Dec 1, 2020
Ghana	Mr Alfred Clayton 'Nini' Bannerman I Jun 12, 2016
Guatemala	Ms Yolanda Parra (de Rubio)
Iceland	Ms Anna Katrin Emilsdottir
India	Mr Chitranjan 'Chit' Kapur ZI Sep 21, 2021
Indonesia	Ms Ratnati Iskandar di Nata
Iran	Mr Azer Kahnemooiypur (Kehnemui) ZI Jul 3, 2019
Israel	Ms Zohar Arshavsky (Ariel) E s Adi Ariel
Italy	Mr Francesco Brioschi
Japan	Ms Yoriko Konishi (Meguro)
Jordan	Mr Farouk El-Aref
Korea	Mr Hee Joon 'John' Park I Jul 27, 2018
Lebanon	Ms Gladys Kerbage E d Hala Achkar
Malaya	Ms Jawahir Binte Haji Ali
Mexico	Mr Francisco Arellano Belloc Jr
Nigeria	Mr Mohammed Amine Liman
Norway	Mr Johan Jurgen Holst
Pakistan	Mr Anis Khan Satti
Philippines	Mr Raul L Contreras
South Africa	Mr Dicks Loubser

Switzerland	Mr Romano Kunz
Thailand	Ms Vacharie Naewboonien
Turkey	Mr Salih Sezgin Bingol
UK	Ms Judith Reader (Dryhurst) I Jun 24, 2017
Vietnam	Ms Than thi Hoai 'Phuong' (Mrs Ta Ngoc Diep)
Yugoslavia	Ms Vesna Gasparevic

1957

Argentina	Mr Tomas N de Estrada E son Santiago de Estrada
Brazil	Ms Norma de Lacerta Blum E
Ceylon	Mr Jayantha C B Dhanapala E
Denmark	Mr Niels Fisch-Thomsen
Egypt	Ms Nadia Hetata
Ethiopia	Mr Mesfin Binega
Finland	Ms Irjaleena 'Irja' Lammi (Eriksson) I May 6, 2019
France	Ms Catherine Orcel (Baud) E
Germany	Mr Norbert Scholz
Ghana	Ms Amelia Addae (Djabanor) E d Gloria Oddoye
Iceland	Mr Gudjon Gudmundsson
India	Mr Padmanabh 'Gopi' Gopinath
Indonesia	Ms Beatrice 'Nonna' Kairupan
Iran	Ms Nahid Sarmad E niece Moujan Morton
Israel	Ms Daphna Rabinowitz (Cohen-Mintz) ZI Mar 31, 2020
Italy	Ms Diana Bedini I May 12, 2018
Japan	Ms Yumiko Morii
Jordan	Mr Hisham F Qaddumi
Korea	Mr Eric Young-Koo Lee
Lebanon	Mr Ziyad Husami
Morocco	Mr Mohamed Amine El Yacoubi Soussane
Nigeria	Mr Boniface Offokaja
Norway	Ms Lucie Paus (Faulk) I May 2, 2019
Pakistan	Mr Amin Jan Naim
Philippines	Mr Edward Dennis Normandy III E
Singapore	Mr Lim Heng Loong 'Peter' I Mar 8, 2019
South Africa	Ms Susan Rennie ZI Dec 22, 2020
Sudan	Mr Mahgoub Obeid Taha
Thailand	Ms Chotima Danitanand (Pathmanand) I Mar 2, 2019
Turkey	Ms Selma Sacir
UK	Ms Sara Chatt (Wood) I Sep 2, 2015
Vietnam	Mr Pham Trong 'Le' E
Yugoslavia	Ms Mirka Misic (Durovic)

1958

Argentina	Ms Vivian Salomon (De Hoic) I Mar 2, 2019
Brazil	Ms Suzana 'Suzie' Rigoleth (Cooper) I Jun 2, 2016
Ceylon	Mr Mahipala 'Mike' Udabage
Denmark	Mr Mogens Bent Poulsen (Svahn)
Egypt	Mr Ahmed Ahmed Attia
Ethiopia	Mr Yilma Taddesse
Finland	Ms Ritva Aulikki Fabrin (Luukkainen)
France	Ms Françoise Monier
Germany	Mr Gerd Greif
Ghana	Mr Tetteh 'Ben' Kofi
Greece	Ms Angeliki Laiou
Iceland	Mr Björn Fridfinnsson
India	Mr K R 'Krishnan' E
Indonesia	Ms Sjarmaini Sjarif
Iran	Ms Minoo Taavon (Payami)
Israel	Ms Ruth Loeb (Belkin) E
Italy	Ms Marcella Bassani (Mottino)
Japan	Ms Yukiko Yoshimura (Nunoi)
Jordan	Mr Michael Qustandi Karam ZI Jul 26, 2021
Korea	Ms Sangmie Choi
Lebanon	Mr Ibrahim Houri I Jun 8, 2016
Malaya	Ms Lee 'Hup Suan'
Morocco	Mr Omar Boury
Nigeria	Ms Foluke Ademoye (Adun)
Norway	Ms Arnlaug Leira I May 2, 2019
Pakistan	Ms Naila Aziz (Ahmed) I June 1, 2016
Panama	Ms Shirley Kris (Tractenberg) (not attend) E d Tanya Tractenberg
Philippines	Ms Patrocinio 'Patsy' Pagaduan (Schweickart)
South Africa	Ms Rina Thom (Pauw) E d Annalie Pauw
Sudan	Mr Beshir Abdel Gadir
Thailand	Mr Saroj Chavanaviraj I Mar 3, 2019
Turkey	Mr Onder 'Al' Guler I by Mehmet Fatih Oztarsu
UK	Mr John Torode I Jul 11, 2017
Vietnam	Ms Nguyen Thieu 'Nga' (Hamilton) E d Joy Marini
Yugoslavia	Mr Trivo Indjich

1959

Argentina	Mr Adolfo José Crosa
Brazil	Ms Alice 'Evelyn' Munro E sis Jocelyn Herrington
Burma	Ms Khin Aye 'Eva' Daniel
Ceylon	Mr P 'Tissa' M Fernando ZI Oct 1, 2021
Denmark	Mr Ejvind Bonderup I Mar 5, 2019

Egypt	Ms Nadia Adb-el-Salam Balbaa (Zaki)
Ethiopia	Ms Bizuayehu 'Bizu' Agonafir
Finland	Ms Kaarina Honkapohja (Lehtonen) ZI Oct 1, 2021
France	Ms Catherine Marin I Sep 8, 2015
Germany	Mr Jörg Ingo Weber
Ghana	Mr Nii Tetteh-Churu Quao I Jun 3, 2017, PI Aug 19, 2016
Greece	Mr Constantinos 'Gus' Fliakos
Iceland	Mr Jon Gunnarsson
India	Ms Nalini Nair (Radhakrishnan) ZI Feb 22, 2021
Indonesia	Ms Kustijah Prodjolalito
Iran	Ms Maryam Daftari E
Israel	Ms Daniela Yaffe (Zidon) E
Italy	Ms Ida Bossi I Sep 18, 2015
Japan	Ms Yukiko 'Yama' Yamakami (Shima) I Sep 25, 2015
Jordan	Mr Yasar Durra I Sep 25, 2015
Korea	Ms Esther Suh (Min) I Feb 25, 2016
Lebanon	Ms Nadia Domian (Asfour)
Nigeria,	Mr Hope Allison
Norway	Mr Nils 'Roger' Harboe I May 2, 2019
Pakistan	Ms Rafia Ayub (Khawaja) ZI Nov 5, 2021
Philippines	Mr Edgar G Gimotea
Singapore	Ms Yuen Chooi 'Yeng'
South Africa	Ms Marita Wessels
Sudan	Mr Mohamed Abdalla Hamadien
Thailand	Mr Bisidthisak Subarnbhesaj
Turkey	Mr Hasan Güclüyildiz E
UK	Mr Peter 'John' Goulden I Feb 27, 2016
USA	Ms Cora Vail Brooks I Jun 19, 2016
Vietnam	Ms Phan Thi Ngoc 'Lan' (Mrs Nguyen Pham)
Yugoslavia	Mr Gojko Stanic

1960

Argentina	Mr Pedro Tomas Ephraim
Brazil	Mr James Ward Carvalho
Burma	Mr Maung Aye 'Arthur' Chen
Cambodia	Ms Phalla Khim-tit
Canada	Ms Johanne Claire Turner (Van-der-Wee)
Ceylon	Mr Priyalal 'Lal' Harischandra Kurukulasuriya
Denmark	Ms Lise-Lotte Paludan-Andersen
Egypt	Mr Taher Ahmed Ali Khalifa
Ethiopia,	Mr Teklu Neway PC May 16, 2022
Finland	Mr Leevi J Lätti
France	Mr Eric Dietlin

Germany	Mr Peter Krohn
Ghana	Mr Lordsfield Anani 'Nani' Dzidzienyo PC Aug 28, 2018
Greece	Mr Iordanis 'Jordan' Arzoglou
Iceland	Ms Jona Edith Burgess (Hammer) I Jun 17, 2016
India	Mr Bimal Parshad Jain I Jun 13, 2016
Indonesia	Ms Johanna Zen (Warnak Tohir)
Iran	Mr Khusrow Hosseini Nezhad
Israel	Ms Tamar Liebes (Plesner)
Italy	Ms Franca Amoretti
Japan	Ms Midori Kawagoe
Korea	Ms Chung Sim Park
Malaia	Mr Ismail bin Ibrahim
Nigeria	Mr Aloysius C Nwaogugu
Norway	Mr Knut Sogstad I May 2, 2019
Pakistan	Mr Irfan Majid
Philippines	Mr Jose Conrado Benitez
Rhodesia	Ms Geraldine 'Gerry' Bray (Thompson) E
Sudan,	Mr Ahmed Siddik Osman I Jun 2, 2016
Thailand	Ms Sahadya Hongskula (Prabhavat) I Mar 2, 2019
Turkey	Ms Yildiz Güvenç (Wasti)
UK	Ms Alison Mary MacEwen (Scott) I Jun 4, 2019
US	Ms Lynn Baron (Henson) PC Jul 5, 2022
Vietnam	Ms Cao Thi Phuong 'Khanh' I Apr 26, 2016
Yugoslavia	Mr Milan Vojnovic

1961

Argentina	Ms Catalina 'Kitty' Lang
Burma	Ms Khin Khin Hla 'Mimi'
Canada	Mr Bruce Havelock Johnstone I Jun 22, 2017
Ceylon	Mr P G K 'Gemunu' Fernando
Chile	Mr Pedro Jose Alfonso Gonzalez
Denmark	Ms Kristen Runge (de Lopez)
Egypt	Ms Sanaa Mahmoud Hassan
Ethiopia	Mr Andreas Eshete
Finland	Ms Aino Ruuskanen
France	Mr Denis Favier
Germany	Ms Karin Goetsch
Ghana	Ms Grace Hinson (Mercer) I Jun 6, 2019
Greece	Ms Anastasia Embeoglou (Voskidou)
Iceland	Mr Sverrir Hólmarsson
India	Mr Ashish Banerjee
Israel	Ms Snait Gissis ZI Jul 16, 2020
Italy	Mr Marcello Felli

Japan	Ms Chiseko Shirai
Jordan	Mr Suheil Fuad I Aranki E
Korea	Ms Eun Sook Lee
Lebanon	Ms Mona Nammur (Iskander)
Netherlands	Mr Maarten B Engwirda I May 7, 2018
Nigeria	Ms Abimbola Okenla
Norway	Mr Per Ottar Seglen I May 4, 2019
Pakistan	Mr Jehangir Maklik
Pakistan	Mr Raza Ali I May 30, 2017
Rhodesia	Mr Jeremy William Hodgson E
Singapore	Mr Tan Wee 'Kiat' I Mar 5, 2019
South Africa	Mr Graham Brian Douglas McIntosh I May 7, 2018
Thailand	Ms Chodchoi Boonnag (Pongpairoj)
Turkey	Ms Ayzer Gevgilili
UK	Ms Zoe Allen (Mars) I Jun 15, 2017
US	Mr Mack 'Mickey' Lipkin Jr I July 27, 2018
US	Ms Katherine Anne Powers (Curtis)
US (Hawaii)	Ms Roberta S K Naauao (Jahrling) ZI Jul 17, 2020
Vietnam	Ms Nguyen 'YLang'
Yugoslavia	Ms Veroslava 'Vera' Ivkovic (Tadic)

1962

Argentina	Mr Guillermo Raul 'Willie' Tufro
Brazil	Ms Lygia Maria Sigaud
Burma	Ms Emma Maung Myint I Mar 7, 2019
Ceylon	Mr Muhummad Mauroof
Chile	Ms Fraya Valenzuela (Smith) E
Colombia	Mr Nelson Gnecco
Egypt	Mr Mohamed Sameh M Said Aly
Ethiopia	Mr Alem Seged Habtu E
Finland	Mr Olli Vilhelm Stålström I May 6, 2019
France	Ms Regine Berrivin
Germany	Mr Dieter Noack E
Ghana	Mr Richard Benjamin Turkson
Greece	Mr Emmanuel 'Manoli' Cassimatis I June 6, 2019
Iceland	Mr Rögnvaldur 'Röggi' Hannesson I Mar 6, 2019
India	Mr Shri Cheruverttolil K Koshy
Indonesia	Mr Zaki Fahmy Rachmat
Israel	Mr Joseph 'Yosi' Rinott E
Italy	Mr Marco di Nola
Japan	Ms Tomoko Fujimoto
Jordan	Mr Salah Ahmed Asa'd Ridwan
Kenya	Mr David Makau Mulumba

Korea	Mr Lee 'Chang Ho'
Malaya	Ms Dorothy Chen (Courtin) I Jun 13, 2016
Nigeria	Mr Akinwande 'Bolaji' Akinyemi
Norway	Mr Ragnar R Naess
Pakistan	Ms Dureen Islam
Peru	Mr Fernando Gonzales del Riego Sumar
Rhodesia	Ms Auxilia Sagwette E sis Eugenia Matthews
South Africa	Mr Johannes Cornelius van der Horst I May 8, 2018
Tanganyika	Mr Samuel J Sitta
Thailand	Ms Duangtip Somnapan (Surintatip) I Mar 2, 2019
Turkey	Mr Erbil Coskuner E
UK	Ms Suzanne Reeder (Warner) I Mar 13, 2019
Uruguay	Mr Rodolfo Fonseca
US & staff	Mr Augustus 'Gus' Nasmith Jr I Jun 18, 2016
Vietnam	Mr Cao Duc 'Thac'
Yugoslavia	Ms Branka Kusturin (Petrovic)

1963

Argentina	Ms Dalinda Funes de Marazzo
Austria	Ms Annemarie Biedl (Meierjohann) I May 9, 2018
Belgium	Mr Thierry van Eyll I May 9, 2019
Bolivia	Mr Jorge Manuel Garcia Soruco
Brazil	Mr Silvio de Albuquerque Mota
Chile	Ms Ana Isabel Coddou Charles
Egypt	Mr Raouf El-Gammal
Ethiopia	Mr Abdul Majid Hussein
France	Mr Thierry Jacques Marie Eydoux
Germany	Mr Rainer Frohn
Greece	Ms Irini Spanidou I Jun 9, 2016
Guatemala	Mr Alberto Lau E
India	Mr Shyamal Kumar Gupta
Iran	Ms Shahla Chehrazi I Aug 22, 2018
Ireland	Ms Nuala Connolly (Kelly) ZI Feb 2, 2022
Israel	Mr Gideon Remez E
Italy	Mr Francesco Saverio Trincia
Japan	Ms Hisako Ohashi (Iida)
Jordan	Mr Muhammad Ahmad Saleh
Kenya	Mr Stephen Mwazige
Korea	Mr Kwang-Yup Hong
Liberia	Mr Amos Sawyer E
Malaysia	Mr G Srinivasa Iyer
Mexico	Ms Elba Carrillo Garcia
New Zealand	Mr Alan Hinkley I Jul 10, 2017

Nigeria	Mr Nsa Harrison
Norway	Mr Tord Larsen I May 3, 2019
Pakistan	Mr Aijaz Ahmad
Panama	Ms Marina Diez
Philippines	Mr Edgardo Maranan
Spain	Mr Pedro Perrino
Sweden	Mr Tommy Carlstein I Apr 29, 2019
Syria	Mr Rabih El-Batal
Thailand	Mr Apichai Tantivess I Mar 2, 2019
Turkey	Mr Bilgin Adali
UK	Ms Catriona Trevelyan (Tyson) I Jun 18, 2017
US	Ms Ethel Silverman (Siris) I Jun 7, 2016
Vietnam	Mr Le Minh 'Son'
Yugoslavia	Mr Slobodan Casule

1964

Argentina	Mr Tamim Etemadi
Austria	Ms Eva Schmid (Lack)
Belgium	Mr Christian De Meulemeester
Bolivia	Mr Serban Protopopescu ZI Jan 25, 2022
Brazil	Ms Stella Maria Gardolinski
Cyprus	Ms Solmaz Necati
Dominican Rep.	Mr Jose Miguel Paliza
Ethiopia	Ms Tersit Agonafer
France	Ms Brigitte Orcel (Buffet)
Germany	Mr Klaus Kirchert
Greece	Mr Constantine Sarantis
Guatemala	Mr Rodrigo Diaz
Israel	Ms Rachel Lev (Pinkus) E
Italy	Mr Vincenzo 'Enzo' Camporini I Mar 6, 2019
Japan	Ms Atsuko Sakurauchi
Jordan	Mr Gabriel 'Gaby' A Khoury
Kenya	Mr Michael Wamalwa
Lebanon	Mr Salah Abu Izzeddin
Liberia	Ms Jerusha Holder
Malaysia	Ms Chua 'Chooi See'
Mexico	Mr Léon Felipe Ferrer I Oct 14, 2022
Nepal	Mr Bharat Bhagat Shrestha E
New Zealand	Ms Barbara Church (Dawson) Cs T Mckinley, S Ransom, d Ana Connor
Nigeria	Mr Abdurrahim Dangana
Norway	Ms Kristina 'Merethe' Rigland (Brodtkorb) I May 2, 2019
Pakistan	Mr Zahid Iqbal

Panama	Mr Mario Alberto Julio
Puerto Rico	Mr Juan 'Rafael' Caballero
Sierra Leone	Mr Hamid Kamara
Spain	Mr Jose Sala PI Jul 3, 2019
Sweden	Mr Torbjörn Lodén I May 9, 2019
Thailand	Ms Rachanee Pisitkasem (Sodsathit)
Trinidad & Tobago	Ms Baidwatee Permanand
Turkey	Ms Aysel San (Yontar) E
UK	Ms Helga Thorne (Kimpton) I Apr 18, 2019
US	Mr Lewis 'Lew' Andrews
Vietnam	Ms Le Thi 'Phuong'

1965

Afghanistan	Mr Assad Allah Ansari
Australia	Mr Michael 'Mike' Jones I Dec 3, 2015
Austria	Ms Monika Kalista I Sep 14, 2015
Bolivia	Mr Carlos Prado
Brazil	Mr Julio Cesar Machado Pinto
Denmark	Mr Joergen Peder Clausager E
Dominican Rep.	Mr Pablo Barinas
Egypt	Ms Mona Zulficar E
Ethiopia	Mr Aklog Birara
France	Ms Guillemette de Sairigné I Jun 28, 2019
Germany	Mr Maxmilian Herberger
Greece	Ms Lisette Iplicjian
Israel	Mr Gavriel Galore
Italy	Mr Pietro Iani I May 27, 2019
Japan	Ms Yoko Nishimagi (Tan)
Kenya	Mr Peter Ruoro (Chege Mbitiru)
Liberia	Mr Emmanuel L Shaw II
Malaysia	Mr Eddie Teo I Mar 5, 2019
Mexico	Mr Jorge Meixueiro
Nepal	Mr Govind B Chipalu
New Zealand	Mr David Winnard Greig I Jan 23, 2017
Nigeria	Mr Olusegun Bucknor
Pakistan	Mr Farouk Chowdhury
Panama	Mr Herman Bern
Puerto Rico	Mr Angel Luis Robles
Sierra Leone	Ms Hawa Tejan (Jalloh)
Spain	Ms Virginia Luengo
Sweden	Mr Göran Högberg I May 10, 2019
Thailand	Ms Varaphan Nimboonchaj I Mar 3, 2019

Trinidad & Tobago	Ms Annette Toussaint
Turkey	Mr Ertan Tezgor
UK	Mr Peter J Lewis ZI May 26, 2021
US	Mr Stephen Tracy
Vietnam,	Mr Nguyen 'Minh' I Jun 9, 2016
Yugoslavia	Ms Vesna Udovicic

1966

Australia	Mr Gregory Henderson
Canada	Mr Gerald Harvey Ross
Costa Rica	Mr Rafael Sayagues E sis Ana Sayagues
Denmark	Ms Randi Philip Joergensen
Egypt	Ms Magda Darwish
Ethiopia	Mr Kamal Bedri
France	Ms Lucile Verger
Germany	Ms Michaela Ibsen (Firsching)
Greece	Mr Evangelos Magirou
India	Mr Sudhir Prakash E
Israel	Ms Gila Noll (Haber)
Italy	Mr Carlo Cristofori E
Japan	Ms Satsuko Mitsumoto (Taruma)
Kenya	Mr Charles Njuguna Waigi
Korea	Ms Kyong Soon Kim
Liberia	Mr Eugene Peabody
Mexico	Mr Roberto E Novoa
Nepal	Mr Kiran Kumar Bhattarai
Netherlands	Mr Thomas 'Tom' Snijders E
New Zealand	Mr Anthony Steele
Nigeria	Ms Folashade 'Shade' Young ZI Jun 3, 2021
Peru	Ms Rosa Maria Dancuart (Macneil)
Sierra Leone	Mr Mamud Sesay
Spain	Mr Juan Ras Sirera I Mar 3, 2019
Sweden	Ms Elisabeth Mossler (Lundberg) I Mar 15, 2019
Thailand	Ms Amara Chayabongse
Turkey	Mr Halùk Ar
UK	Ms Judith Mullin (Round)
US	Ms Marcia Amsterdam
Vietnam	Mr Pham Toan 'Thien'
Yugoslavia	Ms Sonja Liht

1967

Australia	Mr Kenneth 'Ken' D MacDonald I Feb 14, 2016

Bolivia	Mr Guido Foianini
Canada	Ms Catherine M Beamish
Ceylon	Ms Hiranthi Jayasuriya (Walpola) I Feb 11, 2016
Chile	Mr Gonzalo Perez Benavides
Costa Rica	Ms Lucila Escalante (Vargas)
Czechoslovakia	Mr Jan Vanous ZI Jun 25, 2021
Denmark	Mr Niels Olsen
Eqypt	Ms Norma Souccar
Ethiopia	Ms Etenesh Tsige
Germany	Mr Peter Kollross
Ghana	Ms Difie Agyarko (Kusi)
Greece	Mr George Nicolaides
India	Ms Sunita Oberoi
Indonesia	Mr Anak 'Agung' Gde Agung
Israel	Ms Orit Gadiesh I Mar 15, 2019
Italy	Mr Riccardo Fermi
Japan	Mr Toshio Hase I May 8, 2018
Jordan	Mr Wael Toukan
Kenya	Mr Josphat Kiguru Muhindi
Korea	Mr Woo-Hyun Sohn
Mexico	Mr Vicente Fuentes
Netherlands	Mr Pieter Muysken
New Zealand	Mr Michael Keys E
Nigeria	Mr Jacob O Akindele
Peru	Mr Jaime Ponce
Sierra Leone	Mr Edwin Kamara
Singapore	Ms Sandra Anne Krempl ZI Jan 12, 2022
South Africa	Mr Louis van Schaik E
Spain	Ms Alberta 'Tina' Parayre I Mar 24, 2019
Sweden	Ms Charlotte Svenson
Turkey	Mr Ahmet Danis
UK	Ms Ceridwen Roberts I Sep 2, 2015
US	Mr William 'Bill' Migniuolo I Mar 13, 2019
Yugoslavia	Mr Bozidar Roganovic

1968

Argentina	Ms Alba Noemi Zaretsky (de Saleh)
Australia	Ms Beryl Lorraine Trigg (Kennedy) ZI Sep 4, 2020
Ceylon	Mr Krisantha 'Kris' Weerasuriya ZI Dec 21, 2021
Chile	Mr Carlos Alejandro Miranda
Colombia	Mr Daniel Vargas
Costa Rica	Mr Eduardo Augusto Doryan
Denmark	Mr Rolf Molich-Pedersen I May 28, 2019

Ecuador	Mr Patricio N Aguirre Andrade
Ethiopia	Mr Mammo Muchie
Finland	Mr Erkki Liikanen I May 5, 2019
France	Mr Jeanloup Margotton
Germany	Ms Katrin Schumann (Riquelme)
Ghana	Mr Emmanuel Awumbila Noggoh I Jun 9, 2016
Greece	Mr Panayiotis 'Takis' Momferratos
Indonesia	Mr Ronny Adhikarya SI Jun 27, 2018
Iran	Ms Farideh Nikoo (Faye DeWitt)
Israel	Mr Simon Abraham 'Avri' Ravid I Jun 7, 2016
Italy	Mr Amilcare Mantegazza
Japan	Mr Kazuaki Ueno
Kenya	Mr Joseph 'Joe' G Karanja
Korea	Mr 'Young-Ho' Kim
Malaysia	Mr Mustapha bin Mohd Nor
Netherlands	Mr Richard van Zuilen
New Zealand	Mr Mark Abbot I Oct 8, 2019
Nigeria	Mr Nurein Etamesor
Peru	Mr Francisco Landaveri
Philippines	Mr Zachery Labez
South Africa	Ms Marilyn van Heerden
Spain	Ms Elena Gimenez (Moreno)
Turkey	Mr Oguz Baykara
UK	Ms Katrina McLeod
US	Mr Craig Watson E
Vietnam	Mr Vu Duc 'Vuong' E
Yugoslavia	Mr Kosir 'Nikki' Miklavz

1969

Argentina	Ms Marta Mariana Desperbasques
Austria	Ms Ilona Hak (Stevens)
Ceylon	Mr Nirmalan Ranjit Appadurai
Chile	Ms Carola Oyarzun I May 27, 2019
Colombia	Mr Arnold Schiemann I May 27, 2019
Costa Rica	Mr Enrique de Mézerville
Ethiopia	Ms Azeb Zereyohannis
Finland	Mr Mikko Syvanne I May 25, 2019
France	Mr Philippe Altuzarra I May 25, 2019
Germany	Ms Jutta Hennig I May 27, 2019
Greece	Ms Irene Boni
India	Mr Vinod Kumar Sapra
Iran	Mr Said Tavakoli Parsan E
Israel	Mr Amos Paran I Aug 31, 2015

Italy	Ms Maria Christina 'Stella' Leonetti I May 11, 2018
Japan	Mr Takahito Hino
Kenya	Ms Ibtisam Salim
New Zealand	Mr Gregory Nigel 'Greg' Taylor I Mar 22, 2019
Nigeria	Mr Dalha Usman
Norway	Mr Peter Magnus I May 24, 2019
Philippines	Mr Rodel Rodis I May 25, 2019
Singapore	Mr Wu Dah Wei 'David' E
Spain	Mr Raimundo Viana
Switzerland	Ms Yvette Daoudi I May 27, 2019
Turkey	Ms Hatice Tiryaki
UK	Mr Roger van Schaick I March 13, 2019
US	Mr Steven Bell
Vietnam	Mr Ta Dong 'Tam'
Yugoslavia	Mr Ugljesa 'Ugi' Zvekic SI Oct 5, 2017, I May 12, 2019

1970

Argentina	Mr Gustavo Bazan I May 30, 2019
Austria	Mr Curt Cheaure E
Belgium	Mr Jan Op De Beeck
Brazil	Mr Eduardo Faerstein
Ceylon	Ms Priyanthi Kannangara (Fernando) E
Chile	Ms Gloria Esbry
Colombia	Ms Marta Valeria Goenaga (De Bedout)
Ethiopia	Mr Gizachew T Wobishet
France	Mr Christian Dennis I Sep 8, 2015
Germany	Ms Rita Kellner (Stoll) ZI Jun 23, 2020
Ghana	Mr Augustine Aduna
Greece	Ms Chrysy Karydi
India	Ms Sindhushree Rao (Khullar)
Iran	Mr Bahram Bern Niamir E
Israel	Ms Orit Furman
Italy	Mr Pietro Comba I May 27, 2019
Japan	Ms Koko Sakurai (Taylor)
Kenya	Mr Matthew Mweu Nthumbi
Malaysia	Mr Jomo Kwame Sundaram E
Mexico	Mr Saul Escobar Toledo
New Zealand	Ms Marama Reweti
Nigeria	Mr Henry Ijoh Ejembi
Norway	Ms Liv Eli Brynhildsvoll I May 3, 2019
Philippines	Ms Sarah Hernandez (Perry)
Switzerland	Ms Therese Kohler (Guenter)
UK	Ms Alice Knight (Heady)

US	Ms Rona Wilensky
Vietnam	Ms Nguyen Don Hang 'Phuong' (Qually)
Yugoslavia	Ms Melpomeni Korneti

1971

Argentina	Mr Alejandro Tanoue
Austria	Ms Sylvia Stein Krumholz
Belgium	Ms Marianne Van Den Broeck
Brazil	Ms Silvia Gutfilen
Ceylon	Mr Sherille Ismail I Jun 4, 2016
Chile	Ms Patricia Cecilia Steinfort
Colombia	Ms Yamir Ramirez
France	Mr Sylvain-Stephane 'Sylvain' Merino
Germany	Mr Joachim Larisch ZI Aug 29, 2022
Ghana	Ms Bemma Baabo Donkoh
Hong Kong	Mr Patrick Shing Chuen Lay E
India	Mr Venkata Sita Ram 'Sitaram' Yechury
Indonesia	Mr Iftikar Sutalaksana
Iran	Mr Mohammed Mehdi Rostami
Israel	Mr Allon Warburg
Italy	Mr Claudio Treves I May 26, 2019
Ivory Coast	Mr N'gbra 'Bruno' Tano
Japan	Mr Fuminori Ishikoso
Kenya	Mr Hudson Ahmed Liyai
Lebanon	Mr Kamal Fuad Badr
Mexico	Ms Jasmine Aguilar
New Zealand	Mr Ian G Taylor I Nov 5, 2019
Nicaragua	Mr Marvin Anthony 'Tony' Bowie Anderson
Nigeria	Ms Florence Ezekwe E
Norway	Mr Are Lysberg
Pakistan	Mr Haider Ali Khan ZI Apr 21, 2021
Philippines	Ms Maria 'Cecilia' Gomez
Singapore	Ms Susan Agnes Liu
UK	Ms Margaret M Bray
US	Mr Stephen DeWitt Cooke
Vietnam	Mr Nguyen Tan 'Tai'
Yugoslavia	Ms Vesna Smitran

1972

Austria	Mr Paul Pilger
Brazil	Ms Nina Romanos
Chile	Mr Carlos Trujillo
Colombia	Ms Gloria Inés Palma ZI May 4, 2021
France	Mr Eric-Paul Bonnigal

Germany	Ms Claudia Nagel
Ghana	Mr John Wilberforce Osei-Dadzie
India	Mr Rajeev Motiwala
Indonesia	Ms Maria 'Jeanne' d'Arc D.R. Ambar
Israel	Ms Keren Robin (Levi)
Italy	Ms Donatella Soria
Ivory Coast	Mr Boka Assa
Japan	Mr Takeshi Yagi
Kenya	Ms Sheila Adhiambo Oluoch
Lebanon	Ms Randa P Hakim
Nigeria	Ms Evelyn Erokwu (Mbanefo) E
New Zealand	Ms Teresa Gavigan (Penman) I Feb 11, 2016
UK	Mr Michael Portillo I Jul 9, 2017
US	Mr Brien Danko
Yugoslavia	Mr Tomislav Smole

Notes

Chapter 1: An Invitation

1 Int Monika (Austria 65).

2 Childers, *The Evolving Citizen*, 35–6. See also Palladino, *Teenagers*.

3 On cultural cold war see Wilford, *The Might Wurlitzer*; Saunders, *Who Paid the Piper*.

4 Honeck, *Our Frontier*, 207; Palladino, 92. 'Youth' can also be a 'lifestyle or form of social experience' and represent 'newness and change'. Norwig, 'A First European Generation?', 252. See also Alexander & Sleight (eds), *A Cultural History of Youth*.

5 Oram Report, 6.

6 eg. Fieldston, 'The Nursery's Iron Curtain'; Holt, *Cold War Kids*; Kordas, *The Politics of Childhood*; Peacock, *Innocent Weapons*.

7 See Kotek, *Students and the Cold War*; Kotek, 'Youth organizations'; Guillory, 'Culture Clash'; Honeck, *Our Frontier*.

8 Helgren, *American Girls*, 19.

9 Grieve, *Little Cold Warriors*.

10 Chatelain, 'International Sisterhood'; Koivunen, 'Overcoming Cold War Boundaries'; Koivunen, *Performing Peace and Friendship*; Helgren, *American Girls*, 58.

11 Jobs, *Backpack Ambassadors*.

12 Berghel, '"What My Generation"'; Berghel, '"Remove Our Troops"'. See also Chafe, *Civilities and Civil Rights*; Elliott, 'We Should Live'.

13 NYHT to 1962 is available online through the New York Public Library. I am forever indebted to Kate Robertson for her assistance in accessing it.

14 Workum, 'Mechanisms Exposed"; and very recently, Blake 'The World They Wanted', MA thesis.

15 My emphasis. Bio Tomas (Argentina 57); Buchanan, 'Chukka Pony'.

16 The 14 missing countries were mainly those that sent delegates only once or twice. Those who sent more were Kenya (11), Peru (7), Costa Rica (5) and Sierra Leone (4).

Chapter 2: Genesis

1 New York Board of Education Circular, May 1946, F44/2 Reid, LOC.

2 The Student Federalists were founded by Harris Wofford, also a Forum speaker, to promote the idea of world government among students and young people. Niles Cushing become a renowned expert in low-income housing, Harris L Wofford Jnr became a US senator, Stephen Schwebel became president of the International Court of Justice, and was an adult speaker at the 1952 Forum. Leonard Polisar became a corporate lawyer.

Notes to pages 11–18

3 Laura Marvin to 'Sirs', Apr 19, 1946, Ellis White, Asst Dir Laboratory School, Pennsylvania State Teachers College to *NYHT*, Apr 24, 1946, *NYHT* to Laura Marvin, May 6, 1946, *NYHT* to Ellis White, May 6, 1946, F44/2 Reid, LOC. Laura later ecome a theatre critic and writer (as Laura Hitchcock).

4 Krismann, *Encyclopedia*, 457–9; Kluger, *The Paper*, 6–7, 462; Obit. J H Whitney; Kahn, *Jock*.

5 *NYT* Sept 28, 2006. Other women included Sonia Tomara and Marguerite Higgins. The *Tribune* was 'woman-conscious'. Livengood, *Americana*, 100.

6 Helen Reid's bulging folder of membership cards is at F31/4 Reid, LOC.

7 Second Women's Conference on Current Problems (1932), Program, D237 F12770 Reid, LOC.

8 Speakers in 1949 included Dwight Eisenhower, Hubert Humphrey, Clifford Case, Franklin D. Roosevelt, Jr, Adlai Stevenson, Henry Cabot Lodge, Jr, Estes Kefauver, Margaret Chase Smith, Wayne L Morse, John Foster Dulles, and Lucius Clay. *NYHT* Oct 27, 1949, 1; Oct 30, 1949, F3; Oct 26, 1952, F2.

9 *NYHT* Nov 19, 1948, 16.

10 *NYT* Nov 21, 1943, 26. Anna Fett points to concerns about 'a postwar epidemic of juvenile delinquency'. Fett, 'The Teen-Age Program', 4.

11 See Hale, *The Freedom Schools*; Berghel, '"What My Generation"'.

12 *New York Amsterdam News* Dec 4, 1943, 3B; Obit. W Wallace.

13 *NYT* Dec 8, 1946, 54; Dec 12, 1948, 52; Dec 7, 1952, 50; Grogan, 'Australian Lad' Ten years later, delegates came from Denmark, England, Germany, Israel, New Zealand, Norway, Okinawa, the Philippines, and Sweden.

14 Eg Camp Rising Sun, established 1929 in US for younger boys from home and overseas. The *Sun News-Pictorial* Youth Travel Scheme to Britain in 1950s for young teenage Australian boys. Chinner & David, *Australia's Schoolboy Ambassadors*.

15 Email Robin (Australia *Mirror* 56) Jun 15, 2020. In 1961 there was no visit to UN; the day trip to Washington included the Smithsonian but not the White House. Email Anders (Sweden *Mirror* 61) Jul 16, 2020. Program, 19th Annual *New York Mirror* Welfare Fund Youth Forum. Cuttings 'Youth Forum's Resolutions', Mellbourn papers. Graeme better remembered his 2 months' post-forum travels, staying with families around the US, courtesy of Rotary Club contacts. Email Graeme (NZ *Mirror* 61) Jun 4, 2021.

16 *NYT* Oct 26, 1947, 29; Obit. D Gordon.

17 Konkle, 'A Preliminary Overview'. For high school journalism and citizenship education see also Dennis, 'Prior review', 2. Examples of more localized forums: 1944 YMCA high school forum in Charlotte North Carolina; 1945 Emerson Junior High forum in Cleveland; 1948 NY Board of Education radio station WNYE 'Junior High School Forum'.

18 Kuriki, 'History-Mission'; Obit. D Watt. Other examples include the controversial 1926 Floating University taking a shipload of American university students on an

Notes to pages 17–21

8-month 'educational' cruise. Pietsch, *The Floating University*. Students International Union (SIU), founded in 1924, survives today, IWA 'IWA History'. Salzburg Global Seminar, established in 1947 also survives. Salzburg Global Seminar, 'Our History'; Ryback, *The Salzburg Seminar*, 11. See also Tournès & Scott-Smith, *Global Exchanges*; Fass, 'Intersecting Agendas'.

19 Honeck, *Our Frontier*, 88–90. Clara Leiser's Youth for All Nations network of penpals. *NYHT* Mar 8, 1948, 14; *NYT* May 15, 1991.

20 AFS, cited in Fett, 'The Teen-age Program', 8. On AFS see also Scribner, 'American Teenagers'.

21 For Ekataria (Kaiti) Myrivili, Assistant Cultural Attaché, US Embassy, Athens, 1951–69: the US 'represented all the democratic ideals'. Lalaki, 'The Cultural Cold War'; see also Sussman, 'United States Information Service Libraries'.

22 Etheridge, 'Die antideutsche Welle: The Anti-GermanWave, Public Diplomacy, and Intercultural Relations in Cold War America', in Gienow-Hecht (ed.) *Decentering America*, cited in Cohn, '"In between propaganda"', 400.

23 The USIA worked closely with the International Educational Exchange Service (IES, 1952–59) and the Bureau of Educational and Cultural Affairs (ECA, 1960–78). For an outline of administrative history and relationship, see https://eca.state.gov/about-bureau/history-and-mission-eca. USIA and USIS are both used in this book. Officials worked for the USIA but delegates knew it as USIS.

24 Hansen, USIA *Public Diplomacy*, 2, 4, 27-29; Pillsbury Interview, ADST; Frankel, 'Cultural Affairs Officer'; Arndt, *The Resort of Kings*. On libraries see See Sussman, 'United States Information Service Libraries'.

25 National Security Council, Progress Report on US Policy toward Japan by the Operations Coordinating Board, October 19, 1955, Declassified Documents Reference System 298664-i1-10, in Cohn, 'In between propaganda', 401; Spaulding cited in Fett 'The Teen-age Program', 14.

26 US BECA, 'The Teenage Student Exchange Program', B220/F28, BECA, Arkansas; US BECA, *Educational and Cultural Diplomacy*, 1960, 57; US BECA *Educational and Cultural Diplomacy*, 1962, 52; US BECA, *International Exchange* 1967, 23–4. Fett's 'The Teen-Age Program' delves deeply into the development of the US State Department's program using previously classified documents. On the use of private sector see Lucas, 'Beyond freedom'; also Laville & Wilford (eds) *The US Government*; for focus on child welfare, see Fieldston, *Raising the World* esp. ch. 4.

27 Redefer-JHW, Oct 31, 1961, F147/B3 Whitney, Yale; Fieldston, 'The Junior Marshall Plan', 25, 32. In 1948 the Marshall Plan, or European Recovery Program, provided US aid to Europe to assist with rebuilding. See also Papanek, 'American Youth'. Shannon identified benefits for the USIS of involvement in exchanges in Iran. Shannon, 'Losing Hearts', 1.

28 Edward Murrow, in *USIA Correspondent* April 1963, in Hansen *USIA Public Diplomacy*, 9.

29 Cohn, '"In between propaganda"', 398; see also Gienow-Hecht, '"How good are we?"'; Laugesen, 'American Publishers'. Wilford suggests that the influence ran both ways between intellectuals and the government. Wilford, *The Might Wurlitzer*.

30 Koivunen, *Performing Peace*; N Apr 1961, 14; Ints Ollie (Finland 62), Mack (US 61) See also Peacock, 'The perils of building'; Piccini, '"There is no solidarity"'.

31 Int and Email Mack (US 61) Jan 2023; NYT, Feb 21, 1967. See also Krekola & Mikkonen, 'Backlash of the Free World'.

32 Note attached to invitation to OR to tea with Forum delegates and Board of Education, March 1947, B93/F197 Ogden Reid, Yale. Huffman told *Herald Tribune* historian Richard Kluger in 1982 that 'Whitie claims credit' for the idea. RH-Kluger Jan 8, 1982, B6/F131 Kluger, Yale.

33 See Slappey, 'The Youth Forum'.

Chapter 3: Leading the Way

1 Getty Images, caption, photo of Helen Hiett Sep 25, 1940; *Evening Observer*, Dunkirk (NY) Jun 21, 1941, 15. See also *The Times and Daily News Leader,* San Mateo (Cal). Oct 25, 1940, 3. It is a career barely acknowledged by posterity, soon to be remedied by Mabel Gardner, whose PhD thesis at Western University, Ontario has Hiett and her journalism at its center.

2 Klansmen owned the *Pekin Times* 1923–25. Gardner, 'Helen Hiett'; Smith, *A History of Illinois*, 140; ancestry.com; Olar, 'Pekin'; Yearbooks: Pekin High School, 1926, 9; 1927, 13–14; 1931, 58–60, 86, 89, on ancestry.com; Olar, 'News From Days'.

3 Hiett, *No Matter Where*, 16; Scott-Smith, 'Building a Community', 90; 'Harold Lasswell', *Britannica*; Gardner, 'Helen Hiett', 3. International House was an internationalist youth initiative, founded in 1932 by John D Rockefeller Jr, hoping that by living & studying together, international students would build global friendships and understanding.

4 Helen Hiett to Sandy, Dec. 6, 1936, Hiett, Smith College, cited in Gardner, 'Helen Hiett', 7.

5 *Kingston Daily Freeman,* Mar 15, 1938, 4. The North Carolina Congress of Parents and Teachers and Salvage Committee of Kingston NC 'painted a barrel red, white and blue, christened it the "Helen Hiett Barrel" and placed it on Kingston's courthouse square'. It was a collection point for scrap rubber for the war effort and was 'doing so well due to Helen's great radio popularity that more "Hiett Barrels"' were planned. The *Anniston Star* in Alabama reported with some degree of amusement that Helen had been advised of the distinction, but sadly did not record her reaction. (Jul 8, 1942, 2); on female radio correspondents see Hosley, 'As good as'.

6 Frances Witherspoon, review, *NYHT* Apr 2, 1944, D16 ; Hiett, *No Matter Where*, 316, Author bio, back dustflap.

7 Hiett was 'a member of Forum staff' in 1945: *NYHT* Oct 31, 1945, 1A; Nov 4, 1945, G5; Nov 9, 1945, 21. She was 'director' in 1946. *NYHT* Nov 14, 1946, 32.

8 See Lalaki, 'The Cultural Cold War'; Laville, *Cold War Women*; Laville, 'The committee of correspondence'; and on an earlier era, Sluga *Age of Internationalism*.

9 Ints Anon, Hameeda (Pakistan 52).

10 Ints Arnlaug (Norway 58), Susan (SA 57).

11 Ints Christine (Greece 53), Margi Waller; Kluger, *The Paper,* 462.

12 Whitie married Joan Brandon, college-age daughter of *Herald Tribune* staffer Dorothy Brandon. Mrs Wallers (1): Lucynda Roberts (div 1942, d 1993); (2): Ruth Cornish is memorialised in Minsk. *NYHT* Aug 16, 1947, 12A; US Mission Belarus, 'US Embassy, UN and Belarusians Remember'; Clark, 'Speech'. Short-term, ostensibly non-governmental, The Committee for the Marshall Plan was established to promote the passing of the European Recovery Program and was a front for the State Department. The United World Federalists was a non-partisan, international organization promoting global disarmament, cultural freedom and peace. Wala, 'Selling the Marshall Plan'; United World Federalists, 'Finding Aid'; Fuchs, 'The World Federation'; Yoder, 'The United World Federalists'.

13 N May 1957. Int Margi Waller; Int & Email Mark Waller Jun 27, 2020.

14 *NYHT* Aug 2, 1961, 13.

15 Don Cook for *NYHT*; internal memos; HHW-JHW, Aug 11, 1961, Ted Waller-JHW, Aug 18, 1961, B147/F3 Whitney, Yale; Helen Waller Death Report, B0392 NARA; *NYHT* Aug 25, 1961, 26. Ted died in 2010 at 94, after marrying 7 times (including to Irene twice) and having one de facto partner. He must have had charm. His son said: a bit of a 'rascal, who, when he was not drinking, had 'great instincts' (Ints M & M Waller 2020).

16 Kern House Enterprises operated Forum World Features, a commercial news service that served as a channel for information the CIA wished to promulgate. Whitney's cousin was Tracy Barnes of the CIA. Saunders, *Who Paid*, 136, 261, 285; Whitney Foundation Papers, Yale.

17 Anon, Letter, 1962; '1963 World Youth Forum' Booklet A, Courtin papers; 'For the Files: Re: *Herald Tribune* Forum', Dec 7, 1962 & Memo-Paul Ward, Dec 7, 1962, *NYHT*WYF, SLC. Herbert Wieschhoff was Director of the UN Department of Political and Security Council Affairs.

18 JHW-Wieschhoff, Nov 19, 1962, B147/F3 Whitney, Yale.

19 Huffman Resumé, Boal Papers; ancestry.com; Email Susan Boal Feb 23, 2021; Int Haider (Pakistan 71).

20 Solomon-Paul Ward, Dec 7, 1962, *NYHT*WYF, SLC; Miller-JHW, May 28, 1963, B147/F3 Whitney, Yale.

21 Ints Emmanuel (Ghana 68), Mikko (Finland 69); Emails Aysel (Turkey 64) Mar-Apr, 2021, Monika (Austria 65) Oct 2, 2022.

22 Ints Rita (Germany 70), Haider (Pakistan 71).

23 Int Anon; High School Forum Expenses 1948, F47/1 Reid, LOC; HHW, 'Essential operations of the High School Forum Office', Oct 30, 1956, F609 B51/F609 Ogden Reid,

Yale; RH-MacJannets, Sep 27, 1971, B138 MacJannet, Tufts.

24 Emails Daniel Brent Sep 27, Oct 7, 2021; Ints Snait (Israel 61), Christine (Greece 53), Sylvia (Staff).

25 Int Christine (Greece 53); HWW-ORR, Nov 15, 1955, B51/F609 Ogden Reid, Yale.

26 RH-Gus, Jan 11, 1966, Nasmith papers; Ints Emmanuel (Ghana 68), Gus (US 62); N Apr 1960.

27 Ints Hameeda (Pakistan 52), Snait (Israel 61), Avri (Israel 68), Anon.

28 Jeanne Brockman had experience at the Experiment in International Living and became executive assistant of the National Association of Foreign Student Advisors. Stella Stern, Helen's longest serving assistant (1948–54), was then AFS Forum director (and married in June 1954). Connie Jackson (1957–58) later worked for the Institute of International Education. Mary Warner (1956–57) became a well-known historian (as Mary Blanchard). Trinka Peterson (1967–68) joined publishing firm Harcourt Brace; Connie Freeman (1969–70) did a PhD and then became a diplomat. Anne Counes (1962–65) was already in her 30s with a Masters in American Literature from NYU, in 1962. She had worked for McKinsey and Company and the American Association of University Women. She vanishes from the records after 1965, although she may have been the Anne Counes who died in 2010, living in a studio apartment on the fringes of Greenwich Village in New York, in a 'protective service occupation'.

29 N Sep 1956.

30 Ints Chitranjan (India 56), Jorge (Uruguay 53). N Dec 1958. 1959 volunteers: Eddie (Malaya 50), Purificacion (Philippines 52), Susan (SA 57), Judith (Canada 53), Chitranjan (India 56) and Jorge (Uruguay 53). 1960 volunteers: Susan (SA 57), Jorge (Uruguay 53), Raja (Jordan 54), Cora (US 59), Direk (Thailand 53) & Sarah Lawrence College student and ex AFS student, Andrea Cousins, daughter of World Federalist Association president and *Saturday Review* editor Norman Cousins.

31 N Dec 1959; N Jun 1960. Alumni fellows 1960: Gerhard (Germany 54), Thuraya (Lebanon 54) and Tila (Chile 54), chosen by an external committee of Prof. Ethel Alpenfels (NYU), Dr Ethel Huggard (Bd of Education), & Charles Jones (Whitney Foundation). 1960 delegates on the panel were Alison (UK), Tamar (Israel), Bimal (India), Jordan (Greece) and Anani (Ghana). 'The World We Want Panel with *Herald Tribune* Forum' at the Association for Supervision and Curriculum Development, Mar 7, 1960, Scott papers. Alumni fellows 1961: Myrtle (India 52), Marlene (SA 55); 1962: Jayantha (Ceylon 57), Mahine (Iran 50).

Chapter 4: Follow the Money

1 On private/public cooperation see Laville & Wilford (eds), *The US Government*; Osgood, *Total Cold War*; Van Vleck, *The Empire of the Air*.

2 Cameron-OR, Oct 6, 1958, B51/F609 Ogden Reid, Yale.

3 https://www.in2013dollars.com/us/inflation/1948?amount=23000. $1000 in the 1950s generally was the equivalent of about $12,000 in 2024.

4 Forum Costs: 1946: Memo, Jun 25 46, F44/2; 1947: F45/6; 1948: F47/1; 1949: F48/3 Reid, LOC.

5 Forum Costs 1950: F48/3; 1953: F48/8 Reid, LOC; Casimir also suffered ill health (V and D Parmentier, pers. comm. Feb 2024) Negotiations eg 1958: Correspondence: Freeman, Cameron, & Phillips, Jun 1958, Oct 6, 1958, F609/B51 Ogden Reid, Yale.

6 Forum Costs: 1954 & 1955: B94/F199 Ogden Reid, Yale; RH 'Statement of the Executive Director on the status of the World Youth Forum', Sep 6, 1966, B147/F2, Whitney, Yale; RH, 'A frank statement to our alumni', Jul 1971, Hennig papers.

7 Oram Report 3; WJ Johnson-teachers, Mar 1957, Lammi papers.

8 Scharrer-WR, Mar 12, 1949, HHW-WR, Apr 7, 1949, F47/8 Reid, LOC.

9 'Comments on the 1952 Forum for High Schools', F48/8 Reid, LOC; TV1954 'Habits and Customs of Nations', IULMIA.

10 Stabler-Kerbage, Feb 26, 1956, Kerbage papers.

11 Helen proposed a series of editorials to replace it, as 'an extension of the Forum idea and a retention of the franchise rather than an abandonment of it'. As well as contributing 'some new and dramatic editorial ideas', it would 'save a substantial amount of money'. The *Tribune* saved the money, and no editorials appeared. OR-HHW, Sep 14, 1956; HHW, letter announcing cancellation, nd, B51/F609 Ogden Reid, Yale.

12 Cameron-HHW, May 8, 1956, Cameron-OR, Jan 8, Mar 26, May 13, 1958, B51/F609 Ogden Reid, Yale.

13 Cameron-HHW, May 8, 1956, Cameron-OR, Jan 8, Mar 26, May 13, 1958, B51/F609 Ogden Reid, Yale; RH-Kluger, Jan 8, 1982, B6/F131 Kluger, Yale; HHW-Steele, Jan 6, 1960 [sic] 1961, B147/F3 Whitney, Yale.

14 JHW-Redefer, Nov 6, 1961; Anne Counes, Briefing Notes for JHW on Louis E Dieruff High School, Nov 1963, B147/F3 Whitney, Yale.

15 JHW-Wellington, Apr 18, 1963, B147/F3 Whitney, Yale.

16 US BECA, *Educational and Cultural Diplomacy*, 1962, 52.

17 US Dept of State, '*NYHT* Youth Forum', Background Paper 1959, B219/F17 BECA, Arkansas; Int and Emails Emmanuel (Ghana 68). Stella also enlargedthe USIS library & established an exhibition room to introduce American films, lecturers, musicians, and drama to Ghanaians. She visited villages throughout Ghana. Her collection of African art forms the basis of the Albany Art Museum in Georgia. Davis papers (Coleman Family).

18 *Chicago Daily Tribune*, Feb 7, 1949, 4.

19 'Proposed *NYHT* Forum for High School Students', Mar 30, 1949, encl. in Chartrand-HHW, Apr 5, 1949, 47/F8 Reid, LOC.

20 Horne, 'The Cosmopolitan Life', 431; *Indonesian Observer* Apr 3, 1959, in N Apr 1959. Nonna's connection (if any) with the CIA in Indonesia is unclear. Perhaps it was coincidence. She reportedly married a Permesta army member, was imprisoned, later moving to the US to work for the UN. (N Apr 1960, pers. comm. other delegates).

21 Indicating the Forum's connections, Helen suggested she might 'ask our mutual friend, Cord Meyer, Jr., who is now in the top C.I.A. echelon, what's up'. Ogden had 'no objection' but she must not 'use his name'. HHW-OR, Dec 19, 1956, B51/F609 Ogden Reid, Yale. On the CIA and covert funding see eg Wilford, *The Might Wurlitzer*; Saunders, *Who Paid the Piper*; Paget 'From Stockholm to Leiden'.

22 FL Redefer (NYU)-JHW, Oct 31, 1961, B147/F3 Whitney, Yale; Paget, 'From Cooperation', 74; HHW, 'Proposal, A cooperative relationship between the *Reader's Digest* and the *NYHT* High School Forum,' Jul 23, 1956, B94/F198 Ogden Reid, Yale.

23 HHW-Steele, Jan 6, 1960, F3/B147 Whitney, Yale; JFK in Program 1961, Ali papers.

24 US BECA, *International Exchange 1967*.

25 N apr 1959; HHW, 'Proposal, A cooperative relationship', Jul 23, 1956, B94/F198 Ogden Reid, Yale.

26 Dept of State, '*NYHT* Youth Forum,' Background Paper 1959, B219/F17 BECA, Arkansas. The *New York Mirror* Forum had the same deal but for far fewer delegates. At least one delegate to the *Mirror* Forum thought that the State Department paid for flights. Email Robin (*Mirror* 59) Jun 2020; RH-Alumni, Feb 1973, Hennig papers; Van Vleck, *Empire of the Air*, esp. Ch 1 and 265–6; TWA, *Skyliner* Mar 31, 1960, 3. Exchange programs to the US became less popular as youth lost faith in their independence after covert CIA involvement in the World Assembly of Youth and other initiatives was exposed. On enterprise and propaganda see Osgood, *Total Cold War*, esp Ch 7.

27 Int Jona (Iceland 60); see eg *Pan American World Airways Teacher*, X (5) May 1954; TWA *Skyliner* Feb 4, 1960, 6.

28 Despite his father being a member of the Kenyan government, Michael could not afford the extra flight. The Forum used a series of connections. Frances Ann Dougherty was not only an 'interested party at the Institute' of International Education, but, 'the former Mrs John Hersey—author of *The Wall*—and knew Mrs Reid at that time'. Counes-JHW on Mrs Frazer Dougherty, May 1964, B147/F3 Whitney, Yale.

29 Obit M Price; JHW-Wellington, Apr 18, 1963, May 18, 1964; Wellington-JHW, Apr 24, 1963; Counes-JHW on Greyhound, May 1964, B147/F3 Whitney, Yale.

30 Solomon-Taylor, Jun 20, 1958; handwritten note, Taylor-Bornholdt, Jul 1, 1958; Taylor-Solomon, Jul 1, 1958, *NYHT*WYF, SLC. Laura Bornholdt succeeded Esther Rauschenbush as dean in 1957.

31 Parton-HRR, May 22, 1952, B48/F7 Reid, LOC; Taylor-Fox, Ford Foundation, Aug 10, 1955, *NYHT*WYF SLC; *NYHT* Mar 28, 1955, 20.

32 Margaret Freeland, Sec, 'Recapitulation of Student Exchange Workshop Discussion at Curriculum Committee Meeting April 12, 1955'; Raushenbush & Bozeman, 'Evaluation of HT Foreign Students Exchange Program as it concerned Sarah Lawrence College' May 16, 1955; Taylor-Fox, Aug 10, 1955, Raushenbush-Taylor, Sep 3, 1954, *NYHT*WYF SLC.

33 Raushenbush-Taylor, Sep 3, 1954, Jill Whedon-Taylor, Jan 14, 1957, Solomon-

Taylor, Jun 20, 1958; Taylor-Bornholdt, Jul 1, 1958; Taylor-Solomon, Jul 1, 1958, *NYHT*WYF, SLC.

34 Correspondence Jun 1960, Petition Nov 1966; Marjorie Christiansen-Raushenbush, Feb 7, 1969, *NYHT*WYF, SLC.

35 Parton-HRR, May 22, 1952, F48/7 Reid, LOC; HHW, 'Proposal, A cooperative relationship', Jul 23, 1956, B94/F198, Ogden Reid, Yale.

36 *Junior Scholastic* 43(5) Oct 10 1958, 10; *Scholastic Teacher* 70(1) Feb 1 1957, 1; 'The World We Want High School Assembly' Program 1962, Warner papers. Another sponsor was *American Observer*, published by Walter E Myer's Civic Education Service Inc. In 1968 CBS-owned KMOX-TV, co-sponsored a visit to St Louis for a 'Forum', with the St Louis Council on World Affairs.

37 *Monocle* Mar 19, 1953, 4; Colonial Williamsburg, the Hampton Institute, the Richmond International Council Inc were also involved: 'Tour of 1957 High School Forum Delegates to Richmond' Itinerary, B94/F198 Ogden Reid, Yale; Field Trip Schedule 1966, Nasmith papers.

Chapter 5: The Chosen One

1 Int Cyrus (Iran 50).

2 Information for Delegates 1952 F48/8 Reid, LOC. Ambassador KGA (Anthony) Hill is listed on the Alumni Association website as a (self-identified) delegate for 1954 from Jamaica but appears nowhere in the records. He possibly attended the *Mirror* Forum.

3 Later Nobel Peace Prize winner & Canadian Prime Minister.

4 Places were limited to 40 in 1967: 1967 Selection Procedure guidelines, Nasmith papers; National Security Council, 'Statement of US Policy' 1960, US Dept State Office of Historian; Aloreibi & Carey, 'English in Libya'.

5 Recommendations for 1951 Forum, F48/4 Reid, LOC.

6 Indo China was Vietnam, Cambodia, & Laos.

7 See Walker & Sobocinska (eds), *Australia's Asia*.

8 Benelux was Belgium, Netherlands, & Luxembourg.

9 Recommendations for 1951 Forum F48/4 Reid, LOC; HHW-Steele, Jan 6, 1960, B147/F3 Whitney, Yale; HHW-OR, May 15, 1956, B94/F198 Ogden Reid, Yale.

10 Institute of International Education, *Open Doors* 1973, 9.

11 Bios Agung (Indonesia 68), Difie (Ghana 67); 'Dedo Difie Agyarko-Kusi', Wikipedia; Background Files on Youth and Teenagers Programs, 1966, 1967, B1 EDX 11, NARA.

12 Recommendations for 1951 Forum F48/4 Reid, LOC.

13 Correspondence Jun-Jul 1963, B147/F3 Whitney, Yale; Bio Gaby (Jordan 64).

14 Helen told Whitie Reid in Dec 1949 that Jordan had not replied to the invitation for 1950, and Afghanistan, Saudi Arabia and Yemen were 'unable, *apparently,* to send delegates' (my emphasis). To alumni, Helen was more tactful. Afghanistan said 'nothing

could be done because of the prolonged illness of the Minister of Education'. Yemen could not meet 'the conditions of the invitation', perhaps, suggested Helen, because English was not taught there. HHW-WR, Dec 9, 1949, 47/F8 Reid, LOC; N Nov 1949.

15 1967 Selection Procedure guidelines, Nasmith papers; Fett, 'US People to People', 725; see also Osgood, *Total Cold War*; N Sep 1955; *NYHT* Nov 28, 1955, 8; Nov 18, 1956, 50; Nov 17, 1957, 34; Dec 1, 1958, 14.

16 Rita Taylor-Mr [sic] V Titova, Jul 28, 1958, B 94/F200, Ogden Reid, Yale; Blechman, 'Valentina Titova'.

17 Declined: in 1960: Jordan, SA; in 1963: USSR, Poland, Hungary, the Czech Republic, Afghanistan, Algeria, Iraq, the Ivory Coast, Mali, Senegal, Tanganyika, and Venezuela. 'Planning the 1963 World Youth Forum', Courtin papers.

18 'Rules for the Selection of Student Delegates to the *NYHT* Forum for High Schools', Mar 1949, F48/4 Reid, LOC.

19 Standardization was after Helen Waller's death, possibly Bob Huffman's initiative (or assistant Anne Counes' influence?). It occurred when Virginia Wieschhoff was director. 'Procedure for the Selection of the Delegate', 1963, 4–5, Courtin papers.

20 1967 Selection Procedure guidelines, Nasmith papers; Int Sherille (Ceylon 71).

21 Thor (Norway 48), 'The World We Want', Johansen papers; Salazar 'The World We Want', in *Teardrops Dry*; Dorothy (Malaya 62), 'Unity in Diversity' excerpt in 'Young Worlds '62', Courtin papers; Email Louise (Belgium 49) Jan 16, 2019; Josephine (Australia 53), Scrapbook, Glen-Doepel papers; Int Hiranthi (Ceylon 67); 'Procedure for the Selection of the Delegate', 1963, 4–5, Courtin papers; 1967 Selection Procedure guidelines, Nasmith papers.

22 Int Amos (Israel 69).

23 N Apr 1959. Committee members included: Edgar (Philippines 59), Eddie (Malaya 50), Hakeem (Netherlands, 53), Judith (Canada, 53). N Jun 1959, N Dec 1960.

24 Int Yassa (Jordan 59); Email Dieter (Germany 62) Oct 2021.

25 Bio Meliton (Philippines 50). The biography collection covers the entire period, with 1948, 1949, 1953 almost all missing, and 1947, 1950, 1958 partially represented. Located in various archives: Reid, LOC; NET, Wisconsin, Alumni Association website; alumni personal papers.

26 See Bishop, '"A Worthwhile Trace of Myself": Teenage Autobiographies', seminar paper. The little written on college applications and youth life writing more generally includes: Honeck & Moore, 'War and Conflict'; Magee, 'College Admissions Essays'; Walters, 'A Response'; Flynn, 'Composing as a Woman'; Crocker et al, 'Self-image Goals'; Giebel et al, 'Signaled or Suppressed?'; Van Hout, 'Life is a pitch'; Moore, 'Growing Up'; Moruzi et al (eds), *Children's Voices*; Douglas, 'Childhood and Youth'; Douglas & Poletti, *Life Narratives*; on youth political writing: Berghel, 'What my Generation'; on social media self-representation: Maximova & Lukyanova 'Gender differences online'; Herring & Kapidzic, 'Teens, Gender'.

27 Bios Yuen Chooi Yeng (Singapore 59), Yuen Kum Chuen (Singapore 55); H D Hochstadt, Min Education-Principal Methodist Girls' School, Singapore Sep 3, 1958, re 1959 *NYHT* Forum Contest, Edun 1671/55/, Yuen papers.

28 Among the 'outstanding' things Wee Kiat Tan liked were 'music, reading, writing, animals—especially dogs and cats, bath-tub singing and humor in people'. Bios John (UK 59), Alison (UK 60), Tan Wee Kiat (Singapore 61), Suzanne (UK 62); Brent-Suzanne (UK 62), Oct 20, 1961, Warner papers.

29 Bio Michael (UK 72) In a statement that is fascinating in hindsight, he also wrote 'Never an extremist (happy to fit in with the cool atmosphere generated by British politics), I did for years follow one particular party, until successive disappointments persuaded me that I could only support one group in opposition to another on specific issues, and not as a wholehearted party sympathiser.' He later confirmed it was the Labour Party he had followed. (Email).

30 Email Jinhyun Cho, Apr 2023. See also Malhotra & Lambert-Hurley, 'Introduction', 7; Arnold & Blackburn (eds), *Telling Lives in India*.

31 HHW Welcome letter, 1967, Lammi papers; Bio Irjaleena (Finland 57).

32 Bios Graham (SA 61), Pedro (Chile 61).

33 Bios Yumiko (Japan 57), Johnny (Philippines 54), Cecilia (Philippines 71).

34 Courier-Mail (Brisbane, Australia) Dec 16, 1947, 2; Int Minh (Vietnam 65), Bios Pietro (Italy 65), Usha (India 55), Stella (Brazil 64), Lee Hup San (Malaya 58), Marwan (Syria 52), Veroslava (Yugoslavia 61), Serban (Bolivia 64). Silvio (Brazil 63) thought it 'the best way I could be useful not only to my country, but to all the nations of the world for it is the very function of a diplomat to work for world understanding peace among men.' (Bio) Saroj (Thailand 58) wanted to make himself 'a good son, a good student, and of more benefit to all the human beings of the world' (Bio). See also Bios Thierry (France 63), Carmen (Brazil 47).

35 AFS website; Ints Gerhard (Germany 54), Ceridwen (UK 67), Hiranthi (Ceylon 67), Ronny (Indonesia 68). Tina (Spain 67) & Arnlaug (Norway 58) felt too young for a year away; Teresa (NZ 72) wondered if a year would have been easier. Apichai (Thailand 63) thought the Forum program sounded more interesting and international, although looking back, he joked that missing a part year was more difficult because he was 'a lazy student'. (Ints).

36 Bios Duangtip (Thailand 62), Yumiko (Japan 57).

37 Teachers encouraged Saroj (Thailand 58) & Sherille (Ceylon 71) (Ints); Engwirda, *Per Slot can;* Ints Geneviève (France 56), Sara (UK 57), Jorge (Mexico 65). Josephine (Australia 53) was a state finalist in the British *Daily Mail* Forum in 1951. Her brother William was a state finalist for the New York Forum in 1948.

38 *NYHT* Nov 28, 1955, 8; Bios Jawahir (Malaya 56), Phuong (Vietnam 56).

39 *Stars and Stripes* Europe edition Dec 17, 1948; TV programs 1954, 1957 IULMIA; Yearbook: Malverne High School, 1968 on ancestry.com.au.

40 Email Ines Horton 2022; N Aug 1949; Int Amos (Israel 69).

41 N Apr 1961; Email Alberto (Guatemala 62) Jan 22, 2022; Int Jorge (Uruguay 53).

42 Int Hameeda (Pakistan 52).

43 Delegates attending such schools included Gladys (Lebanon 56), Michael (Jordan 58), Irini (Greece 63), Bilgin (Turkey 63), Merethe (Norway 64), Bahram (Iran 70), Shade (Nigeria 66). (Bios).

44 Email Alberto (Guatemala 62) Jan 22, 2022; N Dec 1958; Ints Minh (Vietnam 65), Jan (Czechoslovakia 67). All five Vietnamese boy delegates until 1966 were from Chu Van An. Lycee Marie Curie supplied most female delegates. Bios Vietnamese delegates; N Dec 1959. At King's College: Hope (59), Nsa (63), Segun (65), Jacob (67), Nurein (68). At Queen's College: Minjiba (55), Abimbola (61), Shade (66).

45 Ints Maarten (Netherlands 61), Pietro (Italy 70), Michael (UK 72); Method of Selection of the United Kingdom Delegates, F47/2 Reid, LOC.

46 N Feb 1957; N Dec 1960. Email Ibrahim (Lebanon 58). Siblings: Yuen Kum Chuen & Yuen Chooi Yeng (Singapore 55, 59); Tissa & Gemunu (Sri Lanka 59, 61); Malaival & Mattanee (Thailand 50, 54), Zohreh & Nahid (Iran 53, 57), Catherine & Brigitte (France 57, 64), Cousins: Nasreen & Naila (Pakistan 55, 58).

47 Lathrop, 'Promotion of International Understanding', v.

48 Bios Salika (Thailand 52), Sanaa (Egypt 61); Int Christian (Norway 48). Chodchai (Thailand 61)'s aunt was the widow of King Rama VI (Bio).

49 Int Arnold (Colombia 69); Bios Nasreen (Pakistan 53), Naila (Pakistan 58), Catherine (France 57), Brigitte (France 64), Mona (Egypt 65). Dennis (Philippines 57)'s mother regretted President Magsaysay 'who loved Dennis so much' had not lived to hear about his Forum experience. N May 1957.

50 *NYHT* Mar 7, 1949, 27; Bios & Ints Beryl (Australia 68), Emmanuel (Ghana 68); Memoir Luis (Cuba 47), Calvo papers.

51 See Fett, 'The Teen-Age Program', 10.

52 Bio Dwarika (Nepal 54).

53 Email Thierry (Belgium 63).

54 Initial advertising for 1948 Forum suggested that one Australian and one New Zealander would be selected, but ultimately two Australians attended. *Daily News* (Perth, Aus.) Dec 12, 1947, 9; *Herald* (Melb., Aus.) Dec 12, 1947, 1; Institute of International Education, *Open Doors 1973*, 9. On gender and Fulbright program, see Jordan & Kirkby, '"An Undesirable Type"'; Garner & Kirkby, *Academic Ambassadors*.

55 numbers were 'even' to within two of each other.

56 N Dec 1958; Bios Usha (India 55), Nalini (India 59).

57 Ints Yukiko (Japan 59), Toshio (Japan 67).

58 *NYHT* Sep 25, 1947, 29; HHW-Cunningham, US Embassy, Saigon, Jun 15, 1949; HHW-WR, Dec 9, 1949, F47/8 Reid, LOC.

Notes to pages 86–94

59 'Selection of Student Delegates to the 1955 *NYHT* Forum for High Schools', B11, Hunsaker, Syracuse; N Oct 1963.

60 Emails Anon, Kris (Ceylon 68) Jan 1, 2022, Beryl (Australia 68) 2020; Ints Anon.

61 D31, 2009.

62 N Dec 1960.

63 Craig (US 68) & Stephen (US 71) were African Americans.

64 Bios Evelyn (Nigeria 72), Teresa (NZ 72), Ian (NZ 71), 'the aim of life is surely to enjoy what one partakes of, and this I seem to do' (Bio), met war-survivor Florence (Nigeria 71).

65 Bios Nina (Brazil 72), Donatella (Italy 72), Randa (Lebanon 72).

66 Oram Report.

Chapter 6: Coming to America

1 Int Azer (Iran 56).

2 D45 2017; Ints Eva (Norway 48), Eline (SA 54), Hameeda (Pakistan 52).

3 Int Eduardo (Argentina 47); Seglen, 'My First Air Flight', Diary excerpt translated, Seglen papers.

4 Ints, Ken (Australia 67), Ibrahim (Lebanon 58), Eeva (Finland 55), Roger (Norway 59), Ceridwen (UK 67); Counes-JHW, May 1964, B147/F3 Whitney, Yale.

5 HHW, 'Orientation Session', report 1955, 2, NYHTWYF, SLC; Int Grace (Ghana 61). This was probably a misremembering. Grace told a similar story in the *Delegate* about Graham 'on the front page' in c1963, having sneaked into Accra after being 'not allowed to leave the airport unless he signed a declaration condemning apartheid which he refused to do'. (D37 2013). Graham said he was detained on a Ghana stopover in 1976 as a SA MP. He did not remember a declaration. (D38 2013).

6 Email Rachel (Israel 64), Dec 14, 2021; Bio Marco (Italy 49); HWW, Letter to Delegates, Nov 14, 1960, 5, Seglen papers. Aged 10, Edward (Philippines 57) visited Washington DC with his widowed mother, national president of Gold Star Mothers, Widows and Orphans. While there, he represented the Philippines at the Cub Scout jamboree in Silver Springs, Maryland. (Bio); Michael (Jordan 58) visited family during the Forum, suggesting that was why he was not on any television programs (Int).

7 Arnlaug (Norway 58)'s older sister had been an AFS student in the US so she also perhaps had an idea about what to expect (Int); HWW, Letter to Delegates, Nov 14, 1960, 4–5, Seglen papers; note on Alison's bio, Scott papers; Ints Alison (UK 60), Annemarie (Austria 63).

8 TV1954 'The Family in America', IULMIA; TV1958 'Conquest of Prejudice', IULMIA; TV1959 'Introduction to the United States', IULMIA; *NYHT* Mar 25, 1955, 15; Int Yasar (Jordan 59). Marwan (Syria 52) 'began reading' English books and *Life* and *Time* magazines in the USIS library, since 'it was founded' (Bio).

9 Int Teklu (Ethiopia 60); *NYHT* Nov 17, 1947, 21; N Aug 1949.

10 Ints Jona (Iceland 60), Nuala (Ireland 64).

11 Int Michael (UK 72).

12 Ints Susan (SA 57), Jona (Iceland 60), Minh (Vietnam 65), Sylvia (staff).

13 Spahr Hull-Grant, '"Orientation" of Students for *Herald Tribune* Forum', Dec 16, 1953, AFSCA.

14 'Report on Orientation Program', Jan 11, 1954, 4; Barrett-Spahr Hill, 'Dates for *Herald-Tribune* Meetings', Apr 15, 1954, AFSCA.

15 American Council for Nationalities, *Americans Abroad*.

16 'A Few Rules', 1960, Scott papers.

17 Diary Anon (64); Orientation Program 1969, Leonetti papers; Washington Field Trip Itinerary 1970, Nasmith papers; Int Haider (Pakistan 71).

18 'FY 1966 Background Statement: Teen-Ager Program', Jan 19, 1965, in Fett, 'The Teenage Program', 18.

19 *The Straits Times*, Jun 2, 1957, 14; 'Comments by Delegates on the 1961 *NYHT* Youth Forum Orientation Week', *NYHT*WYF, SLC.

20 Orientation Session *NYHT* High School Forum 1955, Comments, *NYHT*WYF, SLC.

21 Ints Irjaleena (Finland 57), Tina (Spain 67), Jutta (Germany 69), Léon (Mexico 64), Anon; Conversation Teklu (Ethiopia 60); *D*7 1996; Letter Anon.

22 Ints Snait (Israel 61), Irjaleena (Finland 57), Christian (France 70), Geneviève (France 56), Alison (UK, 60), Helga (UK 64), Ceridwen (UK 67); Ceridwen (UK 67), Forum Report 1967, Roberts papers.

23 Ints Saroj (Thailand 58), Emmanuel (Ghana 68); Diary, Helga (UK 64), Kimpton papers; Ceridwen (UK 67), Forum Report 1967, Roberts papers.

Chapter 7: 'Walking Textbooks' at Host Schools

1 Circular to Principals of High Schools and Vocational High Schools, Nov 6, 1949, F47/8 Reid, LOC.

2 1954 *NYHT* Forum Information, B78/F1 NET, Wisconsin; *NYHT* Jan 3, 1956, 18.

3 HWW Memo, Nov 7, 1952, F48/7 Reid, LOC.

4 Host school lists for 1950, 1952–57, 1959–64, 1966–67, 1969 collated from annual finale programs and lists of host school/family allocations.

5 Ints Susan (SA 57), Anon; HHW-Cameron, Oct 30, 1956, B51/F609 Ogden Reid, Yale; HHW-Prospective Host Schools, Sep 17, 1956, B11, Hunsaker, Syracuse.

6 HHW Memo, Nov 7, 1952, F48/7 Reid, LOC.

7 1963 World Youth Forum Booklet A, Courtin papers.

8 Cross, 'Teacher Memories'; Ceridwen (UK 67), Forum Report, 1967 Roberts papers. Mesfin (Ethiopia 57) also corresponded with her. N Dec 1957.

9 Ints Arnlaug (Norway 58), Annemarie (Austria 63), Minh (Vietnam 65), Judith (UK 56), Direk (Thailand 53); *Morning Call* (Allentown Pa.) Jan 9, 1960, 7; Louis E Dieruff High School, Evaluation Report, in Counes-JHW, Nov 1963, B147/F3 Whitney, Yale.

Longstanding staff member Dr Giles J Warren provided continuity at Westwood High.

10 1954 *NYHT* Forum Information, B78/F1 NET, Wisconsin; Circular to Principals of High Schools and Vocational High Schools, Nov 6, 1949, F47/8 Reid, LOC; HHW-Prospective Host Schools, Sep 17, 1956, B 11 Hunsaker, Syracuse; Suzanne (UK 62), Diary, Warner papers; *FT* Jan 18, 1960, 6, Scott papers; Ints & Emails Susie (Brazil 58), Arnlaug (Norway 58); Ceridwen (UK 67), Forum Report, 1967 Roberts papers. The Dwight School is not to be confused with Dwight Morrow High School.

11 Int Teresa (NZ 72); *FT* Jan 18, 1960, Scott papers; Email Michael (NZ 67) 2016; *NYHT* Mar 8, 1948, 31.

12 Diary Anon; Ints Raza (Pakistan 61), Geneviève (France 56), Emmanuel (Ghana 68).

13 Host Schools Report, Eriksson papers; Ints Emmanuel (Ghana 68), Marco (Italy 49), Serban (Bolivia 64); Ints & Emails Susie (Brazil 58), Arnlaug (Norway 58) Apr 28, Jul 28, 2022; Streicker-RH, Apr 14, 1963, B147/F3 Whitney, Yale.

14 TV1959 'Have Your Ideas Changed?', IULMIA; Diary Anon; *NYHT* Mar 8, 1948, 3; N Jul 1956 (translation from Japanese newspaper). Terence (UK 48) noted the 'UK gets a small group to a high standard, while the US gets more to moderately high standard' *NYHT* Mar 8, 1948, 31.

15 Int Ken (Australia 67); *NYHT* Mar 8, 1948, 31; Email Paolo (Italy 55) Aug 1, 2022.

16 TV1959 'Introduction to America', IULMIA.

17 Ints Jorge (Uruguay 53), Teresa (NZ 72), Léon (Mexico 64), Sherille (Ceylon 71), Emmanuel (Ghana 68), Diana (Italy 57), Geneviève (France 56); Email Sergio (Brazil 53) Apr 12, 2022; Portillo, 'World Youth Meeting', 48.

18 Ceridwen (UK 67), Forum Report 1967, Roberts papers. (NHS is National Health Service); Portillo, 'World Youth Meeting', 48; Suzanne (UK 62), Forum Report 1962, Warner papers; Int Rodel (Philippines 69). The 'recent delegate' was identified as the '1947 delegate from Quito' in Instructions to Delegates, 1952 F48/8 Reid, LOC. Later she was just 'a recent delegate': Instructions to Delegates 1954, B78/F1 NET, Wisconsin; Instructions to Delegates 1962, Nasmith papers.

19 Conversation Teklu (Ethiopia 60); Ints Geneviève (France 56), Per (Norway 61), Erik (Denmark 55), Jona (Iceland 60), Naila (Pakistan 58), Carola (Chile 69), Maarten (Netherlands 61); TV1955 'Does the Key to Peace in this Century Rest with Non-White Peoples?', IULMIA.

20 Ints Hameeda (Pakistan 52), Sandra (Singapore 67), Manoli (Greece 62), Emmanuel (Ghana 68), Michael (Jordan 58), Monika (Austria 65), Beryl (Australia 68), Ken (Australia 67), Gustavo (Argentina 70); Email Sudhir (India 66) Feb 25, 2021; Yearbook, Somerville High School, 1972, 99, ancestry.com.

21 Porter, 'A Voice Is Heard', 40; Int Sherille (Ceylon 71).

22 Esposito, 'Susana Donaso reflects'; Int & Email Beryl (Australia 68) Nov 24, 2020; Int Greg (NZ 69).

23 Email Annalie Pauw (dr of Rina (SA 58)) Nov 25, 2020; Int Gerhard (Germany 54).

24 N Sep 1961; Louis E Dieruff High School, Evaluation Report, in Counes, Briefing Notes-JHW, Nov 1963, B147/F3Whitney, Yale.

25 Workum, 'Mechanisms Exposed', 33.

26 *NYHT* Mar 10, 1950, 20. Few Americans beyond host families and personal friends seem to have been aware of the Forum, based on informal discussions with ex-students of host schools.

27 *NYHT* Jan 26, 1952, 7; Jan 30, 1952, 13; Forum Program 1953; Memo re impact, May 1, 1953 B78/F51 NET, Wisconsin; *Monocle* Feb 21, 1957, 1; *Tidewater Review* Feb 21, 1963, 3.

28 'Discussion workshops, Holy Trinity High School' Johnstone papers.

Chapter 8: Part of the Family

1 Int (by Pamela Hull), Burt (Host 59) 2022; Email Ejvind (Denmark 59) May 8, 2022.

2 Fieldston, *Raising the World*, 19. See also Fieldston, 'The Nursery's Iron Curtain' Section 2. Hiett, *No Matter Where*; Experiment in International Living website.

3 Lucie report to Board of Education in Oslo, in N Dec 1957; Ints Jona (Iceland 60), Howard (Host 70, Summer 70), Emmanuel (Ghana 68).

4 See e.g. 'Receiving Your Forum Guest', 1965, Nasmith papers; Int Anon.

5 *NYHT* Dec 19, 1951, 27; Dec 11, 1953, 25; 'Receiving Your Forum Guest', 1965, Nasmith papers; Int Anon; 'Forum Hospitality', 1961, Johnstone papers. Monika (Austria 65) stayed with a boy.

6 HHW-Faculty Advisors re 1953 *NYHT* Forum, Nov 7, 1952, F48/7 Reid, LOC; Int Annemarie (Austria 63).

7 The *Herald Tribune* also took out life and accident insurance for each delegate. HHW-Faculty Advisors re 1953 *NYHT* Forum, Nov 7, 1952, F48/7 Reid, LOC; Delegate Information, *NYHT* 1963, Courtin papers; Int Ronny (Indonesia 68); Streicker-JHW, Apr 14, 1963, B147/F3 Whitney, Yale.

8 Metropolitan School Study Council, Memo re Entertaining Scandanavian Students, Oct 13, 1947, Johansen papers; 'Receiving Your Forum Guest', Nasmith papers.

9 *NYHT* Mar 23, 1953, 22; Int Niels (Denmark 53); Kurland host family information form 1961, Johnstone papers.

10 Email Mel Citrin, Christopher Columbus High. Hosts: Ed von Kloberg (flamboyant 'lobbyist for the loathsome' i, representing the world's dictators) and Vicki Hochberg (one of the 'Original Six' female Hollywood directors). Obit. E von Kloberg; 'Victoria Hochberg', Wikipedia.

11 Huffman, 'The World Youth Forum'.

12 *NHYT* 'HS Forum Report', Mar 29, 1954, 8; Int Judith (UK 56); *Memphis World* 30, n24 (Oct 19, 1960), 2. Ronny (Indonesia 68) stayed with an African American politician in Richmond (Int Ronny).

13 In the 'Doll test', children were given dolls that were identical apart from skin color.

Many, including African Americans, preferred the white dolls, indicating to the Clarks that '"prejudice, discrimination, and segregation" made African-American children feel inferior, damaging their self-esteem'. Legal Defense Fund (LDF), 'A Revealing Experiment'; John J. Brooks-Clarks, 1958, NMAH; *NYHT* Feb 23, 1958, 29. No 1958 delegates recalled this in interviews when asked. Ritva was not found for interview.

14 Ints Mark (NZ 68), Anon; see also Ints Bruce (Canada 61), Carola (Chile 69).

15 letters home Anon, Jan 2, Jan 20, Mar 9.

16 Email Tissa (Ceylon 59); Ints Geneviève (France 56), Liv (Norway 70), Sandra (Singapore 67), Ken (Australia 67), Carola (Chile 69), Teresa (NZ 72). For Tina (Spain 67) one homestay was 'like living in a movie...they had a dishwasher!'.Teresa (NZ 72) recalled a home with five color televisions and an automatic garage opener. (Ints) Sandra stayed at 138 East 65th Street, Manhattan, Street Easy https://streeteasy.com/sale/1577470?card.

17 Ints Hiranthi (Ceylon 67), Manoli (Greece 62), Arnold (Colombia 69).

18 Int Tan Wee Kiat (Singapore 61); Mrs F Ripatranzone, Comments on the Forum, 5, B78/F1 NET, Wisconsin; Email Dieter (Germany 62).

19 Int Roger (Host 67).

20 N Oct 1958, Ints Peter (Norway 69), Emmanuel (Ghana 68), Emma (Burma 62); Abdurrahim (Nigeria 64) report for Nigerian Ministry of Education, B147/F3 Whitney, Yale; Emails, Sergio (Brazil 53) Apr 12, 2022, Tissa (Ceylon 59) Jun 8, 2020.

21 Connie Walker-delegates, Mar 11, 1969, Hennig papers; Ints Sherille (Ceylon 71), Rodel (Philippines 69).

22 Ints Liv (Norway 70), Hameeda (Pakistan 52), Catherine (France 59), Ibrahim (Lebanon 58); Email Jomo (Malaysia 70) Apr 25, 2021, Anon; Myrtle (India 52) to mother, 1952, reprinted in *Stella Maris College, Madras Yearbook*, 1952, 50.

23 Int Abdul (Sudan 60).

24 Conversation daughters of Probal (India 53); Abeyagunawardene, 'A Friendship'; *NYHT* Feb 11, 1952, 5.

25 Email Sandra (Singapore 67) Jan 13, 2022; Ints Carola (Chile 69), Saroj (Thailand 58), Avri (Israel 68), Robert Esik; Streicker-JHW, Apr 14, 1963, B147/F3 Whitney, Yale.

26 Suzanne (UK 62), Forum Report, Warner papers; Ints Geneviève, (France 56), Rodel (Philippines 69), Anon.

27 Ints Anon.

28 *FT* Jan 10, 1962, Nasmith papers.

29 N Jun 1959.

30 N Oct 1956; Int Anon.

31 N Dec 1957; *NYHT* Mar 24, 1958, 2, 15; article by Mildred Jailer, newspaper cutting nd, Kerbage papers; Int Hameeda (Pakistan 52); Email Sudhir (India 66).

32 Comments on the 1952 Forum F8/48 Reid, LOC.

33 Int Roger (Host 67); Roger Wollstadt on Flicker; FB msg Roger (Host 61) Jul 5, 2021.

34 Int Robert (Host 66).

35 N Oct 1958; N Feb 1957; Int Annemarie (Austria 63); See also N Sep 1955; N Oct 1956; *D45* 2017.

36 N Oct 1956; N Apr 1959; Ints Ronny (Indonesia 68), Irjaleena (Finland 57).

37 Ints Irjaleena (Finland 57), Roger (Host 67), Saroj (Thailand 58); Email Nii (Ghana 59) Jan 29, 2022; *D46* 2018.

38 Ints Avri (Israel 68), Michael (UK 72); *D46* 2018; Conversation Sonali Walpola, Dec 2, 2022; see also Int Michael (Jordan 58).

39 Ints Emmanuel (Ghana 68), Nina Fieldsteel (Host mother 68). Ira is best known as the man who rejected John Lennon's application for permanent residency in 1973, changing his mind three years later *NYT* Jul 28, 1976. Haider (Pakistan 71) was similarly 'adopted' by a host family when forced to remain in the US after the Forum. (Int).

Chapter 9: Adolescent Ambassadors

1 Ints Hameeda (Pakistan 52), Nalini (India 59), Malaival (Thailand 50), Saroj (Thailand 58), Irini (Greece 63), Tan Wee Kiat (Singapore 61), Alan (NZ 63); Report on Orientation Program', Jan 11, 1954, 5, AFSCA; N Oct 57. The haka was often the one they had learned at school. Just as New Zealand's rugby union team, the All Blacks (and, more recently the women's team, the Black Ferns) perform a Māori haka before they play international matches, so too, schoolboy rugby teams often have a school haka, performed by all, no matter their heritage.

2 In 1969 delegates attended a 'Pan Am Day' Lunch and discussed: 'If I were President Nixon I would'. *The Clipper* Mar 3, 1969, 2. Pan Am magazine published: '"How to Drink Norwegian Beer" by Are' (Norway 71), Int Sherille (Ceylon 71); *Adelaide News* (Australia) Mar 10, 1953, 14; letters Suzanne (UK 62), Warner papers.

3 USIS images 60-4754, 60-4755, Osman papers; *Daily Mail* Hagerstown, Feb 25, 1959, 14; Emails & Int John (UK 1959); Email Norma (Brazil 57) Mar 21, 2022; *Life,* Feb 25, 1957, 34; Suter, *Labor Law*, 47. Other TV programs in 1953 included 'Kate Smith Hour' (NBC), 'Garry Moore Show' (CBS).

4 *NYHT* Mar 23, 1959, 18.

5 *NYHT* Feb 25, 1952, 10; Mar 23, 1959, 18; Mar 26, 1962, 20. Email Santi (Thailand 52) Dec 12, 2018; Far East: Indonesia Delegate, Japan Delegate to *Herald Tribune* Forum, B2 NARA; The World We Want Forum Program, F48/8 Reid, LOC; 'Schedule for Field Trip' 1966, Nasmith papers.

6 *NYHT* Mar 7, 1950, 12; Apr 29, 1951, 34; Film: The *Herald Tribune* 5th High School Forum 1950.

7 N Oct 1958; N Dec 1958; N Apr 1960; *NYHT* Mar 7, 1949, 21-31; Mar 23, 1959, 18; Jun 26, 1960, 24; Mar 26, 1962, 20.

8 *NYHT* Mar 7, 1949, 21-31; *Congressional Record,* V95, Pt13, A1809, (Eugene J Keogh on 'The World We Want', House of Reps, Mar 28, 1949). Rosemary Bristow later

worked in American embassies in Athens and Rome, before marrying an Italian and settling in Milan. The other speaker was Betty Polis.

9 *NYHT* Mar 7, 1949, 21-31; Part of McMahon's speech is here: Film: The *Herald Tribune* 5th High School Forum 1950 (at 35:10).

10 Smith, 'A Whole World in Which Live Whole Men', Advance Text, Speeches 1950, F48/5 Reid, LOC.

11 *NYHT* Mar 24, 1952, 21; Email Stephen Schwebel, Jul 17, 2020.

12 Scharrer-WR, Mar 12, 1949, F47/8 Reid, LOC.

13 Film: 1952 *NYHT* Youth Forum, 306.256 NARA; *NYHT* Forum For High Schools Information 1947, F46/1 Reid, LOC; *NYHT* Mar 24, 1958, 16.

14 Antil-JHW, Mar 20, 1964; Lynn Bitz-JHW, Mar 20, 1964, B147/F3 Whitney, Yale; Program 1964, Kimpton papers.

15 Programs, 1967, 1969, 1970, Nasmith papers, Leonetti papers.

16 Taylor-Solomon, Jul 1, 1958, *NYHT*WYF SLC; Ints Eline (SA 54), Jona (Iceland 60).

Chapter 10: Media Darlings

1 Int Emmanuel (Ghana 68).

2 HHW, 'Preparations for the Forum Television Program', B78/F1 NET, Wisconsin.

3 The films from the 1950s are mainly in IULMIA, a few audio recordings are in NARA. Google's 'search the song' app identifies the piece as 'The Statesman', and some passages are identical. Williams was a popular composer of production music. On children & propaganda see Peacock, *Innocent Weapons*.

4 Ints Arnold (Colombia 69), Avri (Israel 68), Roger (UK 69).

5 Ints Geneviève (France 56), Jona (Iceland 60); Conversation Teklu (Ethiopia 60).

6 HHW, 'Preparations for the Forum Television Program', B78/F1 NET, Wisconsin. Maureen (UK), Christine (Greece), Araceli (Philippines), Bernard (Belgium), Josephine (Australia), Tor (Norway), & Abdul (Pakistan) appeared multiple times. Delegates from Uruguay, Turkey, Sweden, Indonesia, Egypt & Canada (who arrived late) missed out.

7 Chitranjan (India 55), Padmanabma (India 56), John (UK 59), Jordan (Greece 60), Judith (UK 56), Sarah (UK 57), Susan (SA 57), & Sanaa (Egypt 61) appeared 4 times each.Girls were 46.5% of delegates with 45% of appearances, boys were 53.5% of delegates with 55% of appearances.

8 Ints Judith (UK 56), Chit (India 56).

9 1963 World Youth Forum Booklet A, Courtin papers.

10 Email Michael (NZ 67).

11 Oram Report, 13; lists of TV programs: Program 1960, Scott papers, Program 1964, Kimpton papers, 1965 catalogue in NARA.

12 N Jun 69, Nasmith papers; TV program list 1969, Leonetti papers.

13 For list of NET stations, Feb 7, 1956, see B53/F2 NET Wisconsin.

Notes to pages 158–167

14 Announced in N Apr 59. Susan (SA 57), Edward (Malaya 50) & Purificacion (Philippines 52) were students at Columbia. Christine (Greece 53) and Vangala (India 54) were living in New York.

15 *NYHT* 1963 World Youth Forum, Annual Assembly Program; *NYHT* Apr 8, 1963, 15, *NYHT*WYF, SLC.

16 TV *NYT* Youth Forum 1956 'Are trust territories becoming independent?', YouTube.

17 The US introduced color television in the mid-1950s and, although initially expensive and rare, by 1966 prime time television was routinely in color.

18 *The Record*, May-Jun 1950, 27; 'Academy tea honors visitor', newspaper cutting, Dutt papers; TV1958 'Summary of 3 Months in the USA', IULMIA; Int Peter (Norway 69).

19 N Dec 1957; 'Comments on *NYHT* Forum', 1960, *NYHT*WYF, SLC; Saffron-RH, Mar 14, 1964; Carlos Mautner-RH, Jan 4, 1964; Piute Pete-RH, Apr 8, 1964, B147/F3 Whitney, Yale.

20 TV1956 programs and notes IULMIA.

21 *NYHT* Mar 26, 1962, 20; 1963 World Youth Forum Booklet A, Courtin papers; 1964 World Youth Forum Brochure, 7, Huffman papers; *FT* Jan 10, 1962, *FT* Mar 5, 1962, Warner papers. See also *FT* Jan 18, 1960, Scott papers; *FT* Dec 30, 1960, Johnstone papers.

22 D40, 2015; TV1955 'What is the proper purpose of a high school education', IULMIA; Email Saroj (Thailand 58) Dec 29, 2021.

23 *FT*, Jan 18, 1960, Scott papers; *NYHT* Jan 27, 1954, 13.

24 Ints Mack (US 61), Anon; *NYHT* Mar 3, 1957, 9; TV1957 'Are teenagers universally misunderstood?', IULMIA. This last program has not survived in the archive.

25 '1967 World Youth Forum Annual Assembly Program', Nasmith papers; Int Haider (Pakistan 71).

26 This was noticeable in the 1965 recordings. Huffman took up much air time framing questions in several ways, perhaps confusing for delegates with English as a second language, and unnecessary as they had been well prepared beforehand. Films 1965, NARA.

27 Ints especially Diana (Italy 57), Daphna (Israel 57), but this story was one that popped up in other interviews with delegates from different years.

28 Int Susan (SA 57).

29 *Hastings News* 1950, 10, Ansary papers; Email Johanna Jahn, daughter Richard (Australia 54) Jun 8, 2020; Int & Emails Mike (Australia 65); Ints Minh (Vietnam 65), Jona (Iceland 60). The Australian government was becoming increasingly sensitive to international criticism of the official White Australia policy discriminating against non-white migrants to Australia.

30 TV1959 'How Can One Nation Help Another?', IULMIA.

31 TV1959 'Are Women Really Superior', IULMIA; Film: Hall & Bishop, 'The World We Wanted'.

32 TV1959 'Introduction to America', IULMIA.

Chapter 11: 'Reds Under the Bed' ... and Other Obsessions

1 *NYHT* Mar 24, 1958, 15.

2 Suzanne (UK 62) found Americans 'rather worried' about the CND movement and reassured them that only about 5000 of the 58 million people in Britain were 'ban-the-bombers'. She noted that 'I still haven't seen over a fall-out shelter yet!', either relishing the prospect or regarding it as a little ridiculous. Diary Jan 23, 1962, Warner papers; see also reactions to French atomic bomb tests from Africa and UK delegates, N Dec 1959.

3 Int Judith (UK 56).

4 Bios Milan (Yugoslavia 60), Chung Wha (Korea 52), Chang Ho (Korea 62), Kwang-Yup (Korea 63), Minh (Vietnam 65), Agung (Indonesia 67), Rodolfo (Uruguay 62), Edgar (Philippines, 59). Veroslava (Yugoslavia 61) was 'a member of the People's Youth of Yugoslavia' and Branka (Yugoslavia 62) wrote positively of voluntary youth work camps but not of politics. (Bios).

5 Int Ronny (Indonesia 68); Email Joy Marini, daughter of Nga (Vietnam 58) Jan 18, 2024; N Dec 1958; N Apr 1961.

6 Final Forum Program 1956, B11 Hunsaker, Syracuse; *NYHT* Mar 18, 1956, 40; Mar 25, 1956, A4; Mar 26, 1956, A6. Forum staff mentioned the Russian visit 'at our expense' in later correspondence. Rita Taylor-Mr [sic] V Titova, Jul 28, 1958, B94/F200 Ogden Reid, Yale.

7 *NYHT* Feb 22, 1948, A5; Mar 8, 1948, 31; Int Eeva (Finland 55); TV1954 'The United States as Others See It', IULMIA.

8 Diary Suzanne (UK 62) Jan 8, Jan 24, 1962, Report 1962, Warner papers; N Jun 1960. Other delegates discussed communism in the newsletter in relation to their own countries: Myrtle (India 52) described the uprising in Kerala. Two Sudanese delegates discussed the Sudanese revolution. Krishnan (India 58) suggested China had 'lost her credit' in India. N Jun 1959, N Sep 1959, N Apr 1960.

9 TV1957 'What Does the Word Communism Mean to You?', IULMIA.

10 *NYHT* Mar 24, 1958, 15; Nayeri, 'Mahmoud Sayrafizadeh'; see also Sayrafiezadeh, *When Skateboards*; Shone, 'What price my family'. There may have been others studying in Russia who have not been traced.

11 TV1956 'How Can the United Nations Be Made More Effective?', IULMIA; Sanaa (Egypt 61), Tissa (Ceylon 59) in Workum, 'Mechanisms Exposed', 39–40.

12 TV1965 'Can There Be Stability in SouthEast Asia?', 306-voa-eno-t-7017 NARA.

13 D42 2016.

14 South Vietnam was part of the Southeast Asia Treaty Organization, a military alliance involving the US, Australia, New Zealand, Thailand, the Philippines, France, the UK and Pakistan. The last three countries declined to become involved. The Australian government strongly supported US involvement in Vietnam, & sent conscripted troops, prompting similarly vigorous protests. Mike also told me he spotted Adlai Stephenson at the UN, telling him the US should recognize red China. 'We will but not for some

time', Adlai apparently told the enthusiastic Australian, who felt he had demonstrated an admirable degree of prescience. (Int) Ceridwen (UK 1967), Report 1967, Roberts papers; TV1965 'Can There Be Stability in SouthEast Asia', 306-voa-eno-t-7017 NARA; Int Minh (Vietnam 65).

15 Ints Emmanuel (Ghana 68), Joachim (Germany 71), Anon.

16 Leonetti papers, Daoudi papers.

17 TV schedule 1969, Leonetti papers; Int Ugi (Yugoslavia 69).

18 *NYHT* Mar 28, 1955, 19; Bios Yosi (Israel 62), Salah (Jordan 62); Email Yosi (Israel 62) Jul 10, 2020. Salah did not mention the name of the village nor reveal his brothers' fate, but reading accounts of the massacre, it is likely they did not survive. If Mohamed (Egypt) also had a personal trauma in his past, he did not reveal it in his autobiography, which was a very brief bulletproof list of one-line responses to topics.

19 Email Raja (Jordan 54).

20 *NYHT* Jan 31, 1952, 15; HHW-HRR & WR, Jun 23, 1952, F48/8 Reid, LOC; Int Gerhard (Germany 54). In 1955, Gur (Israel 55) & Mohammed Rifaat (Egypt 55) impressed Paolo (Italy 55) with the way 'they spoke as if they were diplomats', despite representing countries at war with each other Email Paolo (Italy 55) Aug 1, 2022.

21 D11 1998; *NYHT* Mar 29, 1954, 19; Emails family of Zohar (Israel 56). Fellow delegates found her intimidating, 'a bit apart'. 'She rightly made the rest of us feel rather juvenile at times', recalled Christoph (Germany) also remembering that 'When Pan American gave perfumes to the girls and pocket knives to the boys as presents, she exchanged hers with one of the boys' D46 2018.

22 Int Anon; Julia Whedon-Taylor, Jan 14, 1957, *NYHT* WYF SLC.

23 Int and Email Daphna (Israel 58) Jul 10, 2020; American Friends of the Middle East-Daphna, Jan 30, 1957, Daphna- HHW, nd, Cohen-Mintz papers.

24 Lim, 'When Sworn Enemies'. When the Oslo Accord peace deal meant that 'suddenly all is changed', and borders opened, Daphna was excited to meet 'her' Jordanian delegate in Amman and 'talked and talked and talked to make up for our Forum when we didn't' D5 1995.

25 Ints Michael (Jordan 58), Ibrahim (Lebanon 58), Arnlaug (Norway 58), Susie (Brazil 58); Email Ruth (Israel 58) Mar 27, 2022.

26 Mrs Alice Schiller, host mother, Curtis High, Staten Island, praised Ruth, who had 'a very difficult time with the six Arab delegates' but had been 'most conscientious in her "job" and gained the respect of all who knew her—pro-Israelis and anti-Israelis as well'. *Jerusalem Post* Apr 25, 1958, 4. It was better in 1959: see discussion of 'Can One Nation Help Each Other' in the previous chapter.

27 Emails Ethel (US 63) Jun 30, 2022, Gideon (Israel 63) Jun 29, 2022.

28 Delegate Evaluation Form: Muhammad Saleh; Correspondence Jun-Jul 1963, B147/F3 Whitney, Yale; Bio Gaby (Jordan 64).

29 Email Rachel (Israel 64) Dec 14, 2021; Int Minh (Vietnam 65). In 1967 Israeli and

Arab delegates were 'great friends'. Int Will (US 67).

30 Int Avri (Israel 68).

31 TV1955 'Does the Key to Peace in this Century Rest with the Non-White Peoples?' IULMIA; *D*41 2015; *D*42 2016; Int Emmnauel (Ghana 68); Email Johannes (SA 62) Jan 7, 2022.

32 N Jun 1960.

33 TV1956 'Where do Prejudices Come From? Part II', IULMIA; TV1955 'Does the Key to Peace in this Century Rest with the Non-White Peoples?', IULMIA.

34 TV1959 'Who is Prejudiced?', IULMIA; TV1956 'Where Do Prejudices Come From? Part II', IULMIA.

35 TV1957 'Roots of Prejudice: Who's Responsible?', IULMIA.

36 Bizuayehu (Ethiopia 59) in Workum, 'Mechanisms Exposed', 39; Conversation Teklu (Ethiopia 60).

37 Int Johannes (SA 62).

38 Email Alberto (Guatemala 63) Jan 22, 2022.

39 *NYHT* Mar 10, 1958, 4; HHW-Mrs William H Maltbie, Feb 10, 1947, F45/2 Reid, LOC.

40 N May 1956.

41 Esposito, 'Susana Donaso reflects'; Ints Ibrahim (Lebanon 58), Jona (Iceland 60).

42 Chafe, *Civilities and Civil Rights*; Suzanne (UK 62) Letter home & Report 1962, Warner papers; *D*46 2018, 10: Int Dorothy (Malaya 62); Forum Itinerary 1962, SLC. US Court of Appeal, Williams v Howard Johnson's Inc suggests that segregation was mandated in public places in Virginia but that private restaurants could discriminate or not as they chose.

43 Dudziak, *Cold War Civil Rights*, 152–153, 167–169.

44 US Dept of State, '*NYHT* Forum for High Schools March 4, 1950,' *The Record*, 25; HHW-OR, B51/F609 Ogden Reid, Yale; TV1958 'The Conquest of Prejudice', IULMIA; N Dec 1959.

45 TV1956 'Where Do Prejudices Come From? Part II', IULMIA.

46 Int Robert (Host 66). On trauma of generations of oppression see Vaughans, 'To Unchain Haunting'.

47 Ints Duangtip (Thailand 62) Emmanuel (Ghana 68).

48 *D*29 2008, 19; TV1955 'Does the Key to Peace in this Century Rest with the Non-White Peoples?', IULMIA; Int Minh (Vietnam 65); Diary Suzanne (UK 62) Jan 23, 1962, Warner papers. In fact, the Englewood problems involved elementary schools rather than the high school. Nevertheless, Samuel (Tanganyika 62) could hardly have avoided noticing the furor.

49 Ints Gerhardt (Germany 54), Snait (Israel 61), Joachim (Germany 71), Peter (UK 65). See also Int Mark (NZ 68); Email Rachel (Israel 64) Dec 14, 2021.

Notes to pages 193–203

50 Interview Ahmed (Sudan 60); Film: Aidi, 'Malcolm X and the Sudanese'; O'Dell 'Following in the Footsteps'.

51 Int Maria (Summer 64); N June 69, Nasmith papers; World Affairs Council of Philadelphia, 'African Nationalism and Independence' program and briefing notes, Leonetti papers.

52 Ints Liv (Norway 70), Mike (Australia 65), Anon; D42 2016. Mike said that the Australian government banned him from accepting There may be corroborating evidence in the National Archives of Australia.

53 Workum, 'Mechanisms Exposed', 29–31; Int and Email Anon (Australia); TV1965 'Can there Be Stability in SouthEast Asia', 306-voa-eno-t-7017 NARA.

Chapter 12: Beyond New York

1 *D*21 Feb 2004; Emails Gideon (Israel 63), Tord (Norway 63) Jun 29, 2022.

2 Report from Colonial Nancy Tier, N Aug 1949; Email Anon. Nancy Tier became the first female commander of CAP in Connecticut and founded the international women's air and space museum.

3 *Dallas Morning News* Jan 24, 1950, Ansary papers.

4 Counes-JHW; JHW-F G Keck May 18, 1964, B147/F3 Whitney, Yale.

5 *NYHT* Jan 23, 1950, 10; Mar 4, 1962, A5; Address to the General Assembly of the State of Tennessee quoted in Ekbladh, '"Mr T.V.A. "', 335; An Indiana University group canceled its tour in 1951 over segregation issues, and a Sarah Lawrence College group also struck problems in the same year. *NYHT* Sep 4, 1951, 21, Dec 9, 1951, A6; Purcell, *White Collar Radicals*.

6 *NYHT* Feb 9, 1952, 22, Feb 20, 1952, 18; 'Schedule for Field Trip' 1966 Nasmith Papers.

7 N May 1956; N Dec 1957; *NYHT* Feb 7, 1958, 3.

8 Conversation Teklu (Ethiopia 60).

9 Bio, Int, Email Tommy (Sweden 63) May 12, 2022; Ints Arnlaug (Norway 58), Saroj (Thailand 58), Eline (SA 1954).

10 Ints Maarten (Netherlands 61), Emmanuel (Ghana 68); Email Tissa (Ceylon 59).

11 RH-Kluger, Jan 8, 1982, B6/F131, Kluger, Yale. Others in 1969 included William O. Douglas, Donald Fraser, Morton Halperin, Robert A Levine. 'Washington Field Trip February 10–14, 1970', Nasmith papers.

12 Johansen papers; Ints Judith (UK 56), Kaarina (Finland 56), Chotima (Thailand 57), Ibrahim (Lebanon 58); *NYHT* Feb 16, 1956, 3.

13 *NYHT* Feb 17, 1960, 17a.

14 Ints Naila (Pakistan 58), Anon.

15 Ints Irini (Greece 63), Anon; *NYT* Jun 1, 1962, 11; Levitan, 'Fourth Estate', 11–13; D34 2011; Engwirda, *Per slot*, 15–22.

16 Counes, Briefing notes for JHW May 1, 1964, F3 B147 Whitney, Yale; N Oct 1957.

17 Ints Judith (UK 56), Tissa (Ceylon59), John (UK 58), Catriona (UK 63). Neither John nor Catriona can remember which host had the painting, but John Hay Whitney owned at least one Picasso, and Juan Trippe's house (recently sold for $84 million) deserved one!

18 *NYHT* Feb 27, 1948, 18a, March 6, 1948, 6a; D46 2018; Int Judith (UK 56).

19 Conversation Teklu (Ethiopia 60); Ints Cora (US 59), John (UK 59); D31 2009; D39 2014.

20 Preliminary notes B6/F131, Kluger, Yale.

21 'Notes for discussion concerning a Joint Sarah Lawrence-*Herald Tribune* Forum undertaking in the Field of International Exchange August 9, 1954'; Raushenbush-Taylor, Sep 3, 1954, *NYHT*WYF SLC.

22 HHW-Taylor (copies to Raushenbush & Solomon) Dec 9, 1955, Doris Wolff-HHW Dec 8, 1955; Solomon-Taylor Sep 6, 1955; Bozeman-Taylor & Raushenbush, May 13, 1955, *NYHT*WYF SLC; Ints Joy Reidel (SLC), Peter Workum. The 2 South American delegates & the Icelandic delegates missed out, while some left after London.

23 HHW-JHW, Jan 6, 1961, B147/F3 Whitney, Yale; Emails Gur (Israel 55), Daphna (Israel 57), Snait (Israel 61).

24 HHW-OR Apr 7, 56; USIS, 'Berlin Visit of *NYHT* for High Schools April 1–7 1956' in HHW-OR, Jun 4, 1956, B51/F609 Ogden Reid, Yale.

25 HHW-OR, May 17, 1956, B51/F609 Ogden Reid, Yale.

26 Lynn, 'Gone to … Ghana!' Report, Scott papers.

27 *NYHT* Dec 20, 1959, 10. NYU had a history of involvement in educational tourism. See Pietsch, *The Floating University*, esp. Ch. 1. In addition, NYU Prof Fred Redefer was a fan of Helen Waller & the Forum. Redefer-JHW Oct 31, 1961, B147/F3 Whitney, Yale; N Apr 1960.

28 Int Anon; N Apr 1960; Lynn, Report, Scott papers.

29 N Apr 1960; N Sep 1960.

30 Program 'The Massachusetts Junior World Affairs Council meets with The World Youth Forum' 1969, Leonetti papers; D49 2020.

31 Geneva Programs, 1969, 1970, Nasmith papers; Int Peter (Norway 69).

Chapter 13: Hamburgers, Milkshakes, Sex, Drugs & Rock 'n' Roll

1 The development of global youth culture is a growing area of scholarship. See most recently Alexander & Sleight (eds), *A Cultural History of Youth*.

2 Conversation Teklu (Ethiopia 60); Diary Per (Norway 61) Seglen papers; Ints Sherille (Ceylon 71), Hiranthi (Ceylon 67), Ibrahim (Lebanon 58), Chit (India 56).

3 Ints Emmanuel (Ghana 68), Tissa (Ceylon 59), Ronny (Indonesia 68), David (NZ 65) Conversation daughters of Probal (India 53); *NYHT* Mar 8, 1948, 31; N Oct 1957, 4; Ceridwen (UK 67), Forum Report 1967, Roberts papers; Email Michael (NZ 67) 2016. The Dominion Museum was the small national museum.

4 Ints Philippe (France 69), Michael (Jordan 58), Susan (SA 57).
5 Int Jan (Czech 67).
6 TV1959 'Have Your Ideas Changed?' IULMIA; Conversation daughters of Probal (India 53); *NYHT* Mar 8, 1948, 31, Sep 22, 1952, 14.
7 *NYHT* Feb 22, 1948, A5. In the same report, Byrnjulf (Norway 48) was similarly discomfited, 'by the bright gay signs in the worlds' greatest entertainment center, Times Square, and in the very midst of these signs the news flashes—the misery of the world—running in lights around the Times Building'.
8 *FT* Dec 30, 1960, Johnstone papers; Email Jorge (Uruguay 53) Apr 6, 2022, Conversation daughters of Probal (India 53); Ints Emmanuel (Ghana 68), Arnlaug (Norway 58), Beryl (Australia 68).
9 TV1955 'What is the Proper Purpose of a High School Education?', IULMIA: TV1956 'How do American Schools Compare with Yours?', IULMIA; Emails Tissa (Ceylon 59) Jun 8, 2020, Aysel (Turkey 64) Mar 28, 2021; *NYHT* Mar 8, 1948, 31; N Apr 1959; Ints Toshio (Japan 67), Mark (NZ 68), Geneviève (France 56), Röggi (Iceland 62), Vincenzo (Italy 64), Jorge (Uruguay 53), Shahla (Iran 63), Anon.
10 Ints Emmanuel (Ghana 68), Geneviève (France 56), Kris (Ceylon 68), Jorge (Uruguay 53); Conversation daughters of Probal (India 53).
11 Ints Alan (NZ 63), Bruce (Canada 61); Email Mike (Australia 65) Jul 15, 2021.
12 Ints Orit (Israel 67), Hameeda (Pakistan 52), Anon; N Sep 55.
13 Workum, 'Mechanisms Exposed', 60–109, esp 60, 92, 109; TV1958 'Summary of Three Months in the U.S.A.', IULMIA.
14 Letter Suzanne (UK 62) Jan 28, 1962, Warner papers; Ints Per (Norway 61), Serban (Bolivia 64). Michael (NZ 67), from a boys' high school in small town New Zealand, noted that 'the schools were co-ed!', adding 'I loved that'. (Email Mar 6, 2016).
15 TV1959 'Where Do We Go From Here?', IULMIA; Workum, 'Mechanisms Exposed', 92; Int Geneviève (France 56).
16 Ints Yassa (Jordan 59), Roger (UK 69).
17 N May 56; Int Alan (NZ 63); Letter Suzanne (UK 1962) Feb 25, 1962, Warner papers.
18 Ints Sherille (Ceylon 71), Anon.
19 Ints Mike (Australian 65), Monika (Austria 65), Anon. The likely instigators of Mike's adventure were Emmanuel (Liberia 65) and Herman (Panama 65). Minh (Vietnam 65) also identified them as 'much older', although they were only 18. (Int).
20 Letter, Anon, Int Anon.
21 Int Bimal (India 60).
22 Ints Mikko (Finland 69), Stella (Italy 69), Rodel (Philippines 69), Greg (NZ 69), Michael (UK 72); Bio Paul (Austria 72).
23 Lynn, 'Gone to … Ghana!' Report, Scott papers; JHW-Charles Tillinghast May 8, 1964, B147 F3 Whitney, Yale.

24 N May 1956.

25 N May 1957.

26 India Information Services Media Release 77, Apr 11, 1953, Dutt papers.

27 Ints & Emails Rodel (Philippines 69), Greg (NZ 69) Jun 2022.

28 Lynn, 'Gone to ... Ghana!' Report, Scott papers; Pan Am, *World Airways Teacher* Mar-Apr 1950, 2, PanAm.

29 N Feb 1957, 2. See eg Poiger, *Jazz, Rock, and Rebels*; Ivaska, *Cultured States*.

Chapter 14: What a Delegate Did Next

1 HHW, Welcome to Delegates letter, Nov 1956, B53/F2 NET, Wisconsin.

2 N May 56, N May 1957; Anna Katrin (Iceland 56) 'I only shiver when I think about how I am going to struggle this summer with my first year of French and my Latin'. (N May 1956) Ahmed (Egypt 58) confessed that his 'school examinations were horrible (to put it mildly) and frankly I am not very anxious to get the results'. (N Oct 1958) Jona (Iceland 60) also went 'straight back to exams'. (Int) Yvette (Switzerland 69) had strong memories of finding it difficult to study alone for her exams, which the school insisted she take when she returned. (Int) On returning students more generally see Soeterik, 'Re-Entry Adjustment'.

3 N May 1956; N Oct 1956; N May 1957.

4 N May 1957; N Apr 1959. Yukiko (Japan 59)'s friends did not like her new interest in Japanese politics and society; if she spoke of 'such things very often they will criticize me as a conceited girl'. (N Apr 1959).

5 N May 1956; N Jul 1956; N May 1957; N Jun 1960; Workum, 'Mechanisms Exposed', 110.

6 N Sep 1955; N May 1956; N May 1957.

7 N May 1956; D22 2004. Diana (Italy 57) 'didn't like America—so different from anything' she knew. (Int) Geneviève (France 56) did 'appreciate mine [her family] a little more than when I left'. Christoph (Germany 56): 'I really wasn't very happy to be German before I went to America'. Afterwards he felt 'at home in this people, and of course in Europe'. N Jul 1956.

8 N Sep 1955; N Oct 1956; N Jun 1959.

9 excerpts from report from USIS Lahore, N Oct 1956; N Jul 1956; N Oct 1957; N Oct 1958; N Sep 1959; Redefer-JHW, Oct 31, 1961, B147/F3 Whitney, Yale.

10 'Marshall Plan 50th Anniversary', May 28, 1997, c-span.

11 Elbert G Matthews, US Ambassador in Lagos-Whitney Apr 28, 1964, B147/F3 Whitney, Yale; D19 2002. Phuong (Vietnam 56) had 'a very good opinion about America' N Oct 1958.

12 N May 1956; N Jul 1956; N May 1957; N Jun 1959; N Apr 1960; N Jun 1960.

13 N Aug 1949; N Jun 1960.

14 N Sep 1959; N Apr 1960.

15 N Sep 1959.

16 N Jun 1960.

17 N Sep 1959; N Dec 1959; Tamar (Israel 52) in N Jun 1959. See also Salih (Turkey 56) N Sep 1959 & Majid (Iran 55) 'our quaint miniature newsletter'. N Dec 1959.

18 Int Hameeda (Pakistan 52); *NYHT* Jan 31, 1952, 15.

19 Int Anon.

20 HHW-Mrs William H Maltbie, Feb 10, 1947, F45/2 Reid, LOC.

21 Int and Emails Beryl (Australia 68).

22 Int Eline (SA54); Louw, *In My Voorterkkerrok,* 46, 159, 162–3.

23 Int and Emails Snait (Israel 61) Jul-Aug 2020.

24 Hasan, *Enemy in the Promised Land,* 51–3; Emails Suheil (Jordan 61) Jan 19-23, 2024.

25 *Haaretz* Apr 9, 1961, Apr 10, 1961. I am grateful to Snait Gissis for her translation. Dayan appears to confuse the two youngsters in his version, making Sanaa's tale even less likely. Perhaps she was playing on his reputation as a philanderer.

26 Int & Emails Snait (Israel 61) Jul-Aug 2020.

27 Diab, 'Enemy of the status quo'. Sanaa collaborated with Israeli journalist Amos Elon on *Between Enemies: A Compassionate Dialogue between an Israeli and an Arab* (1974) and, in 1987, published *Enemy in the Promised Land.* Reviewer Walter Reich was fooled, admiring her courage when she told her disapproving parents she wanted to go to Israel in 1967. He described her as 'a rebellious 16-year-old' (*The Washington Post* Jan 25, 1987). She was nearly 24. President Anwar Sadat was reportedly so upset with Sanaa's visit to Israel (which pre-empted his own by a few months) and her outspokenness on the subject that he 'forced' her husband, Tahsin Beshir, ambassador to Canada, to divorce his wayward wife, or give up his diplomatic post. Fahmy, *Negotiating for Peace.*

28 Horne, 'The Cosmopolitan Life'; N May 1957.

29 Roman (Philippines 55) in N Sep 1960.

30 *NYHT* Sep 22, 1952, 14; Bhattarai, 'Getting Blessings'.

31 Int Susan (SA 57).

32 D 48 2019; Int Anon.

33 Int Arnold (Colombia 69); Taylor-Solomon, Jul 1, 1958, *NYHT*WYF, SLC; Williams College students included Tetteh (Ghana 58), Teklu (Ethiopia 60), Nani (Ghana 60), Andreas (Ethiopia 61), Tan Wee Kiat (Singapore 61), Alem (Ethiopia 62) and Charles (Kenya 66). Jawahir (Malaya 56) won a scholarship to Briarcliff College in the US. Her parents were reluctant to allow her to accept it but when 'people came to congratulate my parents, they were too proud not to let me go'. (N May 56). Jona (Iceland 60) won a scholarship to Smith College, although she does not remember applying, putting it down to a Forum connection. (Int).

34 Email Vuong (Vietnam 68) Jan 21, 2023. Host brother Bruce Norton took him to the

SAT, older host sister Josephine Adaby introduced him to Thomas Snyder.

35 N Oct 1956; N Feb 1957; N Dec 1958; N Sep 1959, N Sep1960. Khanh (Vietnam 60) had information from Than Thi Hoai Phoung (Vietnam 56)'s cousin that she became the youngest female member of the House of Representatives in South Vietnam at the age of 25, later fleeing the country. By 1996 she was working in Macy's jewelry department in Los Angeles and had died of cancer by 2015. She had lost touch with her husband. Email Khanh (Vietnam 1960) Jul 27, 2022. Academic Nu-Anh Tran (UConn) confirmed that Phuong was related to Madame Nhu and part of her Women's Solidarity Group. (pers. comm.). Research on ancestry.com suggests Diep (Vietnam 55) remained in the US, marrying Kan X Dang in 1965 in California, living there and in New York before dying in Chicago in 2011.

36 Int Irjaleena (Finland 57). Jon (Iceland 59) turned down a scholarship to Columbia.

37 *D*19 2002; N Sep 1955; N Dec 1960; Email Eugenia Matthews, sister of Auxilia (Rhodesia 62) Feb 5, 2022.

38 *NYHT* Mar 25, 1955, 15; *D* 49 2020.

39 Int Kris (Ceylon 68). John was a bit of a poster boy at the soup kitchen, which used his story for publicity, NYC Department for the Aging, 'Stimulus at Work'. Unfortunately he had moved on by the time I contacted the center to talk with him.

40 US phone and address records are available online to a far greater extent than in some other countries. Emigrants, however, often change their names: for instance Farideh (Iran 68) vanished in the record after college in the US. I think I found her, after a serendipitous trail of internet and ancestry.com searches as Faye DeWitt, bookshop manager in Canaan, Connecticut, later living in NYC.

41 N Aug 1949; *D*44, Jan 2017.

42 Email Khanh (Vietnam 60) Jan 27, 2023; Int Haider (Pakistan 71). Haider went back to Dhaka briefly but then returned to the US to study and has settled there.

43 On the contribution of Ghanaian intellectuals, including Anani Dzidzienyo, in this field see Gyamfi, 'From Nkrumah's Black Star'; Int Nii (Ghana 59).

44 *D*24 2005; Email Bharat (Nepal 64) Apr 5, 2018.

45 Obit. D Mulumba.

46 These proportions exclude Israel and South Africa, which stand apart from countries in their respective regions. The issue of a 'brain drain' was recognized as a problem in the 1960s, reflected in the two pages of scholarly articles on 'Brain Drain' listed in Spencer & Awe, *International Educational Exchange*, 56–7.

47 N Oct 1957; Int Joan (Staff). In this section I am using delegates' full names because their positions make that appropriate. Women are identified by their married names if that is how they were known as adults in their careers.

48 Email Gideon (Israel 63) Jul 24, 2022; Duke-NUS Medical School, 'Krisanatha Weeasuriya'.

49 She wrote 'the first notable newspaper article' about the Liverpool band. Obit.

M Cleave. Beatles biographer Bob Spitz claimed a Lennon song was inspired by his relationship with her, but that was contested by all concerned. 'Maureen Cleave', Wikipedia. The New Zealanders were variously in music, local government administration, business, education, hospitality, and law. Three of the Australian girls worked in education, one was a doctor and they all married and had children. The Australian boys included two lawyers, a teacher, a radiotherapist, an Anglican priest, and a business consultant.

50 Int Hiranthi (Ceylon 67).

51 Obit. G Nasmith.

52 N Sep 60; N Dec 60.

53 Email Dieter (Germany 62) Oct 3, 2021; Int Jan (Czechoslovakia 67).

Chapter 15: Americans Abroad

1 1966 World Youth Forum Brochure B6/F131 Kluger, Yale; JHW-parents of Summer Forum delegates, Jun 1964, Draft, B147/F3 Whitney, Yale.

2 Int Pamela (Leader). Delegate lists and itineraries for 1964-1973 are in the following papers: 1964 SLC archives; 1965 Bodnar papers; 1967, 1969 Harrington papers; 1967-1971 Nasmith papers. There is no information for 1966.

3 Media Outlets: KNX, LA, KOIN-TV, Portland, KNOX-TV, St Louis, WCAU TV, Philadelphia, WCBS & *Seventeen Magazine*, NY. Huffman, 'The World Youth Forum'; Int Pamela (Leader).

4 'World Youth Forum: European Program Jul-Aug 1971' Nasmith papers; *Philadelphia Tribune* Aug 2, 1970, 7. Surviving photographs show 1964 delegates were all white. In 1965 and 1966 records are incomplete. Of the 1965 cohort, Joan Levy had spent the previous summer with Alliance Française in France, while Susan King and Stephen Tracy had traveled with The Experiment in International Living.

5 Email Clifford (Summer 1973) Feb 1, 2022.

6 Letter Eileen (Leader) Aug 8, 1967, Harrington papers; Email Richard (Leader) Sep 18, 2022.

7 Int Pamela (Leader), Email Eileen (Leader) Jul 30, 2022; Email Ginger (Summer 1964, Assistant) Jul 30, 2022. Eileen was impressed with Michael's attitude to Germany, given that he had lost family in Dachau. 'If we hate, the Nazis will have won', he told her. Michael died aged just 61 in 2010, after a career as a lawyer specializing in ethics, retaining an interest in travel. He made a great impression on Eileen 'his life as a student and adult personify the highest ideals of the World Youth Forum'. D46 2018.

8 Red Bank High, Red Bank New Jersey, 'Log '68', 38; Ginger (Assistant) Report 1967, Nasmith papers; D38 2013. Orel remembered the family did apologize for deserting her for an unavoidable event at their country house, but was nevertheless disconcerted. Interview, Email Orel (Summer 1964) Jan 27, 2022.

9 Ginger (Assistant) Report 1967; Connie (Leader) Report 1969, Nasmith Papers; Ints Alan (Summer 1965); Joergen (Denmark 1965). The main building is now apartments.

10 D36 2012; Ginger (Assistant) Report 1967; Connie (Leader) Report 1969, Nasmith Papers Int Joachim (Germany 1971) In 1969, Eva (Austria 1964) also set up 'an excellent program, taking care of millions of small details for us, sitting at the station for hours'. (Connie Report).

11 Ginger (Assistant) Report 1967; Connie (Leader) Report 1969, Nasmith papers.

12 Interview Maria (Summer 1964): Email Ginger (Summer 1964) Jul 15, 2021; Ginger (Assistant) Report 1967, Nasmith papers.

13 Int Maria (Summer 1964).

14 Int Maria (Summer 1964); see also Int Orel (Summer 1964), Gary (Summer 1964) in D37 2013.

15 Int Maria (Summer 1964); Ginger (Assistant) Report 1967, Nasmith papers.

16 Ginger (Assistant) Report 1967, Connie (Leader) Report 1969, Nasmith papers.

17 Ginger (Assistant) Report 1967, Nasmith papers. Pamela (Leader) also improvised with great success. (Int).

18 D6 1995; Ginger (Assistant) Report 1967, Nasmith papers.

19 Connie (Leader) Report 1969, Nasmith papers.

20 D38 2013.

21 Ginger (Assistant) Report 1967, Nasmith papers.

22 Int Pamela (Leader). William Golden (Summer 70), *the Polygon* (Polytechnic Preparatory Country Day School newspaper, Brooklyn NY), Oct 9, 1970. Reports from 1967 and 1969, however, noted that the delegates 'did not mix as much as they might have' Connie (Leader) Report 1969 Nasmith papers.

23 Int and Emails, Eileen (Leader).

24 Int Anon; A man from the Economic Institute 'spoke to us at some risk to himself and did an excellent job of explaining the proposed economic reform and answering our many questions'. Connie (Leader) Report 1969 Nasmith papers. Cedok was the official travel agency.

25 Ints Jan (Czechoslovakia 67), Pamela (Leader). Fortunately, Jan's family did not suffer badly from his defection.

26 Corey Shanus was the delegate. Email Richard (Leader) Sep 18, 2022.

27 Int Orel (Summer 64); Email Maria (Summer 64); D37 2013.

28 RH-MacJannets Feb 17, 1972, Jul 6, 1972, B138 MacJannet, Tufts.

Chapter 16: 'An Exercise in Futility?'

1 Matt Meyer-RH, Sep 30, 1966; RH 'Statement of the Executive Director', Sep 6, 1966, B147/F2 Whitney, Yale; RH, 'A frank statement to our alumni', Jul 1971, Hennig papers.

2 Oram Report 1968.

3 Cantor, *The Bernie Cornfeld Story*; Huffman, 'The World Youth Forum', 51; Ints Haider

(Pakistan 71), Gus (US 62, Staff); RH-MacJannets, Jun 11, 1973, B138 MacJannet, Tufts. Huffman also unsuccessfully approached Xerox. RH-Gus, Jul 17, 1969, Nasmith papers.

4 Minutes, Meeting of the Trustees of the World Youth Forum, Oct 27, 1976, Nasmith papers. Ruth Bishop's Lipper Foundation gave $2000 in 1972, Standard Oil (later Exxon) gave $1000 annually from 1971-73. Lawrence A Wien Foundation gave $1000 in 1973 Financial Statements, 1972, 1973, B138 MacJannet, Tufts. Information on Forum finances, B138 MacJannet, Tufts. See also MacJannet Foundation website.

5 RH, 'A frank statement', Hennig papers; John Strelau, Rockefeller Foundation-Gus, Jul 20, 1976, Nasmith papers; RH-Board, Oct 6, 1972, B138 MacJannet, Tufts.

6 Satti & Andlinger-alumni, Jan 1971; RH, 'A frank statement', Hennig papers.

7 US BECA 'International Exchange: Leaders for Tomorrow'; US BECA 'International Exchange 1969'; RH, 'A frank statement', Hennig papers; RH-Board, Jun 11, 1973, B138 MacJannet, Tufts.

8 RH-Gus, Aug 11, 1969, Nasmith papers.

9 RH-MacJannets, Sep 27, 1971, Feb 17, 1972, RH-Board, May 20, 1974, B138 MacJannet, Tufts. Staff included Steve Gooch & Bill Perkins (both from ICYE), Tina Buettell, Barbara Joseph.

10 RH-MacJannets, Sep 27, 1971, Jul 6, 1972, RH-Board Oct 6, 1972, B138 MacJannet, Tufts.

11 RH-alumni, Dec 1971, Hennig papers.

12 RH-MacJannets, Sep 27, 1971; 'World Youth Forum Seminar Series 1971-1972'; 'World Youth Forum Seminar on the United Nations, Carnegie International Center, November 16, 1971' B138 MacJannet, Tufts; RH, 'A frank statement'; RH-alumni, Dec 1971, Hennig papers. Experts included Clark Eichelberger, Noel Brown, Ian Berendsen, Cesrt Ortiz-Tinoco, Yasushi Akashi, Gerald Lavin, Alain Vidal-Naquet, Lalit Thapalyal, Sally Swing Shelley.

13 See eg call for host families for exchange programs at Clarkstown High, which lists six programs in which the school is involved. *The Journal News* Apr 22, 1973, 8A.

14 RH-Board, Oct 6, 1972, B138 MacJannet, Tufts.

15 RH-Board, Oct 6, 1972, B138 MacJannet, Tufts. Board Members: Bob Huffman, Ralph H Daniels & George Dessart (CBS), Anis K Satti (Pakistan 56), Gerhard Andlinger (Austria 49), Robert T Macdonald (International Herald Tribune), Alan P Sloan (WCBSTV), James Roosevelt & Ruth Bishop (IOS), diplomat Richard H Nolte, lawyer Peter F Gass, & executives David Haweeli, Richard Gamble & Vernon Jordan.

16 World Youth Forum Course in International Relations 1972-73; World Youth Forum Seminars 1972-73 Program; RH-MacJannets, Jul 6, 1972, B138 MacJannet, Tufts.

17 1973 delegates also included Youth for Understanding student Croatian Jasminka Sabo (later Sohinger) from Loretto Academy in El Paso, Texas.

18 ICYE Board Minutes, Sep 1972, 1973, F 6 B10, Brethren; RH-MacJannets, Feb 17, 1972, B138 MacJannet, Tufts; Scribner, 'American Teenagers', 563.

19 RH-MacJannets, Jan 11, 1973, B138 MacJannet, Tufts; *The Journal News* Feb 27, 1973, p. 6A. See also Board of Directors Minutes Sep 1972, 1973, ICYE B10/F6, Brethren.

20 RH-MacJannets, Feb 17, 1972; RH-Board, Jun 11, 1973; May 20, 1974; RH-alumni, Jan 1974, B138 MacJannet, Tufts; Int John (NZ AFS 1973), *El Paso Times* Dec 29, 1973, 1; *Public Opinion*, Apr 21, 1973, 13.

21 *The Shopper* Oct 21, 1981, 22; *The News* (Paterson NJ) Mar 24, 1976, 44; Giamo, *On the Bowery*, 27. Robert Esik recalled designing his own program after 'getting a list of delegates' names from someone at the World Youth Forum in New York', (Int).

22 RH-MacJannets, Feb 16, 1976, B138 MacJannet, Tufts.

23 "'A World at Stake" program', Press Release, Jan 30, 1976, B138 MacJannet, Tufts.

24 RH-MacJannets, Feb 16, 1976, B138 MacJannet, Tufts.

25 Minutes of the Meeting of the Trustees of the World Youth Forum, Oct 30, 1979, Nasmith papers.

26 Huffman CV, Boal papers.

Chapter 17: A Forum Phoenix

1 Emails Monika (Austria 65) Sep 2022.

2 Oram Report 1968, 8–9; Int Arnold (Colombia 69).

3 N Oct 1956; N Sep 1959. See also N Dec 1958.

4 N Feb 1957; NMay 1957; see also N May 1956; Int Léon (Mexico 64). John (UK 59) had a witty description of the contagious disease of 'Delegatitis', causing delegates to obsessively seek out Alumni: 'Side effects often include severe nostalgia and an obsession with old photo albums and files of yellowing cuttings from the *NY Herald Tribune*'. D7 1996.

5 N Oct 1957; N Sep 1955; N Sep 1959. The Connecticut group was from Pomfret and other schools, funded by Harold Hochschild, whose son Adam was at Pomfret.

6 N Dec 1959; Int Hameeda (Pakistan 52); D7 1996.

7 N Apr 1959; Ints Catherine (France 59), Léon (Mexico 64), Amos (Israel 69); D4 1994; D7 1996; Email Sergio (Brazil 53) 2022. Sara (UK 57) and Niels (Denmark 53) met at the World University Service Conference in 1959 (N Jun 1959).

8 Int Gerhard (Germany 54); When Inga checked her diary she found Gerhard cycled in 1954 but in later years arrived by train. Email Inga (Denmark 54) Aug 8, 2022.

9 N Feb 1957.

10 Obit. M Kovalsky; Ints John (UK 58), Orel & Serban (Summer, Bolivia 64), Tommy (Sweden 63), Pamela (Leader); Emails Tommy (Sweden 63) May 12, 2022, Cliff (Host 69) Feb 1, 2022.

11 N May 1957: The Philippines delegates were Meliton (50), Araceli (53), Roman (55), Raul (56), Dennis (57); D40 2015; N Jun 1961; N Nov 1961.

12 Int Léon (Mexico 64); World Youth Forum slides B74/F1 MacJannet, Tufts.

13 *D6* 1995.
14 Int Catherine (France 59).
15 See eg *D*18 2001.
16 *D*18 2001.
17 *D*45 2017.
18 *D*19 2002.
19 *D*32 2010.
20 *D*22 2004.
21 Numbers from *The Delegate* reports.
22 *D*27 2007; *D*8 2001.
23 *D*18 2001; Int Kiat (Singapore 61).
24 Ints Susie (Brazil 58), Catherine (France 59); *The Delegate* various issues.
25 *D*19 2002, *D*37 2013.
26 Ints 1969 delegates.
27 Int Anon.
28 *D*8 1996; see also *D*9 1997 for responses.
29 *D*7 1996.
30 *D*37 2013; *D*21 2004; *D*22 2004.
31 Email John (UK 59)-Tissa (Ceylon 59) Jun 12, 2020; *D*20 2003, *D*47 2019; *D*48 2019.
32 *D*29 2008; *D*18 2001; *D*35 2011.
33 ZoomUnion Committee: Daphna (Israel 57), Ginger (Summer 64), John (UK 59), Catherine (France 59), Dorothy (Malaya 62), & Alan (Summer 64).

Chapter 18: Changing the World

1 Johan (Norway 56) in Workum, 'Mechanisms Exposed', 41.
2 Oram Report 1968; Email Sergio (Brazil 53) Apr 12, 2022.
3 Ints Sherille (Ceylon 71), Cora (US 59).
4 Ints Hiranthi (Ceylon 67), Gus (US 1962), John (UK 59).
5 Robert A Lincoln Int. ADST; Kaufman, *Soros*, 247.
6 On the shifting relationship between USIS, the State Department and the cultural cold war see Gienow-Hecht 'How good are we?'; Redefer-JHW, Oct 31, 1961, B147/F3 Whitney, Yale.
7 Negative letters did exist, mentioned in Workum's MA thesis. She had access to Helen Waller's Forum archive, which no longer exists. Waller sent a group of alumni to Miami in lieu: Eddie (Malaya 50), Hameeda (Pakistan 52), Purificacion (Philippines 52), Nakchung (Korea 55). N May 56; N Dec 57.
8 Oram Report, 1968, 6; N Jun 69, Nasmith papers.

9 Int Rolf (Denmark 68).

10 TV1959 'Introduction to America', IULMIA; Letter Anon; Ints Anon.

11 Catriona (UK 64), for example, eschewed Oxbridge for progressive Sussex University.

12 Ints Snait (Israel 61), Susan (SA 57), Anon.

13 Int Anon.

14 Comments, 1957 High School Debate; 1958 High school exchange students, YouTube; Buenaventura, 'I talk about my grandfather Johnny Antillon', YouTube.

15 Comments, 1957 High School Debate, YouTube.

16 See Sluga & Horne (eds) 'Cosmopolitanism in World History'. On educational benefits see Hansel & Grove, 'International Student Exchange Programs'.

17 RH-alumni, Jun 9, 1969, Nasmith papers.

18 RH-alumni, Jan 1974, B138 MacJannet, Tufts.

19 Greta Thunberg would surely have not been out of place at the Forum. 'Greta Thunberg', *Britannica*.

Bibliography and References

Books and Articles

Alexander, Kristine and Simon Sleight. Eds. *A Cultural History of Youth in the Modern Age*. London: Bloomsbury Academic 2022. DOI: http://dx.doi.org/10.5040/9781350033085

Arndt, Richard T. *The Resort of Kings: American Cultural Diplomacy in the Twentieth Century*. Dulles Va: Potomac Books 2005

Arnold, David and Stuart Blackburn. Eds. *Telling Lives in India: Biography, Autobiography and Life History*. Bloomington: Indiana University Press, 2004

Berghel, Susan Eckelmann, Sara Fieldston, and Paul M Renfro. Eds. *Growing Up America: Youth and Politics since 1945*. Athens: University of Georgia Press, 2019

Berghel, Susan Eckelmann. '"Remove Our Troops from Vietnam and Listen": Youth Diplomacy and Johnson's Vietnam War.' In Berghel et al. Eds. *Growing Up America: Youth and Politics since 1945*: 114–32.

Berghel, Susan Eckelmann. '"What My Generation Makes of America": American Youth Citizenship, Civil Rights Allies, and 1960s Black Freedom Struggle.' *The Journal of the History of Childhood and Youth* 10, no. 3 (Fall 2017): 422–40

Bhattarai, Madan Kumar. 'Getting Blessings from Ace Diplomat Ambassador Bhinda Shah.' *Spotlight on Nepal* Mar 6, 2018, https://www.spotlightnepal.com/2018/03/06/getting-blessings-ace-diplomat-ambassador-bhinda-shah/

Buchanan, Chris. 'Chukka Pony.' *Prestige* Digital, Aug 18, 2014, https://prestigedigital.net/editors-choice/chukka-pony/

Cantor, Bert. *The Bernie Cornfeld Story*. New York: Lyle Stuart Inc, 1970.

Chafe, William H. *Civilities and Civil Rights: Greensboro, North Carolina, and the Black Struggle for Freedom*. New York: Oxford University Press, 1980.

Chatelain, Marcia. 'International Sisterhood: Cold War Girl Scouts Encounter the World.' *Diplomatic History* 38, no. 2 (2014): 261–70

Childers, Jay P. *The Evolving Citizen: American Youth and the Changing Norms of Democratic Engagement*. Pennsylvania: Penn State University Press, 2012.

Chinner, Errol and Don David. *Australia's Schoolboy Ambassadors: A Record of the Sun-Advertiser-Daily News Sponsored Youth Travel Tours to Great Britain in the 1950s*. Melbourne: Sun Advertiser Youth Travel Association, 2002.

Cohn, Deborah. '"In between propaganda and escapism": William Faulkner as Cold War Cultural Ambassador.' *Diplomatic History* 40, no. 3 (2016): 392–420

Crocker, Jennifer, Marc-Andre Olivier & Noah Nuer. 'Self-image Goals and Compassionate Goals: Costs and Benefits.' *Self and Identity* 8, nos 2–3 (2009): 251–69

Cull, Nicholas J. 'Public Diplomacy and the Private Sector: The United States Information Agency, its predecessors and the private sector.' In Helen Laville and Hugh

Wilford. Eds. *The US Government, Citizen Groups and the Cold War: The state-private network*: 210-26

Diab, Khaled. 'Enemy of the status quo.' *The Guardian*, Jul 6, 2008, https://www.theguardian.com/commentisfree/2008/jul/06/egypt.israelandthepalestinians

Douglas, Kate and Anna Poletti. *Life Narratives and Youth Culture: Representation, Agency and Participation*. London: Palgrave Macmillan, 2017

Douglas, Kate. 'Childhood and Youth.' *a/b: Auto/Biography Studies*, 32, no. 2 (2017): 303-6, DOI: 10.1080/08989575.2017.1288949).

Dudziak, Mary L. *Cold War Civil Rights: Race and the Image of American Democracy*. Princeton: Princeton University Press, 2011

Ekbladh, David. '"Mr T.V.A.": Grass-Roots Development, David Lilienthal, and the Rise and Fall of the Tennessee Valley Authority as a Symbol for US Overseas Development, 1933-1973.' *Diplomatic History* 26, no. 93 (2002): 335-74

Elliott, Cara A. '"We Should Live Like One World" White Children Write About Race and Brotherhood in Letters to Harry S. Truman.' *The Journal of the History of Childhood and Youth* 10, No. 3, (Fall 2017): 402-21 DOI: https://doi.org/10.1353/hcy.2017.0048

Engwirda, Maarten. *Per Slot can rekening: memoires*. Amsterdam: Elsevier, 201.

Fahmy, Ismail. *Negotiating for Peace in the Middle East*. Croom Helm 1983.

Fass, Paula S. 'Intersecting Agendas: Children in History and Diplomacy.' *Diplomatic History* 38, no. 2 (Mar 2014): 294-8

Fett, Anna. 'The Teen-Age Program: the expansion of a US government experiment in international education from postwar Germany and Austria to the early Cold War world.' *Peace and Change* 48 (2023): 132-51

Fett, Anna. 'U.S. People-to-People Programs: Cold War Cultural Diplomacy to Conflict Resolution.' *Diplomatic History* 45, no. 4 (2021): 714-42 doi:10.1093/dh/dhab055

Fieldston, Sara. 'The Junior Marshall Plan: children, world friendship, and internationalism after World War II.' In Berghel et al. Eds. *Growing Up America: Youth and Politics since 1945*: 19-35

Fieldston, Sara. 'The Nursery's Iron Curtain: Children, Childhood and the Global Cold War.' *History Compass* 17, no. 6 (2019): e12547, DOI https://doi.org/10.1111/hic3.12547

Fieldston, Sara. *Raising the World: Child Welfare in the American Century*. Cambridge: Harvard University Press, 2015

Flynn, Elizabeth A. 'Composing as a Woman.' *College Composition and Communication* 39 (1988): 423-35

Fueur, Alan. 'Remembering the Death, but Mostly the Life, of a Storied Newspaper.' *NYT* Sep 28, 2006, https://www.nytimes.com/2006/09/28/nyregion/28trib.html

Garner, Alice and Diane Kirkby, *Academic Ambassadors, Pacific Allies: Australia, America and the Fulbright Program*. Manchester: Manchester University Press, 2019

Giamo, Benedict. *On the Bowery: Confronting Homelessness in American Society*. Iowa City: University of Iowa Press, 1989

Giebel, Sonia, AJ Alvero, Ben Gebre-Medhim and Anthony Lising Antionio. 'Signaled or Suppressed? How Gender Informs Women's Undergraduate Applications in Biology and Engineering.' *Socius: Sociological Research for a Dynamic World* 8 (2022): 1–20 DOI: 10.1177/23780231221127537

Gienow-Hecht, Jessica. '"How good are we?" culture and the Cold War.' *Intelligence and National Security* 18, no. 2 (2003): 269–82, DOI: 10.1080/02684520412331306850

Grieve, Victoria M. *Little Cold Warriors: American Childhood in the 1950s.* Oxford: Oxford University Press, 2020.

Guillory, Sean. 'Culture Clash in the Socialist Paradise: Soviet Patronage and African Students' Urbanity in the Soviet Union, 1960–1965.' *Diplomatic History* 38, no. 2 (2014): 271–81.

Gyamfi, Bright. 'From Nkrumah's Black Star to the African Diaspora: Ghanaian Intellectual Activists and the Development of Black Studies in the Americas.' *The Journal of African American History* 106, no. 4 (Fall 2021): 682–705

Hale, Jon. *The Freedom Schools: Student Activists in the Mississippi Civil Rights Movement.* New York: Columbia University Press, 2016.

Hansel, Bettina, and Neal Grove. 'International Student Exchange Programs—Are the Educational Benefits Real?' *NASSP (National Association of Secondary School Principals) Bulletin* Feb 1986: 84–90

Hansen, Allen C. *USIA Public Diplomacy in the Computer Age.* second edition. New York: Praeger, 1989.

Hasan, Sana(a). *Enemy in the Promised Land: Egyptian Woman's Journey into Israel.* NY: Shocken Books, 1986

Helgren, Jennifer. *American Girls and Global Responsibility: A New Relation to the World During the Early Cold War.* New Brunswick: Rutgers University Press, 2017.

Herring, Susan and Sanja Kapidzic. 'Teens, Gender and Self-Presentation in Social Media.' In Wright, JD. Ed. *International Encyclopedia of Social and Behavioral Sciences.* Oxford: Elsevier 2015.

Holt, Marilyn Irvin. *Cold War Kids: Politics and Childhood in Postwar America, 1945–1960.* Lawrence: University of Kansas Press, 2014.

Honeck, Mischa and Aaron William Moore. 'War and Conflict.' In Alexander & Sleight. Eds. *A Cultural History of Youth in the Modern Age*: 195–216.

Honeck, Mischa. *Our Frontier Is the World: The Boy Scouts in the Age of American Ascendancy.* Uthaca: Cornell University Press, 2018.

Horne, Julia. 'The Cosmopolitan Life of Alice Erh-Soon Tay.' *Journal of World History* 21, no. 3 (Sep 2010): 419–66 DOI: https://doi.org/10.1353/jwh.2010.0021

Hosley, David H. 'As good as any of us: American female radio correspondents in Europe, 1938–1941.' *Historical Journal of Film, Radio and Television* 2, no. 2 (1982): 141–56, DOI: 10.1080/01439688200260101

Ivaska, Andrew. *Cultured States: Youth Gender and Modern Style in 1960s Dar Es Salaam,* (Durham: Duke University Press, 2011)

Jobs, Richard I. 'Youth Movements: Travel, Protest, and Europe in 1968.' *American Historical Review* 114, no. 2 (Apr 2009): 376–404

Jobs, Richard I. *Backpack Ambassadors*. Chicago: University of Chicago Press, 2017.

Jordan, Caroline and Diane Kirkby. '"An Undesirable Type of Fulbright Grantee": Women, Gender and Transgression in the Cold War Asia–Pacific Region.' *Gender & History* 32 no. 2 (Jul 2020): 482–501.

Kahn, E.J. *Jock: The Life and Times of John Hay Whitney*. New York: Doubleday, 1981.

Kaufman, Michael T. *Soros: The Life and Times of a Messianic Billionaire*. New York: Vintage, 2002

Kluger, Richard. *The Paper: The Life and Death of the New York Herald Tribune*. New York: Alfred A. Knopf, 1986.

Koivunen, Pia. 'Overcoming Cold War Boundaries at World Youth Festivals.' In Autio-Sarasma, Sari & Katalin Miklóssy. Eds. *Reassessing Cold War Europe*. London: Routledge, 2013: 175–92.

Koivunen, Pia. *Performing Peace and Friendship: The World Youth Festivals and Soviet Cultural Diplomacy*. Berlin: De Gruyter Oldenbourg, 2022.

Kordas, Ann Marie. *The Politics of Childhood in Cold War America*. Brookfield, VT: Pickering & Chatto, 2013

Kotek, Joël. 'Youth organizations as a Battlefield in the Cold War.' *Intelligence and Security* 18, no. 2 (2003): 168–91.

Kotek, Joël. *Students and the Cold War*. Basingstoke: Palgrave Macmillan 1996.

Krekola, Joni and Simo Mikkonen. 'Backlash of the Free World: the US presence at the World Youth Festival in Helsinki, 1962.' *Scandinavian Journal of History* 36, no. 2 (2011): 230–55, DOI: 10.1080/03468755.2011.565566

Krismann, Carol H. *Encyclopedia of American Women in Business: From Colonial Times to the Present*. Volume Two: M-Z. Westport, Connecticut: Greenwood, 2005.

Lalaki, Despina. 'The Cultural Cold War and the New Women of Power. Making a Case based on the Fulbright and Ford Foundations in Greece.' *Histoire@Politique: Politique, Culture, Société, Revue du Centre d'Histoire de Sciences Po*, 35 (Mai-Août 2018)

Laugesen, Amanda. 'American Publishers, Books, and the Global Cultural Cold War: Alfred A. Knopf Inc. and the United States Information Agency, 1953–1970.' *Australasian Journal of American Studies* 35, No. 2 (2016): 19–37, www.jstor.org/stable/44779789

Laville, Helen and Hugh Wilford. Eds. *The US Government, Citizen Groups and the Cold War: The state-private network*. Abingdon, Routledge, 2006

Laville, Helen. 'The committee of correspondence: CIA funding of women's groups 1952–1967.' *Intelligence and National Security* 12, no.1 (2007): 104–21, DOI:10.1080/02684529708432401

Laville, Helen. *Cold War Women: The international activities of American women's organisations*. Manchester: Manchester University Press, 2002

Lim, Peter. 'When Sworn Enemies Rock 'n' Roll Together.' *The New Paper* Nov 15, 2006, Sophies World https://sophiesworld-sophiesworld.blogspot.com/2006/11/inside-israel-part-1.html accessed Jan 26, 2024

Lucas, W. Scott. 'Beyond freedom, beyond control, beyond the Cold War: approaches to American culture and the state-private network.' *Intelligence and National Security* 18 no.2 (2003) 53–72, DOI: 10.1080/02684520412331306740

Magee, Sarah Kate. 'College Admissions Essays: A Genre of Masculinity.' *Young Scholars in Writing.* 7 (2010): 116–21, https://youngscholarsinwriting.org/index.php/ysiw/article/view/102;

Malhotra, Anishu and Siobham Lambert-Hurley. 'Introduction.' In Malhotra & Lambert-Hurley. Eds. *Speaking of the Self: Gender, Performance and Autobiography in South Asia.* Durham: Duke University Press, 2015.

Maximova, Olga B & Galina O Lukyanova. 'Gender differences online: self-representation and involvement in political communication on Facebook.' *Heliyon* 6 (2020) e05613 www.cell.com/heliyon.

Moore, Aaron William. 'Growing Up in Nationalist China: Self-Representation in the Personal Documents of Children and Youth, 1927–1949.' *Modern China* 42, no. 1 (2016): 73–110

Moruzi, Kristine, Nell Musgrove, Carla Pascoe Leahy. Eds. *Children's Voices from the Past: new Historical and Interdisciplinary Perspectives.* London: Palgrave Macmillan, 2019.

Nayeri, Kamran. 'Mahmoud Sayrafizadeh: The Father of Iranian Trotskyism.' *Our Place in the World: A Journal of EcoSocialism.* Aug 8, 2019. https://www.academia.edu/40121002/Mahmoud_Sayrafizadeh_The_Father_of_Iranian_Trotskyism

Norwig, Christina. 'A First European Generation? The Myth of Youth and European Integration in the Fifties.' *Diplomatic History* 38, no. 2 (2014): 251–60

O'Dell, Emily. 'Following in the Footsteps of Malcolm X.' *Huffington Post* 2015 https://www.huffpost.com/entry/following-in-the-footstep_b_6434534

Olar, Jared. 'News From Days Gone By.' *From The History Room* blog, Jan 17, 2020, https://fromthehistoryroom.wordpress.com/2020/01/17/news-of-days-gone-by-the-1st-pekin-daily-times/

Olar, Jared. 'Pekin Wasn't Always a Welcoming Place.' *The Pekin Daily Times* Jun 21, 2013

Osgood, Kenneth. *Total Cold War: Eisenhower's Secret Propaganda Battle at Home and Abroad.* Lawrence: University of Kansas Press, 2006.

Paget, Karen M. 'From Cooperation to Covert Action: The US government and students 1940–1952.' In Helen Laville and Hugh Wilford. Eds. *The US Government, Citizen Groups and the Cold War: The state-private network.* Abingdon: Routledge, 2006: 66–82

Paget, Karen M. 'From Stockholm to Leiden: the CIA's role in the formation of the International Student Conference.' *Intelligence and National Security*, 18, no. 2 (2003) 134–67, DOI:10.1080/02684520412331306780

Palladino, Grace. *Teenagers: An American History.* New York: Basic Books, 1996

Peacock, Margaret. 'The perils of building Cold War consensus at the 1957 Moscow World Festival of Youth and Students.' *Cold War History* 12, no. 3 (Aug 2012): 515–35

Peacock, Margaret. *Innocent Weapons: The Soviet and American Politics of Childhood in the Cold War*. Chapel Hill: University of North Carolina Press, 2014.

Piccini, Jon. "'There is no solidarity, peace or friendship with dictatorship": Australians at the World Festival of Youth and Students, 1957–1968.' *History Australia* 9, no. 3 (Dec 2012): 178–98

Pietsch, Tamson. *The Floating University: Experience, Empire and the Politics of Knowledge*. Chicago: University of Chicago Press, 2023.

Poiger, Uta G. *Jazz, Rock, and Rebels: Cold War Politics and American Culture In a Divided Germany*. (Berkeley: University of California Press, 2000)

Purcell, Aaron D. *White Collar Radicals: TVA's Knoxville Fifteen, the New Deal, and the McCarthy Era*. Knoxville: University of Tennessee Press, 2009

Ryback, Timothy W. *The Salzburg Seminar: The First Fifty Years*. Salzburg: Salzburg Seminar in American Studies, 1997.

Salazar, Meliton. *Teardrops Dry: A collection of the literature of Mel V. Salazar*. 8 Jul, 2006

Saunders, Francis Stonor. *Who Paid the Piper?: The CIA and the Cultural Cold War*. 2nd ed. London: Granta Books, 2000.

Sayrafiezadeh, Said. *When Skateboards Will Be Free: My Reluctant Political Childhood*. New York: Penguin, 2009.

Scott-Smith, Giles. 'Building a community around the Pax Americana: the US government and exchange programmes during the 1950s.' In Helen Laville and Hugh Wilford. Eds. *The US Government, Citizen Groups and the Cold War: The state-private network*. Abingdon: Routledge, 2006: 83–99

Scribner, Campbell F. 'American Teenagers, Educational Exchange, and Cold War Politics.' *History of Education Quarterly* 57, no. 4 (Nov 2017): 543–49. doi:10.1017/heq.2017.31

Shone, Tom. 'What price my family.' *The Guardian* Jun 27, 2009. https://www.theguardian.com/lifeandstyle/2009/jun/27/said-sayrafiezadeh-family-father

Sluga, Glenda and Julia Horne. Eds. 'Cosmopolitanism in World History.' Special issue *Journal of World History* 21, no. 3 (Sep 2010)

Sluga, Glenda. *Internationalism in the Age of Nationalism*. Philadelphia: University of Pennsylvania Press, 2013

Smith, George Washington. *A History of Illinois and Her People*. Chicago: American Historical Society, 1927.

Tournès, Ludovic and Giles Scott-Smith. *Global Exchanges: Scholarships and Transnational Circulations in the Modern World*. New York: Berghahn Books, 2017.

Van Vleck, Jenifer. *Empire of the Air: Aviation and the American Ascendency*. Cambridge: Harvard University Press, 2013.

Vaughans, Kirkland C. 'To Unchain Haunting Blood Memories: Intergenerational Trauma among African Americans.' In Jill Salberg and Sue Grand. Eds. *Wounds of History: Repair and Resilience in the Trans-Generational Transmission of Trauma*. London: Routledge, 2016: Chapter 11

Wala, Michael. 'Selling the Marshall Plan at Home: The Committee for the Marshall Plan to Aid European Recovery.' *Diplomatic History* 10, No. 3 (Summer 1986): 247–65

Walker, David and Agnieszka Sobocinska. Eds. *Australia's Asia: From Yellow Peril to Asian Century*. Perth: University of Western Australia Press, 2012.

Walters, Caroline. 'A Response to Sarah Kate Magee.' *Young Scholars in Writing* 11 (2015): 96–8

Wilford, Hugh. *The Might Wurlitzer: How the CIA Played America*. Cambridge Harvard University Press 2009

Yoder, Jon A. 'The United World Federalists: Liberals for Law and Order.' *American Studies* 13, no. 1 (Spring 1972): 109–29

Obituaries

Cleave, Maureen. by David Johnson. *The Guardian* Nov 10, 2021 https://www.theguardian.com/music/2021/nov/09/maureen-cleave-obituary

Gordon, Dorothy. *NYT* May 12, 1970, https://www.nytimes.com/1970/05/12/archives/dorothy-gordon-81-moderator-of-times-youth-forums-is-dead-started.html

Kovalsky, Michael. *The Atlanta Journal-Constitution*, May 16, 2020, Legacy.com, https://www.legacy.com/us/obituaries/atlanta/name/michael-kovalsky-obituary?id=16765379

Mulumba, David. *Diaspora Messenger* Oct 22, 2018, https://diasporamessenger.com/2018/10/death-announcement-professor-david-mulumba-montclair-nj/

Nasmith, Augustus (Gus). *Rutland Herald* Feb 19, 2019, https://www.rutlandherald.com/obituaries/augustus-nasmith-jr/article_4c85fb36-3ee9-5b0f-9e5f-5042ecbc4961.html

Price, Martine. *Hartford Courant* Oct 16, 2011 https://www.courant.com/breaking-news/hc-xpm-2011-10-16-hc-exlife-1009-20111016-story.html

von Kloberg, Edward. by Joel Brinkley. 'Edward von Kloberg III, Lobbyist for Many Dictators, Dies at 63.' *NYT* May 4, 2005, https://www.nytimes.com/2005/05/04/politics/edward-von-kloberg-iii-lobbyist-for-many-dictators-dies-at-63.html

Wallace, Walter A. *Princeton Alumni Weekly* Jan 13, 2016, https://paw.princeton.edu/article/memoriam-walter-l-wallace

Watt, Donald B Watt. https://www.washingtonpost.com/archive/local/1977/11/28/donald-b-watt/d8f81d13-16ef-4e77-8e9f-c7f1e8f6600b/ *NYT* Sep 8, 1934, p. 17

Whitney, John Hay. *NYT*, Feb 9, 1982, https://www.nytimes.com/1982/02/09/obituaries/john-hay-whitney-dies-at-77-publisher-led-in-many-fields.html

Encyclopedia entries

'Dedo Difie Agyarko-Kusi' Wikipedia https://en.wikipedia.org/wiki/Dedo_Difie_Agyarko-Kusi

'Greta Thunberg.' *Britannica*, https://www.britannica.com/biography/Greta-Thunberg

'Harold Lasswell.' *Britannica* https://www.britannica.com/biography/Harold-Lasswell;

'Krisantha Weerasuriya.' Duke-NUS Medical School, https://www.duke-nus.edu.sg/core/about/people-leadership/core-visiting-experts/krisantha-weerasuriya

'Maureen Cleave.' Wikipedia https://en.wikipedia.org/wiki/Maureen_Cleave

'Victoria Hochberg.' Wikipedia https://en.wikipedia.org/wiki/Victoria_Hochberg;

Theses and Unpublished Manuscripts

Aloreibi, Abed B. and Michael D Carey. 'English in Libya.' unpublished ms

Bishop, Catherine. '" Worthwhile Trace of Myself": Teenage Autobiographies of the New York Herald Tribune World Youth Forum 1947–1972.' seminar paper, Australian National University Biography Workshop, 2023

Blake, William. 'The World They Wanted: The Japanese Delegation in the World Youth Forum.' MA dissertation, University of Oregon, 2022

Dennis, J. 'Prior review in the high school newspaper: Perceptions, practices, and effects.' dissertation, University of Georgia, 2007

Gardner, Mabel. 'Helen Hiett: The Ambition, Agency and Accomplishments of a Female Scholar, Journalist and Second World War Correspondent.' conference paper, International Graduate Historical Studies Conference, Central Michigan University, 2019

Konkle, Bruce. 'A Preliminary Overview of the Early History of High School Journalism in the US 1775–1925.' conference paper, AEJMC summer conference, Washington, D.C., Aug 2013. https://quillandscroll.org/wp-content/uploads/2014/01/A-Preliminary-Overview-of-the-Early-History-of-High-School-Journalism-in-the-U.S.-1775-1925-.pdf.

Lathrop, John Clarke. 'Promotion of International Understanding Through the Exchange of High School Students: A Project of the Metropolitan School Study Council Providing Exchange Visits Between American, Latin American and Scandinavian Students.' PhD thesis, Advanced School of Education, Columbia University, 1948

Levitan, Stuart Dean. 'Fourth Estate and Chief Executive A Study of Private and Public Relations.' senior thesis New College, Jun 1975, Box 12, Ron Nessen Papers, Gerald R Ford Presidential Library, https://www.fordlibrarymuseum.gov/library/document/0204/1511781.pdf

Richter, Maurice N. 'Camp Rising Sun 1929–1918.' unpublished ms.

Shannon, Matthew K. 'Losing Hearts and Minds: American-Iranian Relations and International Education During the Cold War.' Phd Thesis, Temple University May 2013

Soeterik, Sonja Marieke. 'Re-Entry Adjustment of High School Exchange Students to New Zealand: cross-cultural transition within a loss and grief framework.' Master of Science thesis, Massey University 1998

Van Hout, Tom. 'Life is a pitch: self-presentation in the age of corporate speak.' Symposium on International Business Communication 2015. https://www.wu.ac.at/fileadmin/wu/d/bizcomm/05_Symposien/Symposium_2015/Abstract_VanHout.pdf.

Workum, Emily Lyon (Lee). 'Mechanisms Exposed in Cross-National Experiences: A Study Based on New York Herald Tribune Forums, 1954–1961.' MA Thesis, Columbia University 1961

Websites & Blogs

Abeyagunawardene, Lakshman. 'A Friendship that has stood the Test of Time.' Ceylon-Ananda Blog, Apr 22, 2017, http://ceylon-ananda.com/a-friendship-that-has-stood-the-test-of-time/

American Field Service (AFS). https://afs.org

Bishop, Catherine. 'Filming the World We Want.' Parts 1 & 2 IULMIA Blog 2020 https://blogs.libraries.indiana.edu/filmarch/2020/06/25/filming-the-world-we-want-part-1/

Clark, Helen. 'Speech at the Renaming of Minsk School #130 in Honor of Ruth Waller.' United Nations Development Programme, Apr 25, 2016. Accessed Jun 28 2020 https://www.undp.org/content/undp/en/home/presscenter/speeches/2016/04/25/helen-clark-speech-at-the-renaming-of-minsk-school-130-in-honor-of-ruth-waller-minsk-belarus.html

Comments, 1957 High School Debate, Nigeria, Ethiopia, Ghan, South Africa. Prejudice pt 1, https://www.youtube.com/watch?v=840XWjnt9wc;

Comments, 1958 High school exchange students: Brazil, Ethiopia, Italy, South Africa 'How do you view Americans?' https://www.youtube.com/watch?v=1NDrq73h7To;

Cross, Richard. 'Teacher Memories.' 1958 http://www.dwightmorrow58.com/class_custom8.cfm

Esposito, Mike. 'Susana Donoso reflects.' Latin Caribbean Travel Blog. Dec 4, 2011, http://latin-caribbean-travelblog.blogspot.com/2011/12/susana-donoso-who-participated-in.html

IWA (Institute of World Affairs). 'IWA History.' http://www.iwa.org/history/.

Kuriki, Maya. 'History-Mission.' The Experiment in International Living Sep 15, 2021, https://www.experiment.org/history-mission/

Legal Defense Fund (LDF). 'A Revealing Experiment: Brown v. Board and "the Doll Test".' https://www.naacpldf.org/ldf-celebrates-60th-anniversary-brown-v-board-education/significance-doll-test/

Louis August Jonas Foundation. 'What We Do.' http://www.lajf.org/what-we-do.

MacJannet Foundation. https://www.macjannet.org

NYC New York City Department for the Aging, 'Stimulus at Work.' http://home.nyc.gov/html/ops/nycstim/html/stimulus/osei.shtml (Accessed 2016).

Salzburg Global Seminar. 'Who We Are.' & 'Our history.' https://www.salzburgglobal.org/about/

US Mission Belarus. 'US Embassy, UN and Belarusians Remember International Relief Worker Ruth Waller.' Aug 7, 2019, https://by.usembassy.gov/u-s-embassy-un-and-belarusians-remember-international-relief-worker-american-ruth-waller/;

Contemporary Publications

American Council for Nationalities. *Americans Abroad: Spokesmen for the United States.* New York: American Council for Nationalities Service, 1959

Blechman, Michael D. 'Valentina Titova Bourgeoisie and Proletariat'. *The Harvard Crimson*, Nov 12, 1960. https://www.thecrimson.com/article/1960/11/12/valentina-titova-bourgeoisie-and-proletariat-pwhat/

Congressional Record: Proceedings and Debates of the 81st Congress First Session, Appendix, Volume 95, Part 13, Mar 14, 1949 to May 10, 1949, (Washington: US Government Printing Office, 1949), https://books.google.com.au

Frankel, Charles. 'Cultural Affairs Officer: The Man in the Middle.' *International Educational and Cultural Exchange* Winter 1966: 1–13

Fuchs, Lawrence H. 'The World Federation Resolution: A Case Study in Congressional Decision-Making.' *Midwest Journal of Political Science* 1, No. 2 (Aug 1957): 151–62, www.jstor.org/stable/2109078

Getty Images, caption, photo of Helen Hiett Sep 25, 1940, Getty Images https://www.gettyimages.com.au/detail/news-photo/quite-unusual-is-the-distinction-of-helen-hiett-she-is-the-news-photo/515181362;

Golden, William in *the Polygon* (Polytechnic Preparatory Country Day School newspaper, Brooklyn NY), Oct 9 1970

Grogan, Peter. 'Australian Lad Attends US Youth Forum.' *The ABC Weekly* (Australia) Feb 23, 1952, 8–9.

Hiett, Helen. *No Matter Where*. New York: E.P. Dutton & Co., 1944.

Huffman, Robert S. 'The World Youth Forum.' *International Educational and Cultural Exchange* 6, no. 3 (Winter 1971): 47–54

Institute of International Education. *Open Doors 1973: Report on International Exchange*. New York: Institute of International Education, 1973. http://files.eric.ed.gov/fulltext/ED091958.pdf

Livengood, WW. Ed. *Americana Taught to the Tune of a Hickory Stick*. Women's National Book Association, 1954

Louw, Eline. *In My Voorterkkerrok Voor Die* Wêreld. Johannesburg: Afrikaanse Pers Boekhandel, 1954

Papanek, Ernst. 'American Youth for World Youth: Social Interest in Kilpatrick's Concept of Education.' *Educational Theory* 16, no. 1 (Jan 1966): 59–70

Porter, Joan. 'A Voice Is Heard.' *The American Girl* 35, no. 5 (May 1952)

Portillo, Michael. 'World Youth Meeting.' *Trends in Education*, Oct 28, 1972: 47–50 books.google.com

Slappey, George H. 'The Youth Forum as a Means of Teaching Civics.' *The Social Studies* 30, no. 1 (1939): 33–4

Spencer, Richard E and Ruth Awe. *International Educational Exchange: A Bibliography*, New York: Institute of International Education, 1970

Sussman, Jody. 'United States Information Service Libraries.' *University of Illinois Graduate School of Library Science Occasional Papers* 111 (Dec 1973) https://www.ideals.illinois.edu/bitstream/handle/2142/3815/gslisoccasionalpv00000i00111.pdf?sequence=1

Suter, Ann C. *Labor Law and Practice in the Empire of Ethiopia*. Bureau of Labor Statistics Report No 298, US Dept of Labor, 1966

US BECA: Bureau of Educational and Cultural Affairs. *Educational and Cultural Diplomacy, 1960*. Washington D.C.: US Department of State Publications, 1961. www.books.google.com.au

US BECA. *Educational and Cultural Diplomacy, 1962*. Washington D.C.: US Department of State Publications, 1963. www.books.google.com.au

US BECA. 'History and Mission of ECA.' https://eca.state.gov/about-bureau/history-and-mission-eca

US BECA. *International Exchange: Leaders for Tomorrow. A Review of US Programs for Foreign Students'*, Washington D.C.: US Department of State Publications, 1971 https://files.eric.ed.gov/fulltext/ED055525.pdf

US BECA. *International Exchange 1967*. Washington D.C.: US Department of State Publications, 1968. https://files.eric.ed.gov/fulltext/ED019914.pdf

US BECA. *International Exchange 1969*. Washington D.C.: US Department of State Publications, 1970. https://files.eric.ed.gov/fulltext/ED042395.pdf

US Court of Appeals. Williams v Howard Johnson's Inc Jul 4, 1959, 4 Cir., 268 F.2d 845 https://casetext.com/case/williams-v-howard-johnsons-restaurant

US Court of Appeals. Williams v Howard Johnson's Inc Nov 2, 1962, 2432 210 F. Supp. 295 https://www.anylaw.com/case/williams-v-howard-johnson-s-inc/e-d-virginia/11-02-1962/IJYGRGYBTlTomsSBHIqz

US Department of State. 'NYHT Forum for High Schools March 4, 1950.' *The Record: Department of State International Exchange* VI no. 3 (May-Jun 1950): 24–7. https://books.google.com.au

US Department of State. *International Educational Exchange Program 1948–1858*. Washington D.C.: US Department of State Publications, 1958 https://books.google.com.au

Wollstadt, Roger, 'Millbrun—Rasul Nizam with Loyd and David (1954).' Flickr, https://www.flickr.com/photos/24736216@N07/5941766114

Yearbooks on ancestry.com: Pekin High School; Somerville High School; *Stella Maris College, Madras*

Newspapers & Magazines

New York Herald Tribune (NYHT)
New York Times (NYT)
Pan Am. *The Clipper Pan American World Airways Teacher*
Scholastic Magazines. *Scholastic Voice*, 1946–1981; *Junior Scholastic*, 1937–2011
TWA. *Skyliner*
US Department of State. *The Record*
Others: Australia: *Adelaide News; Daily News* Perth; *Herald* Melbourne; US: *Anniston Star* AL; *El Paso Times* TX; *Evening Observer* Dunkirk NY; *Hastings News* NY; *Jerusalem Post* NY; *Kingston Daily Freeman* NY; *Monocle* Richmond VA; *Morning Call* Allentown PA; *Philadelphia Tribune* PA; *Public Opinion* PA; *Shopper News* Paramus NJ; *Stars and Stripes* Europe edition; *The Journal News* White Plains NY; *The Times and Daily News Leader* San Mateo CA; *The Washington Post* DC

Films

Aidi, Hisham & Sophie Schrago. 'Malcolm X and the Sudanese.' 2020, https://vimeo.com/394471323

Buenaventura, Daniel. 'I talk about my grandfather Johnny Antillon.' youtube https://www.youtube.com/watch?v=kE6iMbhe0qg

Hall, Richard & Catherine Bishop. 'The World We Wanted.' Nerds Make Media, 2022, https://www.nerdsmakemedia.com/confoundinghistory
The *Herald Tribune* 5th High School Forum 1950: The World We Want, Documentary F548 https://www.youtube.com/watch?v=QtUPq17p7cs
Marshall Plan 50th Anniversary', May 28, 1997, https://www.c-span.org/video/?84942-1/marshall-plan-50th-anniversary
New York Times Youth Forum 1956 episode: 'Are trust territories becoming independent?' https://www.youtube.com/watch?v=b8oKL1Fh74s&t=149s
See also in archives: IULMIA and NARA

Archival Sources

(ADST) The Association for Diplomatic Studies and Training

Foreign Affairs Oral History Project, https://adst.org
  Phillip W Pillsbury Jr, Interview by Charles Stuart Kennedy, Feb 28, 1994, https://www.adst.org/OH%20TOCs/Pillsbury,%20Phillip.toc.pdf
  Robert A. Lincoln, Interview by G. Lewis Smith Apr 19, 1989, 'Ceylon-Sri Lanka Country Reader', https://adst.org/Readers/Ceylon-Sri%20Lanka.pdf

(AFSCA) American Friends Service Committee Archives, Philadelphia

General Admin, Programs at the UN, Seminars, *Herald Tribune* Forum Files https://www.afsc.org/project/archives

(Arkansas) University of Arkansas Library Special Collections

Bureau of Educational and Cultural Affairs (BECA) Historical Collection (MC 468
Group VIII Cooperating Agencies Series 1 Agencies
  B219/F17 New York Herald Tribune Youth Forum
  B220/F28 The Teenage Student Exchange Program

Brethren Historical Library and Archives, Elgin

International Christian Youth Exchange (ICYE) Series 13 B10/F7

(HTWYFAA) *Herald Tribune* World Youth Forum Alumni Association

www.htwyfaa.org
Oram Report: Sidney W. Green, Oram Associates, to Board of Trustees, World Youth Forum, 'Interim Report,' Jun 8, 1968

(LOC) Library of Congress Washington D.C.

Reid Family Papers MSS 65491
Part I HRR papers 1899–1970: Box I D237 F12770: NYHT Forum 1932
Part II NY HT 1913–1973 Box II
  Miscellaneous 1936–7: F31/4
  Forum 1946: F43/7; F44/1–8

Forum 1947: F44/9–10; F45/1–7; F46/1–5
Forum 1948: F46/6–7; F47/1–2
Forum 1949: F47/7–8; F48/1
Forum 1950: F48/2–5
Forum 1952: F48/6–8

Indiana University Library Archive

United World Federalists mss., 1928–1988 'Finding Aid' https://webapp1.dlib.indiana.edu/findingaids/view?doc.view=entire_text&docId=InU-Li-VAB8237

(IULMIA) Indiana University Library Moving Image Archive

'The World We Want' and 'Young Worlds' Films Collection https://collections.libraries.indiana.edu/IULMIA/exhibits/show/the-world-we-want/full-episodes-gallery

Miami University Libraries

Pan American World Airways Records, Digital Collections https://digitalcollections.library.miami.edu/digital/collection/asm0341

(NARA) National Archives, Washington DC

Record Group 59: General Records of the Department of State
    Background Files on Youth and Teenagers Programs. 1955–1968
        B1 EDX 11 1966 & 1967
    Central Decimal Files 1910–1963: Death Reports of US Citizens Abroad
        Helen Waller Death Report in Box 0392 (on ancestry.com)
    Series P 229 Issues of 'VOA Radio News' and Related Materials
        B2 Far East: Delegates to the NYHT Forum
Record Group 306: Records of the US Information Agency:
    Moving Images Relating to US Domestic and International Activities
        306.2269 Operation Columbus: 1949 Forum (copied by Richard Hall 2021)
            https://www.youtube.com/watch?v=_qdR2r-I0as&t=1s
        306.2083/ Herald Tribune Youth Forum (1950) (Copied by Richard Hall 2022)
            https://www.youtube.com/watch?v=Kkg8JeNrqBs&t=856s
        306.256 Youth Forum: Film 1952 NYHT Youth Forum (copied by Richard Hall 2022) https://www.youtube.com/watch?v=Haha2h5JcmM
    Production Library Audio Recordings
        Young Worlds 1965 Episodes 2, 3, 4, 5, 6, 9, 11, 13
        Young Worlds 1966 Episodes 5, 6
        Young Worlds 1967 Episode 18

(NMAH) National Museum of American History at Smithsonian

John J. Brooks-Clarks, Acceptance letter for Minnijean Brown, 1958 https://transcription.si.edu/view/23322/NMAH-RWS2015-07996

Sarah Lawrence College Archives (SLC), New York

Community Sponsored Events on Campus Collection 1932–1987 Box 1, *NYHT* World Youth Forum

Smith College, Northampton Sophia Smith Collection
Helen Hiett Waller Papers, 1838–1958, MS 273

Syracuse University Libraries Special Collections Research Center
Herbert C. Hunsaker Papers, Box 11

Tufts University Archives
Donald and Charlotte MacJannet Papers MS 024
    B138 World Youth Forum
    B74/F1 World Youth Forum Slides

US Department of State Office of the Historian Historical Documents
National Security Council, 'Statement of US Policy Towards Libya', Washington, Mar 15, 1960 Document 339, Volume XIII, Foreign Relations of the United States 1958–1960, https://history.state.gov/historicaldocuments/frus1958-60v13/d339

Wisconsin Historical Society State Archives
National Educational Television (NET) records, 1951–1970. U.S. Mss 66AF
    B53/F2 *NYHT* Annual Forum
    B78/F1 The World We Want Printed Materials 1953–1960

Yale University Library, Manuscripts and Archives
John Hay Whitney and Betsy Cushing Whitney Family Papers (MS 1938) Series I
    B147/F2 & F3 'World Youth Forum 1961–1967'
John Hay Whitney Foundation Records (MS 1952)
Ogden Reid Paper (MS 755) Part II *Herald Tribune* 1950–1958,
    Series II: B51/F609 'Helen Walker [sic] (HT, Forum)'
    Series IV:
        B93/F197 'Forum: general correspondence and memoranda'
        B94/F198 'Forum: general correspondence and memoranda'
        B94/F199 Forum: general correspondence and memoranda'
        B94/F200 Forum Program Committee
Richard Kluger Papers (MS 1443) Series I: B6/F131 'Huffman, Robert'

Privately held papers

Ali: Raza Ali (Pakistan 1961)
Ansary: Cyrus Ansary (Iran 1950)
Calvo: Luis Calvo (Cuba 1947) (held by daughter Nilda Cravens)
Cohen-Mintz: Daphna Rabowitz (Cohen-Mintz) (Israel 1957)
Courtin: Dorothy Chen (Courtin) (Malaya 1962)
Davis: Stella Davis (USIS) (held by Coleman Family)

Doaudi: Yvette Daoudi (Switzerland 1969)

Dutt: Probal Kumar Dutt (India 1953) (held by Dutt family)

Eriksson: Irjaleena Lammi (Eriksson) (Finland 1957)

Glen Doepel: Josephine Glen Doepel (Australia 1953) (held by Spratt family)

Harrington: Eileen Gallagher (Harrington) (Summer Leader)

Hennig: Jutta Hennig (Germany 1969)

Huffman: Robert Huffman (Forum Director) (held by daughter Susan Boal)

Johansen: Thor Hjorth Johansen (Norway 1948) (held by daughter Grete)

Johnstone: Bruce Johnstone (Canada 1961)

Kerbage: Gladys Kerbage (Lebanon 1956) (held by daughter Hala Achkar)

Kimpton: Helga Thorne (Kimpton) (UK 1964)

Leonetti: Stella Leonetti (Italy 1969)

Nasmith: Gus Nasmith (US 1962, Staff) (held by author)

Osman: Ahmed Osman (Sudan 1960)

Roberts: Ceridwen Roberts (UK 1967)

Salazar: Meliton and Araceli Salazar (Philippines 1950, 1953) (held by Salazar Family)

Scott: Alison McEwan (Scott) (UK 1960)

Seglen: Per Seglen (Norway 1961)

Tafari: Nebiat Tafari (Ethiopia 1956) (held by son Haddis Tafari)

Warner: Suzanne Reeder (Warner) (UK 1962)

Yuen: Yuen Chooi Yeng (Singapore 1959) at Odds & Collectables, Singapore.

Interviews with people other than delegates
(For a list of Delegates see Appendix 2)

Alan Bodnar (Summer 1965) Feb 3, 2021; Burt, Brody, (Host 1959) (interviewed by Pamela Hull);Ginger da Silva (Summer 1964 & leader) May 7–10, 2018; Nina Fieldsteel, (Host 1969) Jun 26, 2016; Joan Furth, nee Layton (Forum Assistant) Jun 3, 2016; Joy Gillies, nee Reydel Feb 18, 2020; Eileen Harrington, nee Gallagher (Summer leader) Aug 28, 2018; Pamela Jacklin (Summer leader) Aug 3, 25, 31, 2022; Robert Koslow (Host 1966) Jun 9 2016; Roger Lang (Host 1967) Jan 21, 2022; Howard Liebman (Summer 1970) Aug 8, 2022; Kathy Low (Summer 1972) May 27, 2016; Maria Manhattan, nee Scataccio (Summer 64) Feb 19, 2021; Orel Protopopescu, nee Odinov (Summer 1964) Jan 25, 2022; Sylvia Stedman, nee Abraham (Forum Assistant) Jul 24, 2018; Margaret Waller Jun 25, 2020; Mark Waller Jul 7, 2020; John Whitaker, (NZ AFS 1973) Feb 18, 2021; Peter Workum, Jun 29, 2016

Emails with people other than delegates

Susan Boal, Daniel Brent, Mel Citrin, Connie Freeman, Graeme Gainsford, Ellen Goldblatt, Gary Houston, Clifford Jacobs, Rick Kessler, Anders Mellbourn, Glenn Pantel, Robin Room, Stephen Schwebel, Clifford Stevens, Jinx Watson.

General Index

For references to a particular country's delegates see also individual names in the Index of People.

Afghanistan 85, 347
Africa 63, 64, 82, 100, 155, 163, 175, 185–94, 200, 210–1, 233, 239, 243–5, 248, 2, 309–10
African Americans 12, 14, 26, 55, 146, 190–4
   Delegates 87, 255–6
   Hosts 96, 104, 123–4, 134
   Staff 12, 39–40
Alumni 282–300
   Alumni Association/Reunions 1–2, 6–8, 245, 282–302
   Careers 245–50
   Continued connections 7, 34–5, 41–2, 172, 269, 307
   Donors 270–2, 277
   Emigration & brain drain debate 238–45, 254, 296, 299, Appendix 1
   Forum volunteers 41–3, 53, 72, 86, 117, 144, 155, 158, 209, 273, 370
American Field Service (AFS) exchange 17–20, 77, 106, 116–7, 120, 261, 269, 272, 277–80, 344, 351
American Friends Service Committee (AFSC) 69, 95–6, 140, 150
Antisemitism & Holocaust 115, 127, 189, 256, 260, 266, 368
Apartheid 88, 92, 115, 163–5, 185–8, 235–6, 311
Arab countries/Middle East 11, 59, 63, 67–8, 85
   Problems with delegates 67–8, 131, 182–3
Arab–Israeli conflict 3, 16, 64–8, 98, 110, 146, 150, 157, 163–6, 178–86, 207, 234–8, 243, 246, 295, 298, 306, 308, 311
Argentina 65, 111, 167, 232, 235
Asia 11, 51, 63–5, 75, 99, 110, 135, 146, 156, 175–8, 199, 221, 231, 239, 243–5, 248
Atomic energy/bomb 10, 18, 66, 170, 82, 110, 146, 163
Australia 15, 59, 63, 76, 78, 83–5, 114–5, 155, 235, 239, 248

Vietnam War & 88, 165, 176–7
Race 65, 79, 165, 194–5
Austria 15, 38, 65, 78, 85, 114, 187, 258, 292

Belgium 69, 84
Bolivia 85
Brazil 65, 85, 194, 306
Burma 64–5, 85, 129, 172

Cambodia 64, 69, 175, 234
Camp Rising Sun 76, 340
Canada 11, 15, 189, 199, 205
Central America 11, 62, 189
Central Intelligence Agency (CIA) 35, 51–2, 66, 171–2, 208, 278, 302–4
   World Assembly of Youth 51, 346
Ceylon 64, 66, 84–5, 114, 222, 242, 249
China 68, 146, 162, 171, 174–6, 279, 359
Civil rights (US) 3, 5, 14, 42, 54, 97, 107, 124, 169, 177, 188–94, 211, 255
Cold War 2–6, 17–21, 65, 68, 120, 157, 170–6, 195, 208
   Cultural Cold War & Forum 4–5, 19–24, 44, 120, 133–4, 215, 301–5, 310–13
Columbia Broadcasting System (CBS) 46, 255, 268, 281, 347, 368, 370
Communism 2, 6, 146–7, 163, 170–6, 205, 215, 264
   Anti-Communism 16, 21–22, 37, 50, 66, 93, 158, 163, 173–4, 183, 198–9, 233–4, 264–5
   Countries at Forum 22, 62, 68–9, 266–70
   McCarthyism 5, 12, 18, 170–3, 199
   World Festival of Youth & Students 21–3
Cuba 63, 93, 107, 171
Cyprus 64
Czechoslovakia 18, 22, 68, 80, 215, 264–5

Daily Mail World Youth Forum xv, 34, 80, 349

Decolonization & independence 55, 64, 66, 100, 175–6, 187, 194, 199, 210–1, 214, 225, 236, 245, 278

Delegates
  Activism 66, 171, 177, 190–1, 193–4, 234
  Celebrity Status 141, 154, 197–8, 208, 224, 229–32, 308
  Drinking, smoking, drugs 91, 97, 100, 200, 223–5
  Governments/embassies 121, 129, 165–6, 173, 180–1, 200, 204, 265, 287
  Political consequences for 88, 162, 180–1, 185, 195, 234–8, 250, 308
  Problems at Forum 106–7, 121, 129–31, 181–4, 199, 221–3, 237, 307–10
  Public performances, national costumes 64, 85, 107–18, 140–68, 197–9
  Selection 70–89, 92, 133, 183
  Sex, love affairs, dating 136, 219–23, 286–7
  US colleges 42, 60, 76, 138, 164, 172, 228, 238–45, 265–6, 285
  Youth culture 93–4, 96, 100, 108–9, 134, 213–228, 287

Democracy (US) 2, 4, 9, 98, 102, 110, 120, 229, 311
  Challenged 167, 170–71, 175
  Endorsed 16–21, 171–73, 183, 231
  Free speech & 2, 21, 29, 143, 146, 162, 168, 215
  Promoted by Forum 5, 24, 28–9, 52, 95–6, 158, 264, 301, 305

Denmark 53–4, 63, 113, 258

Ecuador 114

Egypt 57, 63, 67, 179, 182, 190, 207, 225,

El Salvador 63

Ethiopia 84, 142, 188, 243, 309

Europe 3, 5, 17, 110, 128, 137, 207–9,
  Alumni 284–5, 288–91, 296,
  Discussion topic 16, 145, 155–7, 161, 178, 187, 194, 299–300
  Huffman 38, 273–4
  Prejudice 99, 230, 306
  Waller 25–8, 48–9, 208

Exchange programs 5, 15–18, 47, 57, 65, 68–9, 76–7, 83, 98, 117, 121, 136, 167, 173, 242, 250, 271–2, 277–8, 291, 312

Experiment in International Living 17–8, 36, 69, 120, 272, 344, 368

Feminism & women's rights 3, 11–4, 35–27, 29, 166–7, 194, 197, 250, 311

Finland 22, 173

Ford Foundation 56–7, 205

Forum
  Celebrities at 2, 30–1, 193–4, 203–5, 218, 311
  Countries represented 62–70, Appendix 1
  Discussion topics 169–95
  Oram Report 4, 88, 268–70, 282, 288, 305
  Speakers at 10, 13, 97, 145–50, 201–3, 211, 275, 280

Forum Aims 2–6
  Internationalist network 2–3, 5, 9, 18, 20–1, 26–8, 35, 44, 50–2, 77–8, 96, 134, 195, 228, 245–51, 275, 282, 302, 305–7, 310
  Containment 11, 16–17, 19–20, 88, 304–05
  Education 23–4, 35, 59–60, 102–18, 127, 142, 145, 148, 152–3, 160, 167–8, 206, 252–80 passim, 304–5

Forum Board of Trustees 37, 253, 270–81, 370

Forum Directors 25–43, 52, 57, 65, 168, 169, 205, 273

Forum Field Trips 2, 9, 42, 48, 52, 59, 105, 125, 139, 189, 192, 196–212, 221–5, 240, 253

Forum Finale 2, 44–6, 53, 103, 116, 140, 144–51, 169, 172, 175, 182, 203, 236, 275, 304, 308

Forum Funding 29, 38–60, 122, 268–81
  Sponsors & 3, 7, 117, 135, 141, 149, 160, 196–9, 209, 212, 254–5, 305

Forum Impact 47–9, 145, 301–12
  On Americans 115–8, 128, 133–9
  On Delegates 212, 215, 228–51, 255, 263–7
  International 53–4, 57, 143–4

Forum Orientation Program 36, 38, 41–2,

46, 56–8, 92, 94–101, 112, 140–1, 150, 162, 220

Forum Staff 38–41, 95, 104, 256, 272–4, 370

Forum TV debates, 2, 6, 46, 59, 97, 103, 135, 152–68, 175, 178–80, 185–7, 208, 219, 224, 237, 275–7, 304–6, 309–10, Appendix 1

France 65–6, 94, 109, 126, 208–9, 259–60, 288–9, 295

Gender & gendered experiences 4, 15, 75–6, 83–6, 122, 155, 169, 178–9, 246–9, Appendix 1

Germany 18, 52, 65, 78, 170, 175, 189, 208–9, 257–9

Ghana 66, 92, 152, 185, 187–8, 209–11, 241–4

Greater Metropolitan Forum/Program 36, 46, 87, 117–8, 158, 252–3, 274

Greece 1, 79, 114, 283, 289

Guatemala 65, 79

Haiti 15, 63, 189

Honduras 63

Hong Kong 64

Host families/students 38, 57, 62, 75, 94–5, 99, 108, 119–39, 143–9, 154, 199, 204–6, 217–23, 270, 280, 304
    continued contact & 240, 244, 284–92, 302
    Problems with 106, 109, 177, 179, 182–3, 306, 308
    Race & 96, 189, 192–5
    Summer Forum 254–5, 257, 263, 265

Host schools 2, 34, 55–6, 69, 102–18, 140, 144, 159, 172–3, 179, 189–93, 228–9, 274–9, 301, 304

Iceland 55, 59, 65, 113, 165–6, 169

Imperialism 17, 157, 176, 236, 310

India 1, 13, 64, 66, 78, 84, 93, 114, 121, 140, 155, 214, 225, 293

Indonesia 51, 64, 66, 81, 171, 224, 233

International Christian Youth Exchange (ICYE) 18, 20, 272, 277

Investors Overseas Service (IOS) 211–2, 270, 274

Iran 67, 69, 85, 174, 244

Iraq 67, 85, 182, 348

Israel 64, 67–8, 98, 150, 156, 163, 166, 184, 282, 295, 299
    Government & delegates 88, 165, 205, 207, 234–8, 308

Italy 65–6, 98, 258, 293, 296, 298

Jamaica 15, 347

Japan 65–6, 85, 110, 163, 215, 221

Jordan 67–8, 84–5, 93, 114, 131, 144, 179, 237, 243, 285

Kenya 55, 83, 185, 187, 242, 245

Korea 65, 69, 75, 171, 176, 221, 230

Korean War 18, 63, 170–1, 174, 176, 239

Lebanon 57, 67, 85, 178, 179, 184, 285

Luxembourg 64

Malaya/Malaysia 64, 85, 224, 245, 293

Marshall Plan 16, 32, 51, 63, 197, 231–2

Metropolitan School Study Council 56, 81, 102, 103

Mexico 65, 99

Morocco 65, 231

Nepal 64, 82–3, 239, 244, 299

Netherlands 80, 84, 113

New York Board of Education 23, 102, 107, 142

New York Daily Mirror Forum 14–16

New York Herald Tribune (*NYHT*) 11–3, 202, 268
    European Edition 34, 64, 205, 208–9, 212, 252, 259, 268, 289
    Forum for Current Problems/Women's Conference on Current Problems 13–4, 28–9, 38, 45–8, 145, 148, 150
    Forum sponsorship & benefits 3, 14, 24, 28–9, 35, 43–50, 60, 200
    Staff 12–3, 39, 48–9, 95, 141–2

New York Times & NYT Forum 16, 49, 158–60, 167–8, 268, 279

New Zealand xv, 63, 79, 84, 115, 141, 176, 187, 248

Nigeria 1, 66, 80, 163, 185, 188, 309
Norway 63, 113, 156

Pakistan 64, 111, 113-4, 134-6, 140, 167, 200, 231, 244
Pan Am & TWA 7, 37, 54-6, 69, 90-4, 141, 143, 204, 224, 236, 277, 356, 360
Panama 69
Peace Corps 97, 201-2
Philippines 15, 64, 76, 159, 169, 176, 225
Portugal 15, 64
Prejudice as Forum theme 135, 157, 169-70, 306, 309-10
President of the US 2, 13, 76, 93, 200-3, 231-2, 277, 306
Puerto Rico 106, 271

Racism & racial prejudice 96, 187-9, 194-5, 213
    Delegates 99, 142, 150, 190, 306
Rhodesia 64, 69, 78-9, 186, 188, 199, 211
Ryukyu Islands 64

Sarah Lawrence College 36-7, 40, 46, 56-8, 94-101, 117, 150, 180, 185, 205-7, 214, 240, 259, 344, 362
Segregation 2, 21, 39, 124, 142, 146, 185, 188-93, 196
Sexism 86, 98-9, 273
Singapore 1, 114, 141, 224, 293-4
South Africa 64, 78, 150, 163-4, 185-8, 235-6, 243, 293-4, 298, 308
South America 11, 16, 63, 79, 82, 205, 212, 219, 234, 239, 243-5, 363
Soviet Union/ USSR/ Russia 68-9, 109, 138, 166, 172-6, 190-1, 210, 264-5
Spain 69
Sudan 65, 84, 190, 233
Summer Forum 40, 46, 118, 158, 252-67, 285-7, 304
Sweden 63, 84-5
Switzerland 32, 65
Syria 67, 69, 85, 179, 182

Tanganyika 64, 193, 348

Tennessee Valley Authority (TVA) 144, 146, 159, 197-9, 212
Thailand 64, 85, 114, 134, 143-4, 153, 169, 176, 293

United Kingdom (UK) xv-xvi, 65-6, 74, 80, 100, 112-5, 153-5, 187, 203, 214, 203, 238-9, 260-1
United Nations (UN) 32, 89, 130, 190, 269
    Delegates' careers at 203, 245-9
    Destination 135, 164, 177, 202-3, 211, 236
    Discussion topic 71, 157, 162, 169-76 passim
    Speakers from 10, 15, 146-7, 203, 275
    UNA 36, 80, 189, 199, 205, 235
United States
    Delegates from 86-7, 100
    Delegates' Impressions of 3, 95, 107-15 119-40 passim, 142, 144, 152, 157, 213-29, 257, 279
    Delegates' Preconceptions about 76-7, 92-4
    Modernity & 18, 29, 54, 76, 93, 142-4, 152, 187, 196-8, 213-6
United States State Department/USIA/ USIS 18-23, 51, 68, 81, 93-6, 147, 174, 191, 285, 343
    Delegates as publicity for 6, 53-4, 127, 142-5,148, 197-8, 231, 303-4
    Funding for Forum 272, 278-9
    Non-financial support for Forum 3, 11, 18-22, 38, 47, 72-3, 87, 96, 188-91, 197-201, 208-10, 238, 278-80, 284, 302-4
    Selecting delegates 19-20, 50-4, 65
    Speakers from 97, 149, 259, 263-4
Uruguay 79

Venezuela 15, 63, 348
Vietnam 66, 76, 80, 115, 165
Vietnam War 3, 18, 131, 171-2, 176-8, 234-5, 240-1, 244, 269, 278, 307
    Anti-war activism 5, 88, 97, 115, 165, 201, 211, 235
Voice of America (VOA) 53, 140, 143, 150, 197, 239

Yemen 85
Youth 3, 38, 88, 158, 267, 310-2
  Activism of 3-5, 14, 38, 66, 157-8, 171, 177-8, 190, 192-3, 233, 263-5, 305, 310
  Cold War warriors 4-5, 11, 17-23, 51-4, 69, 153, 252, 310
  Forums for 14-7
  Hope for future, as 4, 11, 14, 27-8, 153, 310-2
  Teenagers & youth culture 3, 213-27, 306, 311

Youth for Understanding YFU 20, 277-9
Yugoslavia 10, 22, 66, 68, 115, 163, 171, 174-5, 263-4

Index of People

Plate numbers are in bold type.

Abbot, Mark (NZ 68) 78, 124, 217
Abraham, Sylvia (staff) 39, 95
Addae, Amelia (Ghana 57) xii, 92, 164, 188, 229
Adhikarya, Ronny (Indonesia 68) 77, 122, 137
Agonafir, Bizuayehu 'Bizu' (Ethiopia 59) 84, 188, 191
Agung, Anak 'Agung' Gde (Indonesia 67) 66, 127-8, 135-7, 171
Agyarko, Difie (Ghana 67) 66, 99, 163, 247
Ahe, Khin (Eva Daniels) (Burma 59) 129
Ahmed, Naila Aziz (Pakistan 58) 82, 113, 149, 158, 181-2, 202, 287, 288, 350, **3**
Ahmed, Nasreen Nazir (Pakistan 55) 82, 250, 286, 350, **3**
Ajluni, Raja 'Roger' Mafouz (Jordan 54) 179, 180, 243, **48**
Akhund, Hameeda (Pakistan 52) 30, 41, 79, 90, 114, 129, 134, 140, 218, 249, 285
Akindele, Jacob O (Nigeria 67) 99, 163, 185
Akinyemi, Akinwande 'Bolaji' (Nigeria 62) **24, 28**
Alfonso, Pedro Jose (Chile 61) 75
Ali, Raza (Pakistan 61) 109, **14**
Allen, Zoe (UK 61) 81
Allison, Hope (Nigeria 59) 230, 233

Alper, Barbara (Summer 64) **45**
Altuzarra, Philippe (France 69) 214
Amber, Maria 'Jeanne' (Indonesia 72) **44**
Amoretti, Franca (Italy 60) 233
Andlinger, Gerhard (Austria 49, Board) 78, 271, 370
Andrews, Katherine (volunteer) 39, 273
Andrews, Lew (US 64) 40, 253, 273, 287, **45**
Ansary, Cyrus (Iran 50) 61-2, 197-8, 288
Antillon, Johnny (Philippines 54) 76, 155, 309
Aranki, Suheil Fuad I (Jordan 61) 236-7, 291
Ari, Gur Ben (Israel 55) 179, 207, 299, 360
Arshavsky, Zohar (Israel 56) 180, 236, **21**
Arsotegui, Hernan (Nicaragua 47) 288
Arzoglou, Iordanis 'Jordan' (Greece 60) 1, 289, 298, 344
Asa'd Ridwan, Salah Ahmed (Jordan 62) 179
Attia, Ahmed Ahmed (Egypt 58) 181, **23**
Auerbach, Nurit (Israel 54) 96, 115, 180, 236
Ayub, Rafia (Pakistan 59) 93, 111, 167
Aziz, Nadira (Pakistan 50) 144
Azzara, Denise (teacher) 107, **10**

Bacciagaluppi, Marco (Italy 49) 92, 109-10
Bakal, Vivian (Summer 68) 264

Balbaa, Nadia Adb-el-Salam (Egypt 59) 166, 229
Ball, Marie (host) 95, 138
Banerjee, Ashish (India 61) 98, 216, **14**
Bannerman, Alfred 'Nini' (Ghana 56) 187, 191, 229, 241, 244
Barakat, Akram Z (Jordan 55) 179
Bargman, Jorge (Uruguay 53) 42, 79, 111, 142, 216, 218, **48**
Baron, Lynn (US 60) 209–10, 224, 226
Barrett, Winnifred 'Winni' & Leslie 'Barry' (AFSC) 95
Bassani, Marcella (Italy 58) 137, **29**
Bazan, Gustavo (Argentina 70) 114, 295
Bedini, Diana (Italy 57) 112, 232, 365
Belafonte, Harry 2, 203, 218, 275
Benitez, Jose Conrado (Philippines 60) **13**
Bergman, Ingrid (speaker) 2, 203
Berrivin, Regine (France 62) 196
Bertram, Christoph (Germany 56) 156, 161, 247, 294, 300, 360, 365
Bhagat, Dwarika Ram (Nepal 54) 82
Biedl, Annemarie (Austria 63) 93, 106–07, 122, 137, **51**
Bijur, Polly (Summer 67) 262
Binega, Mesfin (Ethiopia 57) 142, 188, 352
Bingol, Salih Sezgin (Turkey 56) 240, 366
Bishop, Ruth (IOS, Board) 295, 248, 279, 276, 281, 370
Bitz, Lynn (student) 149
Bliss, Robert (teacher) 279
Blum, Norma (Brazil 57) 142, 214
Bodner, Alan (Summer 65) 258
Bonderup, Ejvind (Denmark 59) 53–4, 119–20, 128, 137
Bossi, Ida (Italy 59) 234, 249, 290, **9**
Boury, Omar (Morocco 58) 181, **23, 29**
Braun Cantillo, Eduardo (Argentina 47) 91
Bray, Geraldine 'Gerry' (Rhodesia 60) 80, 108, 186, 188, 201, 210–1, 250, 289–91
Brent, Norma (staff) 39, 74
Brioschi, Francesco (Italy 56) 161
Bristow, Rosemary (host, speaker) 145

Brockman, Jeanne (staff) 39, 344
Brody, Burt (host) 119–20, 128, 137
Bromberg, Dave (staff) 40, 218
Brooks, Cora Vail (US 59) 86, 204, 288, 294, 302, **48, 49**
Brown, Minnijean 124
Brynhildsvoll, Liv (Norway 70) 126, 194
Burgess, Jona (Iceland 60) 55, 94–5, 113, 120, 150, 154, 165–6, 190, 202, 221, 250, 365, 366, **1**
Burgi, Peter S (Switzerland 49) 158
Calvo, Luis (Cuba 47) 82
Cameron, Barney (*NYHT*) 44, 48–9
Camporini, Vincenzo (Italy 64) 217, 300
Canada, Geoffrey (Summer 69) 255
Cao Duc, Thac (Vietnam 62) **4**
Cao Thi Phuong, Khanh (Vietnam 60) 233–4, 367
Carlestam, Jan (Sweden 48) 90
Carlstein, Tommy (Sweden 63) 287
Carrillo Garcia, Elba (Mexico 63) 221
Carter, Philip D (*NYHT*) 141–2, 221
Casper, Gerhard (Germany 54) 77, 115, 180, 189, 193, 286, 289, 344
Cassimatis, Emmanuel 'Manoli' (Greece 62) 114, 126, 295, 299, **28**
Charoenphol, Direk (Thailand 53) 107, 241, 344
Chatelain, Marcia 5
Chatt, Sara (UK 57) 92, 371
Chavanaviraj, Saroj (Thailand 58) 100, 131, 134, 137, 140, 149, 162, 169, 175, 200, 241–2, 349, **18**
Cheare, Curt (Austria 70) 290
Chehrazi, Shahla (Iran 63) 221
Chen, Dorothy (Malaya 62) 71, 248, 290, 292, **4, 28**
Cho, Sophie (Burma 52) 286
Choi, Sangmie (Korea 58) 149
Chowdhury, Farouk (Pakistan 65) 83
Christensen, Johnny (Denmark 48) 204
Church, Barbara (NZ 64) 249

Clark, Kate (host) 124, 134, 148
Clausager, Joergen Peder (Denmark 65) 258
Cleave, Maureen (UK 53) 155, 248, 357
Comba, Pietro (Italy 70) 80
Connolly, Nuala (Ireland 63) 954, 182
Contreras, Raul (Philippines 56) 80, 229, 288
Cooke, Stephen (US 71) 351
Cornfeld, Bernie (IOS) 270
Corry, Hazel Barbara (UK 48) 204
Counes, Anne (staff) 49, 55, 106, 198, 203, 224, 344
Cousins, Andrea (volunteer) 344, **48**
Crosa, Adolfo José (Argentina 59) 72, 167
Cross, Richard (student) 106
Cruz, Roman A (Philippines 55) 80

Da Silva, Ginger (Summer 64, Leader) 192, 253, 256–64, 273, 290–2, 296, 299, **45**
Daftari, Maryam (Iran 59) 166, 247
Danitanand, Chotima (Thailand 57) 201, 238
Daoudi, Yvette (Switzerland 69) **32**
Davis, Stella (USIS) 50
Dayan, Moshe 236–8
De Estrada, Tomas (Argentina 57) 7, 231
Dennis, Christian (France 70) 100
Desperbasques, Marta Mariana (Argentina 69) 82
Dhanapala, Jayantha (Ceylon 57) 144, 230, 246, 250, 302, 344
Di Nola, Marco (Italy 62) 257
Dietlin, Eric (France 60) 223
Dodson, Christine (staff) *See* Sifenou, Christine (Greece 53)
Donkoh, Bemma Baabo (Ghana 71) 247
Donoso, Susana (Ecuador 47) 114, 190
Dougherty, Frances Ann 55
Duarte, Sergio (Brazil 53)112, 247, 285, 302
Dubrovina, Ludmila (speaker) 172–3
Dulles, Eleanor Lansing 52, 208
Dulles, John Foster 19, 52, 208, 340
During, Sven Ingemar (Sweden 48) 94
Durra, Yasar (Jordan 59) 72, 93, 220–2, **39**

Dutt, Probal (India 53) 131, 155, 159, 214–6, 218, 225, **35**
Dzidzienyo, Lordsfield Anani 'Nani' (Ghana 60) 150, 190, 211, 221, 244, 344, 366

Eckerson, Ione (teacher) 106, 108
Ehrnrooth, Casimir (Finland 48) 110, 216
Eisenhower, Dwight 12, 53, 68, 201–2, 301, 304, 340, **37**
El-Aref, Farouk (Jordan 56) 230, **21**
El-Batal, Rabih (Syria 63) 182
El-Far, Mohamed 'Rifaat' (Egypt 55) 179, 360
El-Gammal, Raouf (Egypt 63) 182
Emilsdottir, Anna Katrin (Iceland 56) 226, 265
Engwirda, Maarten (Netherlands 61) 77, 80, 113, 200, 202, 292, **cover**
Ephraim, Pedro Tomas (Argentina 60) 232
Erlendsdóttir, Gudrún (Iceland 55) 219, 248
Erokwu, Evelyn (Nigeria 72) 87–88
Escudero, Leonor (Argentina 47) 232
Eshete, Andreas (Ethiopia 61) 216, 366
Esik, Robert (teacher) 279, 308
Esser, Paul Biery Jr (teacher) 105–07, 116
Etamesor, Nurein (Nigeria 68) 186, 350
Etheridge, Brian C 18
Evans, Lynn (Summer 67) 256
Ewald, Sabine (France 55) 284
Ewing, Donald 'Peter' (Australia 48) 108, 110, 174, 215

Fabrin, Ritva Aulikki (Finland 58) 124
Falck, Lucie (Norway 57) 120, 228, 248
Faulkner, William 21
Favier, Denis (France 61) 117
Fender, Patricia (UK 48) 108, 110
Fermi, Riccardo (Italy 67) 258
Fernandez, Pablo (Uruguay 47) 82
Fernando, P G K 'Gemunu' (Ceylon 60) 350, **14**
Fernando, Priyanthi (Ceylon 70) 249, 299
Fernando, Tissa (Ceylon 59) 125, 128, 167, 176, 200, 203, 214, 217, 350, **8**

Ferrer, Léon (Mexico 64) 99, 112, 284, 286, 289
Fieldsteel, Nina & Ira (host parents) 138
Fieldston, Sara 21, 120
Filippini, Paolo (Italy 55) 110–1, 360
Fisch-Thomsen, Niels (Denmark 57) 123, 229, 371
Fliakos, Constantinos 'Gus' (Greece 59) **9**
Flicker, Bernard (Summer Leader) 256, **45**
Folson, Marion B (speaker) 172, **15**
Fonseca, Rodolfo (Uruguay 62) 171, **28**
Freeman/Walker Connie (Staff, Summer Leader)129, 201, 205, 255–7, 262–3, 344
Fridfinnsson, Björn (Iceland 58) 169
Friedman, Doris 'Freddie' later Wolff (staff) 39, 41, 241
Fuchs, Stuart (Summer 64) **45**
Fuentes, Vicente (Mexico 67) 286

Ga'afer, Hussein Mohamed (Egypt 52) 117
Gadeish, Orit (Israel 67) 163, 218, 247, 284, 289
Gadir, Beshir Abdel (Sudan 58) 181, **23**
Gainsford, Graeme (*Mirror* Forum) 16
Gallagher, Eileen (Summer Leader) 255–6, 264–5
Gardolinski, Stella Maria (Brazil 64) 76
Gavigan, Teresa (NZ 72) 88, 108, 126, 349, **44**
Gevgilili, Ayzcr (Turkey 61) 117
Gimotea, Edgar (Philippines 59) 166, 171, 348
Gissis, Snait (Israel 61) 41, 88, 100, 180, 193, 207, 236–8, 308
Glen-Doeppel, Josephine (Australia 53) 43, 71, 77, 141, 349
Goetsch, Karin (Germany 61) 98
Golden, William (Summer 70) 264
Goll, Thelma (Liberia 53) 62, 308
Gordon, Dorothy Lerner (*NYT* Forum director) 16, 49, 158–9, 167
Gottlieb, Roger (Summer 64) **45**
Goulden, John (UK 59) 92, 110, 142, 159, 166, 204, 242–3, 246, 288, 294, 298, 300, 371–2

Grant, Barbara (AFSC) 95–6
Greif, Gerd (Germany 58) 30
Greig, David (NZ 65) 214
Güclüyildiz, Hasan (Turkey 59) 166
Guler, Onder 'Al' (Turkey 58) 149, 162, 202, **29**
Gurney, F Taylor Dr (USIS) 61

Haber, Nancy (Summer 64) **45**
Haji Ali, Jawahir Binte (Malaya 56) 77–8, 161, 229, 367
Hak, Ilona (Austria 69) 287
Hakim, Randa P (Lebanon 72) 88
Hall, Richard 6
Hamadien, Mohamed Abdulla (Sudan 59) 233
Hannesson, Rögnvaldur 'Röggi' (Iceland 62) 138, 217
Hansen, Annelise (Denmark 48) 204
Hanssen, Merete Bjorn (Denmark 48) 110
Hanum, Inajat (Indonesia 53) 143
Harboe, Nils 'Roger' (Norway 59) 91, 290, 295
Hasan, Sanaa (Egypt 61) 81, 163, 176, 180, 236–38, 257
Hase, Toshio (Japan 67) 217
Hellart, Bill (Summer leader) 256
Hennig, Jutta (Germany 69) 99
Hesse, Lebrecht Wilhelm 'Fifi' (Ghana 55) 92, 185–7, **19**
Hetata, Nadia (Egypt 57) 180
Hiett, Helen *See* Waller, Helen Hiett
Hinkley, Alan (NZ 63) 141, 218, 221
Hinson, Grace (Ghana 61) 92
Hodgson, Jeremy (Rhodesia 61) 79, 92, 186
Hogan-Shaidali, Syed Adam Edward 'Eddie' (Malaya 50) 203, 226, 245, 344, 358
Holst, Johan (Norway 56) 40, 156, 175, 217, 246, 287–8, 301, **10, 48**
Honeck, Mischa 4, 17
Honkapohja, Kaarina (Finland 59) 22, 142, 167, 201
Hoover, Herbert 13, 46

Hopkins, Keith (UK 53) 155
Houri, Ibrahim (Lebanon 58) 80, 91, 130, 181–2, 190, 201, 213, **3, 11, 23, 29**
Houston, Gary (Summer 64) 267, **45**
Hudgins, Alvin (Summer 70) & Bill (Summer 69) 255
Hudson, Peter Anthony (UK 54) 174
Huffman, Robert Smyser 'Bob' (Forum Director) **31, 45**
   Background/personal life 36–7, 52, 278–9, 281
   Connections & lack of 43, 97, 205, 253, 270–1, 276–7, 280
   Delegates & 37–8, 41, 43, 195, 240, 244, 246, 265
      Difficulties with 158, 165, 177, 190, 196, 221–2, 305
      Muhammad (Jordan 63) & 67–8, 182–3
   Forum survival & 46, 49, 70, 99, 124, 268–81
   Gender balance/sexism & 86, 87, 273
   Political views 37–8, 176–8, 183–4, 201, 311
   Staff 39–41, 43, 259, 276
   Summer Forum & 252–8, 267, 274
   TV debates & 156, 158, 162–3, 178, 184
Husami, Ziyad (Lebanon 57) 80, 180, 231

Iani, Pietro (Italy 65) 76
Ibrahim, Ismail bin (Malaya 60) **13**
Indjich, Trivo (Yugoslavia 58) 93
Iqbal, Zahid (Pakistan 64) 100
Islam, Dureen (Pakistan 62) **28**
Ismail, Sherille (Ceylon 71) 70, 112, 114, 129, 213, 222, 302, 356, **22**
Ivkovic, Veroslava 'Vera' (Yugoslavia 61) 76, 359
Iwasaki, Kikuko (Japan 53) 143, 286
Izzeddin, Salah Abu (Lebanon 64) 95, 184

Jacklin, Pamela (Summer Leader) 253–4, 256, 265–6, 287
Jacobs, Clifford (Summer 73) 255–6
Jahn, Richard (Australia 54) 165
Jain, Bimal Parshad (India 60) 223, 344
Jansen, Joseph 'Jay' (Ceylon 56) 229

Jayasuriya, Hiranthi (Ceylon 67) 71, 77, 126, 138, 213, 249, 302
Johansen, Thor Hjorth (Norway 48) 71, 201
Johnson, Lyndon 176, 200, 203
Johnstone, Bruce Havelock (Canada 61) 136, 218
Jones, Christina (Summer 66) 285
Jones, Michael 'Mike' (Australia 65) 88, 165, 177, 178, 195, 218, 222, 235, 249, **43**
Jorgensen, Erik Stig (Denmark 55) 113, 192, **19**

Kahnemooiypur, Azer (Iran 56) 90, 240, 298–9
Kairupan, Beatrice 'Nonna' (Indonesia 57) 51, 224, 233,
Kalicki, Jan (Summer 64 & Leader) 280, **45**
Kalista, Monika (Austria 65) 37, 114, 222, 248, 258, 354, **6**
Kamara, Edwin (Sierra Leone 67) 163
Kaput, Chitranjan 'Chit' (India 56) 41, 137, 155–6, 161, 175, 213–4, 243
Karam, Michael (Jordan 58) 114, 181, 214, 350, 351, **23**
Karanja, Joseph 'Joe' (Kenya 68) 186
Karibo, Minjiba Felicia (Nigeria 55) 92–93, 185, 230, 350
Karydi, Chrysy (Greece 70) 248
Kellner, Rita (Germany 70) 230, 290, 299
Kennedy, Edward 'Teddy' 201, 202
Kennedy, John F 'Jack' 'JFK' 53, 55, 77, 200–4, 278, **cover**
Kennedy, Robert 4, 202–3, 211
Kerbage, Gladys (Lebanon 56) 48, 134, 350, **21**
Kerby, Maurice (Haiti 47) 189
Kessler, Richard 'Rick' (Summer Leader) 256, 266
Keys, Michael (NZ 67) 108, 157, 214, 219, 364, **16**
Khalifa, Taher Ahmed Ali (Egypt 60) **20**
Khan, Haider Ali (Pakistan 71) 37, 163, 244, 270, 307, 356
Khim-tit, Phalla (Cambodia 60) 175, 234

Khoury, Gabriel A 'Gaby' (Jordan 64) 68, 184
King, Martin Luther 4, 149, 194, 211
Kirsimagi, Ines later Horton 78
Kluger, Richard (*NYHT*) 12, 31, 205
Kollross, Peter (Germany 67) 258
Konishi, Yoriko (Japan 56) 110, 134, 201
Korneti, Melpomeni (70) 247
Koslow, Robert (host) 136, 191
Krempl, Sandra Anne (Singapore 67) 114, 126, 131
Kris, Shirley (Panama 58) 62
Krishnan, K R (India 58) 231, 359
Kunz, Romano (Switzerland 56) 228, 231
Kure, Lorraine (Pan Am) 55, 94
Kurland, Roger (host 61) 123, 136
Kurukulasuriya, Priyalal Harischandra 'Lal' (Ceylon 60) 229
Kurz, Esther (Host 69) **41**
Kusturin, Branka (Yugoslavia 62) 263, 359

La Boulle, Louise (Belgium 49) 62, 71, 79
Lababidy, Thuraya (Lebanon 54) 80, 344
Lack, Eva (Austria 64) 369
Laffont, Eric (France 54) 234
Laiou, Angeliki (Greece 58) 79, 287
Lammi, Irjaleena 'Irja' (Finland 57) 75, 99, 100, 109, 137, 229, 241
Lang, Catalina 'Kitty' (Argentina 61) 93
Lang, Roger (host) 127-8, 135
Lange, Christian (Norway 49) 82
Larisch, Joachim (Germany 71) 177, 193, 258
Larranaga, Alfredo (Peru 47) 62
Larsen, Tord (Norway 63) 182, 196
Lätti, Leevi J (Finland 60) 107-8, 202, 295
Lau, Alberto (Guatemala 63) 79, 188
Layton, Joan & Robert (see Levy)
Lee, Chung Wha (Korea 52) 155
Lee, Hup San (Malaya 58) 76
Lee, Young-Koo 'Eric' (Korea 57) 137, 174-5, 239
Lehtinen, Eeva Kaarina (Finland 55) 91, 284
Leira, Arnlaug (Norway 58) 30, 106, 108-9, 349
Leonetti, Maria Christina 'Stella' (Italy 69) 223, 296
Lev, Rachel (Israel 64) 92, 184, 284
Levy, Joan (staff) 39, 273
Levy, Joan (Summer 65) 368
Lewis, Peter (UK 65) 8, 193
Liebes, Tamar (Israel 60) 201, 287, 344
Liebman, Howard (Summer 70) 120, 287
Liht, Sonja (Yugoslavia 66) 248, 263
Liikanen, Erkki (Finland 68) 247, 299
Lim, Heng Loong Peter (Singapore 57) 98, 181, 224
Liman, Mohammed Amine (Nigeria 56) 187
Lipkin, Mack (US 61) 22-4, 202, 217
Loeb, Ruth (Israel 58) 181-2
Loubser, Dicks (SA 56) 186-7, 229
Louw, Eline (SA 54) 90, 150, 200, 235-6
Lysberg, Are (Norway 71) 356

MacDonald, Ken (Australia 67) 91, 110, 114, 126
MacEwan, Alison Mary (UK 60) 80, 92, 344
MacJannet, Charlotte & Donald (sponsors) 256, 271
Magnus, Peter (Norway 69) 128, 160, 212
Mahmood, Riaz (Pakistan 52) 90, 117, 286
Mahmoud, Farouk Ezzat (Egypt 56) 228
Malcolm X 193
Malik, Jehangir (Pakistan 1961) **14**
Malla, Bhinda (Nepal 52) 155, 215, 239, 247, 285
Mantegazza, Amilcare (Italy 68) 100
Mantyla, Marja 'Kaarina' (Finland 56) 201
Maranan, Edguardo 'Ed' (Philippines 63) 137
Marin, Catherine (France 59) 1, 72, 77, 129, 249, 285, 288, 290-1, 293, 295
Marshall, Thurgood (speaker) 42, 203
Martineau, Geneviève (France 56) 77, 109, 112, 113, 125-6, 132, 154, 217, 220, 221, 228, 298-9
Marvin, Laura 10-11
McCane, Charlotte (Summer Leader) 255

McCullough, Constance (Summer 64) **45**
McIntosh, Graham (SA 61) 75, 92, 291, 293, 299
Medina Quiroga, Cecilia (Chile 53) 247
Meixueiro, Jorge (Mexico 65) 77
Mellbourn, Anders (*Mirror* Forum) 16
Meloney, Marie, (Missy, Mrs William Brown) (*NYHT*) 13, 28
Meylan, Robert (teacher) 279
Michael, Michael L (Summer 67 & Assistant 68) 256
Migniuolo, Will (US 67) 361
Misic, Mirka (Yugoslavia 57) 174-5
Mitchell, Dawn (Summer 73) 255
Mitchell, Erica (Canada 47) 45, 62, 308
Mojdara, Malaival (Thailand 50) 140, 226, 350
Molich, Rolf (Denmark 68) 305
Monier, Françoise (France 58) 159
Morii, Yumiko (Japan 57) 75-6, 163
Mota, Silvio de Albuquerque (Brazil 63) 76, 349
Muchie, Mammo (Ethiopia 68) 186
Muhindi, Josphat (Kenya 67) 164
Mulumba, David Makau (Kenya 62) 190, 245
Munro, Alice 'Evelyn' (Brazil 59) 194
Myint, Emma Maung (Burma 62) 128, **28**

Naauao, Roberta (US Hawaii 61) 87
Nagel, Claudia (Germany 72) **44**
Naguib, General Mohamed 225, **35**
Naim, Amin Jan (Pakistan 57) 285
Nair, Nalini (India 59) 84, 140, 200, 219-20, 232
Nair, P Balakrishnan (India 50) 223
Nammur, Mona (Lebanon 61) 80
Nasmith, Gus (US 62, staff) 40-1, 156, 211, 249, 256, 258, 261-2, 265, 270, 273, 276, 281, 283, 288, 299, 302
Nelson, Terence Albert (UK 48) 214, 215, 353
Neway, Teklu (Ethiopia 60) 94, 99, 113, 154, 188, 199, 204, 211, 213, 366, **20**
Nezhad, Khusrow Hosseini (Iran 60) 232

Nguyen Thieu 'Nga' (Vietnam 58) 172, **52**
Nguyen, Diep Ngoc (Vietnam 55) 241
Nguyen, Minh (Vietnam 65) 76, 79, 95, 107, 171, 177, 184, 192, 364
Nguyen, Ylang (Vietnam 61) **14**
Niamir, Bahram (Iran 70) 176, 299, 350
Nikoo, Farideh (Iran 68) 367
Nixon, Richard 203, 278, 356
Nizam, Rasul (Pakistan 54) 136, 282
Nkrumah, Kwame 66, 210, 244
Noack, Dieter (Germany 62) 73, 127, **28**
Noggoh, Emmanuel (Ghana 68) 37, 40, 50, 82, 100, 109, 112, 114, 121, 128, 138-9, 152, 177, 185-6, 192, 200, 214, 216, 218
Normandy, Dennis (Philippines 57) 80, 224-5, 288, 350
Nwaogugu, Aloysius C (Nigeria 60) 107
Nyunt, Richard W Htun (Burma 50) 286

Odinov, Orel (Summer 64) 257, 266, 287, **45**
Offokaja, Boniface (Nigeria 57) 188
Ofuatey-Kodjoe, Wentworth Bosman 'Kiddy' (Ghana 54) 150, 235-36
Okenla, Abimbola (Nigeria 61) 92
Oluoch, Sheila (Kenya 72) **44**
Orcel, Brigitte (France 64) 82, 95, 224, 350
Orcel, Catherine (France 57) 82, 350
Osei-Dadzie, John (Kwabena) (Ghana 72) 242
Osman, Ahmed Siddik (Sudan 60) 130-1, 172, 193, **13, 20**
Oyarzun, Carola (Chile 69) 113, 126, 131, 296

Paasche, Eva (Norway 48) 90
Pagaduan, Patrocinio 'Patsy' (Philippines 58) 100, 169
Paget, Karen 52
Paik, Nakchung (Korea 55) 155, 219, 373
Palma, Gloria (Colombia 72) **44**
Paludan-Anderson, Lise-Lotte (Denmark 60) 223, **13**
Paran, Amos (Israel 69) 72, 78, 296, **41**
Parayre, Alberta 'Tina' (Spain 67) 99, 349, 355

Park, Chung Sim (Korea 60) **13**
Park, Hee Joon John (Korea 56) 161, 230, **7**
Parmentier, Casimir 45
Pavyar, Mahbonoo (Iran 52) 131
Pearson, Lester 62
Perry, Judith (Canada 53, staff) 40, 58, 287–8, **48**
Pham Trong 'Le' (Vietnam 57) 224, 244
Phan Thi Ngoc 'Lan' (Vietnam 59) **39**
Philips, Nancy (US 1946) 10
Pilger, Paul (Austria 72) 114, 223
Pillsbury, Phillip (USIS) 19
Plesner, Ulrik (Denmark 48) 43, 216, 287
Polisar, Leonard (US 1946) 10
Popper, Wera 'Ferdinanda' (Austria 49) 78
Portillo, Michael (UK 72) 74, 80, 95, 112, 138, 223, 247
Poulsen, Mogens Bent (Denmark 58) 219
Powers, Katherine Anne 'Kit' (US 61) 202
Prabhavat, Sahadya (Thailand 60) 248, **13**
Prakesh, Sudhir (India 66) 114, 135, 290, 293, 299
Price, Martine (staff) 55
Prince, Lorna (Summer 70) 255
Prodjolalito, Kustijah (Indonesia 59) 247
Proropopescu, Serban (Bolivia 64) 76, 109, 219, 287

Qaddumi, Hisham F (Jordan 57) 180
Quao, Nii Tetteh-Churu (Ghana 59) 137, 185, 209, 241, 244, 285, 294, **39**

Rabinowitz, Daphna (Italy 57) 134, 164, 180–1, 299
Raj, Myrtle Dorai (India 52) 114, 130, 344, 359
Ram, Vangala Jaya (India 54) 78, 93, 155, 203, 245
Ramstroem, Jack (Sweden 55) 91
Raushenbush, Esther (SLC) 57, 205–6
Ravid, Simon 'Avri' (Israel 68) 41, 131, 138, 154, 184, 232, 241
Reader, Judith (UK 56) 107, 124, 155, 161, 170, 202, 204, 229, **5, 10, 21**
Redefer, Frederick Lovett (NYU) 20, 52, 231, 304
Reed, Linda (staff) 273
Reeder, Suzanne (UK 62) 74, 107, 112, 132, 141–2, 174, 190, 192–3, 219, 221, 359, **28**
Reid Family (*NYHT*) 11–3, 43, 46, 205
Reid, Helen Rogers (*NYHT*) 11–3, 23, 25, 28–9, 31, 46–7, 51,164, 203, 239, 301
Reid, Ogden (Brown) (*NYHT*) 12, 29, 48–9, 52, 148, 205, 208
Reid, Whitelaw (Whitie) (*NYHT*) 12, 31, 47, 64, 67, 147–8
Reidel, Joy (SLC) 206
Remez, Gideon (Israel 63) 182, 196
Rennie, Susan (SA 57) 31, 78, 88, 92, 95, 104, 164–5, 186, 188, 215, 235, 239, 308, 344, 357, 358, **48**
Reweti, Marama (NZ 70) 79
Rigoleth, Suzana 'Susie' (Brazil 58) 108–09, 295
Rinott, Joseph 'Yosi' (Israel 62) 178, **28**
Robert, Glenn (Summer 64) **45**
Roberts, Ceridwen (UK 67) 77, 91, 100, 108, 112, 177, 214
Robin, Keren (Israel 72) **44**
Rodis, Rodel (Philippines 69) 113, 129, 132, 223, 225, 228
Romanos, Nina (Brazil 72) 88, 121, **44**
Roodt, Marlene (SA 55) 92, 185–7, 344, **19**
Room, Robin (*Mirror* Forum) 15
Roosevelt, Eleanor (speaker) 2, 10, 13, 203–04
Roosevelt, James (IOS, Board) 149, 205, 270, 370
Runge, Kirsten (Denmark 61) 203, **cover**
Ruoro, Peter (Chege Mbitiru) (Kenya 65) 83, 242
Rusten, Per Friis (Norway 55) 91, 283

Sabo, Jasminka (Yugoslavia 73 YFU) 370
Sadat, Marwan (Syria 52) 76, 351
Sagwette, Auxilia (Rhodesia 62) 79, 186,

242, **24**
Said, Mohamed 'Sameh' (Egypt 62) **28**
Salazar, Araceli (Philippines 53) 80, 357, 371
Salazar, Meliton (Philippines 50) 71, 73, 80, 371
Saleh, Muhammad Ahmad (Jordan 63) 67–8, 131, 179, 182–83
Salle, Jean-Claude (France 49) 94, 232
Salomon, Vivian (Argentina 58) 133, 149, 232, **11**
San, Aysel (Turkey 64) 37, 217
Sanders, Leonore (staff) 38
Sandford, Patricia (UK 55) 80
Sapra, Vinod (India 69) **32**
Sardadi, Soesilo (Indonesia 50) 81, 159, 233
Satti, Anis Khan (Pakistan 56, Board) 218, 231, 271, 370
Saunders, Frances Stonor 35
Sawyer, Amos (Liberia 63) 247
Sayrafizadeh, Mahmoud (Iran 52) 175
Scattucio, Maria (Summer 64) 193, 257, 260–1, 263, 266, **45, 46, 47**
Scharrer, Helen (Mrs W Harvey) (teacher) 47, 147–9
Schiemann, Arnold (Colombia 69) 126–7, 153–4, 240, 282
Scholes, Lesley (Australia 55) 162, 230
Scholz, Norbert (Germany 57) 141, 175, 284
Schwebel, Stephen M (speaker) 10, 146–7
Scott, Craig (host) 134, 148
Sedee, Gustav Albert 'Gus' (Netherlands 49) 231–2
Seeger, Pete 42, 203–5, 218, 275, **39**
Seglen, Per Ottar (Norway 61) 91, 113, 213, 219, **2**
Sesay, Mamud (Sierra Leone 66) 136, 191
Shanus, Corey (Summer 73) 266
Shaw, Emmanuel (Liberia 65) 247, 364, **31**
Shrestha, Bharat Bhagat (Nepal 64) 244–5
Shriver, Sargent (Peace Corps) 201–2
Siagian, Sabam P (Indonesia 50) 81
Sifenou, Christine (Greece 53, staff) 39–41, 283, 357, 358

Sigaud, Lygia Maria (Brazil 62) **28**
Silverman, Ethel (US 63) 196, 253, **45**
Sitta, Samuel (Tanganyika 62) 64, 193
Skinner, Charles (host) 137
Smith, Joan Lee (staff) 40, 93, 285
Soekader, Tatti Larasati (Indonesia 55) **19**
Soerjomihardjo, Supia Latifah 'Pia' (Indonesia 52) 135
Solomon, Ed (SLC) 36–7, 58, 205–6
Somnapan, Duangtip (Thailand 62) 77, 192, 196
Soria, Donatella (Italy 72) 88, **44**
Souccar, Norma (Egypt 67) 163, 289
Soussane, Mohamed Amine (Morocco 57) 181, 231
Spanidou, Irini (Greece 63) 140, 203, 350
Stabler, Mae Wolff (staff) 38, 48
Stålström, Ollie (Finland 62) 22
Steinem, Gloria 22–3
Stern, Stella (staff) 38
Stevens, Clifford (host) 287
Stone, Victor (Summer 64) **45**
Streicker, Shirley (host) 109, 122, 131, 182–3
Suh, Esther (Korea 59) 229, **39**
Sundaram, Jomo Kwame (Malaysia 70) 120, 129, 247, 299
Supol, Salika (Thailand 52) 81, 143, **40**
Surbarnbhesaj, Bisidthisak (Thailand 59) 144, 308
Syvanne, Mikko (Finland 69) 37, 223

Taavon, Minoo (Iran 58) 149, 191
Tadesse, Yilma (Ethiopia 57) 309–10
Taha, Mahgoub Obeid (Sudan 57) 181, 214–5
Tan Joon Kheng (Singapore 53) 121
Tan Wee Kiat (Singapore 61) 74, 127, 141, 294, 366
Tantivess, Apichai (Thailand 63) 196, 221, 349
Tay, Alice Erh-Soon (Singapore 52) 51, 135, 238, 248, 285

Taylor, Greg (NZ 69) 115, 223, 225, 228
Taylor, Harold (SLC) 56, 58, 150, 206–7
Taylor, Ian (NZ 71) 351
Taylor, Rita (staff) 39–40
Tefari, Nebiat (Ethiopia 56) 161, 188, 191, 226, **cover**
Tejan-Jalloh, Hawa (Sierra Leone 65) 83, 248
Teo, Eddie (Malaysia 65) 195, **12, 34, 43**
Thadani, Usha (India 55) 84
Than thi Hoai Phuong (Vietnam 56) 77, 240, 366, 367
Thant, Khin Ohn (Burma 53) 172
Thomsen, Hanne (Denmark 49) 243
Thorbjornsdottir, Rosa (Iceland 49) 82
Thorn, Rina (SA 58) 115
Thygesen, Niels (Denmark 53) 123, 371
Tier, Nancy (CAP) 197
Tilus, Eeva Rhea (Finland 48) 215
Titova, Valentina (USSR Committee of Youth Organisations) 69
Torode, John (UK 58) 77, 92, 159, 204, 287
Toukan, Wael (Jordan 67) 163
Trevelyan, Catriona (UK 63) 196, 204, 260, 373
Trigg, Beryl (Australia 68) 82, 114–15, 216, 235
Trincia, Francesco (Italy 63) 293
Trippe, Juan (Pan Am) 204, **38**
Truman, Harry S 51, 201, 231, 287, **36**
Turck, Barbara (Summer 64) **45**
Turkson, Richard (Ghana 62) **24**

Udabage, Mahipala 'Mike' (Ceylon 58) 131, 189, **29**
Underhill, Marie (teacher) 106
Utreras, Ines (Ecuador 47) 113

Valera, Purificacion (Philippines 52) 247, 285
Van de Horst, Johannes (SA 62) 186, 188, 298, 299, **24**
Van Eyll, Thierry (Belgium 63) 83
Van Heerden, Marilyn (SA 68) 186
Van Reyen, Jenny Ellen (Netherlands 49) 242, 250, 287
Van Schaick, Roger (UK 69) 154, 211, 220
Van Schaik, Louis (SA 67) 163, 185
Vanous, Jan (Czechoslovakia 67) 68, 80, 138, 215, 244, 265–6, 287, 307
Viana, Raimundo (Spain 69) **42**
Vibulmonkol, Santi (Thailand 52) 143, 153, **17, 40**
Vigorita, Vincent 'Skip' (Summer 67) 258, 262
Vojnovic, Milan (Yugoslavia 60) 171, 226, 234, **20**
Vu Doc, Vuong (Vietnam 68) 240, 307
Vu Huy, Kim (Vietnam 50) 165, 226

Waks, Jay (Summer 64) **45**
Waldvogel, Guy (Switzerland 55) 285
Walker, Gary (Summer leader) 255–6, 262
Waller, Helen Hiett (Forum Director) 29, 34–5, 199, 301 **19, 30**
   Background/personal life (Ted Waller) 25–8, 31–4, 37, 51
   Alumni & 41–2, 53, 92, 158, 245, 282–7
   Clashes 38–40, 44, 47–49, 57–8, 95–6, 206–7, 209
   Connections 52, 59, 97, 203–5, 218, 253, 284
   Delegates & 29–31, 35, 43–4, 214, 221, 239
     Manipulation of 95–6, 104, 140–41, 150, 162–5, 184, 191–92
     Courting controversy with 150, 162–5, 179–82, 235
   Gender balance & 84–6
   Journalistic approach 47,154–6, 163, 184, 208–9
   Political views 27–9, 43, 98, 120, 166, 170–1, 186, 189, 207–8, 235, 301
   TV debates & 93, 111, 152, 154–56, 159–65, 166–67, 170, 187, 194, 221, 235, 297, 306
Wamalwa, Michael (Kenya 64) 55
Warner, John **31**
Warner, Mary (staff) 95, 141, 214, 284, 344
Watson, Craig (US 68) 255, 351
Watson, Linda (Summer 69) 255
Weerasuriya, Krisantha 'Kris' (Ceylon 68) 86, 218, 242, 247

Wellington, Herbert G 'Duke' Snr (sponsor) 56
Wessels, Marita (SA 59) 185, 298
Whitaker, John (NZ 73 AFS) 278
Whitney, John Hay 'Jock' 12, 34–7, 39, 43, 46, 49–50, 52, 67–8, 106, 131, 149, 184, 198, 201, 203, 205, 207, 252, 268, 271
Wider, Willy (Belgium 55) 137
Wieschhoff, Virginia Graves (director) 35–7, 84, 141, 156, 162, 184, 283
Wolff, Doris see Friedman, Doris (staff)
Wolfsberg, Inga (Denmark 54) 214, 236, 286
Woodgate, Elizabeth 'Liz' (Australia 56) 161, 224, 232
Wool, John D (teacher) 109
Woolstadt, Roger (host) 136
Workum, Emily (Lee) (SLC) 7, 32, 206, 219

Yaffe, Daniella (Israel 59) 166
Yamikama, Yukiko (Japan 59) 167, 215, 365
Yoshimura, Yukiko (Japan 58) 149
Yuen, Chooi Yeng (Singapore 59) 73
Yuen, Kum Chuen (Singapore 55) 73, 217

Zulficar, Mona (Egypt 65) 82, 248
Zvekic, Ugi (Yugoslavia 69) 178, 247, 296

www.ingramcontent.com/pod-product-compliance
Ingram Content Group UK Ltd.
Pitfield, Milton Keynes, MK11 3LW, UK
UKHW011301060925
462636UK00001B/81